Electoral Politics in South Africa

Electoral Politics in South Africa

Assessing the First Democratic Decade

Edited by
Jessica Piombo
and
Lia Nijzink

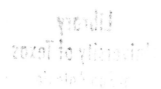

ELECTORAL POLITICS IN SOUTH AFRICA
© Jessica Piombo and Lia Nijzink, 2005.

First published in 2005 by
PALGRAVE MACMILLAN™
175 Fifth Avenue, New York, N.Y. 10010 and
Houndmills, Basingstoke, Hampshire, England RG21 6XS
Companies and representatives throughout the world.

PALGRAVE MACMILLAN is the global academic imprint of the Palgrave Macmillan division of St. Martin's Press, LLC and of Palgrave Macmillan Ltd. Macmillan® is a registered trademark in the United States, United Kingdom and other countries. Palgrave is a registered trademark in the European Union and other countries.

ISBN 1–4039–7123–4

Library of Congress Cataloging-in-Publication Data is available from the Library of Congress.

A catalogue record for this book is available from the British Library.

Design by Newgen Imaging Systems (P) Ltd., Chennai, India.

First edition: December 2005

10 9 8 7 6 5 4 3 2 1

Printed in the United States of America.

CONTENTS

Part 3   Results and Assessment

PREFACE

April 1994 was a time of liberation and hope in South Africa. Millions of South Africans celebrated freedom as they elected a democratic government to end apartheid. Ten years later, South Africa commemorated a decade of democracy. The highlight of the month-long celebrations was the country's third democratic national election on April 14, followed by the inauguration of President Mbeki in a ninety-million Rand fete at the Union buildings in Pretoria. But was there reason to celebrate?

Many achievements have been made over the past ten years. Social services have been extended to the majority. Progress in the provision of houses, water, sanitation, and electricity has been slow, but steady. The Truth and Reconciliation Commission (TRC), although not a perfect exercise, helped the country to heal deep wounds and avoid mass retaliation.

The electoral process has become overwhelmingly peaceful, well managed, and increasingly routine. Political intimidation has decreased considerably, and parties can now campaign in areas where they once feared to tread. Many who lived through the apartheid years marvel at the fact that we can now discuss South African politics in terms of non-violent political competition, rather than by counting politically motivated incidents of intimidation, violence, and intolerance.

But the balance sheet of South Africa's first decade of democracy also shows negatives. The country is still sharply divided between the haves and the have-nots, and inequality is increasing. The HIV/AIDS pandemic is raging in all sectors of society, the full impact of which has yet to be felt. The economy is growing, but at a pace not nearly fast enough to provide sufficient employment. Unemployment and crime continue to be pressing problems.

On the political terrain, competition is increasingly taking place solely among opposition parties, while the ruling party's electoral dominance continues to grow. And, although there were more registered voters in 2004 than in previous elections, fewer people turned out to vote.

This volume brings together contributions from leading and emerging South African and international scholars to assess the quality of democracy and the electoral process in South Africa over the past ten years, with special emphasis on the 2004 elections. It represents the third in a loose series of analyses about democratic elections in South Africa. In contrast to the previous two volumes, we have broadened the perspective to include a retrospective on the past ten years of democracy, oriented toward how changes have affected the context in which elections take place.

Political, economic, and social changes over the past decade have altered the landscape of South African electoral politics. In the opening chapter of this volume, Friedman analyzes the state of South African democracy, its strengths and weaknesses, articulating an argument about the role of identity politics in the process of democratic consolidation. Seekings subsequently looks at social and economic changes that have occurred since 1994 and their electoral implications, while Mattes reviews how changes in public opinion have impacted on people's political preferences and voting decisions between 1994 and 2004. In a chapter on the institutions of representative democracy, Nijzink and Piombo describe how Parliament, which initially spent much of its time on law-making, has become more reactive after 1999. The chapter also discusses how the evolution of the electoral system has worked to cement an alignment of opposition politics that fails to incorporate the majority of South African voters, while enabling the ruling party to absorb some of its longstanding rivals. Kabemba subsequently investigates the organization responsible for administering elections, tracing how electoral administration has evolved since 1994 and highlighting the achievements of the Independent Electoral Commission during its ten-year existence.

Turning to the chapters on political parties, we asked our authors to focus on party tactics and campaign strategies, and to cast an eye toward the development of the parties' fortunes over the past ten years. What were the main issues on which the parties campaigned in the 2004 election and what groups did they target? How did the 2004 election campaign compare with the campaigns of 1994 and 1999? In his chapter on the African National Congress, Lodge describes the ruling party's careful and successful efforts in the 2004 campaign. Booysen, looking at the Democratic Alliance, highlights the problems, pitfalls, and progress in the campaign strategy of the largest opposition party. Schulz-Herzenberg analyzes the demise of the New National Party, while Piper focuses on

politics in KwaZulu-Natal and the fortunes of the Inkatha Freedom
Party. Hoeane reviews how the Pan Africanist Congress, the Azanian
People's Organisation, and the new Independent Democrats fared in the
2004 election. Finally, Naidu and Manqele look at the smallest parties
and their role in electoral politics.

In the last two chapters, the volume turns to an assessment of the electoral process. Davis analyzes the role of the media in the 2004 election by
investigating the question of bias. He presents evidence suggesting that,
despite perceptions of bias, the media were in fact fair in their portrayal
of the various parties. In the final chapter of this volume, Piombo discusses the outcome of the 2004 election at the national and provincial
levels, emphasizing the "normalization" of politics and the contours of
voting trends since 1994. She concludes the volume by looking at what
these trends mean for the future of democratic politics in South Africa.

Overall, this book remains cautiously optimistic about the future
prospects for democracy in South Africa. Some chapters question the
effectiveness of political parties, suggesting a disconnection between
voters and the parties that represent them. Over time, this disconnect
could lead to alienation and voter apathy, but, as most authors argue, the
situation is not yet critical.

In these pages, we have attempted to bring together diverse opinions
on the prospects for democracy in South Africa. We have not tried to
force agreement between the various outlooks of our contributors. If the
result is that the individual chapters contradict each other at certain
points, then this reflects a healthy diversity of opinions on the nature and
quality of South Africa's democracy. We hope that this volume serves
both as a sourcebook for information on the elections, the parties, and
their campaigns and as a contribution to careful analysis and debate on
the electoral process.

Jessica Piombo and Lia Nijzink
August 2005

ACKNOWLEDGMENTS

Many people have contributed time, effort, and support to this project. First of all, we would like to thank the authors. They adhered to a tight production schedule and accommodated our numerous suggestions. They also presented drafts of their chapters at a series of workshops held at the University of Cape Town in April, May, and June 2004, support for which was provided by the Centre for Social Science Research (CSSR). Without these workshops, we would not have had the opportunity to discuss our contributions with each other and the academic community. We would like to extend our gratitude to all the individuals who agreed to serve as discussants, often on short notice and having received the chapters just days in advance. We highly appreciate their flexibility and their excellent comments.

The support of the CSSR has vastly improved this volume. The three workshops at which we brought the authors together were masterfully managed by the CSSR's dedicated staff. We would like to extend a special thanks to Libbi Downes, Kathy Forbes, and others who have helped us with the organization of the workshops and our research fellowships at the CSSR. Allison Stevens provided crucial administrative support and made sure everyone was where they needed to be at the right time. Bob Mattes has proven to be an excellent colleague and collaborator over the years, and we appreciate the fruitful working relationship that we share with him.

The CSSR hosted Piombo twice during the course of this project, providing research and travel support for two trips to South Africa to research the elections and to work on the volume. Nijzink's involvement in this project has also been supported by a research fellowship at the CSSR. The Centre for African Studies of UCT provided office space and a collegial environment in which to conduct our work.

To all our colleagues at UCT, it was a pleasure working with you.

Andrew Reynolds, who edited *Election '94* and *Election '99 South Africa*, has provided sage advice on the approach to this volume, which was much appreciated.

Finally, to our families, without your love and support we would not succeed in any of these endeavors.

PART 1

A Decade of Democracy

CHAPTER ONE

A Voice for Some: South Africa's Ten Years of Democracy

STEVEN FRIEDMAN

Ten years after 1994, South African democracy is healthier than it was expected to be but shallower than it needs to be.

Despite repeated prophecies of doom from those who insist that the electoral dominance of the African National Congress (ANC) precludes the accountability on which democracy depends,[1] civil liberties remain largely intact, and civil society is vigorous and at times able to force changes in government policy, most notably on HIV/AIDS. Despite jeremiads about "voter apathy,"[2] participation in the first two national elections was high, and electoral contest relatively free. Public debate is vigorous.

While these features of the political order often seem to be taken for granted by commentators and politicians, they are considerable achievements. It is remarkable that a society characterized by deep identity divisions and governed by a liberation movement accustomed to viewing itself as the sole voice of the majority[3] and facing no serious electoral challenge should still be essentially democratic after a decade—particularly when we recall that in the 1994 election, research identified some 165 "no-go areas" in which party competition was impossible or very difficult.[4]

But these gains remain unevenly distributed. Civil liberties are not always enjoyed at the grassroots level. This may be because of the persistence of O'Donnell's "brown areas," in which there is low or no presence of the state—where the "state" is understood as "a set of reasonably effective bureaucracies and the effectiveness of properly sanctioned legality."[5] These are areas in which "shacklords," traditional authorities, or other sources of pre- or nondemocratic power may still hold sway.[6] Or, if the allegations of social movement activists are to be believed, liberties may not extend to the grassroots at times because official tolerance of dissent is much more limited at the margins, when protest is led by groups or occurs in places that are outside the mainstream.[7] Equally important, many voters do not enjoy the resources that would enable them to organize to be heard in the public policy debate between elections. Their participation is largely limited to expressing their identities in periodic ballots. Because the poor—about two-fifths of the society—are not heard, their experiences and concerns cannot translate into effective policy. This ensures that they remain mired in poverty and excluded, in a continuing vicious cycle, because participation is largely limited to those with the means to organize.

This chapter attempts to explain why democracy has survived this past decade and to analyze the continued challenge that a lack of voice for the poor poses for democratic quality and survival.

The Double-Edged Sword: Identity, Accountability, and Participation

South African democracy hinges, in important ways, on the expression of identity. This is certainly true of electoral behavior. While scholars and media commentators search for the "issues" on which each election is to be fought, voter behavior contradicts this earnest quest. Thus, despite insistence that jobs, HIV/AIDS and crime were the issues uppermost in the minds of the voters in 2004, those who most lack jobs, have most to lose if antiretroviral medication is not available to the poor, and are most likely to be victims of violent crime voted overwhelmingly for the governing party, while those who have done best out of the economy over the decade, can afford health care, and can buy private security largely supported the opposition.[8] At the local level, a study conducted in three major cities found that satisfaction with local government performance is substantially higher among white than among black voters. Yet in all three cities, black voters overwhelmingly support the majority party and white voters the opposition.[9] The central role played by identity in voting behavior is largely ignored by an intellectual elite convinced that identity voting is irrational and primitive, despite its ubiquity in "established" democracies.

This emphasis on identity must be explained. To insist that electoral behavior is shaped by identity is not to claim that elections are ethnic or racial censuses.[10] If they were, Zulu speaking voters would not divide their support between the ANC and the Inkatha Freedom Party (IFP), and "coloured" voters would not divide theirs between several parties. Nor is race the only determinant of voting behavior. If it were, we would be unable to explain the votes cast for the African Christian Democratic Party (ACDP). Rather, "identity" is used here to denote a social self-definition based on criteria other than socioeconomic interest, on common "webs of meaning."[11] The chief rationale for voter choices is who voters believe they are and their assessment of which party can best provide a vehicle for who they are. Race remains the primary identity, but language, religion, and gender may play a role. So too, on the margins, might "political community:" membership of a group of like-minded people ascribing to similar values. The key point is that, in this context, weighing the programs and policies of parties plays hardly any role. Thus, many black voters will support the ANC even if they lack a job because they believe it expresses their demand for dignity and freedom. Others in KwaZulu-Natal (KZN) will endorse the IFP whether or not their residential areas have been developed because the party is held to protect the tradition they revere. Many white voters will support the Democratic Alliance (DA) even though they know it will not be able to influence government decisions because they believe it says what they think.

An electoral politics based on identity can weaken government accountability and responsiveness where one identity dominates and where one party, in this case the ANC, can project itself as the dominant vehicle of that identity. This is so because, for a period, identity loyalties will ensure that the governing party secures a majority regardless of its performance. What is less often acknowledged is that identity politics can also offer democracy assets.

Unrealized Assets

The first asset is higher levels of electoral participation than we might otherwise expect. Whether voters anywhere behave as if the decision to vote is purely an instrumental cost-benefit calculation is open to serious doubt,[12] but where voters regard casting a ballot as an expression of identity, they are less likely to pass up this opportunity because the outcome of an election is not in doubt. There is no guarantee that this situation will endure indefinitely. If voters become unhappy with the governing party, the salience of identities may cause sharp reductions in electoral participation because disappointed voters might stay away rather than vote for an alternative expression of political identity.

But in South African elections held prior to 2004, in contrast to many new democracies and despite constant claims to the contrary, citizens voted in large numbers. Many more might vote but for a registration system that places the onus to register on the voter. Although failure to register is interpreted by many commentators as a sign of apathy, many who do not register wish to vote but are unable to comply with the reg-istration criteria, which means that registration requirements restrict access to the franchise.[13] In 1999, at least 5 percent of those wishing to vote may have been unable to do so,[14] and in a survey conducted before the 2004 election 60 percent of the quarter of eligible voters who had not registered reported that they were unable to do so for a variety of logistical reasons.[15]

The 2004 election does suggest that this asset may be depreciating. Turnout (as a percentage of registered voters) declined to 77 percent compared with 89 percent in 1999. Whereas attempts to calculate this as a proportion of the adult population demonstrate a confidence in South African census data that many specialists do not share, the proportion of adults voting is clearly less than this figure and might be as low as 57 percent. It is too soon to say whether this means that identities are now less of a spur to voting, but even a 57 percent poll would be equiv-alent to turnout levels in Britain and India, despite the fact that the results of South African elections are widely regarded, with good reason, as foregone conclusions.

Identity politics may also, in the peculiar South African context, provide unexpected sources of accountability. We might expect the salience of racial divisions, with the ANC's dominance of the black African vote, to ensure that minority opinion, expressed through the media and by major opposition parties, is ignored or dismissed as white prejudice. This is partly true. Relations between the ANC and the official opposition, the DA, are not cooperative, and campaigns to hold government account-able are far more likely to succeed if they are black-led. The campaign to win antiretroviral medication for HIV/AIDS patients at public health facilities is a case in point. Criticism is at times dismissed as evidence of prejudice. Identity politics can insulate the government from pressures for accountability, a point best illustrated by the ANC's unwillingness to investigate allegations of corruption in arms dealings.[16]

Given South Africa's history, however, these constraints are less remarkable than the fact that government politicians do continue to feel the need to respond to media criticism or the views of white-led civil society organizations. This is the consequence not of strategic calculation but of a particular racial dynamic. Postapartheid politics has been underpinned by a theme, often not stated overtly, which is pervasive: whites expect a black government to fail and the leaders of that government know they do. It is, therefore, a key preoccupation of much of the new governing elite to demolish these assumptions by demonstrating that black people can govern an industrialized society with a complex market economy. Indeed, the central preoccupation of the post-1994 administrations has been to prove white racism wrong.

This concern is not an unalloyed boon. It weakens the quality of democracy by prompting enthusiasm for technical and managerial solutions rather than for democratic broadening or deepening.[17] It may also impair government effectiveness by prompting reluctance to form partnerships with civil society actors on, for example, HIV and AIDS because it is deemed important to show that government can manage the problem. This may also weaken democracy because government ability to translate law and policy into reality is a key prerequisite of a working democratic order. South Africa, like other democracies, faces the need to ensure that the reach of the state, understood as "a set of bureaucracies, a legal system, and a focus of collective identity for the inhabitants of its territory,"[18] is extended across the whole society. This is essential because democratic liberties cannot be fully enjoyed if unaccountable power-holders can deny citizens the rights that the constitution extends to them, whether the source of their power is tradition, access to the means of violence, resources, or privileged access to the right to erect a home or trade.[19]

The legal order needs to be extended across the entire society if all its citizens are to enjoy rights. And, if the democratic state is unable to translate citizen preferences into policy or policy into implemented reality, the right to participate in shaping public decisions is negated or attenuated. The relationship between state and society, of which the effectiveness of government is an important part, also enables democratic decisions to become reality. Where the desire to refute racism produces unimplementable policy, because it is not based on a plausible assessment of available capacity or has not taken into account a misfit between intentions and social realities, democracy's quality and health are impaired.[20] This is also so where identity divisions prevent the government from forming effective partnerships with key social actors, such as white-owned businesses, whose cooperation is essential to run an effective government.

But the desire to refute racism may also act as a source of accountability. Thus the government may remain engaged with media critics not because it sees this as a route to electoral gain but because it wants to prove its white critics wrong. And, because an important aspect of the desire to disprove white racism is a concern to achieve "world class" status in everything from constitution making to sport,[21] international opinion is often an important influence on government thinking. When international opinion coincides with that of local minorities, as it often does, the effect is to increase accountability in contexts where we would expect the government to lack both inclination and incentive to take dissenting opinion seriously.

Identity politics may also reduce incentives to curb free political activity. First, where one identity is numerically dominant and one party is its overwhelming representative, the stakes of political competition are reduced since the outcome of elections is largely assured. The incentives for conflict on both sides are also much reduced. It could be argued that the continued existence of vehicles for the political expression of minority identities is, in a divided society, useful to political elites on all sides of the divide since it provides a source of solidarity for their support base. Both the ANC and opposition parties are able to rally supporters precisely because other identities find political expression too. Opponents are thus an important asset. A further effect may be to mute the reaction to "disloyal" behavior by the minority. Thus white business persons who openly identify with the opposition may be relatively immune from government antagonism since their political loyalties may be assumed to be an expression of identity and, therefore, an inevitable albeit unpleasant reality.[22]

Unstable Equilibrium?

The pervasiveness of identity politics may, therefore, be the chief reason why democracy has proven relatively robust over the past decade.

It must be stressed, however, that the continued electoral dominance of a particular party does hold longer-term challenges to democratic health against which the trends noted here are an uncertain inoculation. For now, the survival of formal democratic institutions is largely guaranteed by the reality that electoral outcomes are not in doubt. Inevitably, a time will come when they will be, when the governing party faces a challenge from within its own identity group, which places its continued control of government in doubt. It will only be when the major electoral battles are fought within identities as well as between them that we will know how robust democracy really is. The outcome may well be determined by the degree of establishment of precedents and political conventions that shape the way a challenge to the electoral dominance of the governing party will be received. Much of the democratic progress in South Africa in the years immediately ahead may need to be measured against the degree to which understandings and modes of political behavior that will protect democracy when the stakes are raised are established. Thus, in the 2004 election, the battle for KZN was an important bellwether because it was a contest within an identity group in which much hinged on the outcome (in 1994, there was no campaign to speak of; in 1999, the prospect of coalition reduced the stakes).

To place this point in context, one of democracy's key priorities, here as elsewhere, is to provide channels through which social conflicts can be mediated so that their destructive potential is reduced or eliminated. Thus far, one key aspect of conflict, that between rival political organizations, has been resolved in South African democracy largely by the effects of identity politics. In the 1994 election, competing parties resolved the problem of "no-go areas" by largely avoiding campaigning in places assumed to be controlled by another party.[23] Similarly, political conflict has been far less intense than it might have been since 1994 because parties' control of identity segments has often been uncontested (a notable exception being the "coloured" and Indian vote). The key test of the democratic polity will be its ability to continue to resolve conflict when the votes of key identity groups are contested and the outcome may decide who holds power. The black vote is likely to be the test, given the society's demographics. Democracy's prospects over the next decade and beyond will hinge in large measure on whether modes of resolving political conflict become sufficiently entrenched to withstand intense intra-identity political competition.

But, if identities have played themselves out in a way that makes political conflict more manageable, they have also ensured that formal political institutions, Parliament in particular, are not the most important sites of political activity. Lopsided election results and an insistence by both government and larger opposition parties on strict party discipline, make Parliament largely a sideshow as bargaining between the government and key white interests occurs directly, without white-led opposition parties acting as interlocutors.[24] And, although identities may shape voting behavior, they do not define the contest for public resources. There are significant and widening social and economic inequalities within identity groups and so political parties do not express the society's interest cleavages.[25] The key pressure for government accountability is therefore not Parliament but civil society, largely but by no means exclusively, the part that is led by blacks. This, in turn, ensures that propensity to vote does not translate into broad participation in political deliberation. Only those who have the capacity to organize are able to influence the policy debate. It is here that the poor's lack of access to organization acts as a substantive form of disenfranchisement, ensuring the continuance of the "vicious cycle" mentioned earlier.

Poverty and Participation:
The Nature of the Problem

The persistence of poverty and the paucity of peoples' participation between elections are both a symptom of and an explanation for limited democratic quality.

Specialist claims on welfare trends since 1994 differ. But neither the optimistic nor pessimistic conclusions suggest that democracy has brought substantial progress against poverty. One view insists that the gap between rich and poor is widening and that poverty is deepening. It finds statistical support from the official source of government figures, Statistics South Africa (SSA). This is somewhat ironic given that this claim does not reflect well on the government. SSA reports that the Gini coefficient, the measure of income inequality, has grown since 1994 and that many peoples' incomes have declined.[26] Research by independent economists suggests that poverty levels have slightly decreased since 1994 and reports a Gini coefficient significantly lower than that reported by SSA.[27] But even these estimates find that more than one-third of the citizenry live in poverty, that the proportion of poor in the population has hardly declined in ten years, and that the level of inequality is the second highest in the world, behind that of Brazil.[28]

That universal franchise has not prompted a significant decline in poverty or inequality should be surprising since we would expect the poor to use their vote to elect, and then hold accountable public representatives, committed to pursuing their interests, T. H. Marshall noted in the early 1950s that the extension of political rights to the poor, "political citizenship," had enabled them to use the vote to secure growing "social citizenship," increased capacity to participate in the economy and society. The two were related: the poor were becoming active members of society and the economy because their votes were ensuring policies that gave them the means to begin escaping poverty.[29] Based on even the more favorable calculations, this has not yet happened in democratic South Africa. This needs explaining.

The answer lies in the nature of participation in civil society, which is the subject of some misconception. It has become fashionable to bemoan the decline in citizen participation in policy debate since the end of apartheid, when citizens were, it is said, demobilized and so removed from the debate. It seems odd to expect the citizen mobilization achieved when the vast majority of the population was denied elementary human rights to continue after those rights were won. Why should antiapartheid activity have continued after the end of apartheid? The diverse voices of citizens are expressed on a wide range of issues in the media and, at times, on the streets.

A variant of the demobilization thesis suggests that civil society has become increasingly voiceless as the second postapartheid administration under President Mbeki has ignored citizens' groups in its desire to assert its authority and ensure "delivery" of services and public goods. Certainly, citizens' groups do not enjoy the guaranteed access to policy discussions available to them in the first five years of democracy. The Mbeki administration is less inclined to invite civil society organizations into policy formulation than the Mandela government. But the claim that citizens can no longer act to press government to do what they want done is contradicted by the same issue, HIV/AIDS, which seemed to confirm it: the government policy change on this issue is the result of action by citizens ranging from the activists of the Treatment Action Campaign (TAC) and the Congress of South African Trade Unions (Cosatu) to health professionals. Citizens who are able to organize and participate in public policy debates can and do influence government decisions.

Civil society's limitations lie, therefore, not in its lack of energy or independence but in the reality that many South Africans cannot participate in civil society activity and so are unable to influence policy. The absence of a voice for the poor in development policy making is demonstrated by research which, since democracy's advent, has shown significant gulfs between the policy preoccupations of grassroots people and those of the better organized and resourced sections of society who participate in the policy debate. As early as 1994, focus group research showed that grassroots citizens, who often become extremely articulate on political and social issues when speaking their home languages rather than English, showed a sophisticated understanding of the constraints that attempts to dismantle inequality and address poverty faced. But it also showed significant gaps between the desires and needs of people at the grassroots and the assumptions of the policy debate.[30]

The most compelling evidence of this gap is also the most important obstacle to society's attempts to address poverty since 1994—the repeated mismatch between antipoverty policy and programs on the one hand, the circumstances and needs of the poor on the other. Two of many examples may make the point.

The first is that all the key players in our social policy debate—political parties, labor, business, nongovernmental, and civic organizations—spent several years in the National Housing Forum during the 1990s negotiating ways to ensure that poor people gained access to mortgage finance. But research and observed behavior show that the vast majority of poor people do not want mortgaged housing, for a very good reason.[31] In the 1980s, after black people gained the right to own property in the cities, housing market players substantially overestimated the ability of township residents to pay for housing. Many people were persuaded to buy bonded housing only to find that they could not afford the payments. For many poor people, therefore, mortgages are associated with eviction and repossession for not meeting payments, ensuring a reluctance to use this form of housing finance. Yet none of the participants in the policy debate seemed sufficiently in touch with the poor to know that mortgages were not a desired solution to housing need.

The second example is that it took almost a decade of democracy for the mainstream debate to realize that social pensions are the society's most effective means of poverty relief.[32] Through the 1990s, both government and civil society assumed that pensions were a way of keeping some senior citizens from destitution. It was only after an official committee introduced decision makers to the considerable research showing that these pensions were the key form of income support to poor households which included a pensioner, that a key feature of the experiences of the poor and a crucial route to alleviating poverty entered the mainstream debate. The emergence of a basic income grant (BIG) campaign led by Cosatu also played a role. However, it is open to question whether the import has been fully absorbed by policy makers. The level of increase accorded social pensions in the last two budgets, which for the first time acknowledged their importance, seems low given the recognition in principle of the role they play in addressing poverty.[33]

These two examples show the degree to which information about grassroots citizens, which would surely be obvious to public representatives or civic society associations in touch with the poor, elude participants in the policy debate. The obvious conclusion is that the poor are not represented in that debate because, on social policy issues, no one yet speaks for them. Indeed, the tendency to speak of "the poor" as if all poor people share the same circumstances and needs is in itself an illustration of this. Different categories of the poor are poor for different reasons. Gender, illegal immigrant status, lack of industrial skills, or education deficits may all produce different circumstances and needs. The frequent failure to acknowledge the differences among the poor confirms the gulf between those who live in poverty and those of us who take part in policy debates.

Postapartheid South Africa does face a participation problem. But the issue is not that citizens are unwilling to take part in politics or in the policy debate. It is that willingness to vote does not ensure participation in policy discussion. And it is not that civil society has been silenced or fatally weakened by apartheid's end, leaving the citizenry without a means to hold government to account. The problem is that civil society, while vigorous, is also shallow, unable to extend its reach to society's grassroots.

The reality that the grassroots poor still lack a voice between elections also ensures that development policy and programs often misread the needs of beneficiaries and so fail to achieve their intended effect. The lack of a voice for the poor may also hamper policy implementation, reducing the reach of the democratic state. Effective implementation is usually seen as a technical issue, its absence as a symptom of a lack of managerial capacity in the new public service. The institutions responsible for implementation, it is assumed, lack the know-how that would enable them to do the job as it is meant to be done. Clearly, skills and experience do play a role in determining whether intentions are realized. But equally if not more important is the relationship between government and citizens.

Governments face a variety of priorities: which ones they address will depend in large measure on which lobbies are able to attract government attention. If the poor lack a voice, pressure for more effective implementation is unlikely to be directed at measures that really do enhance their quality of life. To illustrate, politicians and officials face little pressure to improve the quality of service in pension queues. The Department of Social Development has undertaken an energetic drive to inspire civil society organizations to help reach more people entitled to social grants,[34] which shows that leadership can at times substitute for active citizen pressure. But approaches that depend on a particular minister or official are far less secure than those that respond to an active citizenry. Where citizens are actively insisting on effective implementation, success is far more likely since the issue moves up government priority lists, making the search for solutions and the appropriate people to achieve them, more urgent. Government effectiveness in fighting poverty, or pursuing many other goals, is far more likely, therefore, when those who would benefit from performance insist on it loudly. The lack of a voice for the poor leaves the implementation of antipoverty policy to the good intentions of government officials and civil society organizations. However good those intentions prove to be, priorities are inevitably driven by those who have a voice and, if the poor lack one, their concerns are likely to take a back seat.

The Vicious Cycle

If limited participation impairs the new democracy's ability to address poverty, poverty in turn has implications for political participation.

It is far more difficult for the poor to participate in public life. Political influence is a product of organization.[35] This requires resources that poor people do not have. A key reason why the poor are unheard may be that, unlike factory workers who *are* heard, most poor people are engaged in dispersed, casual, or informal work in which they lack bargaining power. It is far more difficult for them to act in concert. If factory workers strike, their employer is damaged, but if street traders stop working only they lose income.[36] Poverty also often means separation from access to decision making, not being able to get to those places where government can be reached. It can also, as implied earlier, mean not being able to speak the language in which the policy debate is conducted.

This is not only a limitation on democracy. It also holds consequences for the longer-term survival of the system. If levels of participation are limited, then so are the pressures to ensure that government remains accountable and responsive to citizens. The dangers of corruption, mismanagement, and ineffectiveness then greatly increase. And, if citizens do not feel that the government is listening to them or looking out for them, it is likely that they will not cooperate with it. Since all governments, particularly those that are democratic, need citizen cooperation to govern, this could mean a decline in compliance with government aims. For many, government could become something alien, unable to influence their lives just as they are unable to influence it. The system will remain weak and its future will remain uncertain as long as substantial levels of poverty limit democratic government's reach to many citizens.

A key requirement of an effective democratic system is that it must be inclusive. All citizens must feel that democracy offers them avenues for expression should they wish to use them. Constraints on participation are important not only because the right to participate in public life is an essential democratic right but because they impair the system's inclusiveness and, therefore, its effectiveness.

In some analyses, the inclusiveness of South African democracy is understood purely as a matter of offering a political space for identity minorities, in particular, racial minorities.[37] Clearly, this addresses part of the problem. Since identity politics is primary at election time and continues to matter to some degree between elections, a racial minority that is also identified with a system of minority rule is likely to face the risk of political exclusion. However, at this stage, while most white voters continue to vote for parties that are unlikely to ever win an election, it is difficult to sustain the point that whites are excluded from the South African policy debate. Indeed, it could be argued that their resources, greater access to fluency in English, and their experience of having wielded power in the past continue to give them an inherent advantage, even if they do not enjoy direct access to government decision makers. Continuing to voice the perspectives of minorities remains a key function of opposition parties. But the poor have no similar resources. The constraints on their participation do constitute a form of exclusion, removing a substantial section of the society from the opportunity to participate in public deliberation on policy. The result is that expanding inclusion remains a key task of South African democracy.

Cures That Do Not Heal

In government and society, attempts to provide vehicles for deepened participation may serve only to maintain the democratic deficit at the grassroots.

Where the government recognizes the lack of channels for democratic participation at the grassroots as a problem, its response tends to focus on creating forums or public participation vehicles that are said to allow officials to hear the voice of the grassroots. But because only those who are organized are likely to enjoy a voice, these exercises usually do more to shut out than to let in the voices of poor people. Participation exercises are inherently biased toward the organized. The selection of participants inevitably focuses on those organized enough to be noticed and those possessing the capacities required to participate in them, such as the ability to discuss policy questions in a manner explicable to the powerful, which is usually unavailable to the poor.[38] These attempts to identify grassroots "representatives of the poor" are, therefore, likely merely to anoint some of the organized as authentic spokespeople for those they do not represent.

These realities suggest that the prospects for effective participation in policy debates by the poor rest not on the creation of participation mechanisms alongside representative democracy but in deepening and broadening democratic institutions and practices. Some analysts insist that the solution lies in an end to the closed list proportional representation system that is said to strengthen the hand of party leaderships at the expense of the grassroots.[39] Devolving power to subnational government rather than relegating provinces and municipalities to implementing decisions made elsewhere might enhance participation by poor people, since they are often able only to access those arms of government nearest to them. If those spheres of government accessible to the poor cannot take decisions, poor people are effectively deprived of access to political decision making. It may be no accident that the experiments in pro-poor politics often lauded by activists and academics, such as the Greater London Council, Kerala in India, and Porto Allegre in Brazil, were all the work of provincial or local governments.

These changes are, however, likely to have only limited effect as long as political parties remain as centralized as they are now. A trend within the ANC to centralization, the chief feature of which is the selection of provincial and local government candidates by the national leadership rather than regional and local branches,[40] is mirrored in the other larger parties. In the 2004 campaign, the ANC did not see fit to release the names of its candidates for provincial premier before the election,[41] while the DA left key slots on its election list open, giving its leader the prerogative to fill them.[42] Centralization is also accompanied by an insistence on strict party discipline in subnational legislatures as well as in national parliament. In this context, both the introduction of constituency electoral systems and formal decentralization are unlikely to make a difference, unless accompanied by a change in political approach. In the 1995 local elections, the effect of a ward or constituency system was nullified by the fact that local politicians with histories of civic activism lost ANC nominations to candidates who owed a position by the movement.[43] Local councilors have faced expulsion for not voting their party line. Party discipline has largely ensured that subnational governments act as implementing agents for national government.[44]

Outside government, much has been made by its left critics of the emergence of "new social movements" which seek to mobilize the grassroots poor against government economic and social policy. These movements' intellectual supporters have argued that they provide a new mode of expression for the poor who are ignored by government policy, that they are showing "how struggle in the new South Africa may be rediscovered and re-created."[45] Perhaps the best-known social movement is the TAC, which led the fight for antiretroviral medicines for people living with HIV and AIDS. However, the TAC's incremental approach to change and its willingness to use constitutional mechanisms, such as the courts, the Public Protector, and the Competition Tribunal to pursue its goals, tends to separate it from most of the other movements whose tactics seem more concerned to delegitimize the government than to win concrete gains.[46]

Claims that social movement engagement represents a new form of mass participation lack evidence. The TAC is one of the few social movements to recruit members, so the support base of the others remains unclear. On the rare occasions when the support of the new movements has been tested, they have been found wanting. All sixteen social movement activists who contested the 2000 municipal elections were defeated. Celebrated movement activist Trevor Ngwane received less than 30 percent of the vote in his Soweto ward.[47] In 2004, the Landless People's Movement launched a "No Land, No Vote" campaign that sought to boycott registration. Despite this, more than 3 million people registered for the first time, bringing the total of registered South Africans to over 20 million, the largest registration figure in the country's history.[48] Social movement activists and their intellectual sympathizers insist that these tests do not matter because the influence of social movements is not derived from "traditional" sources of power such as an organized support base. Yet it is hard to see how a movement that canvasses votes but fails to get them, or that exhorts people not to register but fails to persuade them, can be said to be exerting influence. It is possible that the social movements are expressing the concerns of many people, but this remains untested. Even if it were to be demonstrated, it would be difficult to see social movement activism as a significant new force on the political landscape without evidence of an ability to turn support into organized power. The constraints on organizing the poor are great and there is no evidence that social movement activists have given serious attention to how they can be overcome.[49] Until they do, social movement activism is likely to remain a source of alternative social and economic perspectives, but not of political or social power.

Thus far, neither the response of the government nor of those who see themselves as an alternative to it has provided a plausible source of participation for the poor. Within government, an approach that seeks to ensure that representative institutions are closer to the grassroots and that government officials are better attuned to hear the voice of poor people could offer an alternative to current approaches.[50] The first step toward an attempt to deepen democracy in this way would be a recognition among elites that deeper democracy, greater participation, and free political contest—not a simple recourse to technical expertise—are the keys to a society in which poverty is reduced and democracy becomes available to all. Among those who seek to speak for the poor, devising strategies that would stimulate sufficient organization to enable the voices of the poor to be heard remains the central challenge.

The 2004 Election: Farewell to All That?

What, if anything, does the 2004 election tell us about these trends?

The key message was that some of the identity-based assets of the democratic system are wasting. The election result showed that the formal checks and balances on the governing party since 1994 had been products of identity expressions, which reflect a past that is rapidly fading.

In the first two elections, the electoral dominance of the ANC was leavened by results that produced opposition premiers in two provinces and denied it a two-thirds majority in Parliament. This was, however, a consequence of an identity politics that is a product of the past. In KZN, it relied on an IFP vote which, while it may remain significant for some time, is never again likely to be able to deny the ANC provincial power because it erodes as demographic processes, such as black integration into the urban economy, proceed. In the Western Cape, the ANC may have been able to win the premiership because of a shift in the coloured vote that is, in principle, reversible. But the demographic reality that has denied the ANC the province, apartheid-directed restrictions on black African settlement, are themselves eroding and the province is destined to house an African majority.

The 2004 result confirms, therefore, that these checks on majority party power within the system are a product of demographics whose inevitable waning is certain to buttress ANC electoral dominance under current conditions. This is likely to persist until a new opposition capable of winning majority support emerges. Given the dominance of the identity that propels the ANC to power, it seems likely that this new opposition will emerge from within the ANC. The reality that some identity manifestations are waning does not mean that identity will cease to be a key determinant of political behavior.

The political consequences may be less significant than we might assume. The ANC has a two-thirds majority as a result of these shifts. But, in effect, it had one between 1999 and 2004 since it could have mustered the required majority on any issue on which it wanted a constitutional change. And, while non-ANC premierships in KZN and Western Cape did produce some difference in approach in these provinces, most notably on HIV/AIDS, the opposition provinces have not acted as a significant break on ANC power, since it was able to ensure the same broad policy parameters in all provinces. Civil society will remain the chief source of countervailing power, just as it did in the five years before 2004.

Whether this reality is replaced by vigorous party competition when an opposition does emerge out of the ANC will depend on the precedents set between now and then. The fact that the IFP withdrew its complaints from the Independent Electoral Commission (IEC) about alleged electoral irregularities in KZN and accepted the result—and that violence was contained (although not avoided altogether) during the province's campaign does suggest that the principle of alternation of power through the ballot box has passed a test. However, the inclusion of IFP members in the provincial executive does reduce the impact of this advance because the IFP did not lose all access to government office. The political practices that emerge may also depend on whether identity politics is sufficient to maintain relatively high levels of voter participation. Even if that is achieved, however, achieving greater participation by most voters between elections will remain one of the key challenges if the democratic order is to remain in a healthy enough shape to offer a vehicle for democratic invigoration when the opposition of the future emerges.

Notes

1. Hermann Giliomee and Charles Simkins, eds. *The Awkward Embrace: One-Party Domination and Democracy* (Amsterdam and Cape Town: Harwood Academic Publishers and Tafelberg, 1999).
2. One survey reports that "an alarming 13%" of registered voters were planning not to vote in the 2004 election. Only in South Africa, it appears, could a prospective 87% poll be seen as a distressing sign of voter apathy. SABC/Markinor, "Opinion 2004: Possible Turnout, Voter Registration and Apathy" March 26, 2004 (Pretoria and Cape Town: Markinor), 1.
3. Robert Fine, "Civil Society Theory and the Politics of Transition in South Africa," *Review of African Political Economy* 20, no. 55 (November 1993): 71–83.
4. Steven Friedman and Louise Stack, "The Magic Moment: The 1994 Election," in *The Small Miracle: South Africa's Negotiated Settlement*, ed. Steven Friedman and Doreen Atkinson (Johannesburg: Ravan Press, 1994), 310.

5. Guillermo O'Donnell, "On the State, Democratization and Some Conceptual Problems: A Latin American View With Glances at Some Post-Communist Countries," *World Development* 21, no. 8 (1993): 1355–1369.

6. Ivor Chipkin with Paul Thulare, *The Limits of Governance: Prospects for Local Government after the Katorus War* (Johannesburg: Centre for Policy Studies, 1997).

7. Steven Friedman, "SA's Democratic Freedoms Not Necessarily Available to All," *Business Day,* November 26, 2003.

8. For an analysis of identity in the 1999 election see Steven Friedman, "Who We Are: Voter Participation, Rationality and the 1999 Election," *Politikon* 26, no. 2 (1999): 213–224.

9. The three metropolitan areas are eThekwini (Durban), Ekurhuleni (East Rand), and Joburg (Johannesburg). Some 29% of black African residents felt that the council was doing a poor or very poor job. The comparative figure for whites was 18%. In the suburbs, an opposition heartland, 60% of respondents felt the council was doing a good or very good job (SA Cities Network, "State of the Cities Report 2004," Johannesburg: SA Cities Network, 2004).

10. The claim that elections in divided societies have this property is advanced by Donald Horowitz, *A Democratic South Africa?: Constitutional Engineering in a Divided Society* (Cape Town: Oxford University Press, 1991).

11. Clifford Geertz, *The Interpretation of Cultures* (New York: Basic Books, 1973).

12. That they do is claimed by Anthony Downs, *An Economic Theory of Democracy* (New York: Harper and Row, 1957); that they do not is argued by Donald Green and Ian Shapiro, *Pathologies of Rational Choice Theory* (New Haven: Yale University Press, 1996).

13. Graeme Gotz, *Buying In, Staying Out: The Politics of Registration for South Africa's First Democratic Local Government Elections* (Johannesburg: Centre for Policy Studies, October 1995).

14. Calculated by comparing the likely registration figure with intention to vote expressed in surveys. On the first, see Shaun Mackay, "IEC's Sleight of Hand is Not in Electorate's Long-Term Interest," *Synopsis* 3, no. 1 (March 1999); on the second see Rod Alence and Michael O'Donovan, If South Africa's Second Democratic Election Had Been Held in March 1999: A Simulation of Participation and Party Support Patterns (mimeo, Pretoria: Human Sciences Research Council, 1999), 7.

15. SABC/Markinor, Opinion 2004, 3.

16. See, e.g., "War of Words on Arms Deal Cash for ANC," *Business Day*, February 12, 2004.

17. Steven Friedman, "South Africa: Entering the Post-Mandela Era," *Journal of Democracy* 10, no. 4 (October 1999), 3–18.

18. Guillermo O'Donnell, "Notes on the State of Democracy in Latin America" (paper prepared for the project "Desafios de la Democracia en América Latina," sponsored by the Regional Division for Latin America and the Caribbean of the United Nations Development Program, undated).

19. Access to sites on which to build shacks is a crucial source of power in informal settlements. See e.g., Josette Cole, *Crossroads: The Politics of Reform and Repression 1976–1986* (Johannesburg: Ravan, 1988). On the way in which access to trading licenses can buttress unaccountable power see Paul Thulare, "Trading Democracy? Johannesburg Informal Traders and Citizenshi," *Policy Issues and Actors* 17 no. 1 (February 2004) (Johannesburg: Centre for Policy Studies).

20. Steven Friedman, "The Problem With Policy," *Policy Brief* 1 (Johannesburg: Centre for Policy Studies, 1998); Meshack M. Khosa, "Towards Effective Delivery: Synthesis Report on the Project Entitled 'Closing the Gap between Policy and Implementation,'" Social policy series research report no. 98 (Johannesburg: Centre for Policy Studies, February 2003).

21. On the idea of a "world class city" see Johannesburg Metropolitan Council, "iGoli Online: Building an African World Class City," www.igoli,gov.za. For a critique see Steven Friedman, "A Quest for Control: High Modernism and its Discontents in Johannesburg, South Africa," in

Urban Governance Around the World, ed. Blair A. Ruble, Richard E. Stren, Joseph S. Tulchin with Diana H. Varat (Washington DC: Woodrow Wilson Center for International Scholars, 2002).

22. A case in point may be reports that mining executive Bobby Godsell acted as a catalyst to a rapprochement between two opposition parties, the Democratic Alliance and Inkatha Freedom Party, elicited little hostile reaction from the government. Godsell's personal association with the DA and its predecessor liberal parties stretches back several decades.

23. Friedman and Stack, "The Magic Moment," 307–311.

24. Steven Friedman, "Yesterday's Pact: Power-Sharing and Legitimate Governance in Post-Settlement South Africa" (Johannesburg: Centre for Policy Studies, 1995).

25. Servaas van den Bergh and Haroon Bhorat, "The Present as a Legacy of the Past: The Labour Market, Inequality and Poverty in South Africa," DPRU Working Paper 99/29 (Cape Town: Development Policy Research Unit, University of Cape Town, 1999); and Mike McGrath and Andrew Whiteford, "Disparate Circumstances," *Indicator SA* 11, no. 3 (Winter 1994): 47–50.

26. See, e.g., "Statistics South Africa," *Measuring Poverty*, September 7, 2000.

27. Haroon Bhorat, "The Post-Apartheid Challenge: Labour Demand Trends in the South African Labour Market, 1995–1999," Working Paper 03/82 (Cape Town: Development Policy Research Unit, University of Cape Town, 2003); and Laura Poswell, "The Post-Apartheid Labour Market: A Status Report" (Cape Town: Development Policy Research Unit, University of Cape Town, February 2002).

28. Haroon Bhorat, "Labour Market Challenges in the Post-Apartheid South Africa" (paper presented at the Colloquium on Poverty and Development, Cape Town, October 1, 2003).

29. T. H. Marshall, *Class, Citizenship and Social Development* (Westport, CT: Greenwood Press, 1964).

30. Craig Charney, *Voices of a New Democracy: African Expectations in the New South Africa* (Johannesburg: Centre for Policy Studies, 1995).

31. Mary Tomlinson, *From Rejection to Resignation: Beneficiaries' Views on the Government's Housing Subsidy Scheme* (Johannesburg: Centre for Policy Studies, 1996); Mary Tomlinson, *Mortgage Bondage?: Financial Institutions and Low-Cost Housing Delivery* (Johannesburg: Centre for Policy Studies, 1997).

32. See, e.g., Julian May, et al., *Poverty and Inequality Report* (Durban: Praxis Publishers, 1998).

33. Trevor A. Manuel, "South African Budget 2002," Budget Speech by Minister T Manuel, February 20, 2002.

34. See "State Aims to Plant Seeds of Growth in SA by Nurturing Self-Reliance," *Business Day*, February 19, 2004.

35. For an analysis of the use of organization to address poverty under democratic conditions see Adam Przeworski, *Capitalism and Social Democracy* (Cambridge: Cambridge University Press, 1987).

36. Steven Friedman and Ivor Chipkin, *A Poor Voice? The Politics of Inequality in South Africa* (Johannesburg: Centre for Policy Studies, 2001).

37. See, e.g., Arend Lijphart, *Power-Sharing in South Africa* (Berkeley: University of California Press, 1985); Horowitz, "A Democratic South Africa"; and Hermann Giliomee, "The Communal Nature of the South African Conflict," in *Negotiating South Africa's Future*, ed. Hermann Giliomee and Lawrence Schlemmer (Johannesburg: Southern, 1989).

38. Centre for Policy Studies, *Civil Society and Poverty Reduction in Southern Africa* (Johannesburg: Centre for Policy Studies mimeo, July 2002).

39. Giovanni Sartori, "How Could the Constitution Limit Majority Rule?" *Transact* 2, no. 8 (September 1995): 4–12.

40. Thabo Rapoo, "Twist in the Tail?: The ANC and the Appointment of Provincial Premiers," Policy Brief 7 (Johannesburg: Centre for Policy Studies, October 1998).

41. Tom Lodge, "Parties, Not People," *Election Update 2004 South Africa* no. 3 (Johannesburg: Electoral Institute of Southern Africa, March 1, 2004), 2–3.

42. "Tension in DA Ranks Over Gauteng List," *Business Day*, January 27, 2004.

43. Graeme Gotz, *The Process and the Product: The November Local Elections and the Future of Local Government* (Johannesburg: Centre for Policy Studies, 1996).

44. See, e.g., Steven Friedman, "Ethnicity of a Special Type: Race, Ethnicity and Politics in South Africa" (paper presented at the conference on Constitutionalism in Africa, Moorehouse College, Atlanta, 1998). See also Ivor Chipkin, City and Community: Local Government and the Legacy of the "One City" *Slogan* (Johannesburg: Centre for Policy Studies, 1995).

45. Ashwin Desai, *We are the Poors: Community Struggles in Post-Apartheid South Africa* (New York: Monthly Review Press, 2002), 13.

46. See, e.g., critique of the ANC in Desai, *We are the Poors*, 9–12.

47. "Independents could be Future Force" *The Star*, December 6, 2000.

48. Independent Electoral Commission, "Electoral Commission Announces Final Registration Results" January 29, 2004, accessed at http://www.elections.org.za/news.

49. The TAC is in a somewhat different category here but its concern is not to challenge the governing party politically but to win gains from it.

50. Proposals on how this could be achieved are given in Steven Friedman, "The Silent Citizen: Poverty, Participation and the Health of our Democracy" (paper presented at the Foundation of Human Rights conference *In Pursuit of Justice: Celebrating a Decade of Democracy*, Durban January 25, 2004).

CHAPTER TWO

The Electoral Implications of Social and Economic Change since 1994

Jeremy Seekings

Voting behavior in most countries is shaped by voters' social and economic positions. Social and economic changes therefore often have profound electoral implications, eroding support for some parties while improving opportunities for others. Since the end of apartheid in 1994, South African society has changed dramatically, with the rapid growth of the black middle classes at the same time as rising unemployment and declining life expectancy due to AIDS. Inequality has continued to shift from race to class, with growing intraracial inequalities. Yet these social and economic changes have not recast the country's political cleavages. Racial identities have proved resilient and political loyalties seem deep rooted. The major political parties have proved more adept at forging racially based, cross-class than cross-racial coalitions. There are signs of the growing salience of class, but not in the electoral arena.

The Changing Electorate

The electorate changes even if there are no major social and economic shifts in society. Between elections, some voters die, others reach voting age for the first time, some emigrate and others immigrate. Voters also migrate within the country, affecting provincial electoral contests.

South Africa's 2001 Population Census provides an indication of the importance of demographic change in the potential electorate.

South Africa's adult population (i.e., aged 18 years or older) stood at 27.4 million in 2001. Of these potential voters, 4.7 million (or 17 percent) were aged between 18 and 22 years old, which indicates that in 2004, 17 percent of the potential electorate would have been too young to have voted in the 1999 elections.[1] A similar number were between the ages of 23 and 27, meaning that they would have been too young to have voted in the first democratic elections, in 1994. Therefore, one-third of the potential electorate in 2004 was too young to have voted in 1994. This is a largely postapartheid generation of voters, with possibly different perceptions and attitudes to their elders.

Between 1994 and 2004, South Africa's population did not grow uniformly. Lower birth rates and higher emigration rates reduced the white proportion of the electorate. If the election had been held in 2001, 12 percent of the potential electorate would have been white, 9 percent coloured, 3 percent Indian, and 75 percent African.[2] With every passing year, the white proportion has been declining and the African share rising. In the 2004 elections, about 83 percent of the potential first-time voters were African, 8 percent were coloured, 2 percent were Indian, and just 7 percent were white.[3]

These demographic changes will, ultimately, impact on voting patterns as the new generation, with a different racial profile and no personal experience of apartheid, begins to exercise its electoral muscle. This could, in time, erode the strength of support for the African National Congress (ANC). For the moment, however, demographic changes seem to have strengthened the ANC relative to the opposition parties that competed primarily for the declining proportion of white, coloured, and Indian votes.

Income Inequality and Unemployment

Alongside demographic changes, economic patterns have shifted as well. Between the 1970s and 1990s patterns of inequality slowly changed, with interracial inequality declining and intraracial inequality growing.[4] This trend continued after 1994. Data from the 1995 and 2000 Income and Expenditure Surveys (IESs) suggest that the white share of total income declined from about 49 percent in 1995 to about 46 percent in 2000, while the African and coloured shares rose.[5] In 1995, 73 percent of the individuals in the top income decile (the richest 10 percent) were white, and only 18 percent African. By 2000, only 61 percent of the households in the top decile were white, and 25 percent were African.

The racial composition of the top two income deciles shifted dramatically over a very short period of time. There were, by 2000, about as many African households in the top income quintile (20 percent) as there were white households. At the same time, the Gini coefficient for income distribution within the African population rose from about 0.56 in 1995 to about 0.61 in 2000.[6]

These changes in inter- and intraracial inequality reflect a continuing shift from race to class as the basis of inequality in South Africa.[7] Perhaps the most dramatic manifestation of this has been the accelerating growth of the African elite and middle classes. The new African middle class comprises people in salaried jobs (such as managers and university lecturers), professionals, and entrepreneurs and capitalists. Upward occupational mobility, assisted by affirmative action, and reflected in the distribution of salaries has clearly caused more change in patterns of income distribution than black economic empowerment (BEE) through business opportunities.

The best data on black upward mobility into top income categories are data for the public sector. The proportion of managers at all levels who were African rose from 30 percent in 1995 to over 51 percent in 2001, with the total black proportion rising from 40 percent to over 63 percent. Changes in the composition of senior management are more muted, but nevertheless by 2001 there were more black than white senior managers.[8] The 2001 census suggested that there were still more white than black "legislators, senior officials, and managers" (56 percent versus 44 percent) and equal numbers of professionals, but there were many more black than white "technicians and associate professionals" (69 percent versus 31 percent). If these three categories are combined, there are many more black than white people in them (57 percent versus 43 percent, with 41 percent African). The pace of transformation in the private sector is clearly slower than in the public sector, but even a slower pace of change results in significant shifts in the relationship between race and class in South Africa.

The changing racial composition of these high-earning occupations reflects several factors. First, there is a rising supply of African and black graduates from universities and Technikons. Second, emigration has reduced the supply of white professionals and managers, leaving more room at the top for African and black men and women. Third, active policies of affirmative action and, to a lesser extent, BEE have inflated the demand for black and especially African personnel. This last factor provides the growing African middle classes with strong incentives to support the ANC.

If expanding opportunities for upward mobility into or within the middle class provided good reasons for some to vote for the incumbent party, it might be expected that rising unemployment and declining formal employment would have given many other ANC supporters good reasons to withdraw their support. Unemployment rates continued to rise after 1994, from about 20 percent to over 30 percent (in terms of the official, or strict, definition of unemployment) or from about 30 percent to over 40 percent (using the more appropriate expanded definition).[9] Rising unemployment increases inequality. In South Africa, where there is no subsistence agricultural sector to fall back on, unemployment is closely associated with poverty.[10]

In between the prospering middle classes and the impoverished unemployed lies the bulk of the working population. The new Labour Relations Act strengthened the bargaining position of organized labor, so that wages were insulated from the pressures of massive unemployment. Workers in formal, regular employment prospered, as long as they kept their jobs. Facing rising wages despite unemployment, employers sought to reduce their labor costs through either investing in more capital-intensive production or outsourcing labor-intensive activities. The result was continuing "re-segmentation" in the labor market, with a deepening divide between workers in formal, regular employment, mostly with skills, and those in casual or contract employment, mostly unskilled.[11] Across the economy as a whole, the demand for unskilled labor has plummeted. Real average remuneration therefore grew at the same time as formal employment fell.[12]

There is some evidence from surveys on whose earnings changed over time. Data on a panel of African people in KwaZulu-Natal (KZN) show that the real earnings of workers in regular employment rose by 30 percent between 1993 and 1998, compared to an overall average change in earnings of just 7 percent.[13] The earnings of workers in regular employment grew faster than the average for everyone in the panel. Some of this spectacular increase was because new entrants into formal employment had higher wages than those who left. But even among workers who were in formal employment in both 1993 and 1998, earnings rose by 20 percent.[14]

This does not mean that all members of these working classes prospered. The earnings of workers who lost or left their jobs plummeted, because few of the people unable to find formal employment are absorbed into the informal sector. South Africa is unusual in that it is a middle-income developing country with high unemployment and a relatively small informal sector. The few people who do end up in the informal sector tend to earn very low incomes.[15]

If unemployment is one of the most pressing socioeconomic problems of postapartheid South Africa, HIV/AIDS is surely the second. In 2003, an estimated 14 percent of all South Africans were HIV-positive, with more than 1,000 people dying each day of AIDS. For households where breadwinners lose jobs due to poor health, or where children are withdrawn from school to care for sick family members, or for children whose parents die, the consequences of AIDS are clearly massive. Although the evidence is unclear, and much depends on the dynamic responses of employers to the pandemic, it appears likely that AIDS will worsen inequality in South Africa.[16]

Redistribution Through the Budget

The electoral implications of persistent poverty and rising unemployment are muted in part because of redistributive social policies. South Africa redistributes more extensively through the fiscus than any other developing country for which data is readily available.[17] Van der Berg has recently estimated that the Gini coefficient for the distribution of income is reduced by about 18 percentage points (to about 0.50) if taxes and cash transfers are taken into account, and by a further 6 percentage points (to perhaps 0.44) if the value of in-kind public social spending (primarily in the areas of health care and education) is taken into account.[18] This redistribution occurs primarily through three mechanisms: a progressive and efficient tax system; an exceptional public welfare system based primarily on de facto universal and generous old age pensions; and egalitarian public expenditure on education combined with high enrolment rates among poor children.[19]

In South Africa, the top income quintile pays at least three-quarters of all tax, including almost all income taxes and two-thirds of Value-Added Tax (VAT).[20] This is one of the reasons why tax funded public expenditure is redistributive. It also means that there is a narrow tax base, even though the treasury has benefited from improved efficiency in tax collection since 1994. Further increases in tax revenues would require either increasing taxes on the rich, who are already heavily taxed, or extending the tax base through increasing tax rates on the less rich classes. The former might have economic costs, the latter has obvious political costs.

While taxation is primarily paid by the rich, social spending is heavily focused on the poor. Despite the fiscally conservative Growth, Employment and Redistribution (GEAR) strategy, social spending rose in real terms in the decade after 1994 and became more pro-poor.

The proportion of public spending in the areas of education, health, social assistance, housing, and water that was directed toward households in the bottom income quintile rose from 31 percent in 1993 to 33 percent in 1997. The proportion spent on the top quintile was reduced dramatically to just 8 percent.[21] Welfare spending is very pro-poor, especially taking into consideration old-age pensions, disability grants, and the new child support grant. By 2004, almost six million people—or one in seven South Africans—received one or other noncontributory government grant. Education spending also became much more pro-poor after 1994. Teachers in rural areas especially were paid more, teaching posts were allocated from richer to poorer schools, and nonpersonnel expenditure was concentrated on poor schools.

South Africa might be exceptional in terms of the scale of redistribution from rich to poor through the budget, but this does not mean that poverty is eliminated. South Africa has a generous and inclusive system of social assistance. Yet, this safety net has a loose weave and many poor people fall through the holes.[22] Crucially, there is no cash support for households that include no pensioners, no disabled people, and no young children, that is, for households that are poor because they include unemployed people who are able-bodied and of working age.

To address this problem, the government-appointed Taylor Committee (the Committee of Inquiry into a Comprehensive System of Social Security in South Africa) recommended the conditional and phased introduction of a basic income grant (BIG) paying R100 to every South African, regardless of income or need. Even if financed out of increased sales taxes, a BIG would entail substantial redistribution and poverty reduction.[23] The ANC-led government did not accept the proposal. The welfare system thus continues to achieve very uneven poverty reduction, despite being redistributive. The in-kind benefits of public expenditure on education are also of limited advantage to the poor, given the low quality of much public education and the poor prospects for the less skilled in securing well-paid jobs. Finally, pro-poor expenditure on health care did not mean the provision of antiretroviral drugs to poor people with AIDS. While rich people could access drugs through medical aid schemes, poor people died.

Inequality and Identity

Under apartheid, South African politics was unsurprisingly racialized. With deracialization, but persistent inequality, massive unemployment, and a devastating AIDS pandemic, one might have expected politics to realign around class. Discontented voters might be expected to defect from the incumbent ANC, and support existing or new parties that would champion the interests of the poor majority against those of the increasingly multiracial elite. To date this has not happened, in large part because class has not eclipsed race as the primary basis of social identity and few poor people hold the government responsible for their continuing poverty.

The first requirement for a more class-oriented politics is that political attitudes must begin to orient around class rather than other social cleavages. In South Africa, citizens continue to select racial identities in preference to class identities in surveys. The 2000 Afrobarometer survey, for example, found that South Africans volunteered racial, ethnic, or linguistic identities five times more often than class ones (a higher ratio even than in Nigeria). Friedman has argued that South African politics revolves around racial identity rather than class interests. This, he suggests, may be good for democracy but bad for redistribution, as "identity politics . . . may limit both prospects for reducing inequality and the threat which it poses to the survival of formal democratic politics."[24]

At the same time, there are indications of a rising class consciousness. In early 2003, the Institute for Justice and Reconciliation included in its "Reconciliation Barometer" a question on South Africans' perception of the biggest division in the country. The precise wording was:

> People sometimes talk about the divisions between people in South Africa. Sometimes these divisions can cause people to feel left out or discriminated against. In other circumstances it can lead to anger and even violence between groups. What, in your experience, is the biggest division in South Africa today?

The options presented to the respondents were:

- The division between different political parties, like the ANC and IFP.
- The division between poor and middle income/wealthy South Africans.
- The division between those living with HIV/AIDS and other infectious diseases, and the rest of the community.
- The division between members of different religions.
- The divisions between Black, White, Coloured and Indian South Africans.
- The divisions between South Africans of different language groups.

The wording of the question might have led respondents to select either race (i.e., the fifth option), because of the reference to discrimination or parties (i.e., the first option), because of the reference to violence. Only one in five of the respondents selected the fifth option, with a similar proportion selecting the first option. More, 30 percent, selected the second option: class. Within each racial group, class was the most popular option: 29 percent of white and African respondents pointed to class as the biggest division in South Africa, and a slightly higher proportion of coloured and Indian respondents. Interestingly, responses do not seem to be related to household income.

The apparently limited salience of class consciousness does not mean that poorer people are content. South Africans prioritize job creation and crime as by far the two most important problems facing the country and express strong discontent with the government's performance on both issues. Yet, there are few signs of a distinct consciousness among the unemployed. One reason for this is that state policies that might contribute to unemployment, and hence inequality, are unusually opaque. It is not easy for poor people to trace the links between the state's industrial and labor market policies and unemployment and poverty, even if these policies contribute to rising capital intensity and productivity rather than job creation.

Indeed, although South African voters, including the ANC's own supporters, consistently identify unemployment as the most important problem facing the country *and* rate the government's performance on unemployment as very poor, they do not generally hold the government *responsible* for unemployment. The ANC-led government might be responding inadequately, but the causes of unemployment are seen to lie elsewhere.[25] South Africa might be unique in having an electorate that returns the governing party to power with large majorities despite poorly rating its performance on the most important issue facing the country.

While material discontent coexists with enduring racial identities among the poor, there are some signs of change in public attitudes. Mattes reports that surveys show declining confidence in the economy and trust in government. By 2000, he found that only one in three African respondents expected the economy to improve over the following year, and barely half said that the president was interested in their opinions (with even a smaller proportion saying this of Parliament). A sense of relative deprivation also seemed to be increasing:

Even in 1995, despite one of the highest rates of income inequality in the world, only 32 percent of South Africans said they were worse off than others. This was largely due to the fact that black South Africans tended to compare themselves to other blacks rather than to whites. By mid-2000, however, this figure had increased sharply to 50 percent. In the same survey, 31 percent of blacks said their lives were worse now than under apartheid, up sharply from 13 percent in 1997.[26]

Activists to the left of the ANC see data such as this and hopefully claim that there is a growing tide of militant class consciousness among the poor. Desai suggests that popular consciousness is even being internationalized, becoming part of the global struggle against "neoliberalism." Radicalized by their experiences of eviction or disconnection for nonpayment of rent or service charges, "the poors," as they have come to be known in the South African vernacular, "have begun making connections between their situation and that of people, first in Soweto and Tafelsig [Cape Town], but then also in Bolivia, South Korea, America's prisons, Zimbabwe and Chiapas."[27] There is little evidence, however, that this militant class consciousness extends beyond small circles of activists in particular areas.

Overall, the available evidence suggests that racial identities have proved resilient, even as a consciousness of class has increased. The resilience of racial identity is in part due to constant reinforcement by the ANC, both as the government and as a competitive political party. As the governing party, the ANC has taken political advantage of a range of pro-poor policies that it inherited in 1994 and strengthened thereafter. The party is adept at building new clinics and schools in areas where it is electorally threatened, such as the Eastern Cape in 1999. The recent willingness of the ANC to spend more on social policies might indicate a growing concern to retain the support of the rural poor. Given the fact that pro-poor policies are presented in terms of racial redress, they are bound to have an impact on people's identities, especially since redistribution through the fiscus is extensive, as shown earlier.

The ANC also plays the race card effectively in elections, preserving a racial cross-class coalition.[28] Whatever his intention, the effect of President Mbeki using the racialized discourse of "two nations" can only be to shore up racial identities and racialized allegiances. Racial privilege, rather than inequality more broadly, is the ANC's target. ANC supporters have remained loyal to the ANC in part because they give the party credit for democratization. The strength of partisan identification with the ANC is similar to the strength of partisan identification with the Democratic Party (DP) in the United States after a similar defining moment in American politics, the New Deal.

Even if public attitudes were more focused around class rather than race, there might be little opportunity for these attitudes to translate into more class-oriented political behavior. Two features of the political system serve to constrain change in the patterns of political activity. First, the ANC commands sufficient patronage to keep most senior black politicians on board, denuding most opposition parties of high-profile black leadership. The electoral system provides the ANC leadership with an important source of patronage: places on the ANC electoral lists. Control over appointments in both state and parastatal sectors, and opportunities for both legitimate and illegitimate business activities, all serve to keep aspiring black elites behind the party. Second, and partly in consequence, the major opposition parties are not attractive to disillusioned ANC supporters.[29] The result is that the party system remains racialized. As Friedman puts it, there is no class-based party competing for power; insofar as struggles over class occur, it is within not between racialized alliances.[30]

AIDS, like unemployment, is yet to have clear electoral implications. The government's nonresponse to AIDS prompted strong criticism from opposition parties and the emergence of the Treatment Action Campaign (TAC), a high-profile activist organization. The TAC successfully used the courts and media to effect changes in government policy. But the TAC is not a mass organization and public criticism of government policy has not led voters to support other political parties. HIV-positive people are not a well-defined political constituency. This might be due to the lower importance that voters attach to health, compared to other issues such as unemployment and crime. South Africans do not seem to acknowledge that there is a major problem with AIDS. Even if the problem is acknowledged, the government might be seen as responding poorly, but is not held responsible.

Expectations of Mobility

There is another possible explanation for the acquiescence of poor voters. Voters might be making decisions about political allegiance and protest based not so much on current social or economic positions as on their expected future positions. Citizens' perceptions of opportunities for upward mobility might be expected to shape their identities and allegiances as well as their judgments on the legitimacy of inequality. The perception that economic liberalization might promote a more meritocratic society might explain why poor voters in a number of new democracies have endorsed market reforms, even when those reforms have heightened inequality.[31]

In South Africa, there is evidence that expectations are shaping political behavior. Most poor voters have remained loyal to the ANC in part because they are patient in waiting for their expectations of change to be fulfilled.[32] Perhaps these voters' expectations of future improvements are more important than their experiences of hardship, even deepening hardship, now. At its height, apartheid entailed an unprecedented system for improving the opportunities open to white people while restricting those open to black people. With the end of apartheid, the distribution of opportunities has surely moved in a more meritocratic direction.

There is indeed some "absolute" upward mobility by black South Africans. Absolute mobility is due to changes in the overall class structure: an expansion of higher-class occupations pulls in some individuals from lower-class backgrounds. In the late twentieth century, the expansion over time of semiskilled, skilled, and white-collar employment meant new opportunities for upward mobility for many African people.[33] It is not unusual for a young office worker to have a father who was a semi-skilled or skilled worker in manufacturing and a mother who was a domestic worker, and grandparents who were farm workers, unskilled migrant mine workers, or who never had formal employment and never left their homes in the reserves.

But access to new opportunities is clearly not spread evenly across all sections of the African population. More room for African people at the top has not meant that all Africans face similar chances of getting there. The relative mobility rate for individuals from lower-class backgrounds is lower than that for individuals who start off in higher classes. The dismantling of racial discrimination, improved public and private schooling, and policies of affirmative action and BEE have changed relative mobility rates. Some, mostly urban, African households enjoy greatly superior access to the new opportunities. They have the educational qualifications required for skilled employment, and the social capital (or contacts) necessary to secure such employment. Other African households, especially in remote Bantustan settlements, lack education and social capital. This underclass is "truly disadvantaged" in terms of its marginalization in the labor market, that is, its lack of access to opportunities.[34] Such disadvantage also seems to be reproduced between generations. In other words, the children of poor parents face immense difficulties in rising out of poverty.[35]

The HIV/AIDS pandemic only aggravates these problems. Trends in intergenerational and intragenerational mobility as well as in morbidity and mortality due to AIDS suggest that the poor suffer enduring disadvantages in a range of respects. Children growing up in poor households are likely to be disadvantaged in terms of both human capital (i.e., educational attainment) and social capital (in terms of connections in the labor market). They are much more likely to spend their lives in intermittent employment and unemployment, with their employment comprising unskilled and often casual work and their spells of unemployment being long. They are also more likely to fall sick and die, leaving dependents in an especially weak position.

The currently available analysis of and evidence on mobility suggest that the South African economy is something like a game of snakes and ladders. The snakes are the shocks of job loss, the disability or death of a breadwinner due to AIDS, and perhaps also the experiences of crime and social obligations that wipe out the savings of entrepreneurs and inhibit capital accumulation. The ladders involve, above all, getting a job, and also, less directly, acquiring social and human capital. The snakes appear to be distributed fairly randomly, meaning that people in all sorts of social or economic positions are vulnerable. Retrenchment, AIDS-related morbidity and mortality, and even the loss of savings affect both poor and well-off households. But the ladders are not distributed randomly. Relatively disadvantaged households are less likely to find ladders than relatively advantaged ones. They are less likely to acquire the human and social capital that helps secure any employment and especially better-paid employment. Spells of unemployment are likely to be longer, the effects of AIDS-related morbidity or mortality more enduring, and the experiences of crime or social obligations more devastating.

Unfortunately, little research has been conducted on the relationship between disadvantage and perceptions of opportunity and future prospects, or between these and a wider range of social and political attitudes. How do people in different positions in society assess their prospects? How do they perceive the possibilities of encountering either snakes or ladders? And what do they anticipate would be the consequences of sliding down a snake or climbing a ladder?

Attitudinal surveys have indicated that African citizens have been, in general, optimistic about the future, although their optimism may have declined at the very end of the 1990s. They are more positive than citizens in, for example, Brazil in their assessment of the chances of poor people to escape from poverty, and are more likely to attribute poverty to laziness. Their support for the ANC has been closely linked to their optimism about the future. It is unclear, however, whether optimism is related to perceived current or prospective opportunities, or how such perceived opportunities are in fact congruent with real opportunities.

Leaving aside methodological and evidentiary concerns, there are good reasons to doubt whether, less than ten years after the fall of apartheid, new patterns of stratification are likely to lead to clearly differentiated social attitudes or political responses. The ANC is clearly adept at marshalling its resources, both symbolic (as in the charisma of the inimitable Nelson Mandela) and material (as in the construction of new clinics and schools), in order to ward off electoral challenges. In local government elections, critical independent candidates have generally struggled to make headway against official ANC candidates even when the latter were regarded as having performed poorly. Anecdotal impressions suggest that discontent with the government over unemployment is becoming more politically consequential, especially as the ANC elite is seen as feathering its own nest. In the longer term, the pressures on the ANC might intensify, and with them the incentive for the ANC to tackle the factors that appear to trap so many families in disadvantaged trajectories. In the shorter term, however, the more likely outcome of discontent is lower voter turnout rather than intensified electoral competition.

The Politics of Redistribution

One reason why social and economic changes have not had visible electoral implications is that disputes are, to a considerable extent, contained within the ANC alliance. At a rhetorical level, and sometimes substantively, Congress of South African Trade Unions (Cosatu) and the ANC have clashed over policy. Some scholars view both the ANC and Cosatu as having sold out or betrayed the more radical objectives of the antiapartheid struggle.[36] The ANC's neoliberal policies—especially trade liberalization, privatization, fiscal austerity, and cost recovery in urban services—are seen as being against the interests of the poor and working class. Other scholars see South Africa as moving instead toward a class compromise, in which business has done well but labor has also secured gains, notably through labor market policy.[37] The ANC itself argues that the poor have benefited from social policy, with the social wage helping to make up for low (or no) wages earned in the labor market.

Elsewhere we implicitly agreed with *some* of the ANC's claims in arguing that there was a "double class compromise" in South Africa, in terms of which business secured broadly pro-business macroeconomic policies, the working class secured higher wages, and the poor secured pro-poor social policies.[38] We suggested that the poor exerted some power through the ballot box, that is, that the electoral power of the poor was one factor in the ANC's pro-poor social policies. The weakness of this argument is that some of the gains apparently made by the poor were actually gains won by other, nonpoor social groups. For example, the big increase in pro-poor social expenditure after 1994 was in education, where increased spending on teachers' salaries certainly did not result in matching improvements in the quality of schooling enjoyed by poor children. Increased spending on the poor reflected in large part a transfer to teachers, who are definitely not poor. This points us to a central issue in the politics of redistribution in South Africa: the social groups with the political power to extract concessions from the state or capital are nonpoor groups. Very few of Cosatu's members are in the poorest half of the population in South Africa. Most live in households with incomes above the median but below the mean, meaning that they are disadvantaged relative to the rich (mostly white) minority but they themselves enjoy a position that is privileged relative to the poor. Some Cosatu-affiliated unions, including the South African Democratic Teachers' Union (Sadtu) have membership mostly in households with incomes above even the mean.

The limits to change in the politics of distribution in South Africa are evident in two recent political controversies. The first is the debate (or rather non-debate) over the BIG. The "BIG Coalition" brings together a range of human rights and church groups, as well as Cosatu, but only the unions are capable of mobilizing mass support. The unions support the BIG in part out of self-interest, not because union members would benefit directly from the grant but because of indirect benefits. The grant would reduce the pressures on workers to support dependent kin and might also deflect criticism of the unions' demand for high wages (which arguably undermines job creation). But these indirect benefits are insufficient to lead the unions to push the issue and threaten their alliance with the ANC, and so Cosatu has not forced the ANC to seriously consider the proposals. Unions do not organize the poorest of the poor, but actually represent relatively privileged sections of society.[39]

Second, several South African cities have seen a resurgence of "social movements," mobilizing around municipal services and linked into antiglobalization activist networks.[40] These mobilizations are typically single-issue protests (including protests against evictions for nonpayment of rent or bond payments, disconnections of electricity and water supplies for nonpayment, and so on), and involve very localized constituencies.

More important, they entail conflict over the symptoms of inequality, that is, an inability to pay for municipal services or for housing, not over the causes of inequality, such as low quality public schooling, high unemployment, and government policies that undermine labor-intensive growth. It is difficult to see these localized and ephemeral conflicts cohering into a truly mass movement of any consequence.

Electoral pressures might push the ANC-led government into pro-poor spending, but this is likely to be more discretionary (such as new schools, clinics, or public works programs) rather than programmatic (such as a BIG). The uneasy balance of power between established "white" business, aspirant "black" business, and organized labor is unlikely to shift enough to allow for major reforms in government strategy. Without policies that encourage the growth of low-wage jobs for the unskilled unemployed and those that promote more efficient use of public spending on education, inequality is unlikely to diminish.

Notes

1. The assumption here is that the age structure in 2004 is roughly the same as in 2001.
2. Throughout this chapter, the conventional racial labels will be used: "black" refers to coloured, Indian, and African South Africans, while "African" refers to members of the Bantu/indigenous African groups.
3. These figures are for 2001, using the census data, but 2004 would have been broadly similar.
4. Andrew Whiteford and Dirk van Seventer, "Understanding Contemporary Household Inequality in South Africa," *Journal of Studies in Economics and Econometrics* 24, no. 3 (2000): 7–30.
5. It should be noted that survey data from Statistics South Africa (SSA) have clear flaws. The figures reported here use weights calculated by Ingrid Woolard and Charles Simkins, not the weights suggested by SSA. Findings on some inequality trends are very sensitive to the choice of weights, and to the choice between income and expenditure data.
6. Some of these calculations were done by Murray Leibbrandt, and reported in Jeremy Seekings, Nicoli Nattrass, and Murray Leibbrandt, "Inequality in Post-Apartheid South Africa: Trends in the Distribution of Income and Opportunities and their Social and Political Implications" (paper for the Centre for Development and Enterprise, Johannesburg, September 2003). See also Whiteford and Van Seventer, "Understanding Contemporary Household Inequality."
7. Jeremy Seekings and Nicoli Nattrass, *From Race to Class: The Changing Nature of Inequality in South Africa* (New Haven, CT: Yale University Press, 2005).
8. Kevin Thompson and Ingrid Woolard, "Achieving Employment Equity in the Public Service: A Study of Changes between 1995 and 2001," DPRU Working Paper no. 02/61 (Cape Town: Development Policy Research Unit, University of Cape Town, 2002).
9. Nicoli Nattrass, "The Debate about Unemployment in the 1990s," *Journal of Studies in Economics and Econometrics* 24, no. 3 (2000): 73–90; Nicoli Nattrass, "The State of the Economy: A Crisis of Employment," in *State of the Nation: South Africa, 2003–2004*, ed. John Daniel, Adam Habib, and Roger Southall (Pretoria: Human Sciences Research Council, 2003), 141–157.
10. Haroon Bhorat, Murray Leibbrandt, Mmuzi Maziya, Servaas van der Berg, and Ingrid Woolard, *Fighting Poverty: Labour Markets and Inequality in South Africa* (Cape Town: University of Cape Town Press, 2001); Jeremy Seekings, "Visions of Society: Peasants, Workers and the Unemployed

in a Changing South Africa," *Journal of Studies in Economics and Econometrics* 24, no. 3 (2000): 53–72.

11. Bridget Kenny and Eddie Webster, "Eroding the Core: Flexibility and the Resegmentation of the South African Labour Market," *Critical Sociology* 24, no. 3 (1998): 216–243.

12. Johannes Fedderke and M. Mariotti, "Changing Labour Market Conditions in South Africa: A Sectoral Analysis of the Period 1970–97," *South African Journal of Economics* 70, no. 5 (2002): 830–864; Haroon Bhorat and James Hodge, "Decomposing Shifts in Labour Demand in South Africa," *South African Journal of Economics* 67, no. 3 (1999): 348–380; Lawrence Edwards, "Globalisation and the Skills Bias of Occupational Employment in South Africa," *South African Journal of Economics* 69, no. 1 (2001): 40–71; T. Simbi and Michael Aliber, "The Agricultural Employment Crisis in South Africa" (paper presented at the Development Policy Research Unit and Trade and Industrial Policy Secretariat Forum, Muldersdrift, September 2000).

13. Paul Cichello, Gary Fields, and Murray Leibbrandt, "Are African Workers Getting Ahead? Evidence from KwaZulu-Natal, 1993–1998," *Social Dynamics* 27, no. 1 (2001): 130. A panel study involves the same panel of respondents being reinterviewed at different points of time.

14. Ibid., 132.

15. A. Berry, M. von Klottnitz, R. Cassim, A. Kesper, B. Rajaratnam, and D. Van Seventer, *The Economics of Small, Medium and Micro Enterprises in South Africa* (Johannesburg: Trade and Industrial Policy Strategies, 2002); Charles Simkins, "Employment and Unemployment in South Africa" (unpublished paper, 2003).

16. Nicoli Nattrass, *The Moral Economy of AIDS in South Africa* (Cambridge: Cambridge University Press, 2004).

17. Jeremy Seekings, "The Broader Importance of Welfare Reform in South Africa," *Social Dynamics* 28, no.2 (2002): 1–38.

18. Servaas van der Berg, "Redistribution through the Budget: Public Expenditure Incidence in South Africa, 1993–1997," *Social Dynamics* 27, no. 1 (2001): 140–164.

19. Nicoli Nattrass and Jeremy Seekings, "Democracy and Distribution in Highly Unequal Economies: The Case of South Africa," *The Journal of Modern African Studies* 39, no. 3 (2001): 471–498; Seekings, "Broader Importance."

20. Michael McGrath, Catherine Janisch, and C. Horner, "Redistribution through the Fiscal System in the South African Economy" (paper presented to the Economics Society of South Africa Conference, Potchefstroom, 1997); see also Servaas van der Berg, "Trends in Racial Fiscal Incidence in South Africa," *South African Journal of Economics* 69, no. 2 (2001): 243–268.

21. Van der Berg, "Redistribution."

22. Michael Samson, "The Social, Economic and Fiscal Impact of Comprehensive Social Security Reform in South Africa," *Social Dynamics* 28, no. 2 (2002): 69–97.

23. Pieter Le Roux, "Financing a Universal Income Grant in South Africa," *Social Dynamics* 28, no. 2 (2002): 98–121; Haroon Bhorat Samson, "A Universal Income Grant for South Africa: An Empirical Assessment," in *A Basic Income Grant for South Africa*, ed. Michael Samson and Guy Standing (Cape Town: University of Cape Town Press, 2003), 77–101.

24. Steven Friedman and Ivor Chipkin, "A Poor Voice? The Politics of Inequality in South Africa," Centre for Policy Studies Research Report, 87 (Johannesburg: Centre for Policy Studies, 2001): 16. See also Steven Friedman, chapter in current volume, and Friedman, "Who We Are: Voter Participation, Rationality and the 1999 Election," *Politikon* 26, no. 2 (November 1999): 213–224.

25. Nattrass and Seekings, "Democracy and Distribution;" Jeremy Seekings, "Unemployment and Distributive Justice in South Africa: Some Inconclusive Evidence from Cape Town," CSSR Working Paper no. 24 (Cape Town: Centre for Social Science Research, University of Cape Town, 2002).

26. Robert Mattes, "Democracy Without the People: Economics, Institutions and Public Opinion in South Africa," *Journal of Democracy* 13, no.1 (January 2002): 32.

27. Ashwin Desai, "Neoliberalism and Resistance in South Africa," *Monthly Review* 54, no. 8 (2003): 18.

28. Gavin Davis, "Encouraging Exclusivity: The Electoral System and Campaigning in the 1999 South African Election," Master's thesis, University of Cape Town, 2003.

29. Robert Mattes and Jessica Piombo, "Opposition Parties and the Voters in South Africa's 1999 Election," *Democratization* 8, no.13 (Autumn 2001): 101–128.

30. Friedman and Chipkin, "A Poor Voice?" 11–12.

31. Nancy Birdsall and Carol Graham, *New Markets, New Opportunities: Economic and Social Mobility in a Changing World* (Washington, DC: Brookings Institution Press, 2000).

32. Craig Charney, "Voices of a New Democracy: African Expectations in the New South Africa," Research Report no. 38 (Johannesburg: Centre for Policy Studies, 1995); Nicoli Nattrass and Jeremy Seekings, "Growth, Democracy and Expectations in South Africa," in *Economic Globalisation and Fiscal Policy*, ed. Iran Abedian and Michael Biggs (Cape Town: Oxford University Press, 1998), 27–53.

33. Owen Crankshaw, *Race, Class and the Changing Division of Labour under Apartheid* (London: Routledge, 1997).

34. Jeremy Seekings, "Do the Unemployed Constitute an Underclass?" CSSR Working Paper no. 32 (Cape Town: Centre for Social Science Research, University of Cape Town, 2003).

35. Jeremy Seekings, "Social Stratification and Inequality at the End of Apartheid," CSSR Working Paper no. 31 (Cape Town: Centre for Social Science Research, University of Cape Town, 2003).

36. Dale McKinley, *The ANC and the Liberation Struggle* (London: Pluto Press, 2001); Patrick Bond, *Elite Transition: From Apartheid to Neo-Liberalism in South Africa* (Pietermaritzburg: University of Natal Press, 2000); Hein Marais, *South Africa, Limits to Change: The Political Economy of Transition* (Cape Town: University of Cape Town Press, 1998).

37. Glenn Adler and Eddie Webster, "Towards a Class Compromise in South Africa's 'Double Transition': Bargained Liberalization and the Consolidation of Democracy," *Politics and Society* 27, no. 3 (1999): 347–385.

38. Nattrass and Seekings, "Democracy and Distribution."

39. Heidi Matisonn and Jeremy Seekings, "The Politics of a Basic Income Grant in South Africa, 1996–2002," in *A Basic Income Grant for South Africa*, ed. Michael Samson and Guy Standing (Cape Town: University of Cape Town Press, 2003), 56–76.

40. Desai, "Neo-Liberalism and Resistance."

CHAPTER THREE

Voter Information, Government Evaluations, and Party Images in the First Democratic Decade

ROBERT MATTES

This chapter proceeds from the assumption that citizens vote for the political party they think is best fit to govern them and protect their interests. As political scientist V. O. Key succinctly put it: "Voters are not fools."[1] Or, in Christopher Achen's formulation, voters are "neither geniuses nor saints. . . . Voters do not ignore information they have, do not fabricate information they do not have, and do not choose what they do not want. . . . They are required only to do the best with the information they have."[2]

But how do voters judge which party is best fit to govern? And on what kind of information or experience do they base these judgments? An idealized, but unrealistic version of democratic elections presumes that voters gather information about policy positions contained in party manifestos or articulated in election campaigns, compare them with their own preferences, and then vote for the party that comes closest to their own beliefs. But obviously, few voters are ever aware of what is contained in party platforms. Parties may feature just a few issues in their campaigns. Parties may have an incentive to blur the distinctions between themselves and others, or simply not to talk about policy issues at all, concentrating on other matters such as performance or projecting attributes such as compassion, strength, or competence.[3]

More important, policy positions are basically no more than promises about what a party would do if it were in office, and as such, not a very reliable source of information. A more reliable indication of what parties might do in future is simply what they have done in the past, either in or out of government.

But if voters make decisions on the basis of past performance, one might ask "how could the ANC have done so well in the 1999 elections, and again in 2004?" "Hasn't this government presided over a massive increase in the number of HIV infections? Isn't South Africa supplanting Uganda and Botswana as the world's epicenter of the pandemic? Hasn't this government fiddled with a Presidential AIDS Commission stuffed with dissident scientists, dragging its feet needlessly in providing drugs to extend lives or prevent mother to child transmissions, in the face of a massive reduction in adult life expectancy? Hasn't this government presided over a substantial rise in most categories of crime, especially violent crime, since 1994,[4] while its ability to prosecute and convict has declined?"[5]

"Hasn't this government mismanaged a sluggish economy that has shed 500,000 formal jobs, driving unemployment, broadly defined, to almost 40 percent and depriving hundreds of thousands of households of the income needed to make ends meet, while it refuses to implement a modest basic income grant? Hasn't the income of the bottom two-fifths of all households actually decreased since 1994, increasing inequality?[6] Hasn't this government failed to build the business confidence necessary for both domestic and foreign investment, thereby limiting growth to around 3 percent, while it regards a growth rate of 6 to 7 percent as a prerequisite to cutting unemployment and reducing inequality?"

One would expect such an "objective" social situation to create the grounds for a massive political realignment, rather than two landslide reelection victories. However, over the very same period this government has facilitated the construction of 1.6 million low-cost houses and built 56,000 new classrooms. Massive infrastructure projects have given 9 million people access to clean water and provided sanitation to 6.4 million and electricity to 2 million. This government now provides various forms of social grants to 7.4 million people. The poor now have access to free medicine and more than 700 new clinics. Over 5 million needy children get a fifth to a quarter of their daily nutritional needs through school feeding programs.[7] Relatively low inflation means that working South Africans are able to keep up with the cost of living. The national budget deficit has shrunk from 8 percent to around 2 percent of Gross Domestic

Product. Public and private affirmative-action initiatives in education, business ownership and hiring have created a sizeable black middle class that is now surpassing its white counterpart in absolute size.[8]

The point is that an "objective" analysis of developments on the ground does not necessarily tell us whether voters perceive government as serving their interests. Existing voter loyalties, or what political scientists call "partisan identification," do not change easily. Thus, the intense loyalties forged by apartheid and the struggle against it may withstand short-term disappointment. However, voters do learn, and they do not ignore what they learn. What voters learn about political parties and government and not the objective socioeconomic circumstances might shift their loyalties.

Cognitive Awareness of Politics

How do voters learn? What kind of information is the basis for their evaluations? To what extent have the developmental changes described earlier increased voter access to and use of political information?

Ronald Inglehart and Russell Dalton have provided strong evidence that the post–World War II exponential growth in access to formal education and electronic news media in Western Europe and the United States—what they call "cognitive mobilization"—has steadily reduced the effect of structural factors like class or religion on the vote. Instead, a more sophisticated generation of voters who are less likely to rely on party labels and are more likely to gather information about government performance and alternative party positions has emerged.[9] In South Africa, one would expect that the government's intensified efforts to improve access to formal schooling and matriculation rates would gradually increase the number of citizens with the requisite cognitive skills to deal with complex political information. But at this point in time, a review of demographic data from surveys conducted by the Institute for Democracy in South Africa (Idasa), Afrobarometer, and the *Washington Post*/Kaiser Family Foundation between 1994 and 2003 reveals no clear evidence of any trends among the adult population, either in terms of a reduction of the number of people without formal education or an increase in the number of people who have finished high school or have some university education.

One would also expect that the government's massive electrification projects would enable more people to watch television news; or that the partial deregulation of South Africa's airwaves would diversify the types of political information to which voters are exposed. Both developments would be expected to bring down the costs of obtaining political information. However, the Idasa and Afrobarometer surveys show that radio, which provides comparatively less news than TV or print media, remains the most pervasive source of news. As of 2002, nine in ten survey respondents said they received news from the radio (91 percent), while eight in ten (79 percent) said they got it from television "every day" or "a few times a week." Just one-half of all voters (53 percent) read newspapers with the same frequency.

There is no evidence that access to news has significantly increased over the past decade. In fact, the frequency with which people get news from the radio has only now slightly passed the levels measured immediately after the 1994 election; the use of television news has almost caught up, but newspaper readership still lags significantly behind where it was in 1994 (see figure 3.1).

The use of news media and the level of formal education are indications of the amount of political information to which voters are exposed and the cognitive skills they have to make use of that information. But they

Figure 3.1   Use of news media (% every day/a few days a week)

Source: Idasa, Afrobarometer.

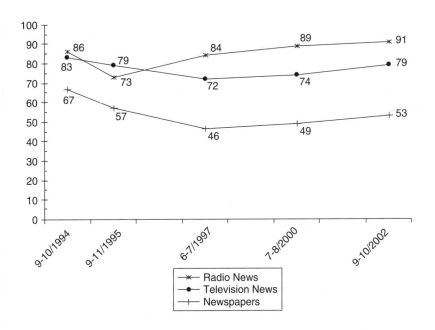

do not tell us whether citizens are more or less politically aware or cognitively engaged in the political process. The Idasa and Afrobarometer surveys also asked people about their interest in politics and the frequency with which they engage in political discussion. The answers demonstrate that, since 1994, just one-twentieth to one-tenth of the electorate "frequently" speak about politics with their family or friends; more than one-third consistently say they "never" do this. Similarly, we find that only one-tenth to one-fifth frequently "follow what's going on in government and public affairs" (see figure 3.2).

Political discussion and interest form a composite construct known as "cognitive engagement," which motivates voters to gather information from available sources.[10] The level of engagement among the South African public is relatively low. In fact, the size of South Africa's "attentive" public is the smallest in southern Africa (see tables 3.1 and 3.2). Such low levels of engagement lead us to expect that South Africans are relatively ill-informed, even though they have the highest levels of formal education and media use in Africa.

Measuring the amount of information that voters possess is notoriously difficult, raising questions about which information is most important, and whether respondents should be able to recall a correct answer, or merely recognize it when presented to them. But however one looks at

Figure 3.2   Political discussion and political interest
Source: Idasa, Opinion '99, Afrobarometer, Markinor.

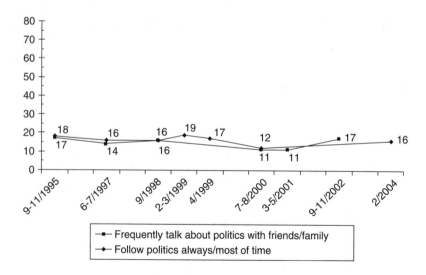

Table 3.1   Political discussion, Southern Africa (%) (1999–2000)

	Zimbabwe	Namibia	Malawi	Botswana	Zambia	Lesotho	South Africa
Frequently	25	20	19	14	14	13	11
Occasionally	38	41	45	38	40	27	52
Never	34	37	36	46	44	59	37

Question: When you get together with your friends, would you say you discuss political matters?

Source: Afrobarometer.

Table 3.2   Political interest, Southern Africa (%) (1999–2000)

	Lesotho	Zambia	Zimbabwe	Namibia	Malawi	Botswana	South Africa
Always, most of the time	31	22	21	18	17	15	12
Some of the time	17	32	27	49	32	23	37
Only now and then	20	17	17	14	30	21	28
Hardly at all	29	26	30	12	20	38	22

Question: Some people seem to follow what's going on in government and public affairs most of the time, whether there's an election going on or not. Others aren't that interested. Would you say you follow what's going on in government and public affairs?

Source: Afrobarometer.

it, evidence abounds that large proportions of the South African electorate remain in the dark about many of the important policy issues of the day.

For example, a 1995 Idasa survey tapping public opinion on the debate about the final constitution found that more than one quarter of all voters (28 percent) were unable to offer any thoughts as to what rights should be included in the constitution. Almost one half (48 percent) mentioned one right, but were unable to offer a second, and three-fifths (61 percent) were unable to offer a third.[11] After years of debate between the government and labor unions about the Growth, Employment, and Redistribution (GEAR) program, the 2000 Afrobarometer found that just 12 percent of South Africans said they had ever heard of GEAR. The 2003 *Washington Post* survey found that despite the major controversies raging in the media about South Africa's stance on land seizures and human rights in Zimbabwe and the U.S. invasion of Iraq, one-fifth of voters (19 percent) did not know who Robert Mugabe was. One third (32 percent) admitted to interviewers that they did not know who George W. Bush was.

Beside these anecdotal questions, the 2000 Afrobarometer offered a more systematic attempt to find out what information voters have across Africa. In each country, respondents were asked to name their vice president, minister of finance, member of parliament (MP) for their constituency, and local councilor (see table 3.3). Almost six in ten (57 percent) South Africans could correctly give the name of Deputy President Jacob Zuma. This was substantially lower than the proportions of Batswana (84 percent), Malawians (79 percent), Zimbabweans (73 percent), and Namibians (71 percent) who could name their vice president. A far lower proportion (38 percent) of South Africans could supply the name of Minister of Finance-Trevor Manuel- though this trend was also observed elsewhere. Reflecting the obstacles created by the country's electoral system of Proportional Representation with party lists, just 1 percent of South Africans, by far the lowest in the region, could even hazard a guess as to who their MP or Local Councilor was supposed to be. While one might argue that the cross-national comparison is irrelevant because of different electoral systems, I contend that the absence of identifiable MPs or local councilors in South Africa means South African voters lack the "cognitive hook" around which voters in other countries focus their attention and follow the political process.

Thus, even while South Africans have relatively high levels of media use and formal education (at least compared to Africa), they remain relatively unengaged and uninformed about politics. Whether and how this limited amount of cognitive awareness shapes voter evaluations depends on whether voters are looking at opposition parties or the government.

Voters with little formal education or access to news media can still acquire information about government performance from conversations with friends and colleagues who pay more attention to politics than they do.

Table 3.3 Political knowledge, Southern Africa (%) (1999–2000)

	Malawi	Zimbabwe	Botswana	Zambia	Namibia	South Africa	Lesotho
Vice president/Prime minister	79	73	84	58	71	57	41
The minister of finance	26	42	14	26	37	38	6
Member of parliament for this constituency	85	55	73	46	24[a]	< 1	1
Your local councilor	NA	59	55	31	6[b]	1	10

Question: Can you tell me who presently holds the following offices? Table provides percentages giving the correct answer, but excludes all cases where it was not possible to determine whether the answer was right or wrong.
[a] Regional councilor [b] Excludes those who don't live in area with local government.

Source: Afrobarometer.

They can also use what Samuel Popkin calls "low information reasoning" and look to their own direct or indirect experiences to evaluate government performance.[12] Do they see more or less jobless people on the streets? Are their salaries keeping pace with the cost of living? Are their monthly bond or hire purchase payments increasing or decreasing? Do they see houses being built, water pipes being laid, and electricity lines being strung? Are more friends and family dying from AIDS-related illnesses?

In contrast to the high visibility of government performance, opposition parties tend not to have widely known track records, unless they have recently been in government. Voters cannot look to their everyday experience to infer how an opposition party has been doing. They must be able to either remember salient actions the party has taken in the past (while in opposition or as a governing party either at national or subnational levels), or they must obtain information on what the party says it would do if elected. Obtaining this information requires a strong interest in politics that encourages the mental storage of such details, or avid media use. Even then, information is difficult to obtain because the actions or promises of opposition parties usually receive far less attention and are therefore less visible than government actions.

Government Evaluations

Voters are likely to pay the greatest amount of attention to government performance on the issues that matter most to them.[13] To determine what the salient issues have been, we turn to a question asked by Idasa, Afrobarometer, and the *Washington Post* since 1994: "What are the most important problems facing this country that the government ought to address?" The question was open-ended and allowed respondents to give up to three answers in their own words. Consistent with an unemployment rate moving toward 40 percent and a sharp increase in violent crime, jobs and crime have consistently topped the public agenda, mentioned since 1997 by three-fifths to three-quarters of respondents. Reflecting the massive inequalities in access to basic services bequeathed by apartheid, housing, education, and health have also consistently received a significant amount of emphasis from the public, usually from between one quarter to one-third of respondents.

Since 2000, growing numbers of voters have also listed poverty, AIDS, and to a lesser extent corruption as important problems. In contrast, issues of violence and discrimination, which were major public preoccupations in 1994 and 1995, quickly fell to the wayside in the ensu-ing years. It is also interesting to note the many issues that typically pre-occupy a large amount of elite attention that are consistently *not* mentioned by ordinary citizens: inequality, wages, incomes and salaries, land, environment, affirmative action, death penalty, or anything remotely related to foreign policy such as immigration, Zimbabwe, mil-itary readiness, or war and peace.

Voter Evaluations of Specific Government Performance

For voter perceptions of how the government has performed on these and other issues, we turn to a set of questions from Markinor, Opinion '99, and Afrobarometer surveys. Over the past decade these surveys asked people to rate how well they think government is handling a range of policy areas. Perhaps the clearest conclusion that emerges from these data is the extent to which South Africans are ready and able to discriminate across policy areas, criticizing government in some areas and praising it in others. They are clearly *not* so constrained by preexisting political loyalties as to offer uniform, rose-coloured assessments of government performance.

South Africans have experienced increasing crime and joblessness and have expressed serious criticisms of government performance in the two areas they consistently cited as the country's most pressing prob-lems. But people have also experienced, either personally or in their immediate surroundings, profound social change with the construction of houses, sanitation, electricity, water, and health clinics and the avail-ability of medicine—issues prioritized by a large proportion of voters— and have rewarded government with far higher levels of approval in these areas.

We can divide the survey questions into four main policy areas: (1) macroeconomic management; (2) equality, redistribution, and nation building; (3) welfare and development; and (4) political governance. In the area of macro economics (see figure 3.3), public evaluations of the government's "handling of the economy" have fluctuated widely, rising above 50 percent during periods of economic expansion, but also plum-meting below 30 percent during periods of high interest rates and infla-tion. And although inflation has been one of the success stories of the government's economic plan, voters have been far less impressed with the government's ability to control prices. The trends follow those of over-all economic performance, but are generally at least 10 to 20 percentage points lower, suggesting that voters are not so much concerned with the

Figure 3.3 Evaluations of government performance-macro-economic management (% well/very well)

Source: Opinion '99, Markinor, *Washington Post*/Kaiser Family Foundation, Afrobarometer.

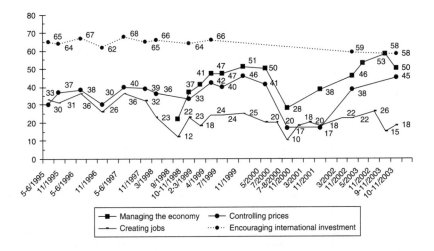

actual *rate* of inflation as the fact that prices are out of their reach. As mentioned earlier, voters are extremely critical of government attempts to "fight unemployment by creating jobs." Voter evaluations on this issue have taken a long downward path over the past decade. The only issue in the area of macroeconomics where the government receives positive reviews is "attracting foreign investment," where two-thirds to three-fifths consistently approve of government performance. However, in this case one struggles to ascertain what experiences are the bases of these evaluations.

On average, South Africans are positive about government efforts to promote equality, redistribution, and national unity (see figure 3.4). Almost three-quarters say government has promoted gender equality well or very well. Solid majorities have also approved of its handling of affirmative action in the civil service, and majorities have generally seen government attempts to narrow the income gap in a positive light. Markinor has also recently begun asking people about government policy in ensuring "access to land," and between 60 to 66 percent have given positive marks in 2002 and 2003. Finally, while it took a noticeable dive after Thabo Mbeki assumed power, the public has been positively impressed with government attempts to "unite all South Africans into one nation."

Government also tends to receive fairly positive marks in the broad area of welfare and development (see figure 3.5). Government distribution

Figure 3.4 Evaluations of government performance-equality, redistribution and nation building (% well/very well)

Source: Opinion '99, Markinor, *Washington Post*/Kaiser Family Foundation, Afrobarometer.

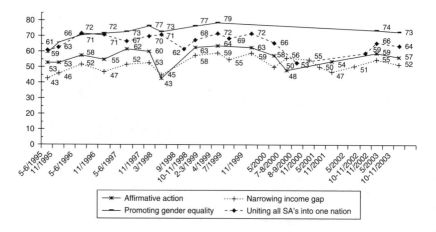

Figure 3.5 Evaluations of government performance-welfare and development (% well/very well)

Source: Opinion '99, Markinor, *Washington Post*/Kaiser Family Foundation, Afrobarometer.

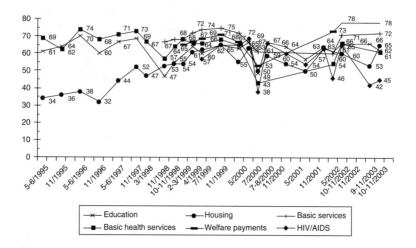

of welfare payments has steadily increased in popularity and is now one of its most well-received areas of performance. South Africans have also positively evaluated the provision of health services as well as basic services like water and electricity over the past decade. Whereas citizens were highly critical of government housing policies from 1995 to 1997, since

Figure 3.6   Evaluations of government performance-political governance (% well/very well)

Source: Opinion '99, Markinor, *Washington Post*/Kaiser Family Foundation, Afrobarometer.

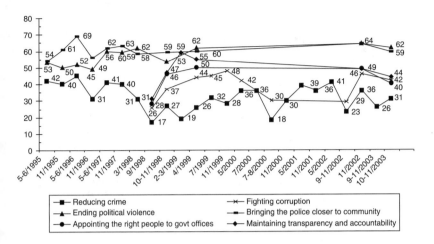

1998 a majority of them have consistently approved of the government's provision of housing. Public opinion toward the government's AIDS policy has varied widely since the question was first asked in 1999, but has been on a clear downward trend in 2002 and 2003.

Finally, in the broad area of political governance, citizens have been extremely critical of government efforts to control crime, even as they have been generally positive about the government's ability to end political violence and its attempts to bring the police close to the community. Government efforts in fighting corruption have received more favorable reviews in 2002 and 2003 after two years of quite critical assessments. This trend has been matched by improving evaluations of government appointments to high office, and government efforts to promote transparency and accountability (see figure 3.6).

Voter Evaluations of Overall Government Performance

South African voters *do not* turn a blind eye to the massive problems of joblessness or criminal violence. They, in some way, *balance* these assessments against government performance across the spectrum. When asked to offer an overall judgment, voters have given broadly positive marks. Public approval of government performance has been relatively positive over the past decade, though there has been a sharp difference in degree between the widespread popular acclaim for the job done by Nelson

Figure 3.7 Evaluations of overall government performance

Source: Markinor, Idasa, Opinion '99, Afrobarometer, *Washington Post*/Kaiser Family Foundation.

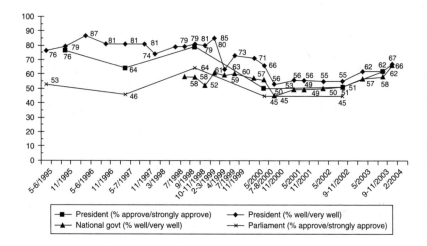

Mandela (averaging in the 70–80 percent range, depending on question wording) and the mere majority approval of Thabo Mbeki. Fluctuations in job approval of the national government as a whole have closely followed trends in approval for the president, but are generally 5 to 10 percentage points lower (see figure 3.7).

Such high approval ratings clearly do not show the type of massive dissatisfaction that one might expect in a society with 40 percent unemployment and declining life expectancy. But as we have seen, this is not because South Africans fail to realize how bad things are, or that, playing Pollyanna, they simply turn a blind eye to these problems. Rather, they balance significant disappointments in certain areas against a range of impressive achievements in others. This suggests that South Africans were broadly satisfied with the performance of the African National Congress (ANC) government over the first ten years of democratic rule.

Partisan Identification and Voting Intentions

How have these evolving performance evaluations translated into partisan attitudes and election results? To answer this, we turn to survey questions that have measured the concept of *partisan identification* since 1994. Partisan identification taps the extent to which voters "identify with" or "feel close to" political parties much in the same way as they identify with social groupings. While this "identification" is analytically separate from the actual vote, it underlies the voting choice of most voters.[14]

Party identification is first learned through socialization from one's family and social milieu at a young age, largely because young adults have little other information about politics. However, we now know that party identification is constantly updated by a voter's evolving evaluations of political parties, their leadership and their performance.[15] As voters accumulate experience and information about parties their identification may change. If a chosen party, whether in government or opposition, performs well, voters may stay loyal to that party. However, if the party does not perform well or a better alternative is presented, loyalties may weaken and party identification may change accordingly. We have firm evidence that the party identifications of South Africans, especially whether or not they feel close to the governing party, are strongly influenced by performance evaluations.[16]

The changing ratio of people who identify with a party versus those who are nonpartisan or "independent" indicates the maximum number of potential "floating voters" whose party support is in doubt at the start of a given election campaign. In the first South African National Post-Election Survey conducted by Idasa in 1994, an astounding 88 percent said that there had been "one particular party" that they "felt especially close to" when asked to reflect back on the historic inaugural election. This extremely high degree of partisan identification may be accounted for in part by the politically charged, euphoric period of late 1994, and partly by a unique question wording, but we have never again registered such a high degree of partisanship.[17]

Since we have moved to the use of the internationally accepted indicator, the proportion of partisan identifiers in the electorate has fluctuated in a fairly wide band between 58 and 43 percent (see figure 3.8). Black (African) voters have consistently been much more likely to identify with a party than the minority (white, coloured, or Indian) voters. Yet beside the stratospheric 89 percent recorded after the 1994 election, no more than 65 percent of the black electorate have told survey researchers that they felt close to a party. This is the first indication that we are not dealing with the highly enthusiastic and loyal black electorate often depicted in popular discourse. In fact, these data yield the perhaps surprising finding that the average proportion of "nonpartisan" South African voters is higher than in France and the United States (approximately 40 percent), Germany (approximately 30 percent), and the United Kingdom (around 10 percent).[18]

Figure 3.8 Partisan identification (% identifying with any party)

Source: Idasa, Opinion '99, Afrobarometer, *Washington Post*/Kaiser Family Foundation.

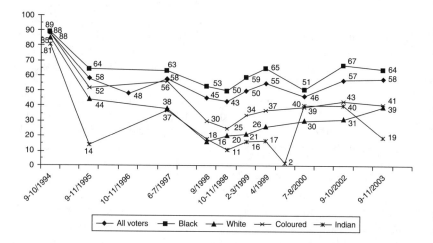

While relative stability in partisanship has been the dominant theme among black voters, trends among minority voters can best be described as de-alignment. More than 80 percent of white, coloured and Indian voters said they had "felt especially close to a party" prior to the 1994 election. Yet just one-fifth of white, one-quarter of coloured, and one-tenth of Indian voters identified with any party by late 1998, though there has been some movement back toward partisanship since then.

Once we divide the electorate into partisans and nonpartisans, we ask those voters who identify with a party, "which party?" In the 1994 Post-Election Survey, the ANC held a three to one advantage over its closest competitor, the National Party (NP). That ratio grew even larger by 1998, mostly as a result of the collapse of the NP and the inability of other parties to pick up sympathies of those voters.

More fluctuation can be observed in the partisan sympathies of minority voters. The demise of the New National Party (NNP) was nothing short of spectacular. NNP partisanship plummeted from about half of the minority voters in 1994 to one in ten coloured voters and just 3 percent of white and Indian voters in 2003. Although the insurgent Democratic Alliance (DA) failed to establish a meaningful support base among coloured and Indian voters, it did manage to garner the sympathies of one-quarter of white voters by 2003 (up from just 3 percent in 1995).

Figure 3.9 Partisan identification (% identifying with a specific party)

Source: Idasa, Opinion '99, Afrobarometer, *Washington Post*/Kaiser Family Foundation.

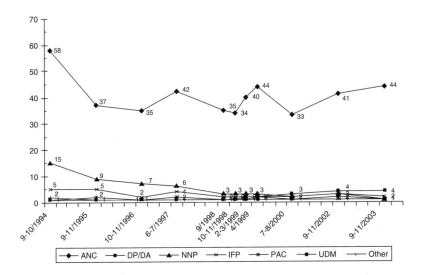

Yet perhaps the most important point to be drawn from these data concerns the nature of the ANC's support base. The ANC won 63 percent and 68 percent of the popular vote in 1994 and 1999, and earned the partisanship of 60 percent of the total electorate in 1994. Since then, partisanship for the ANC has never registered more than 45 percent of the populace, and never more than 60 percent of black voters. Since 1995, the pro-ANC predispositions embodied by party identification have fluctuated between 33 and 44 percent of the total electorate and between 41 and 55 percent of black voters.

Since 1995 Markinor opinion polls have asked people how they would vote "if an election were held tomorrow" (and offered them a mock secret ballot). The data reveal that the ANC's professed voting support dipped from 65 percent in June 1995 to 51 percent in September 1998, returning again to over 60 percent in mid-1999, declining again between elections, and rising back to near 60 percent in February 2004 (see figure 3.10).

Thus, voting support for the ANC tends to be significantly larger than its partisan base. This is especially visible within the black electorate: although the ANC has been able to garner between eight and nine out of every ten black votes at election time, between three and four of every ten black South Africans have been dissatisfied with the president's performance, and around one-third or more have said they felt close to no

Figure 3.10 Voting intentions (% party vote if elections were held tomorrow)

Source: Markinor, Idasa, Opinion '99, Afrobarometer.

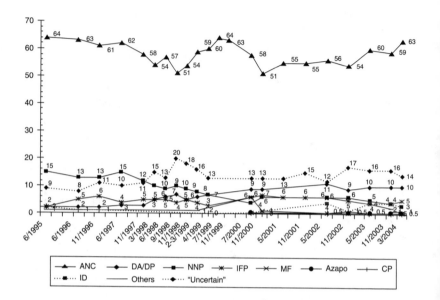

political party. This suggests that many nonpartisans vote for the ANC because they see it as a better option than any other party. It also suggests that many nonpartisans, even those who are dissatisfied with the government, do not see any feasible alternative to the ANC.

Party Images as a Source of Voter Information

Dissatisfaction alone will not lead a person to vote against the ruling party, especially if that person has previously been an ANC supporter. In order for dissatisfaction with the ANC to translate into votes for other parties, people need to consider those parties worthy of their votes. In turn, people must possess enough information about other parties to form such opinions in the first place. Yet, as argued earlier in this chapter, it is likely that voters possess far less information about opposition parties than about the governing party. This makes the primary task of the opposition, convincing voters that they are worthy alternatives to the ruling party, all the more difficult.

The information gap is confirmed by answers to an Opinion '99 question that asked respondents how well each party had performed a range of party activities, such as rallies, report-backs, or parliamentary questioning. While most people had an opinion—and an overwhelmingly positive one—about the ANC, pluralities or majorities were unable to offer an opinion about the Democratic Party (DP), Pan African Congress (PAC), Freedom Front (FF), and the then newly formed United Democratic Movement (UDM). Only the NNP and the Inkatha Freedom Party (IFP), two parties with significant track records from the apartheid era as well as in provincial governments since 1994, had lower levels of "don't know," but they also had very high levels of disapproval (see table 3.4).

With little direct experience and track record to go on, voters may have to rely on party or candidate *traits and attributes* to provide clues as to how an opposition party would actually perform in government. These clues could include some basic facts about the personal history of a party or leader (e.g., whether they supported, collaborated with, or opposed apartheid), or whether they project an image of competence or compassion, or even more basic factors such as the party leader's skin color, language, accent, and dress. Clues such as these provide informational shortcuts as to how inclusive a party is likely to be in its policies and orientations. In a society like that of South Africa, an image of inclusiveness would seem like a prerequisite to any political party hoping to build a multiethnic or multiracial coalition. It is also likely to shape how voters evaluate a particular party.

We can gauge perceptions of inclusivity by examining responses to a question asked in the 1994 Idasa Post-Election Survey as well as in two separate Opinion '99 surveys. Respondents were asked whether they felt a party "represents the interests of all in South Africa or looks after the interests of one group only?" Significantly, large proportions of voters

Table 3.4 Evaluations of party performance[19]

	September 1998			April 1999		
	Fairly well/ Very well	Not very well/ Not at all well	Do not know enough about	Fairly well/ Very well	Not very well/ Not at all well	Do not know enough about
ANC	69	26	5	72	21	7
NNP	22	58	20	21	55	37
IFP	16	55	29	16	56	24
DP	19	33	48	22	37	40
PAC	16	40	44	16	46	37
UDM	11	27	62	15	36	49
FF	7	39	54	7	45	49

Source: Opinion '99.

were not able to offer this most basic assessment, even in the 1999 survey conducted *at the end* of the election campaign. In all cases, the number of "don't knows" are far higher for opposition parties than for the governing ANC (see table 3.5).

Moreover, the data in table 3.5 also illustrates that opposition parties have a difficult time in obtaining a positive image among those who know something about them. While approximately three-quarters of those who could offer an opinion of the ANC saw the party as inclusive, majorities of those who knew something about the IFP or the FF had a negative image, seeing these parties as exclusive. Significant pluralities of those who could offer an opinion of the DP/DA and PAC saw them as exclusive.

Opinion '99 also asked the same type of questions about each party with respect to its perceived ability to run the government if elected, whether the party was believable, and whether it could be trusted. Each obtained the same general patterns of responses. Described in the language of a campaign spin doctor this means that the ANC enjoyed high levels of "positives," while all opposition parties (whether historically white or historically black) had both high levels of "unknowns" and high levels of "negatives." A focus on the views of nonpartisan black voters (which amounted to 35 percent of all black voters at the time) shows that they had similar, if not more negative images of the opposition.

Further analyses of these data show conclusively that images of inclusiveness shape other party images like credibility or trustworthiness. And inclusiveness appears to be a necessary, though certainly insufficient condition for voters to support a party.[20] Thus, black voters who are

Table 3.5 Who do parties represent?

	September–October 1994			September 1998			April 1999		
	All	Only one group	Don't know	All	Only one group	Don't know	All	Only one group	Don't know
ANC	77	17	6	71	25	4	75	21	4
UDM	NA	NA	NA	22	5	74	33	5	62
NNP	39	38	24	32	44	24	29	22	49
DP	39	14	47	24	20	56	28	22	49
PAC	24	36	40	26	23	51	28	25	47
IFP	16	54	30	20	46	34	27	41	32
FF	8	49	43	6	36	57	8	36	55

Source: Idasa, Opinion '99.

dissatisfied with the government perceive very little alternative because they have thoroughly negative images of virtually all other parties. This gives them the options of either voting for the ANC as the least bad alternative, or simply not voting.

Floating Voters?

While we have already detailed the existence of large numbers of nonpartisan, potentially "floating voters," we need to look more closely to determine just how likely they are to shift their vote. Being a floating voter implies, first, being aware of alternative parties, and second, knowing something about them and about why they might offer a better option. This would require some awareness of what a party would do differently to the present government if it were elected. I have already argued and presented evidence that this is extremely difficult for many voters in South Africa.

Yet, difficult is not the same as impossible. Some citizens do possess information and, hence, can form educated opinions about various parties. In order to identify nonpartisan voters who might have access to such information, Dalton has developed a framework that categorizes voters by whether they are partisan or nonpartisan on one hand, and whether they are "cognitively mobilized" or not on the other. Cognitive mobilization refers to whether a respondent *either* has at least some university education *or* is "very interested" in the election campaign, factors that should aide voters to gather information and form opinions about the various parties more easily. The two dimensions in the framework yield the following four categories.

- *Apoliticals* are not attached to any party and thus ideally open to persuasion, but they are harder to reach because they are less educated and uninterested in the political process.
- *Ritual Partisans* are mobilized into politics on the basis of their strong partisan attachments, rather than information and psychological engagement.
- *Cognitive Partisans* identify with a party but are intellectually engaged and support parties based on the information at hand.
- *Apartisans* are independent of parties, but unlike the apoliticals, engaged and informed. It is among these voters that the greatest volatility and unpredictability in voting exists.[21]

For purposes of comparison, I have replicated this analysis for South Africa using Opinion '99 data. It reveals that four-fifths of the apparently "floating" nonpartisan voters fall into the "apolitical" category and only one-fifth qualify as "apartisan," or those more likely to act as rational floating voters. It is also instructive to note that the proportion of "apartisan" voters in South Africa in 1999 was twice as small as that measured in the United States nearly fifty years earlier (see table 3.6).

I have also constructed a longer time series within South Africa to test for any growth in the proportions of "cognitive partisans" and "apartisans."[22] It shows that the proportion of "apartisans" has remained at 10 percent or less over the past decade, and the proportion of "cognitive partisans" has remained at roughly 15 percent or less. Thus, only about one-quarter of the electorate meets Dalton's definition of a cognitively mobilized voter. What this means is that even though South Africa has a relatively large proportion of nonpartisan voters, the vast majority of these voters probably do not have the information or cognitive skills that would enable them to shift their partisan allegiances on the basis of ongoing party performance or party policy positions (see table 3.7).

Table 3.6 Cognitive skills and partisanship, United States and South Africa compared

	United States			**South Africa**	
	1952	**1980**	**1992**	**1998**	**1999**
Apoliticals	16	19	16	47	37
Ritual Partisans	42	28	20	34	40
Cognitive Partisans	32	35	41	10	15
Apartisans	16	18	24	9	8
Total	100%	100%	100%	100%	100%

Source: Dalton, 1996: fn. 9, p. 219; Opinion '99.

Table 3.7 Cognitive skills and partisanship over time

	1994[a]	**1995**	**1996**	**1997**	**1998**	**2000**	**2002**
Apoliticals	11	35	44	36	46	45	34
Ritual partisans	69	47	33	46	33	36	44
Cognitive partisans	19	11	14	12	11	10	13
Apartisans	1	7	8	6	10	10	9
Total	100	100	100	100	100	100	100

[a] 1994 data uses those who "urged someone to vote in a specific way" as the cognitive indicator because there was no item on either political interest or political discussion.

Source: Idasa, World Value Survey, Opinion '99, Afrobarometer.

Conclusion

The partisan alignment that emerged from South Africa's first democratic election in 1994 was largely the result of three main developments. First, the ANC had been, by far, the principal force in the successful struggle against apartheid, thus securing the deep gratitude of a large number of voters. Second, the NP had been the progenitor and defender of the apartheid regime, which caused the misery of millions of black South Africans. Moreover, widespread perceptions that it was either impotent to stem political violence in the early 1990s or was actively fomenting it, robbed the NP of any chance to capitalize on the initial goodwill earned by FW de Klerk among the black electorate.[23] And finally, the NP and De Klerk managed to engage the ANC in negotiations that resulted in a settlement seen to safeguard the interests of minority voters.[24]

The public opinion data reviewed in this chapter yield four main conclusions about partisan politics *since* 1994. First, even while the South African government has made major efforts to expand access to formal education, there is no evidence that the South African electorate is any more educated than it was a decade ago. Even though there has been a massive expansion of the number of people with access to electricity, voters are no more likely to get news from television (or newspapers) than they did ten years ago. If anything, voters appear to have become less interested in or engaged with politics over the past decade.

Second, with some important exceptions, voters have been generally satisfied with the performance of the ANC government. When voters have been asked to reach an overall assessment, their "averaged" opinion has been a generally, though not overwhelmingly positive view of the performance of the government and the president. Thus, the overall balance of pros and cons has not been so negatively tipped against the government as to alter the initial balance of partisan alignments formed in the 1994 election.

Third, public satisfaction with government performance and expressed voting intentions as revealed to survey researchers have typically not equaled the type of voting support that the ANC has received on election day. In other words, the "electoral dominance" registered by the ANC in South Africa's first three national elections has not been matched by a form of "preference" dominance in which South African voters are overwhelmingly satisfied with government performance. But the data reveal that the ANC has been able, through both an effective election campaign as well as the lack of an effective opposition, to stimulate sharp increases in support in the run-up to elections.

Finally, South African voters generally have very negative images of opposition parties, and many have no opinions of them at all. When voters dissatisfied with government performance look for alternatives, they are faced with a range of opposition parties about which they have only minimal information. Party images, often based on no more than a few facts about a party's history and other basic attributes such as race, accent, and dress of a party leader, tell them for whom to vote, or more probably, for whom not to vote. Thus, dissatisfied voters must either swallow hard and vote for the ANC as the least bad alternative or simply not vote at all. Given the sharp decline in voter turnout displayed in the 2004 election, the evidence suggests that this latter option looks increasingly attractive to South African voters.

Notes

I want to thank Cherrel Africa, Jeremy Seekings, and other participants in the Centre for Social Science Research Elections 2004 Seminar Series for their comments on an earlier draft of this chapter. I also want to thank Anneke Greyling and Michael Gordon of Markinor for providing additional data for this chapter.

1. V. O. Key, *The Responsible Electorate: Rationality In Presidential Voting, 1936–1960* (Cambridge: Harvard University Press, 1967).
2. Christopher Achen, "Social Psychology, Demographic Variables and the Linear Regression: Breaking the Iron Triangle In Voter Research," *Political Behavior* 14, no. 3 (1992): 195–211, 198.
3. For a discussion of various types of campaign issues, see Russell Dalton, *Citizen Politics: Public Opinion and Political Parties in Advanced Industrial Democracies* (Chatham, NJ: Chatham House, 1996), 96–219.
4. David Bruce, "Suspect Crime Statistics Cannot Obscure Grim Truth," *Sunday Independent*, June 10, 2001, p. 9; Michael Dynes, "South Africa's Huge Steps On Long Walk to Prosperity," *Sunday Independent*, August 26, 2001, p. 4; S. Pedrag, "Crime Out of Control In South Africa," *MSNBC News*, May 29, 2000, accessed at www.msnbc.com/news.
5. *The Economist*, February 24, 2001.
6. Andrew Whiteford and Dirk van Seventer, *Winners and Losers: South Africa's Changing Income Distribution* (Johannesburg: WEFA, 1999), 11–19; Debbie Budlender, "Earnings Inequality In South Africa, 1995–1998," in *Measuring Poverty In South Africa* (Pretoria: Statistics South Africa, 2000).
7. Reg Rumney, "A Question of Perceptions," *Mail & Guardian*, August 3–9, 2001, p. 15; Howard Barrell, "Back to the Future: Renaissance and South African Domestic Policy," *African Security Review* 9, no. 2 (2000): 87; "Housing: A Good News Story," *RDP Monitor* 7, no. 5 (May 2001): 2; "Electricity: Seeing Clearly Now," *RDP Monitor* 6, no. 7 (July 2000): 2; Josey Ballenger, "Troubled School Feeding Plan Is Still Essential," *Reconstruct* 11 (October 1998): 1; and Judith February, "Political Debates Lack Substance," *Business Day*, April 5, 2004, p. 7.
8. Whiteford and van Seventer, *Winners and Losers*.
9. Dalton, *Citizen Politics*, 215.
10. Michael Bratton, Robert Mattes, and E. Gyimah-Boadi, *Public Opinion, Democracy and Market Reform in Africa* (Cambridge: Cambridge University Press, 2004).
11. Robert Mattes, Jennifer Christie, and Cherrel Africa, "Public Opinion and the New Constitution," Institute for Democracy in South Africa, Public Opinion Service Reports #4 (Cape Town: Idasa, 1996).

12. Samuel Popkin, *The Reasoning Voter: Communications and Persuasion in Presidential Campaigns* (Chicago: University of Chicago Press, 1994).

13. Dalton, *Citizen Politics*, 15–39.

14. Angus Campbell, Philip Converse, Donald Stokes, and Warren Miller, *The American Voter* (New York: John Wiley, 1960).

15. Key, *The Responsible Electorate*; Morris Fiorina, *Retrospective Voting In American Presidential Elections* (New Haven: Yale University Press, 1979); and Achen, "Social Psychology."

16. Robert Mattes, Helen Taylor, and Cherrel Africa, "Judgement and Choice in the 1999 South African Election," *Politikon* 26, no. 2 (1999): 235–247; and Robert Mattes and Jessica Piombo, "Opposition Parties and the Voters In South Africa's 1999 Election," *Democratization* 8, no. 13 (Autumn 2001): 101–128.

17. In 1994, the question read: "Regardless of how you actually voted on Election Day (in April) was there one particular political party which you felt especially close to?" Thereafter, the question has read: "Do you usually think of yourself as close to any particular political party/ies?" The latter question follows the international standard.

18. Dalton, *Citizen Politics*, 209.

19. The survey asked: "Political parties could be involved in a wide range of activities such as developing policies, raising issues and debating in parliament and the media, holding public meetings and rallies, report backs to constituencies, etc. Think about each of the political parties and please tell me whether you thought they performed _____. If I come to a party you haven't heard of or you feel you do not know enough about, just say so. How would you say ___ has performed these activities?"

20. Karen Ferree, "The Microfoundations of Ethnic Voting: Evidence from South Afrcia" Afrobarometer Working Paper Series no. 40 (East Lansing / Accra / Cape Town: Afrobarometer, 2004).

21. Dalton, *Citizen Politics*, 213–216.

22. Because the political interest item was not asked in a consistent fashion over this time period, I have used those people who either "frequently" engage in political discussion, or have at least some university education.

23. Robert Mattes and Amanda Gouws, "Race, Ethnicity and Voting Behavior," in *Elections and Conflict Resolution In Africa*, ed. Timothy Sisk and Andrew Reynolds (Washington, DC: United States Institute of Peace, 1998).

24. Robert Mattes, *The Election Book: Judgment and Choice in South Africa's 1994 Election* (Cape Town: Idasa, 1995).

CHAPTER FOUR

Parliament and the Electoral System: How Are South Africans Being Represented?

LIA NIJZINK AND JESSICA PIOMBO

This chapter aims to chart the development of two institutions central to the functioning of representative democracy in South Africa: the electoral system and the National Assembly (NA).[1] We review how developments since 1994 have shaped the institutional context in which political parties operate and compete for power. The chapter first considers how the NA has developed over the past ten years, reviewing the performance of Parliament and its role in the consolidation of democracy. The second part of the chapter focuses on the electoral system, reviewing the debate around electoral reform and discussing changes that have been introduced since 1999. In the conclusion, we suggest what the implications of these institutional developments are for the future of representative democracy in South Africa.

Parliament in the Past Decade

In 1994, South Africa's first democratically elected parliament was expected to play a very different role than the essentially undemocratic, unrepresentative, and largely inactive parliament of the apartheid regime. According to the Constitution, South Africa's parliament is meant to overcome the legacies of the past by enriching the political system with the values of multipartyism, accountability, responsiveness, and openness. Parliament is designed to instill constitutional values into the political system and be a central agent in the realization of human rights and the transformation of the country. In addition, Parliament is meant to provide a link between government and the people by educating the public about the democratic dispensation, by ensuring public participation in its processes and by being a role model for good governance and democratic values.[2] But how realistic are these constitutional expectations? Ten years after the first democratic elections, it seems appropriate to assess whether Parliament has evolved in the way it was envisaged. Has Parliament, being the country's main representative institution, lived up to its many challenges? How has it performed over the past ten years?

From Legislation to Oversight?

In the period immediately after the 1994 election, Parliament played a central role in the new democratic system. A major part of its work was to serve as the Constitutional Assembly and finalize the new South African Constitution, which it did in 1996. The first democratic parliament was also confronted with the task of passing an extensive government program of legislation intended to replace apartheid laws and address the most immediate problems of a society deeply divided by racism, poverty, and inequality. In fulfilling this legislative task, the first parliament passed a total of 494 bills, an average of almost 100 bills per year. The legislative load decreased considerably during the second parliament. From 1999 to 2003, Parliament passed a total of 313 bills, resulting in an average of about 63 bills per year. In other words, looking at the number of bills passed, Parliament has become less active in the course of the past ten years. (see table 4.1)

The decrease in legislative output between the first and second parliament is not surprising. One would expect the workload to diminish once the first legislative program of the new African National Congress (ANC) government was put in place. Thus, the relatively heavy workload of the

Table 4.1 Number of bills passed by Parliament per year

1994	52	1999	60
1995	89	2000	70
1996	108	2001	69
1997	108	2002	75
1998	137	2003[a]	39

[a] Number of bills passed until November 2003.
Source: Annual Reports of Parliament.

first parliament must be seen as a result of the transition to a democratic regime, whereas the decline in the number of bills passed during the second parliament can be regarded as a sign of "normalization." However, the decrease in legislative output also suggests that Parliament could be in danger of losing its central role in the democratic system if it fails to take an active stance and shift the emphasis in its activities from legislation to oversight and representation.

Such a shift is particularly important in the context of a system of governance in which the initiative in public policy making lies with the executive. The South African parliament, like many of its counterparts elsewhere in the world, has a limited responsibility for making laws. Legislation is primarily prepared and drafted by the executive and presented to Parliament for approval. It is Parliament's responsibility to provide opportunities for public debate and public participation in the law-making process and to ensure that the legislation that is passed reflects policy choices acceptable to the majority.[3] Some parliamentary committees, especially in the first democratic parliament, have been proactive and have redrafted and amended government legislation in a number of policy areas, most notably in the Justice portfolio, but not all committees have equally impressive track records when it comes to the scrutiny of government bills.[4] Committees and individual Members of Parliament (MPs) also have the right to initiate legislation, which is, unusually, enshrined in the constitution, but so far legislative initiatives from individual members and committees have been scarce.[5] In other words, Parliament's law-making activities are to a large extent limited to debating and passing government legislation. Therefore, it is imperative that Parliament extends the emphasis in its work beyond law making to include monitoring and overseeing the executive and the implementation of its policies, especially after the main legislative framework of the ANC government has been put in place.

The second parliament recognized that taking its responsibility of overseeing the executive more seriously could be the next step required to find its place in the political system in the longer term. In 1999, the NA established a subcommittee of the Rules Committee to discuss Parliament's oversight responsibility. The committee commissioned and discussed a report on how to strengthen oversight practices.[6] In addition, portfolio committees started to include oversight in their yearly programs and some began to undertake so-called oversight visits.[7]

These initiatives, however, so far have not resulted in vigorous oversight practices. The Report on Parliamentary Oversight and Accountability identified a number of resource and logistical problems that were restricting committees in their oversight activities but it did not address the crucial issue of political attitudes. As Nijzink has noted elsewhere,

> even if all the resource and logistical problems could be solved, committees would only be transformed into instruments of oversight if committee chairs are not afraid to occasionally antagonize the minister; if the opposition is not set on turning every committee meeting into a mini-plenum; if committees succeed in focusing on policy implementation; and if members regard their committees as efficient parliamentary units established to develop expertise and manage information, rather than extensions of the party political divide.[8]

These attitudinal changes have not yet happened. Instead, partisan power relations in parliamentary proceedings seem to have increased to the detriment of accountability and transparency.

Certain parliamentary committees that are typically less driven by partisan considerations than others, such as the public accounts committee or the committee dealing with members' initiatives for legislation, have become dominated by partisanship. Public accounts committees usually are less driven by partisan considerations when they conduct their business and assess whether money has been spent in accordance with budget decisions. Yet, after the 1999 election, rather than following common practice and appointing a member of an opposition party to chair the Standing Committee on Public Accounts (Scopa), the ANC nominated an Inkatha Freedom Party (IFP) member, Gavin Woods, as the chairperson. Since the IFP was a partner in the ANC-led government, the appointment was seen as a partisan attempt to influence committee procedures. The role of the Scopa has become the topic of even more explicitly partisan power play and debate, after alleged irregularities surrounding an arms deal appeared on the committee's agenda.[9]

Furthermore, although a parliamentary Code of Conduct was introduced in 1997 and Parliament keeps a Register of Members' Interests to prevent conflicts of interest among representatives, there have been several instances when Parliament failed to hold its members accountable. Prominent members, such as Winnie Madikezela-Mandela and former deputy president Jacob Zuma, have not taken Parliament's internal processes of oversight as seriously as they should. On a number of occasions the need to act decisively on any allegations of irregularity involving MPs seemed to have given way to more partisan considerations. Several ministers, including Defence Minister Mosiuoa Lekota, have been accused of not fully disclosing their financial interests, yet without repercussions from the side of Parliament. The chief whip of the ANC in the first parliament, Tony Yengeni, was accused of and convicted for corruption but Parliament left it to the ANC to decide on his resignation, while the party thought it best to depend on Yengeni's own conscience for this decision. In the second parliament, a new scandal broke around the irregular use of travel vouchers by more than a few MPs. Again, Parliament seems to have been slow in acting on allegations of any wrongdoing.

The lack of oversight practices and Parliament's reluctance to hold its members to its code of conduct not only circumscribe the institution's independence, but are also beginning to undermine the public image of Parliament. South Africans do not seem to regard Parliament and its members as particularly trustworthy, a fact that further erodes the ability of Parliament to exert its power in the face of executive dominance. Public opinion data from the Afrobarometer surveys show that the level of trust in Parliament decreased between the first and second parliament. The Afrobarometer asked people, "how much of the time can you trust Parliament to do what is right?" and found that the percentage of people answering "most of the time" has sharply decreased, from 57 percent in 1998 to 34 percent in 2000. The same trend can be seen in figures for parliamentary job approval. In 1998, 64 percent of South Africans approved of the way Parliament performed its job. According to the Afrobarometer surveys, this dropped to 45 percent in 2000. Also, 45 percent of South Africans think that most or almost all MPs are involved in corruption. This perception has been more constant over time: 41 percent in 1997, 44 percent in 1998, and 45 percent in 2000.[10] Clearly, these trends, especially in perceptions of corruption, indicate that Parliament has a pressing problem with regard to its public image and its responsibility as a role model for good governance.

The Role of Committees and Parties in Parliament

The previous section underscored the necessity for Parliament to become more active in terms of overseeing policy implementation and holding its own members and the government accountable if it wants to ensure a central role for itself in the years to come. One way of addressing these issues would be to take the role and powers of parliamentary portfolio committees more seriously. The most important role of portfolio committees is to gather the information that is needed to take informed decisions about public policy and to develop expertise in the relevant policy area. Committees do the detailed work that underpins most parliamentary output and that is impractical if not impossible to do in plenary sittings. Because committees deal with the details of legislation and policy issues, party political differences will not always dominate, which leaves room for more problem-oriented discussion. Furthermore, committees can act as a contact point with the public, being the most practical forum for public participation. Thus, committees have the potential to provide a source of expertise outside the executive, a forum for public hearings, and less partisan, more problem-oriented discussions.[11]

Portfolio committees have considerable powers, at least on paper, to develop their potential. These powers are listed, unusually, in the Constitution itself. According to section 56, the NA or any of its committees may:

1. summon any person to appear before it to give evidence on oath or affirmation, or to produce documents;
2. require any person or institution to report to it;
3. compel in terms of national legislation or the rules and orders, any person or institution to comply with a summons or requirement in terms of paragraph (1) or (2); and
4. receive petitions, representations, or submissions from any interested persons or institutions.

Committees in the South African parliament do request organizations and individuals to make submissions or present reports, but they seldom use their other powers. They are able to function without relying on the tools provided in the constitution. In the context of party political realities, these powers are clearly regarded as a last resort. Committees with a majority of members being members of the ruling party are understandably reluctant to summon ministers or government officials.[12] Nevertheless, committees could be more assertive in compelling the executive to attend their meetings and report on certain matters. Portfolio committees often deal with a piece of government legislation without the minister being present. Some portfolio committees even extensively amend the government draft of a bill with the help of the legal drafter of the department without the minister being there. In many parliamentary systems, it would be unthinkable that the minister who takes political responsibility for a draft bill is absent from committee deliberations. In the NA, it is apparently not regarded as a problem. In fact, it is sometimes impossible to distinguish between the government draft and the version amended by the committee.

In other systems, the power to summon people is only given to parliamentary committees in the case of an official inquiry. In other words, these powers are reserved for more extreme instances where overseeing government policy implementation warrants setting up an inquiry process with witnesses and special hearings. In the South African system such a process does not have to be decided upon in order to use the power to summon. All committees have these powers to use at their discretion, which might, paradoxically, be the reason why they are not being used. Because the extensive powers are always available, even the threat of using them is not an instrument in the hands of Parliament vis-á-vis the executive. It is as yet unclear whether this is simply a consequence of the institutional design or points to a more general tendency toward fusion in South African executive–legislative relations.

A clear trend in the past ten years of parliamentary politics is that parties and partisan considerations increasingly dominate parliamentary proceedings, even in areas where one would expect individual MPs to be able to deal with certain aspects of their work in an atmosphere of slightly relaxed party discipline. Public accounts committees, for example, are typically less partisan than others. The same is true for the avenue of private member bills and even for certain forms of parliamentary questioning when MPs can raise issues that arise during the time they spent in their constituencies. In all these areas we find that there is less scope for individual MPs to make their mark outside the realm of strict party discipline. During the second parliament, Scopa proceedings have become overly politicized, as noted earlier. The committee on members' legislative proposals has not managed to avoid the process becoming subject to majority rule right from the start, and even questions during question time are no longer allocated on a first come first serve basis. Instead, they are now allocated to parties according to their relative size in the House. The ANC apparently saw its members making little use of question time, whereas the opposition was more active in submitting questions. This situation seems to have been the reason for the ANC proposal to introduce a partisan element in the allocation of time to members during question time.

Changing the procedures for questioning in such a way seemed a rather defensive move from the side of the ANC, but typical of the style of the ruling party in Parliament during the last five years. Regardless of its overwhelming majority, the ANC seems to have become more reluctant to engage in open and robust deliberations. Most of the opposition, on the other hand, seems to be stuck in a largely rhetorical and confrontational style instead of choosing the route of constructive criticism. Again, this polarization could be a sign of the "normalization" of parliamentary politics, but one could also interpret it as an indication that Parliament is losing its central role and is not the main forum to debate issues of public concern.

The growing irrelevance of Parliament is also signaled by the fact that politicians do not seem to regard becoming an MP as an important career goal. The ANC's practice of deploying its members together with turnover rates in Parliament of 40 to 50 percent[13] probably prevents this. Although Parliament seems to have become, to some extent, a training ground for ministerial talent, the governing party docs not seem to regard Parliament as an institution central to the overall goal of transforming the country. For example, during his first term President Mbeki made it clear that Parliament was not very high on his list of priorities. Mbeki reluctantly agreed to four question times per year when he would personally come to Parliament to answer questions and gave former Deputy President Jacob Zuma the task of dealing with Parliament in his absence.

Transformative Legislature or Arena Parliament?

One way of assessing the performance of Parliament is to look at what Polsby calls its "transformative capacity."[14] Does Parliament have an independent capacity to mould and transform proposals from different sources into laws? If so, is this capacity frequently exercised? Polsby actually classifies legislatures using a continuum with transformative legislatures on the one end and arena type parliaments on the other. In transformative legislatures a crucial transformation occurs between inputs from the political system and the final result of the legislative process. The internal structures and cultural norms of the institution as well as the division of labor within Parliament are crucial for the way in which the legislature functions. The output of the legislature is primarily influenced by the following factors: the committee structure and appointment processes, the policy preferences of individual legislators, informal legislative groupings, and the operation of rules of internal procedure and customs such as seniority.

Arena parliaments, on the other hand, serve mainly as formalized settings for the interplay of significant political forces in the political system. The more open the regime the more varied, representative, and accountable the forces in the arena are. The main function of an arena type parliament is to question and debate government policy. In order to understand the policy making role of an arena parliament one needs to study the social background of members, their links with civil society, the strategies of government and the civil service, the organization of parliamentary parties, and, more importantly, extra-parliamentary party politics. In other words, the impact of external forces is decisive in accounting for parliamentary outcomes.

Polsby proposes that the main influence on the independence or transformative capacity of legislatures lies in the character of parliamentary parties. There are three important ways in which this works. First, the broader the coalition embraced by the dominant parliamentary group, the more transformative the legislature. Second, the less centralized and hierarchical the management of the parliamentary party, the more transformative the legislature. Last, the less fixed and assured the legislative majorities on certain issues, the more transformative the legislature.[15]

When we apply this theory to the South African case, we see that the dominant party in the South African Parliament is fairly coalitional, in other words, the ANC embraces a diversity of social interests, while the opposition parties are far less coalitional. Looking further at the way parties control the process of candidate selection and nomination, we would have to classify South African parties as centralized and hierarchical. And finally, when we look at voting patterns in Parliament we consistently see the same fixed majority, in other words, there are no shifting majorities according to the issue that is under discussion. All in all, we would expect the South African parliament to have a limited transformative capacity and thus be placed more toward the arena side of Polsby's continuum.

Parliament in the First Ten Years: An Assessment

Perhaps one would have expected the first and second democratic parliaments to shape policy or at least significantly contribute to policy making, especially with regard to the pressing issues of poverty, unemployment, and social inequality. The need for widescale economic and social transformation seemed to call for an active role of the country's main representative institution. However, the South African parliament has not developed into a transformative institution, with the independent capacity to transform input from the political system into policy outcomes. If anything, Parliament has become less active and more reactive over time. This, on the one hand, raises questions about the centrality of Parliament in the consolidation of democracy. On the other hand, one could take it as another sign of "normalization" of South African politics. Few parliaments around the world are the main agents of political or societal change. Initiative in public policy making lies primarily with governments and in the era of globalization many far-reaching decisions are made in international fora.

Furthermore, if the trend toward a reactive parliament is accompanied by a stronger emphasis on Parliament's oversight responsibility it does not necessarily constitute a problem in terms of the consolidation of representative democracy. But, although Parliament has begun to study and discuss its oversight responsibility and portfolio committees undertake so-called oversight visits on a more or less regular basis, we have not yet witnessed vibrant oversight practices in Parliament.

During the past decade, Parliament seems to have evolved more as an arena type of legislature in the sense that it has mainly served as a public forum to debate government policy. However, even as a public arena Parliament has not performed very well during the past five years. The challenge of overcoming the apartheid legacy of a gap of mistrust between government and citizens has only partially been met. The representative capacity of Parliament and its members has not been fully utilized—not even within the limits of the current system of proportional representation, closed party lists, and allocated constituencies—and the image of Parliament among the public is not particularly good. Although Parliament is obviously more representative in makeup than before 1994, it has not become the main forum for forging links between society and the state.

In other words, there are many remaining challenges. Some of these simply exist for all parliaments in parliamentary systems and relate to overseeing executive action. There are other challenges that seem to be linked to the way MPs are elected, more specifically those related to the representativeness and responsiveness of Parliament and its members. These issues have given rise to an ongoing debate on electoral reform, which we discuss next. Finally, some challenges might be more typical for parliaments in young democracies: those related to the development of the institution and its image among the public. It is in this area that the South African Parliament has made some progress over the past ten years, specifically in terms of institution building. But much remains to be done before the country's main representative institution is meeting all the expectations set out in the Constitution and is playing a central role in building a lasting democratic culture.

Debating Electoral Reform

The question of electoral reform has been on the table in South Africa for some time and still shows no sign of having been resolved. Central to the debate is the growing realization that the system of proportional representation (PR) based on closed party lists shows tendencies that could cause problems for the consolidation of democracy. Possible problems revolve around issues of accountability and visibility of MPs, and weak connections between representatives and their constituencies. These issues formed the core concerns that motivated parties from different sides of the political spectrum to advocate reform of the electoral system on the provincial and national levels.[16]

The debate on electoral reform began around the December 2000 local election, yet did not result in any action until March 2002, when the ANC established an Electoral Task Team (ETT), headed by Dr. F. van Zyl Slabbert, to review the system and suggest whether or not any changes should be made.[17] The team began its deliberations in May 2002, and was given the task of completing and submitting its report to Home Affairs Minister Mangosuthu Buthelezi by November 2002. The task team considered three types of electoral systems: the current party-list system of PR; a mixed system with single-member constituencies balanced by proportional elements; and a constituency system, including single- and multi-member constituencies to ensure proportionality. The team evaluated the different systems according to four criteria: fairness, inclusivity, simplicity, and accountability.[18] The ETT commissioned Professors Roger Southall (Human Sciences Research Council) and Robert Mattes (University of Cape Town) to undertake a "comprehensive survey of voters' involvement in, and understanding of, current politics and the electoral system." Working with four South African research survey companies the survey was to be completed and analyzed by late August 2002.[19] The ETT also convened a two-day conference to debate various electoral systems and their likely impact in South Africa, the results of which were published in a report on September 10, 2002.[20]

The task team delivered its report to the cabinet in January 2003. The document reflected disagreement among the members of the team. The majority recommended a moderate change to the current electoral system and rejected the option of a mixed system of single-member constituencies balanced by party-list elements to ensure overall proportionality.[21] They argued that the country already had a mixed system, since the nine provinces constituted nine multimember districts.[22] The majority report recommended breaking down these large provincial constituencies, thus increasing the nine existing constituencies to sixty-nine new ones, demarcated according to existing municipal and district council boundaries.[23] According to this proposal, the NA would include 300 constituency representatives elected in the new districts, in addition to 100 members elected through proportional representation with closed national party lists. These recommendations, including the rejection of single-member constituencies, were based on the logic that the needs of fairness, representivity, and inclusivity outweighed the concern with accountability, even though each was important.

In contrast, the minority report felt that the current system should be retained.[24] Advocates of this view argued that the six major political parties that had participated in the two-day conference, as well as the majority of South Africans, were happy with the current system. Furthermore, the minority argued that the logic advanced by the majority view was not adequate to justify changing the closed-list PR system at the national and provincial levels. If the main concern was accountability, the minority argued, then Parliament should strengthen constituency offices, rather than "tinkering with the electoral model."[25]

The cabinet decided on March 6, 2003 to follow the minority recommendation, agreeing to retain the current electoral system and to reconsider changing it for the 2009 national and provincial elections. Buthelezi argued that there simply was not enough time to change the electoral system before the 2004 election.[26] The members of the task team had anticipated this reaction. In their report, they noted that from the outset, the team had been concerned that any suggestion for change that involved extensive reeducation and redemarcation of existing boundaries was simply impractical, given the time constraints due to the late date at which the reform evaluation had been initiated.[27]

The decision to maintain the current system reflected not only these practical concerns, but also additional factors. The Southall-Mattes survey had found a high degree of satisfaction with the current party-list system and a high level of knowledge about how the system worked. Southall and Mattes found that 74 percent of voters were "satisfied with the way we elect our government." This evaluation seemed to be based on voters' assessment that the system was fair, inclusive, representative, and effective: 72 percent of voters felt that the current system was "fair to all parties," 81 percent that it ensured "we include many voices in Parliament," 78 percent that it gave voters "a way to change the party in power," and 68 percent that it helped voters "hold the parties accountable for their actions."[28] Therefore, according to the views of most South Africans, there was little that was wrong with the current system. The impetus for electoral reform seemed to be originating primarily with political analysts, academics, and people actively involved in the political process.

The ANC, however, had seemed reluctant to change the system even before the minority report recommended that no changes be made.

The ANC's official position on the matter, taken by the National Executive Committee (NEC) in its July 2002 regular meeting, supported retaining proportional representation for national and local elections. The party argued that the system had been adopted before the 1994 election for purposes of inclusivity, and that, eight years later, the country still needed "to harness our inclusive political system in the interest of nation-building and national unity."[29] In theory, this position left room to adopt a new electoral system that combined constituency elements with proportionality, indicating that the party could genuinely be contemplating electoral reform. Yet, an ANC discussion document prepared for the 51st National Conference in September 2002 argued for retaining the current system. While stating that the party would consider different options, the document concluded that

> [t]he current system in place affords a great degree of stability. It allows for fair representation and gives a voice to all. It has certainly allowed for a greater degree of participation of women, people with disabilities and other targeted groups than any other system could. The system is also simple and familiar to voters.[30]

In the light of this preference, the decision to follow the minority recommendation was not surprising and one could even question the sincerity of the official statement that the issue of electoral reform will be reconsidered before the 2009 election.

Electoral System Changes since 1999

Although the matter of reforming the electoral system remains unresolved, between 1999 and 2004 there have been two major changes to the institutional framework that structures elections and party politics in South Africa. The first was the introduction of a new electoral system for the local tier of government in December 2000. The second was the creation of window periods to allow sitting MPs to switch parties in October 2002 and March–April 2003. We provide an overview of these institutional changes and highlight how they have impacted on the party political landscape and structured electoral politics over the past five years.

The 2000 Local Election: Introducing Constituency Elements

The local election in December 2000 was the final step in the creation of a new system of local government, which replaced the transitional governing arrangements that had been in place since 1994.[31] The new system included a demarcation commission, which set the boundaries of the new local governments, and established 6 metropolitan councils, 41 district councils, 5 cross-border municipalities and 232 local councils. The number of local administrations was thus reduced from 864 to 284 and the number of local councilors from 12,000 to approximately 8,000. The new metropolitan councils, also called unicities, amalgamated several urban local administrations into larger, more integrated municipal areas. Most of the new unicities were renamed in the process: Pretoria became Tshwane; Durban—eThekwini; Port Elizabeth—Nelson Mandela Metropole; and the East Rand became Ekurhuleni. Johannesburg and Cape Town retained their original nomenclature. Apart from the unicities, the new system comprises local councils in the smaller cities and towns and district councils covering wider geographic areas with lower population density.[32]

The demarcation process began as early as 1998, although the remaining legislation governing the new local government system was enacted in 2000.[33] This included the new Municipal Electoral Act, which established a mixed electoral system to elect the new local councilors.[34] This electoral system was engineered to maintain overall proportionality, in accordance with the Constitution, by pairing party-list electoral rules with plurality-based constituencies. Roughly half of the local councilors were to be elected through closed party-list PR, and half through a first-past-the-post (FPTP) ward system. The novel aspect of this system was the provision for ward candidates. Any person who was a resident of the municipality in which the ward was located and who appeared on that municipality's segment of the voters' roll could register to contest for a ward-candidate seat. In order to register as a ward candidate, an individual needed only fifty signatures, thirty-five of which had to be voters registered in the ward. This meant that candidates did not have to be members of a political party in order to contest the election. In other words, independent candidates could now participate in local elections.

About 690 independent candidates registered to contest the December 2000 local election, including approximately eighty ex-ANC councilors and a host of politicians who had left the newly formed Democratic Alliance (DA) because they felt that the New National Party (NNP) had sold its supporters out by joining forces with the Democratic Party (DP).[35] Across the country, trade unionists, grassroots activists, and civic organizers began to form alliances with independent candidates and residents' associations. Some of the ex-ANC councilors coalesced into a loose forum, called the Anti-Privatisation Forum. This forum and several ratepayers associations remained politically active after the 2000 local election.[36] Even though many independent candidates did not actually win local council seats, the introduction of ward candidates made the system, at least at the local level, less party dominated.

Another important aspect of the 2000 local election was a realignment in opposition politics. Many of the smaller parties saw the support they had received in the 1999 national and provincial elections decrease in the local election. For example, the United Democratic Movement (UDM) experienced a decline from the 3.42 percent it had earned in the 1999 national election to just 1.4 percent in the 2000 local election. More important, in advance of the election, the DP and the NNP had decided to merge, thus creating the DA. A constitutional prohibition on floor crossing prevented the parties from merging at the national and provincial levels, but nothing prohibited them from registering a new party to contest the local election. Therefore, in June 2000, six months before the election, the parties formed the DA and subsequently ran a joint election campaign. This realignment represented the first time that opposition parties in South Africa agreed to cooperate beyond the level of temporary electoral pacts or an agreement to create a coalition government. The new alliance was an attempt to integrate parties at the organizational level. The fact that the parties involved in the merger represented minority opposition voters rendered the new party open to criticisms of being anti-black and pro-white, a defender of minority privilege.[37]

Despite these charges, the DA performed surprisingly well in the local election. It won nearly 25 percent of the votes nationwide, securing 1,407 of the almost 8,000 local councilor seats, and control over many local governments in the Western Cape, including Cape Town.[38] The DA took control of the Cape Town municipality with 54 percent of the vote against the ANC's 36 percent. The DA also secured more than 30 percent of the vote in three metropolitan areas of Gauteng, polling 35 percent in Tshwane (Greater Pretoria), 33 percent in Johannesburg, and 30 percent on the East Rand.[39] Overall, the DA increased its vote share by 5.69 percent compared to what the component parties had earned in the 1999 national election.

The new party soon proved unstable. The NNP, as the junior partner in the alliance, constantly felt derogated by what it saw as DP imperiousness. Compounding the divisions, the DA was unable to operate as a joint force in the NA and provincial legislatures due to the fact that the constituent parties had to maintain separate party caucuses.[40] By June 2001, the differences came to a head over a fiasco in the Western Cape, when the DA Mayor, Peter Marais (originally an NNP politician), started renaming the streets of Cape Town without following proper procedures.

Marais had a long history as a populist politician and the DA leadership could not agree on how to deal with the situation. Compounding the problem, Marais was accused of corruption and sexual harassment, and again the constituent parties in the DA disagreed on how to deal with the allegations.

The tensions in the DA had been brewing for some time,[41] and by July 2001 the conflicts over Marais, together with accusations of membership rigging and fraud, led to a vitriolic public exchange between high-ranking DA members from the DP and NNP sides.[42] In early November, the NNP officially quit the alliance, after working out an agreement with the ANC that as it withdrew its participation in the DA it would form a coalition government with the ANC in the Western Cape, thus ending the DP-NNP coalition that had ruled the province since the 1999 election. This agreement enabled the NNP to retain provincial power positions in its last remaining stronghold. Yet, quitting the DA also created a serious problem, as the move left the NNP without any representatives at the local tier of government. Therefore, one of the key components of the pact between the ANC and the NNP was an agreement that the ANC would introduce legislation providing for floor crossing, thus enabling the NNP councilors who were "stuck" in DA positions to "come home" to the NNP.[43]

Prejudicing Proportionality? Creating Provisions to Cross the Floor

In late September 2001, the ANC started working on legislation permitting sitting representatives at all tiers of government to switch political parties ("cross the floor") without losing their seats. In January 2002, the Justice and Local Government committees of the NA introduced the floor-crossing legislation. At this point in time, the DA seemed worried about the possibility of losing control over the Cape Town unicity as a result of floor crossing, but the party did not actively oppose the legislation. In fact, when it came to voting in the NA on June 11, 2002, the bill passed with the support of the ANC, NNP, and DA.[44]

The floor-crossing legislation that was adopted in June was actually a package of four separate bills.[45] Together, they provided for the creation of two fifteen-day "window periods" between elections during which members of councils and legislatures could apply to switch from one party to another.[46] The legislation required that in order for a member to defect, at least 10 percent of the party's representatives in the council or legislature would have to agree and follow the move. However, for the initial "transitional" period, this 10 percent minimum would be waived. The waiver signaled a degree of political expediency and the lack of principled motivation of the new legislation.

The floor-crossing legislation set off a constitutional controversy. On the eve of the first window period, which was to commence at midnight on June 21, 2002, the UDM launched an urgent application with the Cape High Court to suspend the legislation. The UDM argued that it had been passed for reasons of political expediency and that it was unconstitutional, since the Constitution stipulated that the electoral system should be based on proportionality. At this point, the DA decided to oppose the legislation, even though the party had voted for it in the NA. The DA and a number of small parties joined the UDM's application, arguing that the legislation violated the Constitution and had been passed to obliterate small opposition parties and cement a political deal between the ANC and the NNP. The ANC's counterargument was that since the will of the people could change in the period between elections, the system should enable adjustments to the composition of councils and legislatures. Furthermore, as the Constitution did not stipulate the exact details of the electoral system but merely that the NA must legislate a system that "results, in general, in proportional representation," the floor-crossing provisions were, according to the ANC, not inherently unconstitutional.

There are indications that the ANC did in fact agree to the floor-crossing legislation because it would help to limit competition from opposition parties, especially the DA. The ANC Chair of the Justice Committee of the NA, Johnny de Lange, publicly admitted that the legislation was motivated by the agreement with the NNP, as well as the ANC's wish to deal with "the DA problem."[47] The ANC's desire to capture the provinces not yet under its control and to recapture control over the Cape Town municipal council were additional motivations for the party's decision to create floor-crossing opportunities.

On June 20, 2002, the Cape High Court suspended the first floor-crossing window period and ruled in favor of the UDM. The Cape Court put the legislation on hold until the case could be reviewed by the Constitutional Court. Several politicians who had already submitted requests to switch parties were caught out by this interdict, and as a result, the high courts in the Western Cape and KwaZulu-Natal (KZN) had to guarantee that these representatives could not be forced to resign from their respective parties until the matter had been settled.

The Constitutional Court did not take up the case until the first week of August and delivered a ruling on October 4, 2002. The court argued that the political motivations behind the floor-crossing legislation were beyond its purview, and that it would focus solely on the issue of constitutionality. The court found that the legislation was not inconsistent with the Constitution's proportionality principle, but that there had been a procedural flaw in using ordinary legislation rather than a constitutional amendment to effect the change at national and provincial levels. Therefore, the court allowed the defection process to proceed at the local level, but ruled that a constitutional amendment was required for defections to take place in the provincial and national legislatures.

After the ruling, the minister of justice introduced the Constitution of RSA Fourth Amendment Bill, which provided for floor crossing at national and provincial levels. The minister also extended protection to the provincial and national representatives who had been exposed in June, stating that they could not be removed from their parties until the amendments had been voted on in Parliament. At the same time, the window for municipal floor crossing opened on October 8 and closed on October 22, 2002. Parliament passed the Fourth Amendment Bill on March 20, 2003, and the national and provincial floor-crossing window promptly opened on March 21.

The cumulative result of both floor-crossing periods was an overall weakening of the opposition and strengthening of the ANC. The ruling party's controversial goal of a two-thirds majority became a reality. After the March–April window period the ANC's presence in the NA had increased from 266 to 275 MPs, representing 68 percent of the NA seats. The opposition, which after 1999 had already experienced growing fragmentation, further disaggregated, as six new parties emerged at the national level, three of which held seats in the NA.[48] The winner among the opposition was the DA, which gained eight MPs, increasing its representation in the NA from 38 to 46 seats.[49] The African Christian Democratic Party (ACDP) also picked up one new MP, thus arriving at seven seats. The UDM, which lost ten of its fourteen MPs, was worst hit, together with the Afrikaner Eenheidsbeweging (AEB), whose sole MP created a new party. The NNP saw its representation decline from 28 to 20 seats and the IFP lost 3 members, thus holding on to 31 seats. The Pan African Congress (PAC) lost its most visible and popular politician, Patricia de Lille, who created a new party, the Independent Democrats (ID).

At the provincial level the changes were perhaps even more significant. The ANC picked up enough defectors to enable the party to win shared control over the Western Cape and KwaZulu-Natal (KZN), the two provinces that had eluded the party in 1999. Thus, the ANC realized

Table 4.2   Seat allocation in the National Assembly before and after the 2003 floor crossing

	ACDP	AEB	ANC	Azapo	DA	FA	FF	IFP	MF	NNP	PAC	UDM	UCDP
Before	6	1	266	1	38	2	3	34	1	28	3	14	3
After	7	—	275	1	46	2	3	31	1	20	2	4	3

NB: This table includes only those parties already represented in the NA before the floor crossing window period opened.

Source: Parliament of the Republic of South Africa, "State of Parties Represented in the National Assembly," April 5, 2003.

its goal of creating a "Parliament of Hope," with the party controlling the NA and all nine provincial governments. At the local level, 555 councilors crossed the floor, with most (61 percent) moving from the DA to the NNP. The ANC gained 22 percent of the floor crossers in the municipal defections. The NNP reconstituted itself at the local level, earning back 340 of its members from the DA and picking up a few additional councilors from other parties.[50] Five new parties formed at the local level,[51] and 21 local councils changed control; most of these were situated in the Western Cape, representing transfers from DA to ANC-NNP control. Interestingly, given heated exchanges between the ANC and the DA, three of the transitions were to ANC-DA coalitions.

Conclusion

What has been the effect of all these developments and, more important, what does it mean for the future of representative democracy in South Africa?

Regarding the electoral system, the long-term effects of the incremental changes have yet to be discerned. The short-term impact of enabling floor crossing is clear: the ANC benefited, while the opposition fragmented even further. With the constitutional ban on floor crossing in place until 2003, party realignments between elections were practically nonexistent, as politicians were reluctant to jump ship and thus lose their jobs midterm.[52] The new floor-crossing provisions have taken away the institutional obstacles for such realignments. Therefore, in principle, they could have the effect of increasing the fluidity of a party system that has crystallized at an early stage in South Africa's democratic development. However, when the 10-percent threshold is enforced, the stabilizing effects of the preexisting system of proportional representation based on closed party lists are likely to be reproduced. It would probably be difficult to convince 10 percent of a party's representatives to defect to another party or form a new party altogether, especially 10 percent of ANC MPs or MPLs. Convincing 10 percent of 279 MPs to defect would clearly require more effort than persuading 10 percent of 20 members. Therefore, future realignments in the window periods for floor crossing are more likely to affect the smaller parties, and will probably not be to their benefit. It is too early, however, for definitive predictions in any direction.

There might be a more positive consequence of the institutional changes, however. In the longer term, the introduction of the provision for floor crossing could work to dilute some of the control party elites have over the career prospects of ordinary MPs. This could, in turn, facilitate Parliament developing into a stronger institution capable of keeping executive dominance in check. Parliamentary committees may be more willing to engage in oversight practices and challenge the party hierarchy if members are not completely dependent on their parties to hold on to their parliamentary seats. This degree of autonomy is important, because if Parliament, being one of the country's main representative institutions, fails to fulfill its potential and live up to its responsibilities, the quality of South African democracy is likely to suffer.

Strengthening Parliament and increasing the autonomy of its members could help to improve Parliament's public image, which further undermines the institution. Electoral reform could also solve image problems and aid accountability, by increasing the connections between parliamentarians and citizens. Under the current electoral system, there seems to be little sense of ownership of Parliament among the public. In an Afrobarometer survey held in 2000, only 0.2 percent of South Africans reported having made contact with an MP.[53] This extremely low level of interaction between voters and their elected representatives provides another rationale to reconsider the electoral system and reopen the debate about electoral reform in advance of the 2009 election. For as long as Parliament remains distant from ordinary South Africans, it will remain tangential to democratic consolidation.

Notes

The views of the authors expressed in this chapter are entirely their own, and do not represent the views and opinions of the organizations and agencies by which the authors are employed.

1. Throughout this chapter we interchangeably use the terms Parliament and National Assembly. Although the South African parliament is bicameral, comprising the National Assembly and the National Council of Provinces (NCOP), we do not include the latter, less important chamber

in our analysis here. For more information about the role and special character of the NCOP, see Christina Murray and Lia Nijzink, *Building Representative Democracy: South Africa's Legislatures and the Constitution* (Cape Town: Parliamentary Support Programme, 2002).

2. Murray and Nijzink, *Building Representative Democracy*.

3. See Susan de Villiers, *A People's Government—The People's Voice: A Review of Public Participation in the Law and Policy-making Process in South Africa* (Cape Town: The Parliamentary Support Programme, 2001).

4. Adam Habib and Collette Herzenberg, "Popular Control over Decision Makers," in *The People Shall Govern! Idasa Democracy Index* (Cape Town: Idasa, 2004).

5. Lia Nijzink, *Members' Legislative Proposals: A Guide for Members of the National Council of Provinces and the Provincial Legislatures* (Cape Town: National Council of Provinces, 2004).

6. Hugh Corder et al., "Report on Parliamentary Oversight and Accountability Prepared for the Office of the Speaker," Faculty of Law, University of Cape Town, July 1999.

7. Annual Report for Parliament 1999.

8. Lia Nijzink, "Opposition in the New South African Parliament," in *Opposition and Democracy in South Africa*, ed. Roger Southall (London: Frank Cass, 2001), 63.

9. Murray and Nijzink, *Building Representative Democracy*.

10. Robert Mattes et al., *Views of Democracy in South Africa and the Region: Trends and Comparisons* (Cape Town: Southern African Democracy Barometer, no. 2, 2000), 35, 39–40, 45.

11. Murray and Nijzink, *Building Representative Democracy*, 60.

12. Ibid., 66.

13. See Piombo, final chapter of this volume.

14. Nelson Polsby, "Legislatures," in *Legislatures*, ed. Philip Norton (Oxford: Oxford University Press, 1990), 129–147.

15. Ibid., 142.

16. In 2000, a new electoral system for the local tier of government was introduced, which we discuss elsewhere in this chapter.

17. The other members of the committee were appointed primarily on the recommendations of the Department of Home Affairs and the Chair of the committee, and included: Raesibe Tladi (Director: Legal Services, Department of Justice and Constitutional Development; Tladi resigned on August 13, 2002 and was not replaced), Zamindlela Titus (Special Ministerial Adviser, Department of Provincial and Local Government), Adv Pansy Tlakula (Chief Electoral Officer, Electoral Commission), S. S. van der Merwe (Commissioner, Electoral Commission), Norman du Plessis (Deputy Chief Electoral Officer, Electoral Commission; appointed by the Minister of Home Affairs), Adv Rufus Malatji (Chief Director: Legal Services, Department of Home Affairs), Professor Jørgen Elklit (Department of Political Science, University of Aarhus, Denmark), Professor Glenda Fick (School of Law, University of the Witwatersrand), Nicholas Haysom (Attorney in private practice), Dr. Wilmot James (Executive Director, Social Cohesion and Integration Research Programme, Human Sciences Research Council), Dren Nupen (Director, Electoral Institute of Southern Africa), Tefo Raditapole (Attorney in private practice); "*The Report of the Electoral Task Team*," (January 2003), section 1.3.2. The entire report is available at http://www.pmg.org.za/bills/030311ett1.pdf.

18. Frederik van Zyl Slabbert, "South Africa: Four Core Values that will be Considered in Choosing a New Electoral System," Electoral Institute of Southern Africa (Johannesburg: EISA), accessed at http://www.eisa.org.za/WEP/southafrica_elesys5.htm, on September 10, 2002.

19. ETT Report, 1.5.1.

20. Norman du Plessis, "An Electoral System For South Africa: Various Options" (Cape Town: Electoral Task Team discussion paper, September 10, 2002).

21. The majority report was endorsed by van Zyl Slabbert, Haysom, du Plessis, James, Elklit, Majatji, Fick, and Nupen.

22. ETT Report, 4.5.1.1.

23. Ibid., 4.1.5.3.

24. The minority comprised members Raditapole, Titus, Tlakula, and van der Merwe.

25. ETT Report 5.6.–5.7.

26. Gordon Bell, "Electoral System to be Changed After 2004," *The Cape Times*, March 6, 2003, http://www.iol.co.za/index.php?set_id=1&click_id=13&art_id=vn20030306062426714C258902.

27. ETT Report, 1.6.

28. Ibid., 2.3.

29. "Future Electoral Systems for South Africa: Discussion Document for National Policy Conference," September 1, 2002 (document prepared for the 51st National Conference of the ANC, December 16–20, 2002), paragraph 8; accessed at http://www.anc.org.za/ancdocs/history/conf/conference51/index.html, on November 19, 2002.

30. Ibid., paragraph 26.

31. For a concise analysis of the system, see David Pottie, "Electoral Legislation—Local Elections," *EISA* (undated) accessed at http://www.eisa.org.za/saelect/locgovt1.htm#1, on August 26, 2000.

32. Information on these government structures can be found at http://www.gov.za/structure/local-gov.htm.

33. There were four separate pieces of legislation that created the system of local elections and local government: the Municipal Demarcation Act (No. 27 of 1998), the Municipal Structures Act (No. 117 of 1998), the Municipal Electoral Act (No. 20 of 2000), and the Municipal Systems Act (No. 32 of 2000).

34. For the text of the act, see http://www.gov.za/gazette/acts/2000/a27-00.pdf.

35. Jessica Piombo, "Time to Reconsider South Africa's Electoral System?" *Mail & Guardian*, November 24–30, 2000. See also William Mervin Gumede and Ferial Haffajee, "Rebellion in the ANC Ranks," *Financial Mail*, October 27, 2000, accessed at http://www.fm.co.za/00/1027/currents/bcurrents.htm.

36. Since December 2000, the Anti-Privatisation Forum has become one of the social movements that has led the revitalization of South Africa's traditionally vibrant, but in the 1990s quiescent, civil society.

37. For example, see "Mbeki Condemns Opposition," *Business Day*, December 8, 2000, accessed at http://www.bday.co.za/bday/content/direct/1.3523.756011-6078-0.00html. Mbeki labeled the new party an "unholy alliance, united by hatred for the ruling party rather than a commitment to serve the interests of the people."

38. Troye Lund, "Analysts Blame ANC Loss on Low Cape Turnout," *The Cape Argus*, December 7, 2000, accessed at http://www.iol.co.za/html/frame_news.php; "DA Loses Five Councils as IE Adjusts Results," *Independent Online*, 7 December 2000, accessed at http://iol.co.za/tempfeat/elections/index.php.

39. Marco Granelli, "Leon Over the Moon at Gains in Black Voters," *The Star*, December 7, 2000, accessed at http://www.iol.co.za/html/frame_news.php.

40. The supporters of the NNP and the DP also had different perspectives on many policy issues and represented distinct interests in South African society. See Robert Mattes and Jessica Piombo, "Opposition Parties and the Voters in South Africa's 1999 Election" (*Democratization*, Autumn 2001, 101–128) for an in-depth analysis.

41. Since at least April 2001, indications of a rift between Leon and van Schalkwyk permeated the media. For just a few examples, see "Leon, Van Schalkwyk Deny Rift," *News 24*, April 2, 2001http://www.news24.co.za/News24/Politics/0,1113,2-12_1005180,00.html, accessed on April 4, 2001; and "DA Letter Causes a Stir," *Beeld*, April 2, 2001, accessed at http://www.news24.co.za/News24/Politics/0,1113,2-12_1004918,00.html.

42. For example, see "Accusations Fly as DP, NNP Turn on Each Other," *Independent Online*, October 10, 2001, accessed at http://www.iol.co.za/index.php?click_id=13&art_id=ct20011010202637682D541428&set_id=1.

43. *Daily News* June 20, 2002; Ashley Smith, "Politics Goes Biblical in the Race for the Cape," *Cape Times* June 10, 2002, accessed at www.iol.co.za/index.php?sf=13&click_id&art_id=ct2002061021534132A21462765&set_id=1.

44. Before the vote, the members of the DA were divided over whether or not the party should oppose the bill (Donwald Pressly, "DA divided over Floor Crossing," *Mail & Guardian Online* March 28, 2002, accessed at www.mg.co.za).

45. The Constitution of RSA Amendment Bill, the Constitution of RSA Second Amendment Bill, the Loss or Retention of Membership in National and Provincial Legislatures Bill, and the Local Government: Municipal Structures Amendment Bill.

46. The window period would open in September of the second and fourth year after an election.

47. Comments reported in "ANC Wipes Parliament's Floor of 'DA Problem,' " *Mail & Guardian*, June 6, 2002, and Carol Paton, "Why did the Politician Cross the Floor?" *The Sunday Times*, June 9, 2002.

48. These parties were: The Independent Democrats, the New Labour Party (Peter Marais), the Alliance for Democracy and Prosperity (Nelson Ramodike in Limpopo), the African Independent Movement (Teresa Millin, formerly of the IFP), Nasionale Aksie/National Action (Cassie Aucamp from the AEB), and the Peace and Development Party (founded by ex-IFP members Jan Slabbert and Farouk Cassim). For a description of these parties, see Marianne Merten, "The Rise of the One Man (and One Woman) Show," *Mail & Guardian*, April 4, 2003.

49. During the window period in March–April, the DP dissolved itself and reconstituted as the DA, finalizing the process that had begun in June 2001.

50. "555 Have Played Political Musical Chairs," *Independent Online* October 24, 2002, accessed at http://www.iol.co.za/index.php?sf=6&click_id=qw1035466561201B224&set_id=1.

51. These were the Universal Party, the Black Consciousness Party, the Sport Party, the Phumulela Rate Payer's Association, and the Belastingbetalersvereneging (Tax Payers' Association).

52. Jessica Piombo, "Constructing Dominance: Institutions, Cleavages and Parties in Post-Apartheid South Africa, 1994–1999" (Ph.D. dissertation, MIT Department of Political Science, Cambridge, MA, 2002).

53. Mattes et al., *Views of Democracy*, 69–71.

CHAPTER FIVE

Electoral Administration: Achievements and Continuing Challenges

CLAUDE KABEMBA

To most, the cornerstone of democracy is the regular holding of free and fair elections, in which multiple political parties are able to participate. The organization of credible and transparent elections is an important feature of the democratic process, yet one that is often overlooked in analyses of democratic consolidation. Since elections are one of the primary ways in which citizens engage with the state and one of the most basic sources of legitimacy for a government, it is important that they be conducted and administered in a competent manner, by an organization that is viewed by most as politically impartial and immune from government meddling. When electoral administrations are politicized or incompetent, election results are frequently contested and resisted by both citizens and the parties that performed poorly in the elections. Therefore, assessing the organization that administers elections is critical in evaluating the progress of democratic institutionalization in South Africa.

This chapter looks critically at the work of the South African Independent Electoral Commission (IEC). The first section focuses on the inception of the IEC, its structure, and independence. The second section briefly looks at the progress the IEC has made since 1994 in organizing elections. The third section reviews the IEC's performance in the 2004 election. The chapter closes by identifying the challenges facing the IEC in future elections.

The Establishment of the IEC: Its Structure and Independence

During the Convention for a Democratic South Africa (Codesa), the organization of inclusive democratic elections that would pave the way for a democratic South Africa was high on the agenda. The critical and by no means easy question of who would administer the first democratic election needed to be answered. The Codesa delegates decided to follow a well-established international model, setting up an organization, separate from government, to oversee the electoral process. In creating this organization, they needed to solve the dilemma of how to establish a body that would be impartial, both in actual fact and in the perception of the public, in a society where stakeholders had yet to build trust among themselves and among citizens. The creation of the IEC was a gamble because had there been any suspicion that the IEC was partisan, the legitimacy of the election could have been called into question, and the transition process stalled or set back.

At the end of the negotiations, South Africa adopted three interrelated statutes that together created the structures to administer elections: the Constitution of the Republic of South Africa (Act no. 20 of 1993), the Electoral Act (Act no. 202 of 1993), and the Independent Electoral Commission Act (Act no. 150 of 1993). Of these three, the Constitution sets the general principles and guidelines with which the electoral system and electoral process must correspond. The specific regulations governing the actual management and administration of elections are enshrined in the Electoral Act, while the third act establishes the body that runs the elections, the IEC. The commission that was created in advance of the 1994 election was a temporary body, replaced by a permanent commission soon after the election.

The responsibilities of the IEC, as currently defined in section 190 of the Constitution (Act 108 of 1996), are:

- to manage elections of national, provincial, and municipal legislative bodies in accordance with the national legislation;
- to ensure that elections are free and fair; and
- to declare the results of those elections within a period that must be prescribed by national legislation and that is as short as possible.

In other words, the IEC is the organization that plans, organizes, and conducts the actual polling process, implementing the electoral rules set out in the Electoral Act.

The Independent Electoral Commission Act establishes the commission and fixes its composition, powers, duties, administrative structure, and financial accountability. The IEC comprises five commissioners, one of whom must be a judge. Commissioners serve for seven years and may only serve two terms.[1] The appointment process to the IEC is transparent and inclusive, and thus promotes the impartiality of the commission. For example, at the time of their appointment, individuals may not hold high political office.[2] The members of the commission are afforded various privileges and immunities. The commissioners can only be removed from office by "the President on the grounds of misconduct, incapacity or incompetence, after a finding to that effect by a committee of the National Assembly on the recommendation of the Electoral Court and the majority vote of the National Assembly on a resolution for removal."[3] The commissioners are not allowed to take up other positions outside the IEC.

Beside the commissioners, the IEC appoints a Chief Electoral Officer (CEO), who heads the administration of the commission and serves as its Accounting Officer. The CEO in turn appoints the remainder of the IEC staff in consultation with the other members of the commission. Gender representation is taken seriously within the structures of the commission. In 2004, the two top positions in the IEC, the chairperson and the CEO, were held by women, Brigalia Bam and Pansy Tlakula, respectively.

The IEC structure expands greatly during elections, and is kept to a small core of employees between elections. The commission is structured to ensure its presence in the nine provinces. The IEC's national headquarters are in Pretoria, with supporting offices in each province. The structure is designed to allow the head office to function as a policy-making unit and a strategic management component, while the core activities such as voter registration and the organization of polling stations are largely the responsibility of provincial and municipal IEC offices. Supervisory functions are located in the nine provincial electoral offices, which coordinate the activities of the municipal electoral offices as well as liaise with the head office and with political parties and security organizations in the provinces to ensure that the process runs smoothly. The 441 municipal electoral offices organize and run the voter registration process and the polling stations. Thus, in practice, the delivery of elections is done through the Provincial Electoral Officers (PEOs) and the Local Electoral Officers (LEOs), who, in most cases, are town clerks based at city metros, local councils, and rural councils.

The independence of the IEC is critical to create confidence in the electoral process. Several aspects of the IEC's structure and operating principles facilitate independence. First, the IEC is a permanent body that is publicly funded. Each year, Parliament approves a budget that has been submitted by the IEC, and then releases funds to the organization. In return, the IEC is requested to report annually to Parliament on its expenditure, but the nature of the expenditure itself is not controlled either by Parliament or the executive. In addition to its public funds, the IEC has also benefited from substantial donor funding. Both types of funds have been effectively and transparently managed. Its financial independence has enabled the commission to discharge its duties efficiently, effectively, with impartiality, and separate from government.[4]

Second, the stipulation that at least one commissioner must be a judge is not accidental. The judiciary plays an important role in managing election-related conflicts and as such the independence of the judiciary is a critical contribution to successfully managing and administering elections. There is a firm public perception that a judge is above politics and will bring to the commission all the qualities associated with an independent judiciary.[5] It is important to note that the IEC does not employ the judge. This commissioner receives no remuneration from the commission, so that he or she is free to offer critical commentary on the organization, without fear of being sacked.[6]

Third, the high moral status of all the commissioners and the fairness of their judgment have enhanced the independence and credibility of the IEC. As Khabele Matlosa puts it, "the IEC is also fairly insulated from undue influences by powerful political actors and, as such, has jealously guarded its independence, thus enhancing its credibility, acceptability and legitimacy before the eyes of all contestants."[7] The IEC's independence and sense of fairness have been demonstrated repeatedly, as commissioners have not hesitated to disagree with and criticize the government on a number of occasions.

Steady Maturation since 1994

In 1994, South Africa organized its first democratic election. In terms of electoral administration, everything needed to be put in place. The new commission had to find the right people and establish a working structure. All South African citizens and permanent residents of voting age could cast ballots. But there were no identity cards and no clear delimitation of district boundaries. With more than 19.5 million people eventually taking part in the election, organizing a smooth electoral process was difficult. To offset the lack of election administration experience of the commissioners, an international Advisory Committee was put in place.

Organizing elections in a divided postapartheid South Africa, with inherited government structures and homelands with very little credibility, was a difficult undertaking. The task was further complicated by the fact that there was a severe time constraint. The commission's first meeting was on December 20, 1993, yet, the election date was set for April 27, 1994. As the IEC put it, "this was accepting what was technically and administratively a virtually impossible task."[8]

In 1994, the political climate was not conducive to holding free and fair elections. In the run-up to the 1994 election, South African society was racked by politically motivated violence; crime and political intimidation were common, and there was a worsening security situation, especially in the province of KwaZulu-Natal (KZN, whose territory included the former Zulu homeland). For example, the Inkatha Freedom Party (IFP) had rejected the interim Constitution, was not in favor of holding elections, and in fact officially boycotted the process until a week before the election was set to open. Because the election would not have been possible in KZN without the cooperation of the IFP, the party's eleventh-hour decision to participate forced the IEC to adjust ballot papers, train additional staff, and create polling stations in large swathes of the province, with just days to go before polling day. The election in KZN was by far the most contentious and controversy-ridden in the entire country. Under these circumstances, the IEC's first responsibility was to work to convince all parties that it was impartial and independent.

It is believed that many mistakes were made in 1994. Overall, the first democratic election was disorganized and somewhat controversial in terms of accuracy and transparency. Most of the problems that occurred related to the lack of a voters' roll, perceived unreliable population statistics, and the ability to vote at any polling station of a person's choice.[9] Additionally, the election result in KZN was thought by many observers to be the product of behind-the-scenes negotiation, decided upon for the purposes of political stability. Yet, the euphoria and excitement that surrounded the election overshadowed the problems that occurred. Anyone who dared to question the credibility of the process would have been identified as a spoiler of freedom for millions of South Africans. Most felt that an imperfect election was better than a civil war.

The IEC was dissolved on the conclusion of its work in late 1994. A new commission, which assumed the same name, was established after the required legislation was passed in 1996. The new commission was established as a permanent body responsible for strengthening constitutional democracy and promoting a democratic electoral process. It was clear that the immediate responsibility of the new body was the compilation of a voters' roll, the demarcation of wards for local government, the review of existing electoral legislation, and the conduct of large-scale voter education before the 1999 election. Again, time became a constraint. The new IEC was appointed on July 9, 1997, with the election (unofficially) planned for June 1999. This timeframe of two years, from the appointment of the commission until the election, proved a daunting challenge.[10] The new IEC also had the task of identifying new voting districts. In 1996, the Electoral Steering Committee recommended the use of the Geographic Information System (GIS) as the basis for determining voting districts that would be the administrative areas for electoral activities. Voters would then have to be registered in their own districts. The voting district system was given statutory sanction in the Electoral Act of 1998.

Since 1999, the electoral process has become increasingly technical with the registration of potential voters and the compilation of a voters' roll being essential elements. During the 1999 election, the IEC experienced few of the organizational problems that had plagued the 1994 electoral exercise. The largest challenge proved to be the compilation of the voters' roll. It had to be created for the first time in advance of the 1999 election.[11] Once the roll was established, the IEC had to ensure that it was accurate, and that it contained only South Africans, since this time only South African citizens were allowed to vote. This proved to be a difficult process, requiring three concentrated registration weekends, and many lawsuits over who could register and what documents were required to register. Ultimately the election was held on time, but for months the registration and the creation of the voters' roll were sticky issues that could have forced a postponement of the election date.

Compared to 1994 and 1999, the 2004 election took place in an atmosphere of greater confidence among all the stakeholders: the IEC, political parties, civil society, and citizens. Time was no longer an issue. The legislative and regulatory frameworks for conducting elections were in place. The voters' roll was established and only needed to be updated. Therefore, the exercise in 2004 was more about trying to perfect the system than to establish it.

The Administration of the 2004 Election

The electoral process and its outcome are dependent on the way the election is managed and administered throughout three distinct phases: the preelection phase, the polling phase (election day), and the postelection phase.[12]

The Preelection Phase

Before elections can take place voting districts need to be identified, voters need to be registered, candidates need to be nominated, parties need to conduct their election campaigns, and conflicts that arise in the course of the electoral process need to be managed. Thus, much of the work of election administration takes place before polling day, in the preelection phase. Without the essential administrative building blocks of effective voter registration and careful delimitation of voting districts, the electoral process inevitably suffers. Without appropriate conflict management, healthy electioneering could escalate into conflicts that damage the electoral process or even result in political violence. In the preelection phase, the IEC's responsibilities include voter registration, the preparation of materials and other logistics for the actual casting of the ballots, the organization of polling stations, and managing conflicts between parties.

Voter Registration

During the preelection phase, the IEC spent most of its efforts attracting potential voters, especially the youth, and its 2004 registration drive can be regarded as a success. As the election approached, the IEC already had a properly compiled register of voters. The task before the commission was to increase the number of registered voters, especially among the section of the electorate that had been too young to register for the 1999 and 2000 elections.

In this process, the IEC demonstrated a genuine willingness to register all eligible voters. Although the onus of registration lies with South African citizens, the IEC tried to make it easier for them by enabling continuous registration at all offices of the Department of Home Affairs, up until the announcement of the election date, when registration officially closed. In addition, the commission arranged two special voter registration drives: on November 8–9, 2003 and January 24–25, 2004. Throughout the registration process, there were other projects such as door-to-door campaigns, the opportunity to use short-message-service (SMS) to check whether a person was on the voters' roll, and the continuously updated IEC Web site. The Web site provided information about where to register and included an interactive feature at which a person could check the voters' roll to make sure his or her name was included.

In contrast to the 1999 election, there were no major disputes around voter registration. However, certain parties accused the IEC of unethical behavior. For example, the Democratic Alliance (DA) in Bloemfontein accused the IEC of allowing a member of the African National Congress (ANC) to manage voter registration.[13] In KZN, the IFP Youth Brigade accused the IEC of allowing ANC Youth League members, not employed by the IEC, to access its registration equipment in Umlazi Township. In most cases, the accusations were not substantiated and the aggrieved parties were unable to take the matter to court. However, such questions around the IEC's integrity, though probably impossible to prevent entirely, should not be considered trivial. They could be a serious warning for future elections.

Two issues that had arisen in 1999 once again came to the fore during the 2004 registration process: the right to vote for prisoners and for South Africans living abroad. In 1994, the IEC had recommended that the issue around the right of prisoners to participate in elections should be resolved well in advance of any future elections.[14] Yet, the recommendation was not taken up by the government. Thus, the issue cropped up again in 2004. This time around, a court ruling establishing the right of prisoners to vote came rather late in the electoral process. The IEC was nevertheless able to immediately begin voter registration for thousands of prisoners across the country. There were more than 70,000 prisoners, many of whom were unable to register because they did not have the required bar-coded identity documents and had no time to acquire them. However, the IEC successfully distributed voter education and campaign materials to prisoners and registered those complying with the electoral regulations. On election day, the IEC sent mobile voting stations to prisons across the country.

The issue of overseas voters was also unresolved. There seemed to be no consensus. In 1994, South Africans overseas had been able to vote at South African consulates and embassies around the world, but, in 1999, only those South Africans who were abroad on official business were able to cast ballots. At the time, this had been a controversial decision, prompting outcries from the opposition that it was an attempt to disenfranchise minority communities, many of whom had moved abroad. In advance of the 2004 election, opposition parties again raised the issue, and this time the ANC conceded and engineered an amendment to the Electoral Act allowing South Africans abroad to vote on a temporary basis, provided that they had registered while still in South Africa.[15]

On February 20, 2004, the CEO of the IEC certified the National Common Voters' Roll. The final voters' roll included 20,674,926 voters. Compared to 18,172,751 registered voters in 1999, this represented an increase of 2.5 million.[16] Women outnumbered men on the voters' roll and made up 54 percent of total registered voters.[17] The IEC was able to register many new voters because there was adequate time for voter registration, especially after the president delayed the announcement of the election date to give potential voters more time to register. The IEC had also invited all political parties to run campaigns motivating people to register. Finally, the registration levels reflected the IEC's efforts to encourage voter participation by increasing awareness, streamlining procedures, and improving access to facilities.

Using figures supplied by Statistics South Africa (SSA), there were 27 million potential voters in 2004. This means that 7 million potential voters were not on the IEC's roll. One could thus conclude that the IEC's registration efforts had not been good enough or call the SSA figures into question. The IEC itself decided to avoid entering into a dispute with SSA and stated that they had simply not found those potential voters as they went around the country. Nevertheless, the issue remains unresolved and needs serious attention. There are many challenges that prevent a 100 percent accurate census of the South African population but the IEC cannot continue to run elections with substantially wrong census data. For one thing, it makes it difficult to judge the IEC's performance in voter registration. Especially because many factors influence whether or not citizens choose to register, it seems reasonable to, for now, judge the IEC on the efforts it made to entice potential voters to register. By this yardstick, the commission performed well in advance of the 2004 election.

Logistics

The IEC had enough time to prepare for the election. By the end of January 2004, the necessary materials, such as voting compartments, ballot boxes, cardboard tables and chairs to be used by election staff, ballot papers and special ink, were ready. Special provisions were in place for disabled and visually impaired voters.[18]

The security of election materials during printing, storage, and distribution impacts on the credibility of elections. To close the pitfalls observed in the previous elections, the IEC introduced a Logistics Information System (LIS), increasing efficiency in dealing with material requirements.[19] Election materials were dispatched from the central warehouse in Pretoria to the provinces. Provincial IEC offices then stored the materials in warehouses located in the different municipalities. From the municipalities, materials were dispatched to polling stations the day before the election opened.[20] All these procedures took place under tight security, and political parties were briefed on the process to increase transparency.

Clearly, a high degree of organization and advanced logistical planning and coordination was involved here, suggesting that the IEC had learned from previous election experiences and was determined to overcome the problems of the past.[21] However, the IEC's approach of dispatching materials weeks before election day did imply a security risk of materials being unduly exposed, especially at the local level. Another disadvantage was the apparent centralization of the process. While the IEC structure is decentralized with provincial offices playing a key role, all the logistical control processes were mounted from the Pretoria head office. The IEC monitored progress in the different provinces through a system of "milestones." This involved targets to be achieved and a national schedule of activities to be followed by each provincial office at specified times. This enabled the IEC to oversee progress from the center and eliminated the danger of some provinces performing below expectations.[22]

Polling Stations

As mentioned earlier, the main focus of the IEC in the preelection phase was to improve voter turnout. The IEC had already undertaken a redelimitation exercise soon after the municipal election in 2000, which was aimed at improving access to polling stations in rural areas. Another measure to encourage participation was to increase the number of voting stations. The IEC increased the number of polling stations from 14,992 in the 2000 municipal election to 16,966 in the 2004 election, an increase of 13.7 percent. Analyzing patterns of voter registration, the IEC determined how many polling stations were needed and where the new stations would be. Most of the new polling stations were situated in former homelands and black residential areas.[23] By increasing the number of voting stations, the IEC reduced the distance the average voter traveled and the time he or she spent in voting, thereby reducing one factor that discourages high voter turnout.

Most often, the IEC used schools and clinics as polling stations. Government departments improved some of these facilities before the election. In other cases, the IEC provided toilets, drinking water, and lighting, all of a temporary nature, in order to improve the circumstances in which voters would cast their votes. In addition, the IEC created 337 mobile voting stations that transported voting materials in minibuses, following preset routes and timetables to provide election services to areas that needed supplemental coverage.

Communication between polling stations and Pretoria was considered critical to the success of the election. The proliferation of the mobile phone had already revolutionized communications during the electoral process. Rather than installing temporary landlines as they had done in the past, the IEC planned to rely heavily on cellular phones to communicate between polling stations, municipal and provincial offices. Compared to the previous two general elections, there was improved cell phone coverage in 2004.[24] All areas where signal strength was questionable were visited by cell phone companies at their own expense and, where possible, they boosted the signal. Only 432 voting stations countrywide had no cellular coverage. In all these stations, the IEC used landline telephones and radios to communicate. The police was also mobilized and its communication network was made available for use in any unforeseen circumstances.

Conflict Management

Elections evoke a degree of tension and are by their very nature open to conflict. For the 2004 election, the IEC had an effective system of conflict management in place, which had been established and tested in earlier elections. Party liaison committees existed at the national, provincial, and municipal levels. These structures gave political parties an opportunity to interact with one another and to stay informed of the various election preparations. Consultations like these, between the IEC and political parties, increased the transparency of the electoral process and played an important role in preventing election-related conflicts.

In addition, conflict management panels existed at national, provincial, and district levels to intervene and mediate in minor disputes. These panels of mediators, comprising representatives from civil society organizations, lawyers, and religious leaders, were tasked with monitoring areas of potential conflict and arbitrating disputes that might otherwise be brought before the Electoral Court.[25] As in earlier elections and in accordance with electoral law, the Electoral Court had final jurisdiction over infringements of the Electoral Act and the Code of Conduct.

All parties that contested the 2004 national and provincial elections signed the Electoral Code of Conduct. As in earlier elections, the purpose of the code was to promote conditions conducive to free and fair elections. As the strengthening of democracy in South Africa depends on a growing political maturity among parties and their increasing tolerance of one another as legitimate players on an open and even political playing field, it is essential for parties to adhere to the rules of the game during their election campaigns. Notably, the strength of the South African electoral process, in comparison to other countries in the Southern African

Development Community, is that most political parties are aware of the Code of Conduct.

Another indication of how far South Africa has come in terms of conflict management is the fact that in the 2004 election the main issue of concern to parties in the liaison committees were incidents of poster vandalism, a minor issue compared to instances of voter intimidation, interparty conflict, and political violence that plagued earlier elections.[26]

Election Day 2004

The 2004 election opened a few days before the official election date of April 14, in order to allow those who qualified for "special votes" to cast their ballots.[27] The IEC enabled election officials and those involved in the electoral process (such as security personnel and election monitors), pregnant women, the physically infirm, and people with disabilities to cast their votes two days prior to election day, if they had applied, in advance, for a special vote. More than 120,330 people applied to utilize the special vote facility.[28] In 1999, there were only 31,950 voters who applied for and were granted special votes. The special voting process went well with only a few minor problems in parts of KZN, the Eastern Cape, and to a lesser extent in Limpopo. In these provinces, pensioners and other people who had not applied for special votes turned up to vote before election day, some out of ignorance and others in an attempt to avoid long queues. They had to be turned away.

On April 14, 2004, South Africans turned out in considerable numbers to vote. Voters formed queues at polling stations long before the polls were due to open. Overall, people demonstrated patience and respect for the voting process. Their commitment to democracy and peaceful participation in the electoral process was definitely a sign that South African democracy was consolidating. The spirit among voters was enthusiastic and peaceful, even in conflict-prone KZN.

Most polling stations opened on time and did not close until every voter in the queue was served—which often meant staying open past the official closing time of nine pm. The few stations that opened late seemed to be located in the Eastern Cape, Free State, Northern Cape, and Limpopo. Only in the Eastern Cape did all polling stations close on time. Other problems encountered on election day were power failures, for example in nine polling stations in Soweto and Roodepoort, in Gauteng. Some stations used candles; in others the national power company (ESKOM) quickly intervened to repair the service interruption or provide generators. Overall, the process on election day was without any major glitches.

International organizations such as the Commonwealth, the United Nations, and the European Union declined to monitor South Africa's third democratic election because they saw no need to do so. They were satisfied that the 2004 election would be free, fair, and conducted in a transparent manner. Polling was instead monitored by approximately 3,000 local election observers and 204 international observer missions from smaller, regional organizations. The local observers concentrated mostly on the province of KZN, where there was fear for political violence. The IEC in KZN put in place an election observation system, the KwaZulu-Natal Democracy and Elections Forum, to deal specifically with election threats. According to most observer groups, voting went smoothly and the process was mostly without problems.[29] The secrecy of the ballot was respected and voting procedures at polling stations were clear.

The Postelection Phase

When the polling stations closed, counting began. The IEC specified that ballots had to be counted within polling stations, which then had to report the results to the provincial electoral offices. Polling stations started counting as soon as they closed, and continued until all ballots were counted, the number of counted ballots were reconciled with the number of ballots distributed, and the results verified. The count was reported to have progressed well throughout the country, although observers did report some irregularities. There were situations in which polling officers had difficulty completing the forms after counting. In other cases, a certain level of negligence was observed, as some polling officers did not seem to know where to take the ballot boxes. In KZN, two ballot boxes were found dumped, one in the Ixopo and another in the Msinga municipality.[30] In the Northern Cape, five ballot books were reported missing, and in North West twenty ballot papers were stolen, although this was not a major problem, since papers without an IEC stamp were invalid. As polling station staff was on duty from the time the polls opened until the counting process was complete, their tiredness might have been a reason for some of the problems that occurred.

Only the IFP in KZN and the Freedom Front Plus (FF+) in the Free State disputed the election results. Both parties claimed that the election in their respective province had not been free and fair. The FF+ quickly dropped its case. The IFP's complaint seemed more sustained, especially when the party realized that the ANC was set to win the majority of votes in the KZN provincial poll. The IFP filed cases with the Electoral Court, alleging that ANC activists had tampered with identity documents in order to enable voters from the Eastern Cape to illegally cast their votes in the KZN provincial ballot.[31] But the IFP also dropped its case and there were no further challenges to the integrity of the electoral process.

The advance in technology and level of skills within the IEC improved its performance. In 1999, the IEC had announced the election results six days after the election. In 2004, the votes were captured, audited by an independent auditor, and announced within three days. This was possible due to the use of advanced information technology that facilitated information processing and networking between different IEC offices in the provinces and linked the provincial results centers with the national center in Pretoria. Polling stations called in their results to the provincial offices, which then put the results into a nationwide database. With computerized checkpoints, the process of reporting results was quick and efficient.

Remaining Challenges

There seems to be no dispute about the constitutional and legal framework within which South African elections take place. There is consensus about most elements of the electoral process, the electoral system and party funding being the exceptions.[32] However, there are still areas of electoral administration that need improvement.

Infrastructure at Local Level

South Africa is a vast country with two sets of infrastructure: one sophisticated, found in mostly urban areas, and the other rudimentary, found in rural areas. South Africa's rural areas still suffer from a lack of transport and communication facilities, electricity, and water. Some communities are located in inaccessible areas, and access is even more problematic during the rainy season. A survey conducted by the IEC in 2002–2003 showed that 39.1 percent of schools have no electricity, 20.8 percent have no toilets, and 27.3 percent have no running water.[33] The country's local government structures, although improving, remain poorly resourced. This situation poses serious challenges to the administration and management of elections. An improvement of the infrastructure at the local level is needed to ease the organizational burden of the IEC in the preparation for and administration of elections.

Voter Education

In the 2004 election the IEC carried out voter education together with local organizations. Like in 1999 and the 2000 local election, limited funding meant that the IEC was unable to undertake a wide and sustained voter education campaign. There is, however, no doubt that more voter education is needed, especially in rural areas and around the issue of the special vote.

Staff Training

The capability and ability of election officers is a key factor in the success of elections. The IEC continues to depend on local civil servants to carry out election duties, as it does not have the permanent staff to cover the whole country. Therefore, the training of local officials is critically important for the administration of elections.

During the 2004 election, political parties complained about what they perceived to be the poor quality of training of the electoral officials operating the polling stations. This, it was claimed, had resulted in a lack of knowledge about procedures and, on occasion, a failure to operate in an open and evenhanded manner. Laurence Piper has argued that problems around capacity and quality of staff affect only the low echelon in the IEC.[34] At the higher levels, the IEC has quality staff but few of them, whereas at the lower levels it has more staff, but less capable people. Apparently, "the head office only has 54.9 percent of approved posts filled. As a ratio of the temporary election staff, the IEC staff only constitutes 0.079 percent."[35] Even the ruling party complained that the senior IEC staff was always too busy with managing IEC business to deal with daily issues that emerged.

The temporary nature of most of the IEC's staff exacerbates the problems, specifically with regard to the quality of training. It would be impractical for the IEC to keep the large numbers of people required to conduct elections on a permanent payroll, but this means that new officials must be trained each time elections are held. The training provided by the commission takes place through a "cascade" system. This approach is rather like photocopying photocopies: after a time, inevitably, the quality of the copies begins to deteriorate. Furthermore, according to observers, the IEC training is little more than a number of general briefings, and polling station officials often have difficulties implementing the nuances of the electoral regulations. It is important that the commission staff should have a much more hands-on involvement at all levels of training, and that the actual training sessions be more thorough. Training should focus not only on the mechanics of the electoral administration but also on the role of elections within the democratic process, explaining the values on which democratic elections are based.

Party Funding

In order for elections to be free and fair, the playing field for political parties should not be too uneven, especially not in terms of the resources they command. The South African Constitution attempts to address this issue in a clause on the public funding of political parties: "To enhance multi-party democracy, national legislation must provide for funding of political parties participating in national and provincial legislatures on an equitable and proportional basis."[36] The management of the current fund for represented political parties is the responsibility of the IEC's CEO. From 1998 to 2003, the yearly sum available has steadily increased: from 1998 to 1999, R52.1 million; 1999 to 2000, R57.8 million; 2000 to 2001, R57.8 million; 2001 to 2002, R62.8 million; to 2002 to 2003, R67.4 million.[37] According to the legislation, 10 percent of the funds are distributed equally among the parties, and 90 percent proportionally based on the share of the vote each party received in the last election. On the basis of this formula, the ANC receives the lion's share of the funding. The funds are distributed only to parties already represented in a legislature, so new parties and parties struggling to gain entrance into the political arena are excluded.

In addition, political parties receive private funding, which has raised concerns as it creates an uneven playing field. The Electoral Act does not provide for a way forward. There are no rules of disclosure governing private funding and the tax status of such donations to parties is unclear.[38] However, some private companies decided to go public on their funding of parties in the 2004 election, which has eased the tension that was created by the Institute for Democracy in South Africa's (Idasa) attempt to take parties to court if they would not reveal the source of their funding. The funding of political parties deserves public scrutiny and the decision by private companies to disclose their contributions helps to increase transparency and reduce corruption. However, it would be better if private funding of parties would, in future, be in accordance with legal requirements backed by strong monitoring and enforcement measures.

Conflict Management

Despite the IEC's mechanisms for conflict prevention and mediation provisions discussed earlier, election-related conflict remains a major threat to democracy and political stability. Though there has been a steady decline in politically motivated violence, the 2004 election was not entirely free of violence and intimidation. KZN was still a trouble spot, with incidents between ANC and IFP supporters occurring throughout the election campaign.

Perhaps the most substantial criticism leveled against the IEC in this respect was that it tends to prioritize peace over justice in election-related conflicts. This view seemed to be shared by both the governing party and the opposition. The ANC complained that the Code of Conduct in KZN was meaningless without some means of enforcing it. The IEC does not have any enforcement mechanisms to create compliance with the code. A complaint must be taken to the police and thus resolving it gets easily delayed in the justice system. The system is simply too slow to provide effective sanctions upon breaches of the code. The ANC source felt that a special court was required to give teeth to the Code of Conduct. The DA argued that "the IEC always wants to mediate," even when the issue at stake is a simple matter of redress for pulling down posters or the like.[39] In short, the IEC was accused of always containing rather than resolving disputes.

Conclusion

There is no doubt that the IEC's performance in the organization of free and fair elections has improved tremendously. There is consensus that the 2004 election was substantially free and fair and in terms of electoral administration, an improvement on the 1994 and 1999 elections. The IEC was very well prepared; it could have conducted the election at any date the president decided on. It was this level of preparedness that allowed the IEC to undertake the registration of prisoners with efficiency despite the time constraint. As mentioned earlier, the 2004 election drew little attention from international observers. This is clearly a mark of confidence in the electoral management and political stability South Africa has achieved in ten years.

However, there is still room for further improvement, especially with regard to the level of service delivery in many rural areas, with a high population density and a lack of infrastructure. Generally, it is felt that this is one of the biggest challenges facing the IEC in future elections. The government can facilitate the future work of the IEC by improving infrastructure in poor voting districts.

Notes

1. Government of South Africa, *Electoral Commission Act, 1996* (Act No. 51 of 1996), A7.
2. Tom Lodge, "South Africa," in *Compendium of Elections in Southern Africa*, ed. Tom Lodge, Denis Kadima, and David Pottie (Johannesburg: Electoral Institute of Southern Africa, 2002), 297.
3. Tom Lodge, *Handbook of South African Electoral Laws and Regulations* (Johannesburg: EISA, 2004), 12.
4. Interim Statement by the EISA Election Observation Mission, *South African National and Provincial Elections April 12–14, 2004* (Johannesburg: Electoral Institute of South Africa, April 16, 2004).
5. Ismail Hussain, "The Role of the Judiciary in the Management of the Electoral Related Conflicts" (paper presented at the Conference on Consolidating Peace and Democracy, Maputo, Mozambique, July 22–23, 2003), 266.
6. Ibid.
7. Khabele Matlosa, "Editorial," *Election Update South Africa* 5 (Johannesburg: EISA, March 30, 2004).
8. "Report of the Independent Electoral Commission on the 1994 Elections" (Pretoria: Independent Electoral Commission, October 1994).
9. "Electoral Commission Report of the National and Provincial Election of 1999" (Pretoria: Independent Electoral Commission, June 2, 1999), 15.
10. IEC, "Electoral Commission Report."
11. The constitution and the Electoral Act (1998) required the commission to produce a national common voters' roll.
12. Electoral Institute of South Africa, *Principles for Election Management, Monitoring and Observation in the SADC Region* (Johannesburg: EISA, 2004), 2.
13. *This Day*, November 13, 2003.
14. IEC, "Report of the Independent Electoral Commission on the 1994 Elections," 85.
15. However, this does not seem to have resolved the issue entirely. Opposition parties wanted all South African citizens living abroad to be allowed to vote, regardless of whether or not the move was permanent. The ANC has consistently rejected this position, arguing that permanent emigrants have chosen to leave South Africa and therefore forfeit their right to vote.
16. Dirk Kotzé, "The IEC's State of Preparedness," *Election Update South Africa* 5 (Johannesburg: EISA, March 30, 2004), 3.
17. Registration information can be found at the Web site of the IEC: http://www.elections.org.za/Statistics1.asp.
18. For the disabled, the IEC provided voting compartments that could accommodate wheel chairs and a ballot paper template was provided for the visually impaired voters.
19. Kotzé, "The IEC's State of Preparedness," 3.
20. Thabo Rapoo, "Election Phase in Mpumalanga: Polling Stations, Ballot Boxes and Other Logistics," *Election Update South Africa* 7 (Johannesburg: EISA, April 26, 2004).
21. Ibid.

22. Kotzé, "The IEC's State of Preparedness," 3.

23. *The Sowetan*, December 12, 2004.

24. This improvement was significant, because in previous elections, cellphones proved unreliable during times of extremely high-call volume, as many calls could not get through in those situations.

25. Lodge, *Handbook*, 15.

26. SADC Parliamentary Forum Observation Report on South Africa's 2004 Elections (Gaborone, Botswana: SADC, 2004), 4.

27. A week before election day, on April 7, the voting process started in 105 South African missions abroad.

28. IEC media release (Pretoria, April 13, 2004).

29. See e.g., Jean-Jacques Cornish, "Observers Give Poll Thumbs Up," *Mail & Guardian*, April 16, 2004, accessed at http://www.mg.co.za/Content/l3.asp?ao=34223.

30. "Two Ballot Boxes Stolen in KwaZulu-Natal," *Independent Online* April 15, 2004, accessed at http://www.iol.co.za/index.php?sf=2902&click_id=13&art_id=qw1082016000525B242&set_id=1.

31. In 2004, a new provision, section 24(A) of the Electoral Act, enabled registered voters to vote anywhere in the country in the national, but not the provincial ballot. For more information, see Nijzink and Piombo, this volume.

32. As discussed in Nijzink and Piombo (this volume), there remains significant pressure from political parties and civil society organizations to change the electoral system.

33. Kotzé, "The IEC's State of Preparedness," 4.

34. Laurence Piper, "A Competent and Wise Head Atop An Average Body: The IEC in KwaZulu Natal," *Election Update South Africa* 5 (Johannesburg: EISA, March 30, 2004), 23.

35. Kotzé, "The IEC's State of Preparedness," 5.

36. Section 236 of the Constitution of the Republic of South Africa (Act 108 of 1996).

37. IEC, "Annual Report on Represented Political Parties Fund: 1998–2003" (Pretoria: Independent Electoral Commission, 2003).

38. Kennedy Mbaya; "The Use of State Resource during Elections in South Africa," in *The Politics of State Resources: Party Funding in South Africa*, ed. Khabele Matlosa (Johannesburg: Konrad-Adenauer-Stiftung, 2004), 69. See also Idasa, "Regulation of Private Funding to Political Parties," Idasa Position Paper (Cape Town, South Africa, October 2003).

39. Thabo Mbeki, "Letter from the President: Our People Must Freely Express Their Will," *ANC Today* 4, no. 13 (April 2–8, 2004).

PART 2

The Party Campaigns

CHAPTER SIX

The African National Congress: There Is No Party Like It; Ayikho Efana Nayo

TOM LODGE

Four features characterized the African National Congress (ANC) election campaigns in 1994 and 1999. First, campaign strategists relied heavily on modern market research techniques, including public opinion surveys and focus group discussions, both to identify loyalists and potential supporters and to select the messages the party would project in its electioneering. Second, despite the importance planners accorded to communicating with the electorate through the media, the ANC also exploited its large and well-organized following through deploying thousands of volunteers in door-to-door canvassing. The combination of advanced electioneering techniques borrowed from American experience and old-fashioned mass party membership mobilization distinguished the ANC from its competitors and made its approach fairly unusual in a more general contemporary context. Third, the content of the ANC campaigns in 1994 and thereafter tended to be upbeat and positive; on the whole, at least with respect to most of its officially sanctioned appeals, the ANC refrained from direct attacks on its rivals, concentrating instead on the issues that would be of most concern to its core constituency. In general, the party's campaigning sought to animate its followers by appealing to their hopes, expectations, and optimism about the future rather than fears or resentments arising from conflicts of the past. Finally, ANC campaigns have been presidential in ethos, a reflection of the political predispositions of the electoral system and the party's own centralized traditions.

With minor qualifications, the ANC campaign in 2004 conformed to these generalizations. It seems likely that the ANC had less to spend in this election than in previous polls; even so it remained the best resourced party, capable certainly of investing in extensive research and in sophisticated mass communication on a national scale. And, to an even greater extent than before the ANC could exploit the advantages derived from incumbency, given the widening embrace of the government's social programs since 1994.

Preparations

Early in 2003, the ANC formed an election planning group, headed by Manne Dipico, who was "redeployed" from his post as premier of the Northern Cape. However, the most important preparations for the 2004 election well preceded Dipico's arrival at Lutuli House, the ANC's head-quarters in Johannesburg. From 2000 onward the party had invested considerable effort in reviving its branch level organization, reconfiguring the branches so that they would be in alignment with local government wards, reviewing and reorganizing membership records and, perhaps most important of all, reigniting activist traditions through the launch in January 2002 of a monthly schedule of voluntary activities that would "recapture the community spirit of letsema, ilima."[1] Each month volunteers would address a specific theme. For example, in January, the month of education, activists would repair schools, attempt to retrieve missing books, and distribute admission forms to parents.[2]

In late 2002 and early 2003, twenty students in the Wits Department of Political Studies interviewed 300 members of fifty ANC branches in Gauteng, KwaZulu-Natal (KZN), and Limpopo. Though not drawn from a systematic sample, the interviews are likely to be roughly representative of the ANC's black membership; about half were women and nearly half were unemployed. The respondents, 124 in number, held executive positions in their branches, and unemployed people were almost as likely to be among these as those who had jobs. At branch level, the ANC is evidently an egalitarian movement. The interviews revealed a high level of activity in ANC branches. Of the respondents, 68 percent attended monthly branch meetings. Thirty percent participated in fundraising events, 36 percent participated in nominations for conference delegates, and 43 percent said they read Umrabulo, the ANC's journal. Most impressively of all, 74 percent undertook voluntary work in the ANC's Letsema campaign. Many respondents could refer to a variety of activities they had undertaken, suggesting that the program had sustained itself over the year. For example, in Alexandra's Ward 75, a particularly active branch, respondents mentioned tree planting, school cleaning, visits to old age homes and prisons, the distribution of information about HIV/AIDS, work at a community crèche, and tidying up a police station. All but three out of twenty-eight respondents from this branch had participated. In only one branch included in the Wits survey, Langaville on the East Rand, was there no evidence of Letsema participation.

To revive its branch organization by the end of the campaign, the ANC claimed well over 400,000 paid up members documented on computerized records. If the group of respondents in the Wits survey was representative, then the ANC's branch life was vigorous. It featured a high degree of activism by members who were prepared to regularly give up time for its political programs and kept themselves informed about party policies. As we shall see, branch members were going to play an extremely (according to press reports more extensively so than before) active role within the ANC's core constituency in the months before the election. Compared to any of its rivals, on the eve of the election campaign, the ANC could claim a significant activist following in most parts of the country.

Despite the emphasis on face-to-face contact with the electorate, the party maintained its commitment to more modern kinds of political marketing. As before, the ANC entrusted the crafting of its media messages to an advertising agency, selecting Ogilvy and Mather from a number of bids. Ogilvy and Mather, incidentally, is partly owned by an empowerment company directed by Nelson Mandela's wife, Graca Machel. The agency's brief included the development of new cost-effective ways through which the ANC could get its message across, and a more restricted use of the posters that predominated in earlier campaigns.[3] Among other projects, the agency developed "eleven creative elements" that displayed ANC advertisements in the 16,000 buses run by the nationwide Comutanet company.[4] Ogilvy and Mather's innovations even included income generation for the party: a cell phone SMS competition in which hopeful contestants would contact the ANC to answer a simple question.

By the beginning of 2004, it was evident that the ANC would have less money to spend than in previous elections. Trevor Manuel admitted to journalists that the election budget was "the smallest yet"; one figure cited in the press was a relatively modest R70 million.[5] In January 2004, the Western Cape party organization had to appeal for donations to enable it to pay rent and telephone bill arrears. Elsewhere, there were widespread complaints by party officials who had not been paid.[6] Judging from public disclosures, the ANC received the lion's share of South African corporate funding, 70 percent of the disclosed support including R2 million from the Standard Bank in March 2004, but local donations were apparently insufficient.[7] As the ANC itself has conceded in court, it remained "heavily reliant upon funding from international sources, including governments, political parties, NGOs and civil society groups."[8] It is likely that these were rather less generous than was the case a decade ago. In this situation, relying on house-to-house canvassing made good sense.

In the same vein, professional market research was supplemented by the party's own efforts to collect information about its supporters' perceptions. As Smuts Ngonyama recalled, "the President said, listen, what is coming out from the surveys, there are a number of messages that are coming out, that are highly confusing and therefore we need to have a direct line with people to get exactly what they are telling us and therefore it is important for us to go to them and have time. . . ."[9] Thus, in late 2003 Dipico's group undertook a nationwide process of consultation, "collecting views from organized sectors." In this process, according to Dipico's spokesman, Steyn Speed, "poverty and unemployment would come across as the biggest challenges." The election planning group also learned "that HIV/AIDS was bound to be the main issue in this election."[10]

Such intelligence partly matched publicly available opinion polling evidence. For example, a national survey mounted by the Kaiser Foundation confirmed that among black respondents unemployment (72 percent) and crime (26 percent) were regarded as the most important problems that the government should address, followed by AIDS (22 percent). Only 12 percent of black respondents suggested that poverty was the priority issue.[11] Both this survey and the ANC's own information indicated that most black South Africans believed that government services had improved generally, including the areas of health care and education, and that considerable reservoirs of public optimism about the future still existed. According to ANC Secretary General Kgalema Motlanthe, "baseline research from focus groups" commissioned by the ANC confirmed that the ANC was vulnerable on issues of crime, corruption, and HIV/AIDS.[12] Contrary to the wisdom among pundits, the pace or quality of national government delivery in general was *not* an issue, despite anger directed at local agencies.

A final important influence on the tone and content of the ANC campaign was a series of government *imbizos* across the country: carefully stage-managed public dialogues between President Mbeki and representative groups of citizens. Like the focus groups, the *imbizos* revealed high levels of displeasure at the performance of the municipal government. The party leadership also learned from polls and meetings that, to quote Motlanthe, the party's "hardest battle (would) be against apathy."[13] Even enthusiastic ANC followers might take the party's victory for granted and not vote and those ANC adherents less satisfied with government performance would need to be convinced that voting was worth their while.

Voter Registration

Ensuring its supporters could vote and extending its support base through voter registration was the first task for ANC activists, especially in KZN, where there was considerable under-registration of the eligible electorate in the ANC's strongholds, the main urban centers, as well as in the working-class, coloured neighborhoods of Cape Town, where the ANC hoped to make fresh converts. As early as October 2003, ANC posters urging voters to register started appearing across the country. In Gauteng, the ANC made a special effort, partly as a response to discouraging opinion polls. In November, Markinor put ANC provincial support at 42 percent. The ANC registration drive in Gauteng concentrated its activity in squatter camps, where most unregistered voters who were likely to support the party resided.[14] In the four months before the Independent Electoral Commission's (IEC) first registration weekend, Gauteng ANC activists visited 350,000 homes, distributed more than a million leaflets, and organized hundreds of public meetings to persuade people to register.[15] Indians in KZN, perceived to be substantially underregistered, were also a particular target of the ANC registration drive, especially in Phoenix, where the party was hoping to do well against the Democratic Alliance (DA).[16] In the Western Cape, interestingly, the ANC's registration activities seem to have been more low key. In the working-class coloured areas of Cape Town, the New National Party's (NNP's) attempts to register its likely supporters attracted much more attention from journalists.

Adoption and Composition of Candidate Lists

While ANC activists consolidated support through registration drives, the party began its elaborate procedures for selecting or reselecting its legislators. The ANC candidate nominations procedure combines an element of democratic choice with powerful consensual traditions that reinforce leadership predispositions. In the first step of the process, branches nominate potential candidates, who are then vetted by list committees. Candidates who are supported by at least three branches and who pass the screening procedure of the list committees are considered at provincial list conferences (which were, in this case, scheduled for October 2003). At most of these conferences delegates vote through a secret ballot to generate lists of candidates for the provincial legislature and the National Assembly (NA). Provincial conference nominations must be arranged in order of precedence and again vetted by list committees, as consensually as possible, though sometimes voting on particular nominees through a show of hands is necessary. Delegates from the provinces assembled at a national list conference (which was scheduled for November 21–22) must confirm candidate lists for the provincial legislatures and agree on the two NA lists, the provincial nominations to the NA, and the more prestigious national list. Decisions made at the national conference are subject to further revision by the secretary general's office, a subcommittee of the National Executive, and the ANC president.

During the nomination procedures for the 2004 election, there was plenty of evidence of delegate assertiveness. Branches began identifying candidates in mid-2003. This gave particular groups within provinces ample opportunity to form factional followings. Nominations seem to have been especially contested in the Western Cape, where at one stage three lists were circulating. There was a so-called Africanist slate led by provincial secretary Mcebisi Skwatsha, with its base in Langa and Gugulethu, that included white and coloured candidates and excluded all serving Members of the Executive Council (MECs). A second list was headed by the MEC for Social Services Marius Fransman, backed by rural coloured branches. And there was a third "middle path" grouping around Ebrahim Rassool and all the MECs as well as Skwatsha, which ultimately prevailed at the provincial conference. Before the conference, Congress of South African Trade Unions (Cosatu) officials circulated a list of people whom they suggested delegates should not support, including the chairperson of the South African Communist Party (SACP) in the Western Cape and Safety and Security MEC, Leonard Amatlakane.

Though vigorously competitive, the Western Cape nominations procedure produced an outcome that met with the approval of national leadership. The conferences in some of the other provinces demonstrated divisions within the ANC provincial organizations that eventually had to be resolved at the national level. In the Free State, a mutinous provincial organization decided that Jacob Zuma and not Thabo Mbeki should head up its slate for the national to national list for the NA. The Free State provincial delegates put Mbeki in fourth position on their list, and accorded only one position in the top thirty to an MEC, while consigning the incumbent premier, Winkie Direko, to position number fifty-two. Direko eventually ended up as candidate number thirty-nine on the "national to national" list. The Free Staters chose Ace Magushule to head up their candidate list for the provincial legislature, a powerful personality blamed by national leadership for much of the factionalism within the provincial organization. National ANC leaders were probably equally displeased with a KZN conference that placed only five Indians on the candidate list for the provincial legislature and failed to place any Indians higher than in the twenty-ninth position. The outcome of the Mpumalanga conference also suggested deep divisions among delegates and at best minority support for premier Ndaweni Mahlangu, who received nominations from only seven branches.

There was evidence of internal conflicts between supporters of rival notables in most provinces except for Gauteng, where delegates refused to rank "national to national" nominations for the NA. These divisions prompted the decision by national leaders to refrain from naming any provincial premier candidates. Zuma explained that "premiers do not play a role in election campaigns."[17] This was in fact true of the ANC campaigns in 1994 and 1999. Then, even in the provincial contests, the ANC had refrained from constructing its electoral appeals around the personalities of its projected premiers, though the party did name its favored premier candidates. In the campaign for the 2004 election, the decision not to name any premier candidates was taken when the ANC released its provisional lists. The accompanying press release on November 24, 2003 noted that premier candidates were yet to be determined and that their names would be inserted later. ANC officials suggested to reporters that this decision was partly prompted by a fear that in divided provinces, disappointed supporters of losing factions might hold back from electioneering.[18]

After their adoption by the provincial conferences, the provisional candidate lists were reviewed at the party's national level. In the case of sitting representatives, the review included evaluations of their work in the legislature and their activities in the constituencies assigned to them. There were a few prominent casualties in this process. John Block, who had headed the provisional Northern Cape list for the provincial legislature, was excised as a consequence of his involvement as an MEC in a corruption scandal. A few of the defectors who had crossed the floor to the ANC were upgraded to electable positions. Former NNP member John Gogotya was moved from position 150 on the provisional "national to national" list for the NA to the just electable position 136. Veteran parliamentarian and SACP member Kay Moonsamy was another beneficiary of "strategic political interventions" by the national list committee.[19] She was one of several of SACP members who were accommodated in good positions on the "national to national" list for the NA in compensation for the influence the SACP had lost in the provincial nominations. (In 1999, the alliance partners had jointly hosted provincial list conferences.) On the whole, though, revisions were quite limited, particularly with respect to the candidate lists for provincial legislatures—even in KZN with its single Indian candidate in an electable position on the list.

As might be expected, the ANC's final national to national list for the NA was headed mainly by serving members of the cabinet more or less in order of seniority as well as three former provincial premiers, Dipico, Molele, and Ramatholdi. The top 280 NA candidates on the ANC lists included 67 candidates who were not African, a slightly lower number than the 71 serving non-African MPs but still telling evidence of the ANC's commitment to "descriptive" representation. Every third position was given to a woman, a practice to which the ANC committed itself in 1994. The lists also demonstrated considerable turnover. Before candidate nominations began, ANC officials were predicting that about half of their candidates would be "new blood," members fresh to parliament. In fact, 78 members of the ANC's parliamentary caucus as on March 26, 2004 were omitted from the ANC's NA lists (though a few of these did appear on the lists for the provincial legislatures).[20] There were thirty-three new names in electable positions on the "national to national" list for the NA, including several notables from provincial politics, and eighty-five new names appeared in good positions on the provincial lists for the NA. Significantly, incumbent parliamentarians who remained in good positions on the lists included several personalities who had emerged as left-wing critics of government policy. Candidate nominations really did signify renewal rather than a purge of the more independent backbenchers.

Electioneering

The Campaign Message

The ANC campaign in 2004 was based on the research the party had conducted in preparation for the election. Thus, the ANC manifesto stated that it was time to "celebrate freedom," referred to improving services, and promised "more" and "better." Job creation, poverty reduction, "turning the tide" against HIV/AIDS as well as "significantly" reducing crime were the salient commitments in the manifesto. The language that was used revived the "people centered" rhetoric of the Reconstruction and Development Programme (RDP) in its references to a contract between government and "each citizen, community and sector of society . . . to build a better South Africa." In the campaign that followed the manifesto launch, the most conspicuous themes projected in ANC slogans were the celebration of democracy's tenth anniversary, the creation of work, and the ending of poverty; the latter two to be advanced through a vaguely defined "people's contract." The ANC manifesto itself was an eloquent expression of the ambiguities in this approach: its opening photographs of cheering party supporters were followed by soberly reflective headings: "Learning from experience: we can do more, better" and "The next five years: The Practical steps." In KZN and the Western Cape, ANC slogans referred to the completion of the "liberation cycle" through an ANC victory in the provincial elections.

In its formal campaign communications, the ANC eschewed attacks on its competitors, refusing to assign them the status of serious rivals. As in 1999, ANC leaders refused to accede to the DA's demand for a televised debate between party leaders. On the whole, the ANC limited attacks on other parties to off-the-cuff remarks and Thabo Mbeki's weekly online newsletters. In *ANC Today*, Mbeki castigated the DA's exploitation of the "danger of an imaginary one-party state" (March 5, 2004), questioned the economic practicality of the Independent Democrats' (ID) manifesto pledges (March 19, 2004), and told "the truth as we see it" about the DA's alliance with Inkatha, a "right wing coalition" to protect white interests (March 26, 2004). Most of the ANC's public references to other parties were more perfunctory in character, contrasting their political impotence with the ANC's strength and its capacity as governing party. People should not cast their votes for "silly parties" such as the NNP, the DA, or the African Christian Democratic Party (ACDP), Mbeki told an audience in Rustenberg, adding, apparently, that if his sister was to arrive home and tell him that she was in love with Reverend Meshoe he would have to beat her. Mbazhima Shilowa noted, "What the DA has to do first is to get elected." And what was the point of voting for a strong opposition, Mbeki asked a meeting in the Eastern Cape, "If they are an opposition, this means they are opposed to everything we stand for—building communities, fighting joblessness and so forth. Why would anyone want to vote for people opposed to these things?"

A subsidiary campaign discourse referred to the ANC's historic status as a liberation movement. In Jane Furse, Mbeki introduced local heroes John Nkadimeng and Nathaniel Masemola to the crowd: "These are your sons, they are the people that changed the country, they always trusted the ANC, your choice is clear." Failing to vote on April 14, Mandela noted in early April, "would be a slap in the face of those who made great sacrifices." And Mbeki's taxi rank speeches in his tour of the Eastern Cape began with the reminder that "you all know who the ANC is and what it has done. It is the ANC of Nelson Mandela, the late Steve Tshwete and numerous other heroes. You therefore know for whom to vote." In these exhortations the ANC was in its heartland, addressing those whom it perceived to be most loyal rather than the audiences that it needed to convert. Such appeals were more likely to resonate among the rural elderly than the urban young, people who in any case were most likely to feel that government had brought about a better life.

The Campaign Strategy

In contrast to earlier campaigns the ANC organized fewer grandiose events. Its major rallies were confined to the launch and the closure of the campaign. Instead, the ANC projected its messages through television. News coverage of an accessible and responsive president meeting his fellow citizens and listening to their concerns communicated a powerful message that capitalized on Thabo Mbeki's rising public trust ratings in opinion polls. Most cabinet ministers and other senior party figures were dispatched around the country to follow energetic schedules of meeting voters on their doorsteps, at taxi ranks and railway stations, in community centers and outside hostels, at apartment blocks, and even in suburban shopping malls, hitherto mainly the preserve of the DA. These campaign activities were not just about generating compelling media photo opportunities, effective as these were in communicating to television audiences the ANC's commitment to public accountability. The primary target of this electioneering was the people being visited and others in their communities. Though the claim by an ANC official that in Gauteng party representatives visited over three million people was probably overstated, in the 2004 campaign the ANC did aim to achieve extensive direct contact with voters. ANC officials claimed that Thabo Mbeki himself visited 5,000 households.[21]

In door-to-door campaigning, major ANC notables were accompanied by councilors, mayors, and other local officials, who constituted units that could address any grievances raised by residents. In every ward, ANC branch members were given lists of houses that they were to visit and report back on.[22] During visits, officials frequently ordered subordinates to immediately sort out the difficulties of claimants unable to access social security grants, or pensioners confronted with huge debts for their unpaid electricity bills. This way, ANC leaders could both deflect responsibility for these problems from themselves and their movement onto errant underlings, show that they listened, and confirm that "only the ANC has the capacity to fight poverty and deal with your problems."[23] Despite the party's goal to induce within poor communities a feeling of co-responsibility in achieving "our aim to create work and beat poverty," a crucial element in the ANC's appeal to people without resources was the power to exert executive authority.[24] As a praise singer in Jane Furse noted before Thabo Mbeki addressed a local assembly, "I may be hungry, I may be poor, but things are good because the ANC takes care of everything."[25] "They know the ANC listens," Thabo Mbeki told journalists after a busy day of street visits.[26]

The government's concern for the needs of its citizens and, more important, the ANC's capacity to address problems effectively was an important feature of the party's electioneering in rural areas. Ronnie Kasrils, national minister of water and forestry, spent much of the campaign period in Northern KZN, making appearances in communities within the Inkatha heartland that were beneficiaries of the activities of his own department. For the first time, it was possible for the ANC to canvass relatively openly in these areas, which gave the party the opportunity to emphasize a message of responsive authority. This message gave the ANC an advantage in campaigning in the region, according to Kasrils.

[C]ertainly the ANC's organization has improved (in Northern KwaZulu-Natal). It has footholds all over. The tolerance factor very much improved. And the gate is open now. People who hitherto hadn't had access, hadn't heard the ANC directly, who I believe would have voted for us in the past, but that had been blocked, their ears are now open. I found everywhere I went very positive responses. Extension of water pipes has made a difference, very much so. In terms of that, alongside other ANC national ministers, we made sure that we had been in that province in the last five years at all the events where water or electricity or roads had been opened with MECs, be they ANC or IFP, and I think people had very much come to realize that although IFP councils might claim credit, people realize its national, that it's the ANC government with its ministers that's had a very positive impact throughout five years of governing. They certainly shifted me around in the campaign very much in the Northern part. What helped as well is that I do have a great deal of respect from IFP mayors. People haven't been able to take me on as though I am an interloper.[27]

Especially in the rural areas of KZN, the ANC used the strategy of exploiting the power of holding office. As one ANC official explained:

[N]obody could stand in the way of the four by four—KZN ministers, Sbu Ndebele, Zweli Mkhize, Mike Mabuyakhulu and Dumisane Makhaye. After all a four by four is a well built car with which to travel on both smooth and gravel roads. They visited the Amakhosi areas which were not easy roads in the past. Meetings were held with the amakhosi. The Makhosi asked for things they wanted done in their areas. For instance, inkhosi yamaHlubi wanted a bridge to be built at Bhekula area near Estcourt. The former MEC for Transport invited to hold a special meeting with the amakhosi. The purpose of that meeting was to develop a program of action to deliver the goods in their respective areas.[28]

Jacob Zuma and other ANC leaders emphasized the themes of peace and political tolerance. An important message in their KZN electioneering was that citizens should be free to choose, "a message" that, according to ANC officials, "has not filtered down to the IFP [Inkatha Freedom Party] membership on the ground."[29] In this context, the militaristic preliminaries at IFP public events helped to underline the ANC's posture as the party of peace—Inkatha's final rally at Nongoma, for example, was heralded by dancing warriors in full battle regalia.

Reaching Minority Voters

Strategic public appearances of ANC leaders underlined the ANC's commitment to winning over voters in minority communities, including whites. Mbeki's appearance at an Afrikaner arts festival in Oudtshoorn; Mbazhima Shilowa's trek across suburban Krugersdorp, preceded by 2000 ululating women led by 55-year-old Jacoba van der Berg; and Thabo Mbeki's unheralded visit to a cluster home complex in Kempton Park were each prompted by the belief that the ANC might succeed in detaching especially white lower-middle-class Afrikaners from the DA and breaking "its stranglehold on minorities."[30] More important, given the press attention these undertakings attracted, they were highly effective in directing a message to racial minorities that they could "be part of the decision-making majority." In the past, Mbeki noted, government had failed "to communicate properly with white citizens" and as a consequence the impression had been created "that the government did not care for them."[31] For the ANC president and his staff, attracting working-class white Afrikaner support was a prospect they took very seriously, despite discouraging signals from opinion polls:

President Mbeki felt very strongly about the minorities, particularly about the white communities. We have this notion that there are no poor whites in the country but he said we must go out and actually look at the socio-economic situation of various minority groups. . . . It was exciting. On the very first visit that we made, the response of the white community around Pretoria informed his approach that he was correct that we need to go in these areas.[32]

ANC efforts to court white votes were evident in the scale of the party's publicity in traditionally white neighborhoods. As one resident of a Durban suburb noted, "in my street alone there were over 300 ANC lamppost posters, over half of which were in Afrikaans . . . accompanied by two pamphlet drops."[33] The ANC's attention to minority voters also included a concerted effort to win over the Indian vote, especially in KZN.

Within Indian communities in KZN, the ANC's electioneering was calculated carefully (in contrast to the DA, which did not craft a specifically Indian targeted campaign). As a group of ANC strategists constituted by the provincial party organization acknowledged, previous failures to win Indian support could be explained by the ANC's own mistakes: the marginalization of experienced Indian activists and too much dependence on supposedly influential notables who were unable to draw their constituencies over to the ANC. In the past, the ANC had also rather neglected the preoccupations Indians had with respect to jobs, affirmative action, crime, and education. ANC strategists felt that the party had done particularly badly among working-class Indians, who tended to be Hindu rather than Muslim. The strategists argued that in the 2004 campaign ANC approaches to Indian voters should be more focused and discerning with respect to the preoccupations of different groups within the Indian communities. They advised that the symbolic content of the campaigning should shift from its customary emphasis on struggle traditions dating back to Gandhi's leadership of the Natal Indian Congress to material issues on which the ANC could deliver. They also argued that the ANC should exploit the diplomatic positions it had adopted on international issues that might appeal to particular sections of the Indian electorate, for example its support for the Tamil Tigers or its warm relations with the PLO. Finally, the party was advised to deploy its Indian "floor crossers" (defectors from other parties) in those localities where they enjoyed substantial personal followings.[34]

The ANC's efforts to capture Indian support reflected this advice. As Adam Habib noted, the party started "speaking of issues that affect the Indian community" and "to treat Indian people like all citizens," rather than as an undifferentiated cultural group.[35] Certainly, the ANC campaign retained features of the party's earlier approach. A sequence of posters in Chatsworth first asked "Who would Gandhi have voted for?"; a second placard with a picture of local resident Ela Gandhi responded: "My grandfather would have voted for the ANC." The *Sunday Times Extra* (an Indian focused newspaper) supplement carried ANC endorsements from celebrities such as filmmaker Anant Singh and beauty queen Prebashni Naidoo. ANC efforts to woo Tamil speakers included an appearance by Thabo Mbeki at a Tamil New Year celebration at Chatsworth stadium, just before polling day, in which he suggested that in the future, Tamil might be taught in schools and more Tamil films broadcast on television.

However, extensive door-to-door canvassing by activists who focused on everyday material concerns was probably as important in defining the ANC's new appeal to Indian voters as any historical or cultural themes evoked in its campaign. In Phoenix, ANC posters went up to announce that teachers would vote "for the ANC," a reasonable prediction given the strength of the South African Democratic Teacher's Union (Sadtu) in Phoenix schools. In a community where teachers still commanded respect and status, this was a strong message. In addressing Indian voters, the ANC was as ready as its rivals to campaign negatively. In one of the ANC advertisements on East Coast Radio, Vivian Reddy told listeners:

I am Vivian Reddy. Much has been written about me. Let me set the facts straight. I am in politics because I want to make a difference. This year I wanted a bigger forum. I joined the DA. It took me one month to realize this was not the party for me or my people. The DA uses Indians, coloureds and Africans like cannon fodder to secure their racist selfish interests. They have a hidden agenda. I joined the ANC because it is the right thing to do. Join the winning team, invest in your future. Vote the ANC.[36]

Reddy was echoing one of the key messages of the ANC campaign. As its architects had explained, "joining the winning side" was a matter of self-interest for Indians. "Precisely because Indians are concerned about jobs, fair application of affirmative action, crime etc. . . . they must vote for the ANC . . . If Indians vote ANC, their needs and interests can be taken more seriously." This was the argument that the ANC hoped would be influential in shifting Indian voter sentiments in the party's favor.

Did Electioneering Make a Difference?

The 2004 election results showed a slight increase in the absolute total of national votes for the ANC, from 10,608,330 in 1999 to 10,878,251 in 2004.[37] This represented a gain of about 270,000 votes in the context of a slightly lower national poll, since the overall turnout was 15,863,554 votes, about 360,000 fewer votes than in the 1999 election. In proportional terms, the ANC's share of the national vote increased from 66.35 to 69.68 percent. With respect to votes for the National Assembly, the ANC improved its performance most significantly in KZN, receiving about 135,000 more votes in the province than in 1999 (in the context of a KZN turnout of 200,000 votes less than in 1999). In the Western Cape, where turnout was about the same as in 1999, the ANC gained 110,000 votes. The party also gained nearly 200,000 votes in the Eastern Cape (where turnout increased) but lost more than 100,000 votes in Gauteng, though with a lower turnout here the ANC's percentage share remained unchanged compared to 1999.

In KZN, the distribution of votes among parties suggested that the ANC's gains were chiefly at the expense of the IFP, which received 230,000 fewer votes than in the 1999 election. This was confirmed by the geographical distribution of ANC gains. These occurred primarily in rural districts in which the IFP had predominated in 1999. For example, in the Zululand district, the IFP received 28,000 votes less than in 1999, whereas the ANC's share of the vote rose by 11,000. In the Eastern Cape, the ANC took votes mainly from the UDM, which lost 80,000 voters. Here, ANC gains were concentrated in the OR Tambo District (the area around Umtata), where the party's support exceeded its 1999 total by 100,000 votes, while the United Democratic Movement's (UDM) share of the vote fell by 50,000. In this district, which had been the main area of UDM support in 1999, voter registration was obviously important in helping to expand the ANC vote. On the whole, the ANC gains in the Eastern Cape urban areas were comparatively modest. Its main growth was among rural voters in the former Transkei. In the Western Cape, 100,000 of the 400,000 or so former NNP voters who changed their allegiances supported the ANC, though it is likely that the ID was the major beneficiaries of the NNP's collapse.

From which sections of the electorate did ANC derive its gains? ANC analysts claimed after the election that they attracted "thousands of new . . . voters among the rural coloured populations in the Western and Northern Cape,"[38] an assertion supported by the ANC gains evident in the West Coast and Karoo Districts of the Western Cape and in the rural municipalities of the Northern Cape. Journalists suggested that ANC successes in rural KZN may have been a consequence of disenchantment with IFP hardliners among the youth.[39] Relatively low turnout among KZN voters also helped the ANC, given that levels of voter registration in the province were higher in traditionally Inkatha affiliated rural areas. Similarly, low turnout in working-class coloured neighborhoods in Cape Town probably benefited the ANC; many coloured NNP supporters seemed to have stayed at home on polling day.

Increases in ANC support in elite suburbs, such as Houghton in Johannesburg and Durban North, probably reflected recent black social mobility rather than new white converts. Significantly, there was no rise in ANC support in Constantia in Cape Town, a reflection of the weakness of the black elite in the Western Cape. The ANC may have been a beneficiary of a shift of white votes in Pietermaritzburg, where a group called the Capital Alliance prompted nearly 50,000 DA voters to support other parties in the provincial poll in protest against the DA's alignment with the IFP (which insisted that the provincial capital should be Ulundi not Pietermaritzburg). In the Free State, the ANC's provincial election coordinator, Pat Mathosa, claimed that significant numbers of young white voters had abandoned the NNP to support his party.[40]

Where and among whom did the ANC's electioneering make a critical difference? The ANC's campaigning was probably decisive among Indian voters. In the main Indian neighborhoods the party registered increases in support: in Lenasia, at the expense of the DA, and in KZN where, according to its rivals, the ANC's performance in Indian townships was amplified by low registration and turnout.[41] In Phoenix in Durban, the ANC improved its showing significantly, from less than 9 percent of the vote in 1999 to 25 percent in 2004, again to the detriment of the DA. The ANC also expanded its support in Chatsworth. In Durban generally, the ANC's share of the historically fluid Indian vote rose from 14 to 22 percent.[42]

In at least two other contexts, in rural KZN and in the Western Cape, ANC campaigning was probably the key factor in converting voters. As noted earlier, in contrast to previous elections, the ANC was able to establish a presence in the IFP-dominated districts of rural KZN, where its posters were as evident as that of IFP and where, more important, its activists were able to conduct door-to-door visits. For example, in Ulundi, on March 27, the ANC organized a daylong program that included pamphleteering, door-to-door visits, loud-hailing, putting up posters, and a mass rally.[43] According to the ANC Youth League's chairperson for the North Coast, Thomas Mashaba, this was the "best planned and managed campaign I've ever participated in."[44] It was in KZN that the ANC concentrated its most important national office bearers. In March 2004, Thabo Mbeki spent ten days electioneering in the province. Jacob Zuma was especially conspicuous in KZN, accompanied by members of the provincial government so that he could provide immediate remedies to citizens' complaints. This tactic worked particularly well when local difficulties could be blamed on the ANC's coalition partners in the province or on IFP aligned municipal administrators. ANC analysts maintained that the 2004 election in KZN was better monitored than any previous contest and that the presence of carefully trained ANC agents in polling stations north of the Tugela for the first time made for a more accurate count; this, they argued, helps to explain the sharp fall in turnout in these districts.[45]

In rural localities, both in KZN and elsewhere, pensions and various kinds of welfare grants constitute a disproportionately important source of livelihood in communities where wage earners are absent and local sources of income very limited. Increases in old age pensions and the recent raise in the age of eligibility for child support grants probably worked to the ANC's advantage. In northern KZN, in IFP heartlands such as Nqutu and Nkandla, journalists encountered a revealing political terminology that demonstrated little concern for the ideological distinctions between the IFP and its main rival. Local people called Mangosuthu Buthelezi "ubaba wama glass"—the spectacles man—a reference to his appearance in the IFP posters. However Thabo Mbeki was "ubaba weqolo"—the man who gives grants.[46]

In the Western Cape as elsewhere, ANC successes were the outcome of very intensive canvassing, but they were also a consequence of a very discriminating allocation of resources and efforts, and indeed, in certain areas, restraint. During the final weeks of electioneering, 3,000 ANC activists undertook door-to-door work, including, officials claimed, 160 members of parliament.[47] In previous elections, the ANC's coloured support was concentrated in middle-class communities (and in the countryside) and it was in middle-class areas such as Macassar and in African townships that the party's canvassing was concentrated. In the Western Cape, the ANC's strategic emphasis seems to have been on mobilizing existing support rather than winning new votes. Interestingly, Ebrahim Rassool told reporters in the election aftermath that the ANC had refrained from "specifically targeting" coloureds as a group.[48] ANC leaders knew that a low turnout in NNP/DA-affiliated coloured working-class districts was likely and would favor their prospects of victory. The stress on canvassing as opposed to mass rallies, a general feature of ANC electioneering nationwide, made particular sense in a province where the intention was to avoid activating hostile voters. In the election aftermath, ANC leaders acknowledged that turnout factors made a critical contribution to the party's result in the Western Cape.[49] As Ebrahim Rassool noted, "coloured voters who did not feel the same hostility to the ANC (as in previous contests) did not vote."[50] Before the election, Rassool had predicted a low turnout among urban working-class coloureds that, he believed, would mainly hurt his rivals.[51] With this constituency, the ANC "softly-softly" approach was not aimed to win votes but rather to "allay fears."[52] Nevertheless, the ANC collected more votes than ever before in the working-class Mitchell's Plain.

Conclusion

At the end of its second term in government, the ANC mounted its most sophisticated and most successful ever election campaign, winning more votes in a reduced poll. Though the huge majority the party obtained will certainly prompt apprehensions about the future health of South African democracy, it is worth noting that the ANC victory was the outcome of a campaign that depended on careful research into voter perceptions and canvassing that was undertaken by a reinvigorated branch organization. If the South African democratic progress depends partly on lively and structured political parties that aggregate public concerns and channel them effectively toward leadership, then the ANC's mobilization of its following in this campaign represents a positive development. Parliamentary elections are also about leadership renewal and here again there is plenty of evidence of the ANC's commitment to this aspect of democracy in the party's candidate nomination procedure.

The essential themes in ANC electioneering were its accessibility, its responsiveness, its incumbent power, and its historical legitimacy.

The party subtly orchestrated these elements in different combinations with varying emphases depending upon whom it was addressing. The reward for these efforts was the addition to the ANC's core support of significant quantities of new votes, from the Indian and coloured minorities and among the rural poor in KZN.

Notes

1. ANC, "Statement of the National Executive Committee of the African National Congress on the Occasion of the Year 90 of the ANC," January 8, 2002, accessible at http://www.anc.org.za/ancdocs/history/jan8-2002.html.
2. Other monthly topics were safety and security, women's emancipation, human rights, health, culture and heritage, the environment, the youth, African and international solidarity, the rights of the child, and rural, urban, and community development.
3. *Financial Mail*, August 8, 2003.
4. *The Star*, March 27, 2004.
5. *Business Day*, November 6, 2003.
6. *The Star*, April 10, 2004.
7. *This Day*, April 16, 2004.
8. *Mail & Guardian*, January 9, 2004.
9. Author Interview, IEC Results Centre in Pretoria, April 15, 2004.
10. *The Star*, January 6, 2004.
11. *The Star*, April 1, 2004.
12. *Financial Mail*, August 8, 2003.
13. *Mail & Guardian*, January 1, 2004.
14. *Sunday Times*, February 14, 2004.
15. ANC, "Assessment of Registration Weekend" (Gauteng Branch Press Release, November 13, 2003).
16. *Sunday Times*, November 9, 2004.
17. *Mail & Guardian*, February 27, 2004.
18. After the election only one of the incumbent premiers, Mbhazima Shilowa, would return to office. In several instances, President Mbeki used his authority to select people from comparatively low positions on the list. Beatrice Marshoff, e.g., was candidate number twenty-three on the list for the Free State legislature. Marshoff was actually moved down during the review process. Dipuo Peters was legislature candidate number twelve in the Northern Cape.
19. The quote is from Amos Masondo, cited in the *Mail & Guardian*, November 21, 2003.
20. *Financial Mail*, August 8, 2003.
21. Ngonyama interview, April 15, 2004.
22. *Mail & Guardian*, April 8, 2004.
23. *Sunday Times*, April 4, 2004.
24. *The Star*, April 2, 2004.
25. *The Star*, March 29, 2004.
26. *The Star*, April 5, 2004.
27. Author's interview with Ronnie Kasrils, IEC Results Centre in Pretoria, April 15, 2004.
28. *NUMSA News*, no. 2, May 2004.
29. ANC in KZN Press Release, March 9, 2004.
30. *Mail & Guardian*, January 23, 2004.
31. *Sunday Times*, April 4, 2002.

32. Kasrils interview.
33. John Daniel, "Third-Time Lucky: The ANC's Victory in KwaZulu-Natal," *Election Synopsis* 1, no. 4 (Johannesburg: Human Sciences Research Council, 2004), 19.
34. ANC KZN, "Note Towards Developing an Approach to Indians in KZN," January 22, 2004.
35. *Daily News*, April 18, 2004.
36. *East Coast Radio*, 15:02, March 29, 2004.
37. Unless otherwise noted, all election results were obtained from the Web site of the Independent Electoral Commission, www.elections.org.za.
38. Michael Sachs, "The Poor Believe in the Poll," *Mail & Guardian*, May 21, 2004.
39. *Mail & Guardian*, April 30, 2004.
40. *This Day*, April 16, 2004.
41. Amichand Rajbansi in *This Day*, April 16, 2004.
42. Adam Habib quoted in *The Daily News*, April 18, 2004.
43. ANC in KZN Press Release, March 24, 2004.
44. *NUMSA News*, no. 2, May 2004.
45. Michael Sachs, "Voting Patterns in the 1999 and 2004 Elections Compared," *Election Synopsis* 1, no. 4 (Johannesburg: Human Sciences Research Council, 2004), 9.
46. *Mail & Guardian*, May 7, 2004.
47. *Financial Mail*, March 26, 2004.
48. *Cape Times*, April 14, 2004.
49. *ANC Today*, April 23, 2004.
50. *Financial Mail*, April 30, 2004.
51. *Cape Times*, April 14, 2004.
52. *This Day*, April 16, 2004.

CHAPTER SEVEN

The Democratic Alliance: Progress and Pitfalls

SUSAN BOOYSEN

South Africa's 2004 election brought the Democratic Alliance (DA) to unforeseen crossroads. As the DA scrambled across the electoral landscape to scoop up old New National Party (NNP) support, pacify and please its existing liberal constituency, and make small inroads into the "black voter market," its multiple ventures exposed dualities, inconsistencies, and unexpected weaknesses. Yet, the DA ran a reasonably successful campaign, helping it to outperform the rest of the opposition parties. The DA was the only opposition party that could register growth of any significance in the 2004 election. Its overall growth of 2.8 percent was only beaten by that of the African National Congress (ANC), which grew by 3.3 percent in 2004. The DA was the only opposition party that won seats in all nine provincial legislatures. It uncompromisingly proclaimed its pride in being an *opposition*. The DA even stated its belief that South Africa owes the existence of democracy, rather than a one-party state, to its presence.

While the DA proved to be the strongest opposition party, the 2004 election demonstrated that the party was not yet on the road to challenging the ANC for power. There were limits to what a professionally oriented and predatory electoral machine, a well-designed election strategy, and apparent voter availability could deliver. Although the DA increased its support and improved its lead on the other opposition parties, these gains were made in the context of an electoral scene where the ANC was able to increase its overall share of the vote, leaving the opposition to compete among themselves within a smaller pool of voters. Therefore, while the DA climbed in the electoral rankings, it may be reaching a plateau of voter support, beyond which it cannot rise unless it changes its tactics.

This chapter explores how the DA's campaign for the 2004 election brought the party to the realization that it needs a new role, strategy, and vision.[1] It maps the tale of how the DA's optimism and expectations ended in modest successes and disappointments. The chapter first assesses the role of the DA as the foremost opposition party in South Africa's multi-party democracy. The subsequent section deals with the details of the DA's 2004 campaign. It explores the problems, pitfalls, and progress that were associated with positioning for power, candidates, campaign messages, and campaign targeting. It then tracks the electoral strength of the DA in the context of opposition party developments. The final section considers the challenges that the DA faces in the aftermath of the 2004 election.

Opposition in Times of Affirmation

The DA's 2004 electoral challenge to prevent the ANC from achieving a two-thirds majority derives much of its meaning from the particular culture of contestation and opposition that prevailed in South Africa in 2004. The test for the DA was to maintain and extend itself in times "not conducive to contestation."[2] Not only did the election coincide with South Africa's celebration of ten years of democracy, it also signaled a period in which recognition of the vulnerabilities of the governing ANC gave way to affirmation of the powerful liberation movement party. In addition, robust opposition was perceived to be unpatriotic. In this context, it would be a trying project for any opposition party to build broad national credibility and penetrate the ANC's support base, especially because the strongest basis for such a campaign would entail attacks on the continued icon of liberation and transformation. The DA's task was further encumbered because it had become the political home for large numbers of voters harboring varying degrees of hostility toward the ANC.

Ten years into South Africa's multiparty democracy, the DA continued to forge its role as the official opposition. By 2004, it was the torchbearer for opposition politics and probably the primary party political watch-dog. The DA's status was asserted amid the preelection decline of both the sizes of individual opposition parties, and the overall percentage space they occupied.[3] In the 2004 election, the DA reversed the first of these trends. It was the only existing opposition party that registered more than negligible growth. Its growth also exceeded the national size of the new Independent Democrats (ID).

These opposition party achievements were not generally celebrated as significant to multiparty democracy, a system that depends on contestation for its effectiveness. The DA campaign, under the slogan "South Africa Deserves Better," was often interpreted as polarizing.[4] The cloud of the DA's 1999 "Fight Back" campaign still hovered, despite the fact that 1999 had witnessed the rebuilding of a party that had been marginal in size and influence after the 1994 election. Thus, the DA's victories were recorded amid a widespread political culture against aggressive, Westminster style, party opposition.[5]

The ANC and sections of the mass media joined forces in an assault on the DA as the main opposition party. This antagonism resulted from a complex interplay of factors, including the "time of celebration" that accompanied the ten-year commemoration of South Africa's liberation, and the overwhelming recognition that despite flaws and lapses, the ANC had made progress. The ANC's message that "the tide has turned" was institutionalized. The ruling party was also honest in recognizing that much remained to be done, a message that was linked to the ANC campaign theme of renewing its contract with the people.[6] In short, the 2004 climate was disadvantageous for practicing opposition politics.

The DA nevertheless stepped in to try and assert itself as a viable, effective opposition. The obvious first line of attack for the DA was to focus on policy failures and lapses in government integrity that had become evident. Equally obvious, the DA emphasized the undesirability of more power for the ANC. It positioned itself as the opposition force that could save the South African voters from ANC power hunger and specters of African politics gone wrong. The DA also questioned the commitment of the president to evacuate office upon the expiry of his second term in 2009.[7] The DA's message that too much power for the ANC is dangerous was further associated with the notion that the ANC lacked the political will to prevent a recurrence of Zimbabwean disregard for human rights in South Africa. The DA strived to persuade voters that the problems in Zimbabwe resulted from too much power for government and too little opposition.[8] Given these messages, it was a small step for DA opponents to project the party as reactionary, opposed to transformation, harking back to the days of apartheid, and as white and racist.[9]

In the course of the election campaign, an anti-"DA as opposition" culture increasingly manifested itself. In reaction to the DA's assertive style of opposition, the dictum seemed to be "any opposition, except the

DA." This could be interpreted as "no opposition," because by 2004 the DA had emerged as the only opposition party of consistent strength. As Desai remarked, the ANC and agencies sympathetic to it tried to "keep the DA on the outside." Desai also referred to a discourse of punishing the DA that was developing amid a real need for contestation.[10] Clearly, constructive and cooperative opposition in the style of the NNP was in vogue and regarded as noble by the ANC.[11]

The DA dismissed the notion that it was conducting a negative campaign.[12] Over the years, it had also rejected the option of cooperative governance with the ANC. In the incumbency period of Nelson Mandela, the party turned down an invitation to become part of a government of national unity.[13] On April 16, 2004 when Mbeki called for opposition parties to become part of a broadly based government, the DA again rejected the option.[14] Party leader Leon clearly stated the DA's position: "We are unashamedly the opposition, we are the reason why this country is a democracy . . . [I]f there was no opposition, this would be a one-party state."[15]

In short, the DA's 2004 campaign and performance was affected by a combination of the culture of affirmation of ten years of ANC governance, conditional support for the notion of party opposition, and the DA's own choice of positioning itself as the savior of multiparty democracy and protector of the people against the "power-hunger" and policy failures of the ANC.

The Campaign: Alliances, Ideology, and Strategy

In 2004, the DA found itself in the highly contested and poorly differentiated domain of opposition party contestation to the right of the ANC. Its challenge was to retain credibility with its existing voter base of liberals and the incongruous ex-NNP, and make inroads into the voting bloc of black and poor people. While trying to meet this challenge, the DA encountered contradictions in its ideological and racial positioning. In order to grow the party needed to target poor and potentially disaffected black voters. Yet, its policy solutions were overwhelmingly free-market, which constituted a policy environment that was essentially incompatible with the party's proposal for a Basic Income Grant. In addition, the DA had to portray itself as a liberal-democratic party, yet it also pursued voters in favor of the death penalty. The DA hoped that its credibility on policy issues could help to realize growth, despite its image as a party for minority groups with a predominantly rich and white leadership.

The DA's Coalition for Change with the Inkatha Freedom Party (IFP) was intended to invoke a semblance of nonracialism in an attempt to induce black voters to enter a new political home. Alliance formation had the twofold preelection purpose of lending credence to the DA claim that it would be strong enough to challenge the ANC, as well as adding black-African legitimacy to a party with a minority-group image. From 2000 to 2001, it was the alliance with the NNP that brought the temporary appearance of a sizeable and united opposition force. When the NNP withdrew and the DA as an interparty alliance collapsed, the new DA registered significant gains against the NNP in the 2003 window period for floor crossing.[16] The DA, however, returned to resembling a white party. The NNP support base of mostly working-class coloured voters in the Western Cape was available for recruitment, but not guaranteed. In 2004, the DA embarked on cooperation with the IFP, forming the Coalition for Change in an attempt to gain legitimacy among black-African voters. The parties hoped to capture provincial power in KwaZulu-Natal. The DA's model was the Western Cape, where it had formed a coalition government with the NNP after the 1999 election.

The remainder of this section further explores the DA's campaign challenges along the themes of the candidate lists, the campaign issues and strategy, and the linkage between campaign messages and targets.

The DA Candidates

At the level of the party branches, the process to nominate DA candidates closed on October 31, 2003, after which party officials vetted the nominations. Each province, working through the executive of its provincial electoral college, completed a list with approximately three times the required number of candidates.[17] The electoral colleges subsequently interviewed the nominees and produced revised lists. In the process of list construction the positions 3, 7, 14, 21, and 28 were left vacant, giving national and provincial leaders a way to ensure that the final lists of candidates would show the required expertise and demographic balance.[18] For the national list, every third position was left vacant. The final lists of DA candidates were launched on February 14, 2004.

As the DA launched its candidate lists with Leon stating that they were "representative and diverse," Idasa commented that the party seemed to be taking note of the issue of racial credibility.[19] Among the efforts to balance the candidate lists were quotas for black candidates, albeit with scope for exceptions. The DA did not "want to go with an all-white team, but if some white person has been incredibly active in building the party or raising money, they should not be discriminated against."[20] Elaborating on the theme of nonracialism at the launch, Leon stated:[21]

> Today . . . we have seen that [the candidates] come from all communities, from all walks of life. In the Democratic Alliance we do not say to one person or another: "This one will represent this group of people, and that one will represent that group." Instead we say: "You, and you, and you, and I—we each represent all of South Africa."

Representativeness featured alongside merit as a criterion for candidate selection.[22] The DA included more black candidates on its lists than in previous elections. The nonracial gist in Leon's statements about the DA candidates represented a tentative break with the 1999 campaign. Yet, Western Cape leader Theuns Botha defended the high proportion of white persons on the provincial list in terms of "retention of expertise."[23] This and the persistent predominance of whites at the top of the national leadership signaled that the DA would continue to be haunted by its racial character. With regard to the DA list, Janet Cherry remarked that "there [were] few African leaders of credibility in either of the 'old white' parties, the DA or the NNP."[24]

The DA Election Manifesto

While discussing election campaigns, the tendency often is to focus on the most visible medium: posters. Yet, as Jonathan Faull argues, "[p]osters and other complementary texts cannot operate in a discourse vacuum, and rely on manifestos, speeches and campaigning to infuse their messages with meaning."[25] The DA manifesto articulated the core of the party's 2004 campaign message, namely that the ANC had failed the people of South Africa. According to the DA, the ANC had not delivered on its 1994 and 1999 election promises and as a result, the people of South Africa had been suffering. Leon proclaimed: "What South Africa needs, is an approach in which the people will lead the way . . . that is what the DA intends to provide."[26] The DA manifesto, which was based on the work of two years,[27] presented a program for "real change," "providing solutions to the most pressing problems we face."[28]

The DA manifesto brought a range of policy positions to the voters:[29]

- The DA's economic policies promised to create millions of real jobs by unleashing the private sector and boosting growth. The DA would create new and sustainable jobs by increasing Gross Domestic Product (GDP) by at least 6 percent per annum.
- A Basic Income Grant (BIG) of R110 per month would be payable to everyone living in poverty and without access to another grant. The DA argued that this was a feasible and properly costed policy.
- An increase in the number of police officers to 150,000 would address crime. The DA promised to train and equip them to have them on the streets by 2005.
- The DA promised swift, decisive action on corruption in both the private and public sectors.
- Free antiretroviral drugs to each person living with AIDS would support the DA's "proven track record of providing antiretroviral drugs." The greater use of generic drugs would ensure feasibility of the initiative within the limits of the current health budget.
- An improvement in education would ensure that all children emerge from school literate and numerate at internationally benchmarked levels, thus being prepared for participation in a modern economy.
- A revision of the ANC's policy on affirmative action would ensure that this "extreme form" of affirmative action no longer restrained investment.[30]

Other DA campaign themes included the revival of nation building, speeding up the privatization of the economy, and addressing the continuing housing problem. Due to a high degree of issue consensus among different segments of the South African voting population, the DA could use many of these issues to target both black-African and white/coloured voters.[31] The DA recognized that the interests of its minority-group voters would best be served through attention to the issues of poverty, development, and unemployment, thus enhancing convergence.

Themes and Phases of the DA Campaign

The DA's broad national campaign, covering all provinces and a diversity of demographic voting blocs, required a collage of messages. The party's message strategy was three-pronged, ranging from the projection of DA strengths and its policy alternatives, to highlighting ANC weaknesses with reference to integrity and policy, as well as the weaknesses of other opposition parties (see table 7.1). These three message themes were used with varying emphases in different phases of the DA campaign.

The interlocking prongs of the DA strategy served, *first*, to highlight the party's strengths and achievements. The DA focused on its status as foremost among the opposition parties, the only opposition party that could effectively oppose the ANC. The DA highlighted its alliance strength, achieved through its relationship with the IFP. Preelection print and radio advertisements punted that the Coalition for Change would achieve 30 percent of the national poll.[32] The DA also devoted much of its campaign to presenting its policy alternatives, which were projected as major party strengths. *Second*, the DA's strengths were twinned with attacks on ANC policies and leadership. DA leader Leon pointed out that the ANC was wrong in stating that there was no need for new policy initiatives. The DA further presented arguments on the

Table 7.1 Three-pronged message strategy of the DA

	Projections of own strengths		Projections of ANC weaknesses		Projections of other parties' weaknesses
DA strategic strength	Strength through alliances	Alternative policies	Attacks on ANC integrity	Attacks on ANC policies	Attacks on NNP and ID
Alternative to government; strongest and fastest growing of opposition parties; only viable opposition party	With IFP can challenge ANC for government over next five years; multi-identity liberal movement	Strong and costed policies on policing, BIG, AIDS, growth and jobs, better on affirmative action, housing, education	Corruption in officialdom, provincial governments; enriching only the few; president seeking third term; poor choice of international friends	Policies have failed, poverty rife, government doesn't care about poor and AIDS sufferers; ANC refuses to acknowledge policy failures	ID a one-woman show; NNP bankrupt and lap dog of ANC; vote for a smaller party (ID) is a wasted vote: it has no researched and comprehensive policy platform
Phases of campaign in which themes were deployed					
Used throughout the campaign period; amplified in later phases	Dominated in the later campaign phases; focused on ability to challenge for power	Throughout the campaign period	Throughout campaign period	Throughout campaign period	Throughout campaign, but higher prominence in later phases

Sources: Multiple media sources; synthesized and categorized by the author.

lack of integrity of the ANC leadership. *Third*, the DA campaign focused on the weaknesses of other opposition parties, counterposing such weaknesses with details of its own strengths. The DA singled out the NNP, Independent Democrats (ID), Freedom Front + (FF+), and Minority Front (MF).[33] The attacks on the NNP were mostly unleashed in the Western Cape, those on the FF+ in the northern provinces, and those on the ID both provincially and nationally.

Although there was no phase in the campaign that exclusively used a particular theme, certain themes predominated specific phases.

- *Start-up phase* (late 2003 to launch in February 2004): The campaign was predominantly about issues, with specific reference to unemployment, crime, health, corruption, and education.
- *Intermediate phase* (February to March 2004): The campaign focused on the credibility of the government, emphasizing that the ANC had been failing the people and suggesting that the ANC had dubious constitutional objectives.
- *Penultimate phase* (March to April 2004): The campaign placed a strong emphasis on the notion that the DA was strong enough to take on the ANC, especially in cooperation with the IFP, and that this challenge would be realized in the following five years.
- *Final phase* (April 2004): The campaign mainly related to the consolidation of the opposition, with emphasis on the need for voters to unite behind the DA and ensure that the party would be strong enough to challenge the ANC.

In different phases of the campaign, the DA presented itself as an alternative government, rather than just another opposition party. In the words of Leon: "We are building the core of an alternative government to the ANC. Our support is continuing to grow among all communities in South Africa."[34] DA strategists highlighted that the DA was challenging the ANC instead of the other opposition parties. The opposite was true, as was attested in the final campaign phases when the DA focused on the consolidation of the opposition. In the words of the DA's Athol Trollip: "We firmly believe that a vote for a smaller party is a wasted vote. We believe in strong opposition and we have seen in the past how smaller parties split the votes."[35] The DA used the "consolidation of opposition" message to scoop up votes that had become available after the disintegration of the NNP, while fending off competing opposition parties. The DA had to counter threats that were posed by the ID,[36] and ensure that there would be no resurgence of the FF+.[37]

The DA spread its message of alliance strength using radio advertisements and joint rallies with the IFP. Its claim was that "together, the DA and its alliances partners" could achieve close to 30 percent of the vote, and over (or in) the next five years challenge the ANC for power: "Together, we are big enough to . . . provide South Africa with an alternative government."[38] In the final stages of the campaign, the DA reinforced its message through radio advertisements on the need to unite the opposition, using matching posters, pamphlet drops, and newspaper advertisements.[39]

Campaign Strategy and Messages in Relation to DA Targets

The DA campaign crisscrossed South Africa, moving from working-class coloured communities in the Northern Areas of Port Elizabeth and Cape Town's Mitchell's Plain, to Mpumalanga, Limpopo, and Soweto in Gauteng.[40] It focused on the areas that had formerly anchored NNP support and ventured into areas dominated by the ANC. By virtue of gains made in the 2000 local government elections, and with some aid from the 2002 local floor crossings, the DA had captured new chunks of support.[41] These had to be defended and consolidated. The party used a series of messages to confirm its core and consolidate its weak support, another to win over available former NNP supporters, and a third batch to recruit weak ANC supporters.

In the DA campaign, white voters featured as the support base. Yet, the need persisted to capture remnants of the disintegrating NNP's support, and to consolidate the white voter gains made in the period since 1999. Polling research of late 2003 indicated that two-thirds of DA support would be white with equal numbers of white-Afrikaners and English-speaking whites.[42] Overall, the DA felt secure in its appeal to white voters, with director of strategy, Ryan Coetzee, saying: "[A]mong white voters, the other opposition parties practically don't exist."[43] DA research among white voters in late 2003 indicated that the party enjoyed 66 percent of their support, the ID 4.4 percent, the NNP 3.7 percent, and the FF+ and African Christian Democratic Party (ACDP) 3.2 percent each.[44]

In recent years, it had already become clear that the DA's constituency was not just white and privileged.[45] The DA started gaining ground on the NNP in the run-up to the 1999 election by winning a series of by-elections in white working-class and lower-middle-class areas. In the 1999 election, the DA had already registered notable Indian middle-class support.

The DA saw two extension targets in the coloured voter bloc and a portion of the black-African vote. The coloured voter bloc would be the easier of the two targets. As a study by Makatees indicated, there was a willingness among coloured voters to experiment with new party options, especially in the void left by the preelection fading away of the NNP.[46] However, it was by no means certain what the destination of this "journey" to find a new political home would be. The ANC appeared to be an option; so did the DA and the ID. The DA had the "racial" advantage. According to the Makatees study, coloured voters felt that a "white" party such as the DA would be effective in defending their interests.[47]

Municipal by-elections in coloured areas had already demonstrated that the DA could not take any of the components of the coloured vote for granted. The ANC would be a significant contender. The results of a 2003 by-election in the Nelson Mandela Metropolitan Municipality[48] indicated how special attention to local community interests could turn coloured voters in favor of the ANC.[49] The DA campaign thus gave prominence to the coloured areas of the Cape Flats. In the wrap-up of the campaign in this community, the DA emphasized the enemy status of the ANC, as well as the fact that the NNP had surrendered the support of these voters to the ANC. The 2004 ballot was the place to correct this transgression.[50] In working to win over the coloured former support of the NNP, the DA dabbled with affirmative action and the perceived exclusion of minority groups from the spoils. This strategy exposed the DA to accusations of stirring the fires of racism.[51] Thabo Mbeki accused opposition parties generally of being determined to "polarise our country," and referred to opposition arguments on affirmative action as "a camouflaged message that black upliftment is contrary to the interests of the white section of our population."[52]

The other expansion target of the DA in the 2004 campaign was doubtful or weak ANC supporters, despite doubts as to their availability to opposition parties such as the DA. As Patrick Laurence noted: "There is no evidence of mass desertion by the poor from the ANC. There may, however, be diminishing enthusiasm for its causes and concomitant scepticism over its ability to deliver on its promises. There is thus a theoretical opportunity for Leon or a rival opposition leader to exploit in the pending election. . . ."[53] The DA, in the person of deputy leader Joe Seremane, acknowledged this constraint. He noted that the DA could only hope to make inroads among these voters once they would vote on the basis of issues, rather than "personality and tradition."[54]

The DA's optimistic preelection projections of success were built on the assumption that the party would be able to convert municipal by-election support from the preceding years into national and provincial votes. Leon noted the DA's demonstrable growth in comparison with past performance levels.[55] The DA was especially hopeful of winning black support in the provinces of Gauteng, Mpumalanga, Limpopo, and KwaZulu-Natal.[56]

The DA approached this challenge using a wedge strategy. It cast doubt on the integrity and performance of the ANC, and stressed that the ruling party was neglecting the needs of the voters, while nurturing elite interests. According to the DA, its own policies could better the efforts of the ANC. Leon stated: "On every major social issue facing the people of South Africa, the president and the ANC are in the wrong. And the DA has the right answers."[57] The DA also tried to capitalize on Mbeki's statement that ". . . we don't foresee that there will be any need for new and major policy initiatives."[58] Leon retorted by saying that "many of the government policies simply are bad and need to be replaced."[59]

The DA's wedge strategy included the message that the ANC could not be trusted. The DA argued that ANC loyalists ran organizations such as the police and the SABC, a situation that threatened the principles and practice of democracy and undermined the constitutional order.[60] The DA cunningly linked their arguments of ANC power hunger to latent minority group fears of the patterns of one-party dominance typical of African states. One of the most prominent examples was the issue of a third term for the president. Whether Mbeki was hoping to have the constitution amended in order to allow him a third term in office was at the core of the early DA campaign, and appeared to many as antiblack sentiment.[61] The implied argument was that in future the ANC might take South Africa down the Zimbabwe route.[62] The DA's primary objective was to create doubt, by associating Mbeki with unpopular and politically corrupt leaders, and fear, by invoking a specter of ANC disregard for constitutionalism.[63]

Thabo Rapoo observes that the DA succeeded in putting the ANC on the defensive.[64] Indeed, the ANC responded to the DA message with counterattacks aimed at delegitimizing the DA. DA leader Leon identified a number of ANC strategies, such as portraying the DA as a right-wing party, the DA's identification of policy and governance problems as unpatriotic, and the DA's criticisms as "hankering after the past."[65] The DA saw the ANC attacks as attempts to avoid public debates about policy failures. Leon referred to Alan Fine, who wrote that "although corruption is an issue for all voters, including the ANC's traditional support base, when the DP exposes government corruption it is 'overstating the case' and 'playing on the prejudices that blacks can't govern.' "[66]

The DA's 2004 Results

In its 2004 campaign, the DA aimed to confirm its standing as the predominant opposition party and initiate the process of consolidating the opposition. It conditionally achieved both objectives. The DA asserted itself as the predominant, albeit small, opposition party and partially consolidated the opposition vote. The DA did not lose support, usurped more of the NNP's previous support, and contained the growth of both the new ID and existing small parties such as the FF+ and the ACDP. However, before and during the campaign the DA failed to convincingly establish predominant status, as small parties continued to capture small chunks of support.

The DA was one of nine opposition parties that contested the elections both nationally and in all nine provinces.[67] It emerged as the only opposition party that won seats in the National Assembly (NA) as well as in all nine provincial legislatures. The DA became the official opposition in seven of the nine provinces, including the Western Cape and KwaZulu-Natal, but excluding the Eastern Cape and the Northwest. In the Eastern Cape, the title went to the United Democratic Movement (UDM). In Northwest, the United Christian Democratic Party (UCDP) beat the DA. Across the nine provinces, the DA scored a total of fifty-one provincial seats, up from thirty-five seats in 1999. Its total gain across the provincial legislatures was sixteen seats, compared to the ANC's fifteen.[68]

Compared to the 1999 election result of the DP, the DA manifested growth of 2.8 percent of the national vote.[69] This growth figure was only matched by the ANC's 3.3 percent. It was, however, noticeably less than the approximately 8 percent growth that the DP had shown in 1999. In the 1999 election, the DP had risen from its 1.75 percent of 1994 to a new height of 9.56 percent, mostly picking up support from the declining NNP. In 2004, the DA was the only opposition party showing growth, apart from the new ID, which accumulated 1.73 percent of the national vote. Among the parties with declining national fortunes from 1999 to 2004 was the DA's coalition partner, the IFP.

The DA election results in the past decade (table 7.2) indicate that both nationally and in the nine provinces, the DP/DA recorded systematic growth from election to election. The advances were relatively small, but without relapse. The three biggest instances of growth were in Gauteng in the period from 1994 to 1999, and in the Western and Northern Cape in the period from 1999 to 2004. In all cases DA growth coincided with the collapse of the NNP support base.[70] The DA's strongest 2004 provincial performance was in the Western Cape. Opinion polls in the run-up to

Susan Booysen

Table 7.2 Democratic Party/Democratic Alliance performance, 1994–2004

	% 1994 (DP)	% 1999 (DP)	% 2004 (DA)
National	1.75	9.56	12.37 (50 seats)
Provinces			
Eastern Cape	2.05	6.29	7.34 (5 seats)
Free State	0.56	5.33	8.47 (3 seats)
Gauteng	5.32	17.97	20.90 (15 seats)
KwaZulu-Natal	2.15	8.16	8.36 (7 seats)
Limpopo	0.21	1.41	3.59 (2 seats)
Mpumalanga	0.56	4.46	6.94 (2 seats)
Northern Cape	1.87	4.77	11.08 (3 seats)
Northwest	0.50	3.26	5.00 (2 seats)
Western Cape	6.64	11.91	27.11 (12 seats)

Source: Statistics supplied by the Independent Electoral Commission, 2004.

the election indicated a consistently rising profile for the DA in the province.[71] Support for the DA in the Western Cape continued to climb, initially peaking at 24 percent, reaching 26 percent with the application of discriminant analysis, and culminating in 27 percent in the provincial election.[72]

The DA made important gains among coloured voters in the 2004 elections. Yet, its successes were not unambiguous. The ANC gained at the cost of the DA in areas of Mitchell's Plain and the northern areas of Port Elizabeth.[73] The expected conversion of black by-election support into provincial and national votes did not materialize for the DA. The exact reasons for this disjuncture would be a major theme for postelection investigations.[74] Statisticians from the Council for Scientific and Industrial Research (CSIR) estimated that 0.4 percent of African voters supported the DP in 1999. This had risen to 1.7 percent black-African support for the DA in 2004.[75] They also reasoned that the slight progress among black-African voters had originated in fallout from the UDM and IFP, rather than in the ANC. The DA's black-African support came from predominantly rural areas of provinces such as Mpumalanga, KwaZulu-Natal, and the Eastern Cape.[76] The DA's James Selfe acknowledged that the party's performance was "not as good as we would have liked," and further noted that "voting behaviour in Africa is different in that it is not predictable on the basis of issue preferences."[77] However, the DA was satisfied that it had the messages and the community presence that could be expected from its side.[78]

Conclusion

By the standards of post-1994 opposition politics in South Africa, the DA's growth was not insignificant. The electoral performance of opposition parties, particularly in the 1994 and 1999 elections, was distinguished by three principal features: the biggest among the opposition parties had shrunk, the total opposition party space had shrunk at the behest of the growing ANC, and a larger number of parties had been sharing the limited opposition space. Whereas the DA did reverse some of these trends in 2004, its gains were tentative. The DA was not on an inevitable path of sustained growth and good fortune. Its uncertain fortunes were related to a diverse and unconsolidated support base, leadership, and incongruous ideological positioning.

As the story of the DA in the 2004 election unfolded, the DA emerged as a party that was, at best, liberal, multifaceted, and engaged in vigorous multipartyism; and, at worst, contradictory in terms of policy, internally inconsistent, and operating as an opportunistic vote-garnering apparatus. Four distinct voter constituencies—the old liberals, the unreformed and reactionary old Nats, the reformed Nats that wished to distance themselves from the stigmatized NNP past, and enclaves of new black support coming from the ranks of old Bantustan politics—were based under one DA roof. This broad church of anti-ANC sentiments persisted, but without the altar of liberation politics and antiracism to which its nemesis, the ANC, genuflects.

With regard to leadership, the DA has been described as two parties, referring to the divergent styles and orientations of Tony Leon and Helen Zille.[79] These dualities continue in the DA's ideological and issue stances. It is a liberal party, yet more neoliberal than the ANC. It wished upon itself the label of social democrat, yet displayed a mixed bag of orientations. In its 2004 campaign the party seamlessly veered into conservative policies and vote-catching issues.

The DA has already indicated the continuation of its 2004 campaign in preparation for 2009: "As the DA, we are involved in a two-phase process. Firstly we need to unite the opposition and take votes away from the ruling ANC. The second phase is to put together a workable alternative to the government and challenge them for power in the next election."[80] In the postelection period the DA has reexamined itself, envisaging a "sweeping revision" in order to prepare for what was described as a long-term assault on the ANC.[81]

Despite the DA being the predominant opposition party, there is a continuous debate in South Africa on whether the DA or some still-to-emerge party will be the "real" opposition of the future. This debate often centers on the need for an opposition challenging the ANC government from the left, and not the center-right of the political spectrum. If the trends of the preceding decade prevail into the next, the DA will continue to make small but systematic inroads into the black-African section of the electorate, possibly capturing chunks of support from both other opposition parties and the ANC. When and if the opposition party from the left arrives, its first challenge might be to match and overtake the DA. Until that happens the DA, either on its own or in an alliance, is likely to remain South Africa's principal opposition party.

Notes

1. See Brendan Boyle, "A Whole New Ball Game for Leon," *Sunday Times*, May 30, 2004, p. 21.
2. Susan Booysen, "History More Important than Policy," *The Star*, April 9, 2004.
3. Susan Booysen, "Ten Years of Opposition Politics in Democratic South Africa—Unfolding Trends" (paper presented at Electoral Institute of Southern Africa, Election Seminar Series, Johannesburg, April 1, 2004), 15.
4. Asserting and promoting this culture of associating patriotism with support for the ANC, Mbeki said that the key challenge for the electorate was not whether the country should have a strong opposition, "responding to the fictional threat of a one-party state," but whether "our people . . . are ready to give further impetus to the process of national reconciliation by acting together in unity in a people's contract" (*ANC Today*, "Letter from the President," April 9, 2004).
5. The DA also acknowledged that this style characteristic had negatively affected the party. See Boyle, "A Whole New."
6. Tony Leon, "ANC Manifesto Lacks Vision, Urgency," *The Sunday Independent*, January 18, 2004, p. 7.
7. The Constitution sets a limit of two terms of office for the president.
8. David Moore, "The Wrong Lessons from Zimbabwe," *This Day*, May 5, 2004, p. 11.
9. See Console Tleane, "DA Reveals Its Racist Attitude," *City Press*, March 7, 2004, p. 18. This analysis is an illustration of widespread media analyses that focused on the DA as being anti-transformation and racist.
10. Ashwin Desai, panelist on the "After 8 Debate" with John Perlman, SAFM, April 21, 2004.
11. Smuts Ngonyama, informal interview with author, April 15, 2004, Pretoria.
12. Linda Ensor, "DA Rejects Negative Campaigning Claims," *Business Day*, March 24, 2004, p. 4.
13. The party that turned down the invitation was the Democratic Party (DP). The DP changed its name to DA after a merger with the NNP that took place in 2000. The DA retained its name when the NNP left the alliance in 2001.
14. *The Star*, April 17, 2004, p. 1.
15. Tony Leon, quoted in *The Star*, March 29, 2004, p. 6.
16. Susan Booysen, "Caveats in Post-Liberation Multiparty Opposition Politics in South Africa: Reconfiguration from 2002–2003" (paper delivered at the 46th Annual Meeting of the African Studies Association, Boston, October 30–November 2, 2003), 18.
17. Dirk Kotzé, "The Nomination Processes of Candidates on Party Lists," *Election Update 2004* 2, no. 16 (Johannesburg: The Electoral Institute of Southern Africa), 2–7.
18. On the balances between racial groups, gender, and defectors on the DA's Western Cape list, see *This Day*, "Crucial Coloureds Fail to Make It to the Top of DA List," February 3, 2004, p. 5.

19. Idasa, "Party Support in South Africa's Third Democratic Election," *Elections Brief* (Cape Town: Political Information and Monitoring Service—South Africa, February 20, 2004). Also see S'Thembiso Msomi, "DA's Quest for Black Votes," *Sunday Times*, February 15, 2004, p. 9.

20. Tony Leon, "I'm Not a Guilty White," interview with Drew Forrest, *Mail & Guardian*, January 30, 2004, p. 4.

21. Idasa, "Party Support."

22. Marianne Merton, "DA to 'Take On the ANC in Its Own Backyard,' " *Mail & Guardian*, January 9, 2004, p. 4.

23. See Sabelo Ndlangisa, in *Sunday Times*, February 29, 2004, p. 7.

24. Janet Cherry, "Elections 2004: The Party Lists and Issues of Identity," *Election Synopsis* 1, no. 3 (Pretoria: CPP, CPS, HSRC, Idasa, 2004), 8.

25. Jonathan Faull, "What is a Manifesto and What Does It Mean?" *Election Synopsis* 1, no. 3 (Pretoria: CPP, CPS, HSRC, Idasa, 2004), 10–11.

26. Tony Leon, quoted in *The Sunday Independent*, January 18, 2004, p. 7; DA Election Manifesto 2004, "South Africa Deserves Better" (Cape Town, 2004), 33.

27. Tony Leon, quoted in *Business Day*, April 6, 2004, p. 9. Also see DA, 2004 campaign pamphlet, "Unite the Opposition on April 14," (Cape Town, 2004).

28. DA advertisement, "South Africa Deserves Better" *Sunday Times*, February 8, 2004, p. 14.

29. DA Election Manifesto 2004; also see SABC NewsNet, April 19, 2004.

30. Tony Leon quoted in Drew Forrest, "I'm Not a Guilty White."

31. See Idasa, "Party Support."

32. DA, 2004 campaign pamphlet, "South Africa Deserves Better" (Cape Town, 2004).

33. Tony Leon, "A Message from Tony Leon," newspaper advertisement, *The Star*, March 16, 2004, p. 6; DA, 2004 campaign pamphlet, "Die Volkstaat is So Dood Soos die Woestyn Waarin die Vryheidsfront sê u Kan Woon," (Cape Town, 2004).

34. Tony Leon, quoted in *Business Day*, April 6, 2004, p. 9. In *Asikhulume*, February 1, 2004, SABC1. Leon emphasized that despite its relatively small size, the DA is in the league of an alternative government.

35. Athol Trollip, quoted in "DA Sees de Lille's Party as Its Biggest Threat," SABC NewsNet, SABC.com, March 16, 2004.

36. One of the DA campaign advertisements on radio stated in a female voice-over: "I like De Lille, but she is just a one-woman show," *This Day*, March 6, 2003, p. 3.

37. Douglas Gibson, interview with SABC NewsNet, "DA brands De Lille's party a one-woman show," SABC.com, March 16, 2004.

38. DA, "South Africa Deserves Better."

39. DA, SABC NewsNet, March 29, 2004.

40. See DA, sponsored political message, "A message from Tony Leon," *The Star*, March 4, 2004, p. 15.

41. Booysen, "Caveats in Post-Liberation Multiparty Opposition Politics."

42. Markinor, Survey of October/November 2003; Marí Harris (Markinor), interview with author, April 13, 2004, Pretoria.

43. SABC NewsNet, April 16, 2004; Ryan Coetzee, quoted in "DA-ID battle intensifies," SABC NewsNet, News 24.com, April 7, 2004.

44. Douglas Gibson, quoted in *This Day*, April 7, 2004, p. 5.

45. The DA also specifically targeted the Portuguese, one of the largest white immigrant communities in South Africa. See *This Day*, March 29, 2004, p. 5.

46. Kenneth Makatees, "An Investigation of the Effect of New Political Alliances on Party Preferences of Coloureds from Working and Middle Class Areas of Cape Town," Master's thesis, University of Port Elizabeth, 2003.

47. Ibid.

48. In December 2000, Port Elizabeth was expanded and renamed Nelson Mandela Metropolitan Municipality.

49. Cedric Frölick, interview with author, August 20, 2003, Port Elizabeth.

50. Theuns Botha, quoted in Mariechen Waldner, "DA Woos Coloured Voters in Battle for Western Cape," *City Press*, April 11, 2004, p. 8.

51. Rasool, quoted in *This Day*, April 7, 2004, p. 4. Also see *Business Day*, April 7, 2004, p. 5; Mathatha Tsedu, in *City Press*, February 15, 2004, p. 18.

52. Thabo Mbeki in *ANC Today*, "Letter from the President," April 9, 2004.

53. Patrick Laurence, "Battle for the Hearts and Minds of the Poor," *Focus* 30 (Durban: Helen Suzman Foundation, 2003): 6.

54. Joe Seremane, quoted in *Rapport*, March 7, 2004, p. 9.

55. Tom Lodge, quoted in *Business Day*, January 14, 2004, p. 7, referring to the fact that the DA's share of the vote in black townships in places exceeded 10%; Tony Leon, quoted in *Mail & Guardian*, January 9, 2004, p. 4; Tony Leon quoted in Drew Forrest, "I'm Not a Guilty White."

56. Tony Leon in interview with Joseph Aranes, *The Star*, April 1, 2004, p. 15.

57. Tony Leon, quoted in "Mbeki Rewriting the Past—Leon," SABC NewsNet, News24.co.za, March 26, 2004.

58. *Business Day*, April 6, 2004, p. 9.

59. Tony Leon, quoted in *Business Day*, April 6, 2004, p. 9.

60. See Yul Derek Davids, "The People's Agenda Versus Election Manifestos of the Political Parties," *Election Synopsis* 1, no. 3 (Pretoria: CPP, CPS, HSRC, Idasa, 2004): 12–15.

61. See Joe Seremane, "Third-Term Question is Not Racism," *City Press*, March 7, 2004, p. 18. The ANC's Kgalema Motlanthe, in a letter to Leon, responded that the issue had not arisen in the ANC. See *This Day*, February 5, 2004, p. 5.

62. See Thabo Rapoo, "Election 2004: Party Campaign Strategies and Tactics," *Election Synopsis* 1, no. 3 (Pretoria: CPP, CPS, HSRC, Idasa, 2004): 18–20, with regard to the DA campaign references to former Haitian leader, Bertrand Aristide.

63. See Omano Edigheji, "Fear versus Freedom: Minority Parties and the ANC," *Election Synopsis* 1, no. 2 (Pretoria: CPP, CPS, HSRC, Idasa, 2004): 16–18.

64. Rapoo, "Election 2004."

65. Tony Leon, "Government Ducks and Dives to Hide Failures," *Sunday Times*, March 14, 2004, p. 16.

66. Tony Leon, "A Form of Cowardice," in *Political Correctness in South Africa*, ed. Rainier Erkins and John Kane-Berman (Johannesburg: South African Institute of International Affairs, 2000), 62.

67. See *This Day*, March 1, 2004, p. 5.

68. Derived from SABC Electoral Database 2004, April 16, 2004 and the Web site of the Independent Electoral Commission, www.elections.org.za.

69. The comparison here is between the DA in 2004 and its predecessor, the Democratic Party (DP), in 1999, rather than the DA in 2000–2001 when it comprised the DP and the NNP.

70. In Gauteng, between 1994 and 1999 NNP support decreased from 23.88 to 3.89%. In the period between 1999 and 2004, the NNP declined in the Northern Cape from 24.17 to 7.52 %. In the Western Cape between 1994 and 1999 the NNP declined from 53.25 to 38.39% and, in 2004, the party further faded to 10.88%.

71. See SABC/Markinor Opinion 2004, 223 and 2004 (conducted October/November 2003 and January/February 2004).

72. Ibid., 2004; Harris, author's interview.

73. The former is from Garth Strachan, author's interview (telephone), April 15, 2004; the latter from Cedric Frölick, author's interview (telephone), April 15, 2004.

74. James Selfe, author's interview, April 15, 2004.

75. Anonymous interview with author on request of interviewee, April 15, 2004. Compare the estimated increase of black-African support for the DA with the estimated increase of white support for the ANC from 8% in 1999 to 16% in 2004.

76. Hans Ittmann, Manager, CSIR Centre for Logistical and Decision Support, telephonic interview, May 12, 2004.

77. Selfe, author's interview.
78. Ryan Coetzee, DA strategist, author's interview, April 16, 2004.
79. Zille is a former Western Cape politician, after the 2004 election deployed in Parliament. ANC sources grant her "township credibility" and see her as a person they could work with; anonymous ANC interview, April 16, 2004.
80. Tony Leon in interview with Joseph Aranes, *The Star*, April 1, 2004, p. 15.
81. Boyle, "A Whole New."

CHAPTER EIGHT

The Inkatha Freedom Party: Between the Impossible and the Ineffective

LAURENCE PIPER

From the perspective of the Inkatha Freedom Party (IFP), the 2004 election was remarkable in two ways. First, the IFP fared worse than ever. Formed by Prince Mangosuthu Buthelezi in 1975, the party is rooted in rural Zulu people of the KwaZulu-Natal province. During the apartheid era, the IFP virtually was the KwaZulu government. After 1994, it was the leading party in the province, and a governing partner of the African National Congress (ANC) at the national level. The 2004 election saw the IFP lose its thirty years of dominance in KwaZulu-Natal to the ANC, and with it, the party's stake in national government.

Second, the 2004 election was notable for the comparative lack of violence and intimidation between IFP and ANC supporters, especially in KwaZulu-Natal (KZN). The IFP, which put forth a major effort to curb the potential for violent action by its supporters, was integral in the submergence of political violence. This decline was significant because violence has been a consistent feature of the rivalry between the two parties since 1980. Politically related killings marred the 1999 and the 1994 election. In 1994, the number of people killed in political violence in KZN was over 1,000. In 1999, the figure was 82. In 2004, an estimated 15 people were killed in election-related violence in the province.[1] The relative absence of violence and intimidation in 2004 is all the more remarkable, as all parties knew this would be the closest race ever.

These outcomes are mostly the result of the IFP's attempt to adopt a new strategy. Since 1994, the party has jettisoned the militant Zulu nationalism of the 1980s and early 1990s in favor of a more inclusive liberal-democratic politics. However, this strategic movement has been incomplete. This is partly because the history of the IFP makes reinvention difficult, as most people think of the IFP as the party for traditionalist Zulus. Mostly, however, reinvention has been hampered by the nature of the IFP as an organization. Increasingly based around the personality of Buthelezi and a politics of courtly intrigue, there is little space for the kind of debate, discussion, and leadership required to effectively pursue liberal-democratic politics.

Consequently, the IFP's postapartheid politics has not so much transformed from militant Zulu nationalism to an inclusive conservative-liberalism as it has become trapped between the two. What this means is that the party continues to rely on rural Zulu people for support, but is less and less able to use traditional leaders and old tactics of coercion combined with appeals to Zuluness. At the same time its efforts to reach out to new constituencies have not worked because the party has not developed the required leaders, policies, or record in government.

The following section will unpack this characterization of the IFP's postapartheid politics more substantially in terms of a rivalry with the ANC, which dates back some twenty-five years. Here, I want to outline how the IFP's postapartheid strategic malaise was manifest in the 2004 election. It must be noted that the IFP's campaign in 2004 had its strong points, not least the significant efforts made by many in the party, including Buthelezi. However, the campaign fell short in getting out the party's core support and in winning over new voters. Add to this an aggressive and effective ANC campaign in the rural areas of KZN and Durban and it is clear how the IFP lost ground in 2004.

There are three main reasons why the IFP's campaign was suboptimal. First, the party put disproportionate emphasis on a national campaign aimed at potential new voters instead of consolidating its core support in KZN. Of particular importance here was the use of scare resources on tactics like rallies instead of the more personal one-to-one engagement that characterized the ANC campaign. Second, the national campaign was ineffective, not least because of a misplaced reliance on the alleged "cross-over" statesman appeal of Buthelezi. Lastly, while the Coalition for Change with the Democratic Alliance (DA) did bring some benefits, they came at a cost both to the IFP's national image and, possibly, its core support.

The other side to the story of the IFP's decline in 2004 was an effective ANC campaign, especially in KZN. The ANC decided to forego a ten-year approach of "pragmatic cooperation" in favor of a return to direct confrontation. The resulting ANC victory in KZN means that the party has finally and irreversibly gained ascendancy over the IFP. This happened because the IFP is organizationally paralyzed between an old strategy, which is increasingly untenable, and a new strategy, which is insufficiently supported. Shedding core support while failing to attract new votes, the IFP is slowly but steadily hemorrhaging to death.

The IFP's Postapartheid Politics

Prior to 1994, IFP politics was associated with militant Zulu nationalism. It was largely defensive politics. At the mass level, the IFP turned to the traditional elite of the KwaZulu homeland and a militaristic and patriarchal Zuluness to defend its constituency against ANC incursions, often using coercive tactics. This strategy was prompted by the IFP's perceived fortunes in relation to the ANC. Indeed, the ANC-IFP rivalry has been the most important influence on KZN politics for some twenty-five years. An uneasy fraternity in the late 1970s gave way to competition and conflict in the 1980s and early 1990s. This was followed by pragmatic cooperation after the 1994 election, until the final "defeat" of the IFP by the ANC in 2004. It has been a history between organizations of the oppressed, and the resulting intimacy has imbued ANC-IFP relations with the emotive register of sibling rivalry. This helps explain *both* the early sympathies between the IFP and the ANC as well as the talk of merger in recent years, *and* the betrayal both sides felt during the long years of violent confrontation. What both believed ought to have been an organic unity somehow dissipated into violence and discord.[2]

By the early 1980s, the basic features of IFP politics of the transition were established. When things went well in relation to the ANC, the IFP presented itself as a black, national, conservative-liberal, anti–apartheid organization using peaceful tactics to bring about change. When things went badly it embraced a defensive Zulu nationalist and provincial pose alongside militant and sometimes violent tactics on the ground. Both expansive and defensive moments coexisted in the party's strategy for twenty years. The reason most people think of the IFP as Zulu nationalist is because for most of this time the party was faring poorly in competition with the ANC. However, there were moments like the commencement of negotiations in 1990 and May 1994 when the party was in a buoyant mood and presented its inclusive, national, and conservative-liberal face.

The basic shape of ANC-IFP relations in the 1980s continued into the 1990s when the rivalry over leadership of the oppressed transformed into a rivalry over the transition to a postapartheid state. Indeed, as the 1994 election drew nearer, the IFP turned increasingly to Zulu nationalism, eventually endorsing the Zulu king's calls for a sovereign Zulu state. Initially, the ANC and its allies behaved in a manner similar to the IFP, especially during the 1980s when ideological and practical confrontation ruled party relations. During the 1990s, the ANC in KZN underwent a strategic shift at the ideological level, embracing Zuluness as part of a multicultural South African nationalism. On the side of the IFP, the Zulu nationalism of the 1980s broadened and deepened into the politics of Zuluness of the early 1990s.[3]

With the advent of democracy in 1994 all this changed. The IFP-ANC rivalry took on new forms in response to changed political conditions. By the 1996 local government elections things could not have been more different. The province of KZN, home to the "Zulu kingdom," was part of South Africa. King Zwelithini no longer advocated an independent Zulu kingdom and IFP leader Mangosuthu Buthelezi was a senior minister in national government. Zulu nationalist rhetoric had all but disappeared from the public language of the IFP. The party was presenting itself as an inclusive, conservative-liberal alternative to the ANC, a party for people of all races and ethnic groups. Political violence had dropped and the IFP and ANC were cooperating closely in both national government and in KZN.

What brought about this change? Partly, the IFP had no choice and was compelled to drop old strategies. Partly, it was charmed into a more constructive orientation. During the provincial constitution-making process of 1995–1996, the IFP learned the hard way that a narrow victory at the polls in KZN made the use of confrontation counterproductive.[4] In addition, the slow but steady return of law and order, and the surveillance by civil society, made the use of coercive tactics increasingly difficult. Furthermore, the Zulu king publicly defected from the IFP after 1994, undermining the IFP's claims to represent the Zulu nation.

At the same time, the election results of 1994 and 1999 gave the IFP a stake in the new order, enabling it to reproduce itself reasonably successfully according to liberal-democratic rules. The election results provided the party with access to national power and status for Buthelezi. Since the launch of Inkatha, Buthelezi's ambition has been to lead South Africa, not just a Zulu kingdom or the province of KZN. The periodic embrace of the Zulu nation and provincial elites was a strategic, and often defensive, response to the frustration of this main goal.

The ANC's charm offensive, which centered on constructively engaging and including the IFP in government rather than confronting and excluding it, has also been important in shaping the IFP's shift in strategy. A lesson learnt from the transition years, the charm offensive was used first with the Zulu king and then with Buthelezi. Driven by the ANC at a national level with Jacob Zuma—a Zulu—as the main player, the charm offensive proved highly effective, not least because it acknowledged Buthelezi's desire for national recognition. Not only was peace the obvious dividend, with militant Zulu nationalism gone, the ANC-IFP rivalry could only be articulated in terms of policy, delivery, and effectiveness. This terrain was advantageous to the ANC as it was the party in power.

Importantly, the IFP's strategic shift after 1994 was incomplete. The party has been unable to develop the leaders, policies, and performance required to reinvent itself as a credible alternative to the ANC. This is because the IFP is simply not an organization conducive to liberal-democratic politics. Increasingly based around the personality of Buthelezi and dominated by internal politics of patronage and intrigue, the party has little tolerance for the open debate and leadership development necessary to become an effective conservative-liberal party. Consequently, the people who do the liberal-democratic work of the party either depart or are pushed, leaving behind a party increasingly populated by "yes-men" (who are often traditionalist). This is consistently the view of those who have left the party, but is also borne out by a brief comparison of the leadership characteristics of those who have left the party over the years, and those who have stayed.[5]

The ANC-IFP rivalry has continued in postapartheid South Africa but in a new form. In KZN, the period from about 1996 to 2002 was a period of pragmatic cooperation between the two parties. The decision to share Pietermaritzburg and Ulundi as capitals best represents this period. That pragmatic cooperation did not bring an end to ANC-IFP rivalry was clearly demonstrated when, in mid-2002, the ANC and other minority parties in KZN outvoted the IFP on the location of the legislative capital, deciding that it should be Pietermaritzburg. While the IFP's Lionel Mtshali used his discretion as premier to declare Ulundi the home of provincial administration, the new functional division of capitals symbolized the end of pragmatic cooperation.[6] The renewed rivalry was confirmed in early 2003 when the ANC in KZN intended to use floor-crossing legislation to win defectors from the IFP and challenge the party for the premiership. In response, Lionel Mtshali threatened to use his premier's prerogative to call an early election in KZN. Concerned about the financial and logistical implications of such a move, the national ANC stepped in and agreed to hold back on floor crossing until after the 2004 election, thus maintaining the IFP's leadership of the province.[7]

In short, the IFP embraced a more constructive strategic orientation since 1994 not because it was doing better in its rivalry with the ANC, but because new political conditions made it prudent to do so. With old strategies increasingly difficult to pursue, the IFP's hope was that the more constructive conservative-liberal approach would win the party new support, perhaps allowing it to reinvent itself as the national party Buthelezi always desired it to be. However, the party's organizational culture has made this nigh impossible. Consequently, the IFP has not been winning new supporters and at the same time has steadily been shedding old support. Thus, many in the party entered the 2004 election with some anxiety.

The IFP Campaign

The IFP seemed positive about its election campaign in 2004. This was the view both of the team around Buthelezi,[8] and the national organizer and national election committee chair, Albert Mncwango. Interviewed after the election, Mncwango declared the IFP's campaign "more comprehensive and better organized than in 1999." He explained "more comprehensive" to mean better focused on "the people's issues of delivery and development." He also described the IFP's internal organization as superior to 1999, remarking that in 2004, "we had more structures in place covering the entire geographical spread of the country and they functioned like a well-oiled machine." Despite this, the IFP did worse because of "a lack of resources" and "incredible rigging by the ANC." Mncwango added that the IFP experienced growing intolerance in the Durban and Pietermaritzburg townships. When pushed he acknowledged that perhaps the IFP failed to get its voters to the polls, blaming this on the costs of transporting people to voting stations.[9]

Not getting its supporters to the polls was probably the key problem for the IFP in 2004, especially in light of an aggressive ANC campaign in rural KZN. It is at the heart of the first of three main shortcomings in the IFP campaign: its focus, its message, and its alliances.

The Focus of the Campaign

The IFP put disproportionate emphasis on a national campaign aimed at winning potential new voters, despite the fact that the party has always depended heavily on rural Zulu voters in KZN. In 1994, the province returned 88.54 percent of the party's national support, and in 1999, 87.27 percent. Nevertheless, in 2004, the party spent nearly half of its limited budget outside of KZN, and used what it considers its main asset, Buthelezi, mainly to pursue new votes.

Consequently, Buthelezi toured the country following a schedule that would have exhausted someone half his seventy-six years. Between the launch of the IFP campaign in Durban on January 18 and the final rally in Nongoma on April 12, Buthelezi attended no fewer than twenty-nine meetings and rallies, three alliance-formation public announcements, eleven walkabouts and meet and greet sessions, and six major press conferences. Buthelezi also visited all nine provinces: KwaZulu-Natal twenty-seven times, Gauteng ten times, the Western Cape five times, and every other province at least once. In addition, Buthelezi and Leon campaigned jointly no fewer than five times, twice in KZN, twice in Gauteng and once in the Western Cape.[10]

The party recognized that its resources were limited. This was reflected in the fact that almost all Buthelezi's traveling was done by car, with a quick-to-assemble media conference kit in the trailer.[11] Moreover, IFP national spokesperson Musa Zondi publicly lamented the IFP's lack of resources, complaining that the IFP could only afford 60,000 posters nationally in comparison with the ANC's (alleged) 1,000,000 in KZN alone. The IFP also had but a handful of cars in comparison with the ANC's many cars and nine election trucks, and far fewer T-shirts. According to Zondi, "wealthy parties are buying their way into power."[12]

However, the issue is not so much that the ANC had more resources than the IFP but rather that the IFP did not spend its resources as wisely as it ought to have done. Indeed, in the view of some IFP leaders, the party seemed to take its rural Zulu vote for granted despite aggressive door-to-door campaigning by the ANC in rural KZN. As one ANC Member of Parliament (MP) explained, this was done by branches and list candidates in rural areas where the ANC had a foothold, and by national leaders in IFP strongholds.[13] The IFP spent most of its money on rallies rather than on door-to-door campaigning. As intimated earlier, an important reason for this was Buthelezi's national ambition. At an IFP preelection meeting the question was asked whether Buthelezi should consider returning to KZN to secure the premiership. In response the party's national whip Koos van der Merwe denounced the suggestion, declaring Buthelezi "a leader of national and international standing, a president in waiting."[14]

All of this is not to say that the IFP did nothing among its core supporters, but rather that it did not make enough effort of the right kind. Thus, while 50 percent of the rallies addressed by Buthelezi were in KZN, it was only in the last six weeks of the campaign that he conducted a significant number of "meet-and-greet" sessions, and even then these were not with core supporters, but mostly with potential new voters.[15] Other IFP leaders like Lionel Mtshali, Narend Singh, and Musa Zondi addressed rallies and events, almost all of which were in KZN.

However, it was at the local level that most one-on-one contact occurred. According to Albert Mncwango, local structures were central to voter registration, party information dissemination, and getting people to the polls.[16] Every one of the IFP's 5,670 branches was required to meet at least twice a week, and was responsible for finding ways and means to meet its objectives. Some IFP leaders complained of a lack of organizers to assist local branches in these activities, a problem again attributed to insufficient resources.[17] It seems that the ANC put more effort and resources into many rural areas in KZN. Thus, one interviewee spoke of IFP organizers addressing a meeting in an IFP area where ANC activists had already been and facing "challenges from our constituency for the first time." After tackling these, the organizer returned some six weeks later to find that the ANC "had already been back and taken things a bit further."

In the rural areas of KZN traditional leaders have been central to IFP efforts in the past, and in 2004 many took part directly in IFP processes. The difference with previous elections was the greater ANC pressure on traditional leaders to play a more politically neutral role and allow access. According to ANC provincial election campaign head Senzo Mchunu, a key part of the ANC strategy was to force access to IFP strongholds where ordinary members could not go by using national leaders like Mbeki, Nqakula, and Zuma.[18] It seems that the awareness of allowing access has spread more broadly among traditional leadership who, in the words of one interviewee, see the ANC as "an anti-traditional cancer" spreading in their areas "but there's little they can do about it."

Perhaps another significant aspect of the campaign worth mentioning was the use of state resources. The premier and several Members of the Executive Council (MECs), including ANC and DA members, decided to advertise the achievements of their departments by placing large adverts prominently featuring their faces in the press and on billboards. In related moves many MECs initiated projects promising great delivery in the weeks preceding the election. The champion here was Narend Singh who, as KwaZulu-Natal MEC of Education, managed to secure excellent coverage for his department's good work, notably a R16 million project in the Ugu municipality. Aptly enough, Singh was the first to complain when the ANC's Mike Mabuyakulu opened a school that his Department of Public Works had built but for which Singh's department had paid!

The Campaign Message

According to Mncwango, the IFP's campaign was conceptualized in late 2003 at the national, provincial, and local levels.[19] Musa Zondi explained that, while tactics to reach voters were different at different levels, the general message of the campaign was the same,[20] portraying the IFP as an inclusive, conservative-liberal alternative to the ANC. There was indeed some diversity in local events. The IFP Youth Brigade hosted a rally at the Westville campus of the University of KwaZulu-Natal, which seemed a hybrid between a charismatic church meeting and a rave. Other rallies, for example, the one in Pietermaritzburg, had a more menacing air with *amabutho* mock fighting and many firearms on display. Despite these differences in style, the campaign message differed only in the extent to which IFP leaders criticized the ANC. Buthelezi conveyed the message in speech after speech, and press conference after press conference. In every instance it was the same. Only the emphasis and order of issues changed in accordance with the audience.[21] Hence, in speaking with business people Buthelezi prioritized economic concerns; with religious leaders he highlighted moral issues; in Indian areas he talked more about corruption; in rural areas he spoke of Zulu history and ANC injustices to the Zulu king and the IFP.

The main problem with the IFP campaign message was that it was tailored to fit potential new voters and not the party's core support. A close look at the style and content of the manifesto and the party's campaign launch on January 18, 2004 in Durban reveals the extent to which the IFP presented itself as an inclusive, conservative-liberal, and powerful alternative to the ANC.

Stylistically, the cover of the manifesto presented Buthelezi as a benign yet accessible grandfatherly figure, welcoming of women and people of all races. This is suggested by him standing head and shoulders above others in the photograph; his protective and inclusive stance in relation to a group of younger women of all races; and his old world yet funky dress style, as revealed by the words, "It's Cool Man," inscribed on his braces.

In addition, the manifesto cover also signals the degree to which the IFP intended to base its national campaign on Buthelezi's person, believing that he was, in the words of one of the IFP's consultants, "a statesman who commanded more respect than the party itself."[22] Many IFP election posters have a picture of Buthelezi in a bow tie, repeating the image of an old-world gentleman.

A moment's reflection reveals how this imagery is precisely the opposite of public perceptions of the IFP as Zulu traditionalist. Indeed the party's concern to distance itself from its Zulu nationalist past was confirmed in the question-and-answer session at the launch of the campaign. When asked "What would you say to those who perceived the IFP as a Zulu party?" Buthelezi's answer was "Who brought you in here?" referring to Suzanne Vos, the party's communications spokesperson, who had ushered us into the room. He cited Suzanne as an example of the many women and people of all races who comprise the IFP. Furthermore, when asked about the Zulu nationalism of the transition years he explained it as the initiative of the king to which he had responded.[23]

The content of the manifesto was summarized in the slogan "Real Development Now." The IFP manifesto identified the five major issues picked up by most parties: HIV/AIDS, corruption, job creation and economic growth, poverty and crime, and foreign policy.[24] It summarized policy proposals in point form, joining these with an overarching depiction of the party as "Caring, Capable and Clean"—the "three C's." In his speech at the launch of the campaign Buthelezi echoed much of this content, criticizing the government's failure to address the major problems of the day, but also framing the IFP as the party with the better policies and leadership to address these issues.[25] In addition, Buthelezi's speech presented the IFP's policies in typically conservative terms as based on common sense and as being more realistic than the left-leaning views of the ANC: "At heart, I fear the ANC remains committed to socialist interventionism . . . [Whereas we believe in] a hand up, not a hand down." Notably, neither the manifesto nor Buthelezi's speech referred to the Coalition for Change with the DA, and when prompted on the issue by a journalist, Buthelezi's response was sparse. However, at the rally after the press conference, Buthelezi presented the Coalition for Change as an initiative of the IFP, intended to provide voters with a choice between two possible "governments of the future."[26] Not once was the DA mentioned.

The obvious problem with the IFP campaign message was that it was not directed enough at the party's core supporters, many of whom are the poorest of the poor and concerned with how government can help in the day-to-day struggle for a better quality of life. The IFP campaign did not really target this section of the electorate despite the fact that poverty in the rural areas remains high, and despite greater ANC access to these areas. According to one source, the IFP also failed to exploit issues on which the ANC was weak like floor-crossing legislation, the Zuma corruption scandal, and even HIV/AIDS.

Perhaps the IFP's focus on potential voters would have been excusable had the campaign been more effective. However, it was not. Relying on Buthelezi's alleged "statesman" appeal to opposition voters was, in my view, a miscalculation. Certainly, Buthelezi used to enjoy significant standing among both black and white South Africans but this has waned significantly due to the IFP's unremarkable record in government, and perhaps most important, due to Buthelezi's often truculent public behavior during the negotiation years. Moreover, there is little that stood out in the IFP message either in terms of issues or policy suggestions. The party has neither developed a national profile through policy development nor has it developed a significant number of quality leaders. In this regard, Premier Lionel Mtshali was a distinct liability, described by one IFP source as "not enjoyed anywhere."

Finally, the IFP failed to get its message of an inclusive, conservative-liberal party across. Not only did the party have insufficient resources to run a truly nationwide poster campaign, it also received only limited coverage in the national media. And when it did, the coverage was often on the issue of violence. This was no accident. Following Mbeki's comments about the state's enforcement of a free and fair election at the ANC launch, the ANC in KZN followed up thick and fast with repeated press releases. To be fair, many of these were in response to actual incidents, not least the harassment and blockages that Mbeki experienced on his two trips around KZN, and the incident Jacob Zuma experienced at the Dalton hostel on the Witwatersrand. The point is not that there was no intimidation, but rather that the ANC was determined to make as much mileage as it could out of the incidents that did occur. In response, IFP leadership, especially Buthelezi and Zondi, repeatedly affirmed peace and urged calm. After a while the IFP stopped engaging with the ANC over violence, partly because the situation calmed down as the election approached, and partly because the party realized that it was playing into the ANC's hands. Indeed, many reports in the media reinforced the association between the IFP and violence. A good example was the TV coverage of the electoral code of conduct. Although signed by all parties contesting the election, SABC and ETV news broadcasts singled out Buthelezi's signing and comments as significant.

Campaign Allies

If the focus and message of much of the IFP's campaign in 2004 was inadequately designed and often reactive, then at least the Coalition for Change offered a positive element. Indeed, the coalition, although primarily initiated by the DA, dovetailed with IFP attempts to forge public links with parties and organizations rooted in opposition voters. The first event along these lines was the defection of the KZN New National Party (NNP) youth leaders to the IFP on January16. This was less a boon for the IFP than it might appear, as the individuals involved had defected from the IFP to the NNP in the first place. Relations with other organizations followed quickly. Between January and April 2004, Buthelezi addressed the Ethiopian Catholic Church in Zion and the Divine Life Society. He met the moderator of the Dutch Reformed Church, and signed an accord with Solidarity.[27] The IFP also secured various agreements with other political parties including the Alliance for Democracy and Prosperity (ADP)[28] and the Freedom Alliance (FA), but the most important alliance was the Coalition for Change with the DA.

Formally constituted in September 2003 but dating back to agreements in December 2002,[29] the Coalition for Change was based on an agreement between the DA and IFP to govern together wherever possible, exchange and share resources to develop policy, deepen democracy, cooperate in government "even where one party would not need . . . the other," and campaign jointly to advance the coalition.[30] However, there seems little doubt that the Coalition for Change was much more the DA's initiative than the IFP's. For one thing, the idea stemmed from the new DA strategy of projecting itself as a party capable of challenging the ANC for power. For another, the ANC had distanced itself from the IFP after ten years of coalition government at both national and provincial level. For the first time since 1976 the IFP ran a real risk of not being in government in KZN and this is what the coalition seemed to be able to prevent.

In addition to providing an alternative route to power, the coalition had the benefit of strengthening the IFP's hand for possible postelection negotiations with the ANC in KZN. The coalition also proved to be the most significant way the IFP attracted national media attention. Through the promise of a potential "future government," the coalition offered the

IFP a way to affirm its status as a national player. Lastly, the coalition helped present the IFP as a party friendly to opposition voters and not just for Zulu traditionalists.

However, the coalition also had its drawbacks. The very existence of the coalition implied recognition that, nationally, the IFP could not take on the ANC by itself. More important, the media portrayed the IFP as a junior partner to the DA not least by talking of Tony Leon as the "official leader of the opposition." This could only boost the DA at the expense of the IFP and help shift opposition support from the IFP to the DA. The coalition possibly also removed grounds for anti-ANC voters in KZN to support the IFP. A vote for the DA would count just as much as a vote for the IFP in keeping the ANC out of power. Lastly, there was evidence that many rural voters accidentally spoilt their ballots by voting for both parties on the same ballot sheet.[31]

The Aftermath

On April 17, 2004, the national and provincial elections ended when the Independent Electoral Commission (IEC) declared them free and fair. The IFP remained the third largest party in South Africa with just over one million votes and 6.97 percent of the national ballot. However, as table 8.1 illustrates, the 2004 election continued the IFP's downward trend in support since 1994. The party has lost 3.57 percent of its support over the last decade, nearly 1 million votes or half of its 1994 backing. This means that the IFP now has just twenty-eight seats in the National Assembly, fifteen down from the forty-three of 1994. A similar story is evident in KZN, as reflected in table 8.2. This is not surprising given that the province supplied 88.56 percent of the IFP's national support. Since 1994, the IFP has dropped 13.5 percent of its support in KZN, losing 834,803 votes provincially. This brings the party's number of seats in the provincial legislature down from a majority of forty-one

Table 8.1   IFP support in 1994, 1999, and 2004 national elections

Party	1994 national votes	1994 national %	Seats	1999 national votes	1999 national %	Seats	2004 national votes	Seats	2004 national %
IFP	2,058,294	10.54	43	1,371,477	8.58	34	1,088,664	28	6.97

Source: Independent Electoral Commission of South Africa.

Table 8.2 Party support in KwaZulu-Natal: 1994, 1999, and 2004 provincial elections

Party	Votes			Percentage			Seats		
	1994	**1999**	**2004**	**1994**	**1999**	**2004**	**1994**	**1999**	**2004**
ACDP	24,690	53,745	48,892	0.49	0.67	1.78	1	1	2
ANC	1,181,118	1,167,094	1,287,823	32.23	39.38	46.98	26	32	38
DP/DA	78,910	241,779	228,857	2.15	8.16	8.35	2	7	7
IFP	1,844,070	1,241,522	1,009,267	50.32	41.9	36.82	41	34	30
MF	48,951	86,770	71,540	1.34	2.93	2.61	1	2	2
NNP	410,710	97,077	14,218	11.21	3.28	0.52	9	3	0
PAC	26,601	7,654	5,118	0.73	0.26	0.19	1	0	0
UDM	–	34,586	20,546	–	1.17	0.75	–	1	1
Total seats							81	80	80
Valid votes	3,664,324	2,963,358	2,741,265						
Spoilt	39,369	46,141	41,300						
Total ballot	3,703,693	3,009,499	2,782,565						
Registered	4,585,091	3,443,978	3,763,406						
% poll				80.78	87.38	72.84			
Votes per seat	44,687	36,585	34,782						

Source: Independent Electoral Commission of South Africa.

in 1994 to just thirty. The IFP is now the second largest party in the province behind the ANC.

The political consequences of the 2004 election were profound for the IFP. For the first time in its existence it found itself out of power in the province of KZN and thus with a radically reduced chance of access to national power. In this context the party publicly threatened to take the IEC to court over alleged election irregularities in KZN. The IFP accused the IEC of declaring the elections free and fair before it had responded to forty-two complaints, most centrally the concern raised over some 371,742 voters who had voted outside of the voting district in which they were registered. Although legal in terms of section 24(a) of the Electoral Act (an amendment passed in 2003 that allowed voters cast ballots outside their home districts), the IFP alleged that many of these voters had been bussed in by the ANC from the Eastern Cape, or illegally registered using IEC registration stickers wrongfully obtained by ANC members.[32]

Some observers characterized this move as an attempt to hold the election result to ransom and thus force accommodation by the ANC. Perhaps it was, as the IFP dropped the case "in the interests of national unity," after the various positions in national and provincial government were allocated. However, there was also genuine outrage at what was perceived as ANC cheating. On its part, the IEC in KZN denied any wrongdoing and argued that the numbers of section 24(a) voters were similar to other provinces. At the same time, the IEC did suggest that the amendment in question be revisited as it created significant logistical problems.[33]

Postelection conflict did not end there. Without a clear majority in KZN, the ANC was able to garner enough support from the UDM, ACDP, and MF to elect 'Sbu Ndebele as the new provincial premier. This left the IFP's access to power at both national and provincial level in the hands of the ANC. At national level, Thabo Mbeki offered the positions of deputy public works minister and deputy sports minister to the IFP's Musa Zondi and Vincent Ngema respectively. In KZN, 'Sbu Ndebele intended to appoint three IFP members in his executive committee. In both cases, the IFP equivocated. With regard to the cabinet positions, the IFP appealed to the president to delay the swearing-in of cabinet members until the party could discuss whether it wanted to go into government with the ANC or remain in opposition. According to one source, however, the real issue was that the IFP elite did not like the candidates Mbeki and Ndebele had chosen as they were "too compliant." Frustrated with waiting for the IFP, Mbeki decided to award the positions to others. Shortly thereafter, the IFP entered into negotiations with Ndebele about the KZN posts and reached agreement on the three IFP MECs to be appointed.

Whatever the reasons for the IFP's behavior in the immediate aftermath of the 2004 election, there can be little doubt that the party is in dire straits. A closer look at the results at both the national and provincial levels confirms that the party is not winning new voters, and that it is slowly but steadily losing its core rural support to the ANC.

The first claim is supported by the fact that the ratio between votes for the IFP in KZN and the rest of the country has been remarkably constant since 1994, remaining in a 1.3 percent range between 87.27 percent and 88.56 percent. Combined with the fact that the vast majority of support for the IFP in KZN (and perhaps Gauteng) comes from rural Zulu people and the vast majority of support outside of the province does not, this lack of change shows that the IFP is failing to attract new opposition votes. In fact, the party lost votes in every province other than the Western Cape where it gained a mere 600 more votes than in 1999. Overall the IFP became slightly more dependent on KZN voters in 2004 (by just 1.3 percent) suggesting that the national campaign achieved even less than in 1999.

The second claim is supported by results from KZN where the IFP showed a significant loss of 100,000 votes from rural areas all over the province, but especially in the north coast and south of Durban. Much of this could be attributed to a lower turnout. Had registered voters turned out at 1999 levels, then the IFP would probably have secured about the same number of votes than in 1999. The question, therefore, is why did so many IFP supporters not go out and vote? This question is sharpened by the fact that ANC supporters did turn out. Indeed, the ANC was the only major party to get more votes in KZN in 2004 than in 1999. The fact that outside Durban, IFP losses were greater than ANC gains suggests a failure by the IFP to mobilize its support.

The IFP's failure to mobilize its core support is only one-half of the story of the 2004 election in KZN. The other half is the success of the ANC. The ANC made gains in Durban and across most rural areas. In fact, for the first time the ANC is the majority party south of the Tukela River. Notably, the ANC improved its 1999 provincial result by gaining 120,000 votes, 80,000 or 65 percent of which were from Durban. Ironically for the ANC, the IFP actually also improved its 1999 result in Durban by some 6,000 votes, though not nearly as much as the ANC. The ANC's effort during the registration campaign was a key factor in this increase: 44 percent of all new registrations in KZN took place in Durban.

Conclusion

Overall, the IFP's strategic decision in the 2004 election to push for a national following undoubtedly hurt the party. Not only did the party fail to break through onto the national scene as a viable alternative to the ANC, but in attempting this route, the party also wound up losing support in its core areas and among core constituents. Therefore, the campaign forces the question of tactics and strategy: should the IFP continue to focus on the attempt to build a national base, or return to a strategy of regionally based mobilization? From the perspective of the party, it is clear that the leadership preferred the first option. In the 2004 election, the IFP invested a disproportionate amount of resources in a national campaign aimed at potential new voters instead of first consolidating its core support in KZN. Yet in pursuing this strategy, the party failed to pursue tactics and put forth messages best suited for its core supporters. Given the ANC's superior resources and better tactics, the IFP found itself perpetually on the defensive.

Furthermore, the party was unable to rely as much as it had in the past on traditional support and old tactics of exclusion and coercion, not least because the ANC explicitly campaigned around these. In addition, the national campaign did not work very well. The party suffered from a significant lack of national profile and failed to sell a distinctive set of issues and policies. It relied on Buthelezi's person and the Coalition for Change with the DA to win over new votes. However, the IFP overestimated Buthelezi's appeal and affirmed the DA rather than itself as the key opposition force in South Africa.

In retrospect, the result of the 2004 election was the worst yet for the IFP at both the national level and in KZN. At national level, the party lost opposition voters rather than gained them, and in KZN it shed significant numbers of its core supporters to the ANC. In doing so, the party continued its downward trajectory evident since the 1994 election. This outcome reflects a strategic impasse, which has plagued the IFP's postapartheid politics. On the one hand, the party has moved away from the militant Zulu nationalism of the transition years, not least as this has become increasingly difficult to pursue. On the other hand, its embrace of inclusive conservative-liberalism has proved ineffective. In my view, this is because the internal political culture of the party is not conducive to such politics.

The shortcomings of the IFP's 2004 campaign are rooted in a fundamental malaise, further evidence of which was the often glum attitude of many IFP leaders during the campaign. Although never openly acknowledged, there seemed to be a substantial belief in the inevitability of an ANC victory. This malaise is portentous of the IFP's future. There does not seem to be any way out of the strategic trap the party finds itself in as long as Buthelezi is the party leader. However, as soon as Buthelezi goes—probably before the 2009 election—the party loses its major link to the traditional elite and its core supporters. Trapped between the impossible and the ineffective, the IFP is slowly but surely hemorrhaging to death.

Notes

1. Cheryl Goodenough, "KwaZulu-Natal," *Election Update '99*, no. 15 (Johannesburg: Electoral Institute of South Africa, 1999), 346.

2. For a fuller characterization and history of this relationship see Laurence Piper, *A Minor Miracle: The Mysterious Disappearance Of Zulu Nationalism In Democratic South Africa* (Pietermaritzburg: University of KwaZulu-Natal Press, forthcoming).

3. Laurence Piper, "Nationalism without a Nation: The Rise and Fall of Zulu Nationalism in South Africa's Transition to Democracy, 1975–1999," *Nations and Nationalism* 8, no. 1 (January 2002): 73–94.

4. Laurence Piper and Kerry Hampton, "The Decline of 'Militant Zulu Nationalism': The Sea-Change In IFP Politics After 1994," *Politikon* 25, no. 1 (1998): 81–101.

5. Compare the list of those senior leaders who have left (Sibusiso Bhengu, Oscar Dlomo, Ziba Jiyane, Frank Mdalose, Walter Felgate, Sipo Mzimela, Mike Tarr, Maurice McKenzie, Ben Ngubane, and Peter Miller), with some who have stayed (Gideon Zulu, Celani Mthetwa, David Ntombela, and Thomas Shabalala).

6. Peter Miller, "Don't be Misled on the Capital Issue," *The Witness*, March 19, 2004.

7. *The Witness*, January 11, 2003.

8. Author's interview with Andrew Smith, consultant to IFP national campaign, April 4, 2004, KZN.

9. Interviewed by author on May 27, 2004, KZN.

10. Statistics compiled from IFP election e-mail alerts and media coverage.

11. Smith interview, KZN.

12. Interviewed by author on February 19, 2004, KZN.

13. Author's interview with John Jeffery, parliamentary advisor to Jacob Zuma, May 2, 2004.

14. Anonymous source, interviewed on May 20, 2004.

15. Smith interview.

16. Interviewed on March 19, 2004.

17. Comment by Musa Zondi on SABC 2 coverage of election 2004, April 16, 2004.

18. Interviewed by author on March 24, 2004.

19. Interviewed by author on February 19, 2004.

20. Interviewed by author on February 19, 2004.

21. Author's interview with John Cayser, IFP media directorate, March 6, 2004.

22. Smith interview.

23. Interview with Mangosuthu Buthelezi, IFP President, on January 18, 2004.

24. Accessible at http://www.ifp.org.za/IFP%20Manifesto.htm.

25. Mangosuthu Buthelezi, "Launch of the 2004 IFP Election Campaign Opening Press Conference Speech," Durban, January 18, 2004.

26. Mangosuthu Buthelezi, "Launch of the IFP 2004 Election Campaign and Presentation of the IFP Manifesto Address," T. M. Shabalala Stadium, Lindelani, Durban, January 18, 2004.

27. A mostly white trade union, the accord spelt out a common position on affirmative action. Notably, on March 11 the DA and Nationale Aksie (NA) also signed the document.

28. The ADP is a party based in Limpopo, where the IFP agreed not to contest the provincial ballot if the ADP supported it.

29. "IFP-DA Joint Leadership Retreat Minutes," *The Kingdom*, December 9, 2002.

30. "Joint Statement by the Inkatha Freedom Party and the Democratic Alliance," Vinyard Hotel, Cape Town, September 15, 2003.

31. Author's interview with Penny Tainton, DA provincial organizer, May 10, 2004.

32. Perhaps what was most notable about the number of votes contested by the IFP was that it was exactly enough to gain back a plurality in the provincial poll.

33. "IEC Official Tells of Voting Nightmare," *The Mercury*, April 23, 2004.

CHAPTER NINE

The New National Party: The End of the Road

COLLETTE SCHULZ-HERZENBERG

The 2004 elections signaled the end for the architects of apartheid, the New National Party (NNP). Shortly after South Africa's third democratic elections the NNP's leader, Marthinus van Schalkwyk, announced that the party would disband and merge with its former political enemy, the African National Congress (ANC).[1] This declaration signaled the end of one of South Africa's more controversial political forces, which had been in steady decline since the 1994 elections. As the creator of apartheid, the National Party (NP) had benefited from forty-six years of uninterrupted rule before becoming a negotiating partner in the successful transition to democracy in 1994. In the historic first elections, the NNP (at the time still called the National Party), was able to secure the second position in Parliament, but by the 1999 elections the party won only half the seats it had earned in 1994. Between 1994 and 1999, the party seemed unable to position itself in South African politics. It had entered into and then withdrawn from the Government of National Unity (GNU); renamed itself the NNP; adopted a vaguely articulated "Christian Democratic" platform, and attempted to become a "nonracial" alternative to the ANC. After being reduced to fourth position in the 1999 election, the party further attempted to transform its political persona by entering into a series of alliances to ensure its future. Such efforts proved futile as the 2004 election brought about the rapid decline and eventual demise of the party. Over this ten-year period, the NNP has mirrored the fate of other "white" parties that attracted support by claiming to protect minority economic and cultural interests only to be rapidly deposed of political power during postindependence democratization.[2]

This chapter provides an overview of the NNP's political strategy since 1994. It outlines trends in party support as well as the key characteristics of the NNP's 2004 election campaign. The chapter then examines the party's election results and the events that subsequently signaled the end of the NNP.

The NNP's Strategic Choices

Starting with the decision to leave the GNU in 1996, the NNP's strategic choices have had significant implications for the party's fortunes in postapartheid politics. One of the most critical choices the NNP made was a decision to enter into an alliance with the Democratic Party (DP). The collaboration between the two parties began soon after the 1999 election, in which the ANC became the largest party in the Western Cape. The combined forces of the DP and NNP, however, held a majority and the two parties entered into a coalition government, thus excluding the ANC from power in the province.[3]

After the successful formation of a provincial government in the Western Cape, the DP and NNP wanted to merge their respective parties into one new party, but constitutional obstacles concerning "floor crossing" forced them to remain separate entities at the provincial and national levels and instead establish an alliance.[4] The objectives of the alliance were twofold: to present a challenge to the ANC's electoral dominance and to strengthen opposition politics. When the 2000 local government election lifted the constitutional constraints to merge at the local level, the two parties were able to form a new party: the Democratic Alliance (DA). The DP's Tony Leon became the DA's national leader, and Marthinus van Schalkwyk of the NNP became the deputy leader. The DA contested the local government election but at the national and provincial levels the DP and NNP continued to exist as two separate entities.

The NNP's decision to join forces with the DP backfired in numerous ways. As the stronger party in the alliance, the DP had set the terms of the merger, which led to a struggle for control between the respective leaders.[5] Being compelled to function as separate parties at provincial and national levels exacerbated these tensions. The DP and NNP also had vastly different values and philosophies, which resulted in different opposition styles and ambitions.[6] These issues led to divisions within the new DA along the old NNP-DP lines.

In October 2001, the NNP expressed its discontent by suspending its membership of the DP/NNP alliance and exiting the DA at the local level. The dissolution of the DA left the NNP with several challenges. First, the DP retained the DA name as well as significant numbers of NNP dissidents. Second, although NNP officials had been reluctant to merge their branch organizations into the new DA framework, the DA had effectively absorbed much of what was left of the NNP's grassroots resources, which the party was unable to reclaim. Thus, the NNP had to reestablish its party structures at the local level. Finally, the NNP had already suffered financial setbacks before entering into the DA. After the 1999 election, the party was practically bankrupt, and the merger-split with the DP stretched its meager resources even further.[7]

Shortly after its withdrawal from the DA, the NNP decided to enter into a third experiment in cooperative governance with the ANC. The first had been the NP's participation in the GNU in 1994. As a partner in the GNU the party had been placed in the precarious position of working with the ANC while opposing it.[8] As a result the NP pulled out of the GNU in 1996 with De Klerk citing the impossibility to influence public policy as the main reason, thus signaling to voters that the NP did not believe in its own constructive, cooperative stance. The second experiment occurred during the 1999 campaign when the NNP purported to be a constructive opposition willing to work with the ANC. Yet, the formation of a coalition government with the DP in the Western Cape prevented this goal from being realized. The third experiment began shortly after the breakup of the DA, when a joint ANC/NNP statement announced that the two parties would enter into a "cooperation agreement" at all levels of government.[9] While they maintained separate structures and policy platforms, the agreement emphasized a cooperative system of governance, reconciliation, nation building, and consensus seeking on policy issues as the rationale of the relationship between the two parties.[10]

These shifts and experiments suggest that since 1994 the NNP has struggled with questions of tactics and strategy, mainly revolving around the dilemma of choosing a constructive or more robust opposition stance in relation to the ANC.[11] The new ANC/NNP pact indicated that the NNP, having tested both approaches, had returned to the idea of working with the ANC. Daryl Swanepoel, the NNP secretary general, shed light on the party's rationale when he stated in 2003: "It is now that the GNU has broken down that we realize exactly how important that concept was . . . because polarization has deepened, and minority communities have become more isolated and marginalized."[12]

Whatever the reasons for the change in NNP tactics, the ANC clearly understood the benefits of cooperation. The agreement presented the ANC with an opportunity to consolidate its support in the much-contested Western Cape province and gain control over the provincial government and many local councils. Similarly, the NNP entered into the agreement in order to hold onto provincial power and the premiership in the Western Cape after the breakup of the DA. Both parties anticipated that they would benefit from continued cooperation. The NNP stood a chance of being rewarded by the ANC if it helped to secure a majority in the province after the 2004 election. Opinion polls prior to the election had indicated that no single party would win an overall majority in the Western Cape.[13] Therefore, an ANC/NNP coalition government was an interesting prospect for both parties.

Before the NNP and ANC could reap the benefits of their new agreement, however, constitutional obstacles had to be removed. Local NNP representatives had been elected as DA members and were therefore still officially bound to the DA. For the DA to reconfigure into two separate parties, the Constitution's anti-defection clause had to be revoked to allow local councilors to "cross the floor" to another party. In 2002, national parliament passed the so-called floor-crossing legislation allowing local councilors, as well as provincial representatives and members of the national parliament, to change political parties without losing their seats. After much legal wrangling, and a constitutional amendment to effect the change at all tiers of government, the National Assembly (NA) passed the required changes with a two-thirds majority vote. The support of the NNP was critical in ensuring that the ANC was able to pass the necessary constitutional amendment.[14]

However, the floor-crossing exercise served to further debilitate the NNP. The legislation included a provision that allowed parties to merge between elections. This was regarded by some as a sign that the ANC anticipated to simply absorb the NNP at a later stage, thus embracing the NNP's voting constituency in the Western Cape.[15] At the end of the window period for floor crossing, the NNP had lost representatives to other parties at all three tiers of government. The majority of losses were representatives who were not enthusiastic about returning to the NNP and chose to remain with the DA.

At national level the NNP lost eight representatives, reducing its seats in Parliament from twenty-eight to twenty. These defections included a number of party heavyweights who had formed the backbone of the NNP's parliamentary experience, such as stalwart of the justice committee Sheila Camerer. In the Western Cape, the NNP lost seven representatives,

Table 9.1 Seat allocation in the Western Cape provincial legislature before and after floor crossing

Party	1999 election	Defections	After floor crossing
ANC	18	+4	22
DP/DA	5	+2	7
NNP	17	−7	10
UDM	1	−1	0
ACDP	1	+1	2
New Labour Party	—	+1	1
Total	42	8	42

Source: Idasa, Political Information and Monitoring Service.

reducing its seats in the provincial legislature from seventeen to ten (see table 9.1). Six defectors left the NNP for other parties while one member, Peter Marais, formed a new party. Nevertheless, the ANC/NNP alliance was able to secure enough seats to form a coalition government in the Western Cape.

At the local level the NNP lost 44 percent of the representatives who had originally been with the party before the merger with the DP. Most of these councilors remained with the DA.[16] Despite these losses, NNP returnees tipped the balance in favor of the new ANC/NNP alliance in a number of formerly DA controlled councils and municipalities, such as the Cape Town Unicity.

Trends in Support for the NNP

These events leading up to the 2004 election conspired to diminish the chances of the NNP. Preelection public opinion surveys offer helpful insights into the electoral milieu, showing the extent to which support for the NNP was declining in advance of election day.

Surveys measuring partisan identification and voting intentions pointed to a steady decrease in national support for the NNP, indicating that the party would suffer great electoral losses. A 2003 Afrobarometer survey placed NNP support at just 3 percent of the national vote, a substantial decrease from the 6.87 percent the party had achieved in the 1999 election.[17] In January 2004, an SABC/Markinor survey found that the NNP stood at around 4 percent, which was confirmed in a Markinor survey held in March 2004.[18]

Opinion polls also indicated that the NNP would find it difficult to retain its support in the Western Cape, the party's regional stronghold. In March 2004, the Markinor survey showed that support for the NNP in the Western Cape ranged between 13 to 15 percent, a sharp decrease from the 38.39 percent the party had achieved in the provincial poll in 1999.[19] The 2003 Afrobarometer survey painted an even bleaker picture, forecasting that only 10 percent of voters in the Western Cape would support the NNP.[20]

Overall, the data indicate the NNP's deteriorating reputation among voters, mainly in response to the breakup of the DA, the realignment of the NNP with the ANC, and the ensuing floor-crossing controversy. Continuous shifts in NNP tactics portrayed an inconsistent and often contradictory image to its supporters and made it difficult for the party to forge and present a coherent political identity.

In the Western Cape, coalition bargaining had undermined support for and popular trust in party politics in the province.[21] In addition, floor crossing influenced the balance of power in the province and seemed to cause further signs of voter alienation and disenchantment. Around the time when the breakup of the DA and the realignment of the NNP with the ANC occurred, nearly one-third of voters in the province (32 percent) stated that they would not vote "if an election were held tomorrow."[22] Due to coalition politics and defections, Western Cape voters were faced with an alternation of government between elections. Such a reshuffling of provincial and party leadership posts without an electoral mandate seemed to undermine popular trust in the Western Cape provincial government. In 1995, while the NP was in power, 32 percent of respondents expressed their trust in the provincial government. In 2002, this had declined to 15 percent.[23]

Coalition politics not only undermined trust in the provincial government, it also affected perceptions of the NNP and its leadership. A Markinor survey released just before the election in April 2004 revealed that 54 percent of non-ANC supporters were of the opinion that opposition parties working with the ANC did not deserve their vote.[24] The NNP's approach of constructive cooperation had already proved vastly unpopular during the GNU years, when many of its supporters left for the more aggressive DP.[25] Surveys carried out in 1999 about public perceptions of opposition politics had already indicated a preference for confrontational opposition among minority groups.[26] After the change of party leadership from De Klerk to van Schalkwyk the NNP had lost significant support.[27] The leadership of van Schalkwyk, nicknamed Kortbroek, or "short-pants," due to his lack of political influence and experience, was problematic for the party. In 2004, public perceptions of the NNP leadership were dismal. Marthinus van Schalkwyk scored low in a Markinor preelection survey measuring the popularity of party leaders. On a scale from 0 to 10, respondents gave him an average score of 2.79, which put him in sixth place on the list of party leaders.[28]

In the same survey, a racial breakdown of the popularity scores indicated that van Schalkwyk was relatively unpopular even among the party's traditional constituencies. He fared badly among white voters, who placed other politicians such as Tony Leon (6.44), Patricia de Lille (5.52), Mangosuthu Buthelezi (4.27), and Thabo Mbeki (3.95) before van Schalkwyk (3.77)! Considering that much of the NNP's support in the 1999 election had come from the coloured community, one would have expected van Schalkwyk to fare better among this constituency. Yet, even coloured voters preferred politicians Patricia de Lille (6.82), Thabo Mbeki (5.52), and Tony Leon (5.51) to NNP leader van Schalkwyk (5.42).

In short, preelection trends in support for the NNP indicated that the results of the April election would not favor the party. The NNP's 2004 election campaign must, therefore, be understood against the background of this sharp decline in support and the party's attempts to reposition itself in order to remain a viable political force.

The NNP Election Campaign

The NNP's campaign strategists were undoubtedly aware of the party's declining support as they attempted to position the NNP in such a way as to counteract flailing public confidence as well as fierce competition from the DA. According to party officials, the NNP decided to depart from the issue-driven tactics of previous campaigns and instead promote its cooperative approach to opposition politics in postapartheid South Africa.[29] The party's campaign message centered on the alliance with the ANC and its benefits for minority constituencies. According to the NNP, the route of pragmatic politics would provide a channel into government decision making. The party would employ the "politics of influence" and thereby take up the role of a constructive opposition. The election manifesto, entitled "You Deserve a Fair Share," framed the NNP as the party best positioned to ensure a voice for non-ANC voters in a multiparty government. The NNP hoped that this message would find resonance among voters who were sensitive to feelings of political marginalization.

Campaign Messages

Although their language was more nuanced and less robust than in previous campaigns, NNP messages still pandered to fears of exclusion from mainstream politics and the economy. The NNP projected images of an unstable political terrain and racial polarization, which justified its role as consensus seeker, negotiator, and compromiser. The party drew distinctions between consensual and confrontational politics, claiming that the latter encouraged instability. An element of cynicism informed the central message to the voters. The NNP presented the election as a choice between cooperation with the ANC and confrontation that could lead to political instability, as witnessed in Zimbabwe.[30]

The NNP election slogans encapsulated the underlying theme that the party would provide the key to government and ensure access to a fair share of decision making and state resources. A critical interpretation of the slogans' language suggests an undertone of pessimism and inconsistency. Notions of exclusion, which formed the backbone of the NNP campaign, contradicted the party's call for nation building and compromise. The NNP's earlier statement that "the country does not belong to the ANC alone; it belongs to all that live in it," seemed to suggest that minority communities had become marginalized under an ANC government. Such notions of exclusion were compounded by the NNP's 2004 election manifesto. "You deserve the right to create a future . . . you can only do this by having access to a fair share . . .," suggested that minority groups still struggled to access state resources.

The NNP manifesto, launched in Stellenbosch on February 20, 2004, prioritized policy issues that promised to resonate with the electorate. Surveys had shown that in the run-up to the election voters regarded unemployment and crime, and to a lesser extent poverty and HIV/AIDS, as the most important problems facing the country.[31] Surveys also indicated that crime and unemployment were the two most pressing issues among NNP supporters.[32] Accordingly, the NNP manifesto promised 1 million new jobs by 2008, economic growth of 4 percent, and stringent measures to deal with crime.

The NNP also boasted an ideological shift to the center of the political spectrum.[33] Its overall policy stance, however, showed inconsistencies. Many proposals were incongruous with the new centrist position and clearly designed to appeal to a more conservative minority audience. The NNP advocated, for example, a particularly conservative "no mercy" policy on crime and a return to the death penalty—policies that promised to be popular among voters, but do not reflect a centrist position.

The NNP manifesto also failed to appeal to a racially mixed support base. Despite the NNP's claim that the party was highly representative, it explicitly rejected affirmative action measures and excluded redistributive or empowerment policies. The acknowledgment that the party targeted a "narrow audience" contradicted NNP hopes for a meaningful role as a broadly representative opposition party.

By presenting itself as a new centrist brand of opposition, the NNP attempted to furnish itself with ammunition against its main adversary, the DA. Van Schalkwyk attacked the DA's Westminster style of opposition, stating that it was not appropriate in complicated societies such as South Africa. Van Schalkwyk further accused the DA of pandering to race politics and protecting white interests. The NNP hoped to gain political mileage from right-leaning rhetoric emanating from the DA. NNP poster slogans such as the "DP + Right Wing = DA" hit at the heart of a shift of right-wing support to the DA, although ironically at the expense of the NNP's white conservative constituency.

Campaign Strategy

In the 1994 and 1999 elections, the energies of the NNP were officially directed toward campaigning against the ANC, but in reality the party split its efforts between challenging the ANC and competing with the DP for the same pool of voters.[34] In the 2004 campaign, the NNP spent more time and resources explicitly fighting the DA.

In 1994, the NP campaign had centered on the need for social and economic stability, depicting the ANC as a dangerous left-leaning party.[35] The 1999 campaign also focused on opposing the powerful ANC government but the NNP attempted to distinguish its approach from the DP's robust style of opposition by describing its slogan "Let's get South Africa working" as a "message of hope."[36] For the 2004 election, the NNP and its new partner, the ANC, had established a strategy in which the two parties would run separate campaigns but work together to ensure similar electoral messages, embracing "the spirit of a new patriotism" and "a people-centred government aimed at reaching consensus."[37]

Yet, during the 2004 campaign national ANC leaders chose not to appear publicly with NNP leaders in the Western Cape. The ANC may have calculated that joint public events would not be popular with its supporters, but the lack of a joint public platform undermined the NNP. The party was keen to demonstrate that its partnership with the ANC in the province had worked, providing stability and improving government performance and service delivery. Yet, without any provincial appearances with the ANC and without a common platform, the NNP found it difficult to make these assertions credible.

During the campaign, the ANC was also reluctant to speculate about the political makeup of the Western Cape provincial government after the election. The NNP's future seemed to depend on the party's access to government power via the ANC but several scenarios relegating the NNP to the sidelines could have played themselves out. In the first scenario, the ANC and NNP together would not achieve the majority of votes needed to form a provincial government. Opinion polls deemed this outcome unlikely.[38] Alternatively, the provincial results could give the ANC an overall majority, in which case the party would have little need to form a coalition with the NNP. Finally, NNP support could turn out to be too little to make the party a worthwhile coalition partner. Just before election day, ANC Deputy Secretary General Sankie Mthembi-Mahanyele stated: "If the NNP is decimated at the polls it will mean it no longer exists and there can be no partnership."[39] Given these uncertainties, the ANC chose not to commit itself to any course of action. This decision made sense from the perspective of the ANC, but also signaled that the cooperation agreement might not be decisive in the process of government formation. This further undermined the NNP's ability to convince voters of the merits of its partnership with the ANC.

The ANC's "wait and see" approach clearly damaged the NNP's poster campaign promising "Marthinus for Premier." After President Mbeki publicly endorsed Ebrahim Rasool as the future Western Cape premier and then retracted the endorsement in March 2004, the ANC remained silent on the issue. But during the last week of electioneering the ANC stated that if it were to win 42 percent and the NNP 10 percent, it would prove difficult to justify giving the premiership to the NNP.[40] This served to further undermine the NNP's campaign strategy, which hinged on the party retaining the position of premier.

Campaign Methods and Target Audiences

According to NNP officials, the NNP campaign was primarily aimed at non-ANC voters. The party targeted minority groups, in particular Afrikaans white and working-class coloured communities. The NNP believed that a large number of South Africans potentially favored a cooperative approach to opposition politics.[41]

However, the NNP message of constructive opposition could not be expected to hold much appeal. Pro-ANC voters had little reason to vote for the NNP because they could simply vote for the ruling party.

Similarly, voters opposed to the ANC had no incentive to vote for the NNP since the party had stated before the election that it would work with the ANC. Furthermore, increasing support for the DA indicated that opposition voters favored a confrontational and robust style over an inclusive approach reaching across a variety of communities. Research on the 1999 election had already shown that parties embarking on "inclusive" campaigns were punished at the polls.[42]

In the 1994 and 1999 elections, "the coloured vote" had taken on special significance for the NNP as it became the pivotal factor in the party's electoral performance. In 2004, the NNP's fortunes at the polls again depended on winning the hearts and minds of the working-class coloured community, especially since the party's white support had been steadily declining. To shore up coloured support, the NNP held public meetings in Hanover Park, Mitchells Plain, and Manenberg, focusing on policy issues such as health, education, crime, and social service delivery.

Although it claimed to be a highly representative party, NNP campaigning in African areas was limited to poster and leaflet drops.[43] In a halfhearted attempt to woo African voters, the NNP released a party document highlighting a survey from the Human Sciences Research Council (HSRC), which indicated that the NNP was the only major party with a mixed support base. Yet, the survey also showed that the NNP's diversity resulted mainly from its coloured constituency, which made up more than 40 percent of the party's support base.[44] Compared to its branch structures in traditionally coloured areas in the Western Cape, the NNP had very little presence in black communities. The Indian population received far less attention from the party in 2004 than in the previous elections. Although the NNP had won 60 percent of the Indian vote in KwaZulu-Natal (KZN) in 1994, the Minority Front, DP, and ANC had since made inroads into this community.[45]

The NNP utilized a variety of methods to reach its target audiences, including paid advertisements and press statements, public meetings and poster campaigns. The party made use of radio advertising, selecting stations that aimed at particular audiences. The NNP also placed posters, distributed leaflets and flyers, and paid for advertisements in newspapers, again choosing to cover the areas of targeted communities.[46] Over 300,000 NNP posters were distributed countrywide, with each province deciding on the placement and language of the posters. The party also tried to make use of the national media, through daily press releases as well as speeches and statements by the NNP leadership.[47] At the grassroots level, party leaders were deployed to make various public appearances and attend meetings with communities and interest groups. The NNP used internal newsletters to keep party structures informed, while direct contact with voters was promoted through the Campaign Bus, street and telephone canvassing, and door-to-door campaigning.

The predictions of very low national support for the NNP probably helped to steer the party's campaign efforts toward its last stronghold, the Western Cape. The NNP held two large campaign events per week, one in the Western Cape and one nationally. The largest event was the NNP Federal Congress and launch of its election manifesto, held in Stellenbosch in February 2004. NNP rallies were also held in KZN and Gauteng to ensure that the party's message would reach a national audience. The NNP further attempted to maintain a national presence by organizing weekly appearances of its leadership throughout the country. Marthinus van Schalkwyk embarked on a national campaign trail. His visits included meetings with community workers in Uitenhage to discuss housing issues and poverty alleviation; visiting an informal market in Chatsworth in KZN; visiting a poor coloured community in Westbury, Johannesburg to discuss crime; and meetings with farming communities in the Free State and Northern Cape.

In the final weeks before the election the NNP played its trump card: former president Willem de Klerk. De Klerk's leadership skills and role in the negotiation process had clearly attracted voters in previous elections. In the run-up to the 2004 election, de Klerk praised the new ANC/NNP pact stating that there was a need for cooperative governance to counteract a "pattern of ethnic reaction" emerging from the DA's "fight back" style of opposition.[48] To attract voters, the NNP boldly used de Klerk's endorsement on its campaign material.

Despite all these efforts, the NNP ran a weak and ambiguous campaign. The party found itself on the horns of a dilemma. Its traditional support bases had responded to negative campaign messages in 1994 and 1999. Since then the party had publicly committed itself to nonracialism and nation building as well as the notion of working within the government. The contradictions in this strategy found expression in the NNP messages, which attempted to balance the old and the new, the negative and the positive. In addition, the NNP attempted to run a dual campaign focusing on the Western Cape while keeping up a national appearance. However, the party had to face the reality that its ability to maintain a national presence had severely weakened since 1994. In the end, the NNP campaign simply spread itself too thinly to be effective.

The NNP's choice to reposition itself and employ the "politics of influence" was also a miscalculation of the interests and concerns of its target audiences. Non-ANC voters, who were looking for a viable opposition to the governing party, did clearly not believe that the NNP could offer this while in collaboration with the ANC. After the election, the NNP leadership admitted that the party's alliance with the ANC had resulted in its dismal performance, but still maintained that a co-governance approach was the best strategy for South Africa.[49]

Another indication of the difficult situation in which the NNP found itself were media reports highlighting the party's inability to repay substantial financial debts to ABSA Bank.[50] In 1994, the NNP's election campaign had been sustained by the white business community and the party's control over state resources (particularly the police and the South African Defense Force, SADF). Without the significant financial support that had sustained the party during the apartheid years, by 2004, the NNP was left unable to muster serious financial backing and reduced to relying on loans that it was eventually unable to settle. The shortage of party funding reflected a lack of public and business confidence in the NNP's ability to influence policy making in the new postapartheid political environment.

The Results

The 2004 election results were catastrophic for the NNP.[51] At the national level, the party lost thirteen of its twenty seats (twenty-one of its twenty-eight seats if one looks at the seat allocation before floor crossing), thus moving from fourth to sixth position and becoming one of the smaller parties in the third democratic parliament. This meant the party won only seven seats in the National Assembly, a decimation compared to the eighty-two seats the party held ten years earlier. Looking at the number of votes, the decline is even starker: the party won 20.39 percent of the national poll in 1994, 6.87 percent in 1999, and just 1.65 percent in 2004. Nationally, the NNP received a total number of 3,983,690 votes in 1994, 1,098,215 in 1999, and 257,824 in 2004. These figures show that in 1999 the party lost 72 percent of its 1994 support. In 2004, the party lost 77 percent of its 1999 support. A comparison of the NNP's results in 1994 and 2004 shows a staggering loss of 94 percent of the party's national support in just one decade.

At the provincial level, what remained of the NNP's electoral presence was concentrated in the Western Cape but even in its last stronghold the party fared badly. With 10.88 percent of the provincial poll, the NNP was no longer the second largest party in the province after the ANC. That position was taken by the DA, which received 27.11 percent of the

Table 9.2 NNP results at provincial level

Province	Vote share (percent)		Seats	
	1999	2004	1999	2004
Eastern Cape	3.22	0.63	2	0
Free State	5.20	0.82	2	0
Gauteng	3.89	0.76	3	0
KwaZulu–Natal	3.28	0.52	3	0
Limpopo	1.70	0.46	1	0
Mpumalanga	2.47	0.46	1	0
Northern Cape	24.17	7.52	8	2
North West	2.29	0.43	1	0
Western Cape	38.39	10.88	17	5

Source: Independent Electoral Commission of South Africa.

votes in the Western Cape. In the Northern Cape, the NNP also moved from second to third place. The party had maintained a strong presence in the province in the 1999 election but showed a sharp decline in 2004. In the Eastern Cape, the NNP moved from fourth to seventh position, becoming practically nonexistent. In KZN, the party was wiped out. In the Free State, the NNP fell from third to seventh position and in Gauteng and the North West, from third to ninth place. In Mpumalanga and Limpopo, the NNP moved from third to eighth position. After the 1999 election, the NNP held seats in all nine provincial legislatures. In the 2004 election, the party only earned representation in two provinces (see table 9.2).

In both 1994 and 1999, the NNP support base had been largely confined to segments of the Indian, coloured, and white populations.[52] The NNP's dismal performance in 2004 highlighted its inability to retain even these constituencies and its failure to broaden its appeal to black communities. Damaging political choices since 1999, including the unpopular cooperation agreement with the ANC, and a poor campaign resulted in a high level of apathy within the NNP support base and led to a significant realignment among opposition voters.

The NNP still received most of its support in the Western Cape, but the province also saw a relatively high level of stay-aways among traditional NNP supporters. Out of the 2,220,283 registered voters in the Western Cape, only 1,621,835 voted. In other words, 73.05 percent of registered voters participated in the election, which made it the lowest poll across all nine provinces. The turnout was particularly low in working-class coloured communities.[53] In contrast, turnout among the

African population was high. A sense of alienation among the youth in the Afrikaans-speaking coloured communities characterized by high unemployment, crime, and substance abuse, seems to have impacted on the levels of voter participation. Whereas in black African areas loyalties to the ANC were strong enough to override issues such as poverty and unemployment, in the coloured communities party identification with the NNP had severely weakened.[54]

In 1994, the NNP's "swart gevaar" campaign found resonance within poor coloured communities where a sense of racial alienation persisted. Ten years on, this sense of marginalization continued. However, the NNP was now seen as not having succeeded in delivering socioeconomic security, despite having been in the provincial government. At the same time, the ANC was perceived to be delivering to the African poor. To some extent, this perception constituted an objective reality since the Western Cape coloured communities did experience significant job losses in the province's clothing and textile industries.[55] The ANC had emphasized the delivery of basic services such as housing, water, and electricity, which, due to the apartheid legacy of uneven development, mainly improved living conditions in black African communities. In short, the material conditions of poor coloured communities did not improve significantly since 1994, which seems to have weakened their support for the NNP.

Another factor that negatively influenced the NNP's electoral performance was the increasingly competitive multiparty environment in the Western Cape. In the traditional NNP stronghold, the 2004 election was highly contested by the NNP, ANC, and DA, as well as the new Independent Democrats (ID). The NNP faced its biggest threat from the DA, which ran an aggressive campaign to consolidate the opposition vote under its banner. The DA strategy was effective in weakening the NNP support base by describing the ANC/NNP alliance as a sellout with slogans such as "The ANC and the NNP are the same" and "You wouldn't vote for the ANC, so why vote NNP?"

Since 1994, and especially over the last five years, an increasingly important threat to the NNP support base has come from the ANC, which tried to remedy its image in the Western Cape. The party revised its campaign style to meet the peculiarities and sensitivities of the province and used provincial ANC leader Ebrahim Rasool's leverage in coloured communities.[56] The ANC was also able to claim responsibility for implementing progressive legislation that has impacted on the lives of the poor in the province. Relative economic stability, the fruits of freedom, and the unyielding ANC approach of nonracialism may have helped a realignment process in the Western Cape in favor of the ANC. The party has attracted the support of middle-class coloured workers who have benefited from the employment equity policies and ideologically associate themselves with newfound democracy.[57] In addition, the ANC has increased its support in the Western Cape's rural areas. This has been attributed to an increase of African migrant workers in these areas and a shift of the NNP's rural coloured support to the ANC.[58]

The introduction of the ID, the new party of Patricia de Lille, further increased party competition and fragmented the vote in the Western Cape. The new party and its charismatic leader found resonance in coloured and white communities. The ID's appeal among women and the youth in particular may have undermined the NNP's efforts to capture both female and young voters. In the past, the NNP had done particularly well among female coloured voters and NNP research showed that the majority of ID supporters were female.[59]

The highly contested multiparty environment served to demonstrate the fallacy of the so-called coloured vote. A preelection Markinor survey found the highest number of uncertain voters among registered voters of minority groups. One in five (21 percent) registered coloured voters and almost a quarter (24 percent) of registered Indian voters were undecided. The percentage of registered white voters was only marginally lower at 18 percent.[60] These data indicated that minority voters, including the coloured section of the electorate, were not predisposed to bloc voting or voting for a certain political party. While 53 percent of Western Cape voters were coloured in 2004, this section of the electorate was indeed more fractured than ever, dividing its support on election day between the ANC, DA, NNP, and ID. This is illustrated by the election results in Mitchell's Plain, formerly a key NNP area, where the vote was now split four ways.[61]

Election results from voting districts in various coloured communities around Cape Town further illustrate this point. In a voting district in Hanover Park, the NNP received 66 percent of the votes in 1999 and 28 percent in 2004, while the DA received 9 percent in 1999 and 35 percent in 2004. The ID obtained 9 percent of the votes in 2004. The turnout in this voting district stood at 60 percent. In another voting district in Athlone the NNP received 55 percent in 1999 and only 17 percent in 2004. The DA obtained 11 percent in 1999 and 29 percent in 2004. The ID received 20 percent of the votes in 2004. The turnout was 60 percent. And in a Mitchell's Plain voting district the NNP received 42 percent in 1999 and 16 percent in 2004, the DA 21 percent in 1999 and 32 percent in 2004, and the ID 21 percent in 2004. Voter turnout was 70 percent.

These examples also illustrate a number of key characteristics of the 2004 election in the Western Cape. First, several parties seriously challenged the NNP in its traditional coloured constituencies. Second, the so-called coloured vote did not exist as a homogenous voting bloc. Third, lower turnout in the coloured communities pointed to growing voter apathy. Together these trends contributed to the dismal performance of the NNP.

The NNP also lost critical support among its traditional constituency of white Afrikaners. The party had hoped that its message of inclusive politics would appeal to a sense of alienation and a loss of power felt particularly among rural audiences within this group. However, the election results did not validate these expectations. White Afrikaners seemed to increasingly support other parties, such as the Freedom Front Plus (FF+), the African Christian Democratic Party (ACDP), and in particular the DA. Two examples from predominantly Afrikaans-speaking-middle-class voting districts demonstrate the shift within the Afrikaner community. In Welgemoed, the NNP received 53 percent and the DA 30 percent of the votes in 1999. In 2004 this pattern of support was more than reversed, with the NNP receiving 24 percent and the DA 58 percent. Similarly, in Bothasig the NNP received 50 percent and the DA 37 percent of the votes in 1999. In 2004, the NNP had shrunk to only 5 percent, while the DA had climbed to 80 percent.

A similar realignment occurred in the English-speaking white suburbs of the Cape Town metro, but here the new ID also made some inroads into the opposition vote. In Plumstead, the NNP received 30 percent of the votes in 1999 but only 5 percent in 2004. The DA received 50 percent in 1999 and 61 percent in 2004, while the ID received 13 percent. In Bergvliet, the NNP received 25 percent in 1999 and 3 percent in 2004. The DA moved from 55 percent to 73 percent, with the ID receiving 10 percent of the votes in 2004.

It is clear that the NNP made no impact among the black African section of the electorate. Ward 38 in the Cape Town metro is a good example as it encompasses six voting districts in the predominantly black African areas of Guguletu, Crossroads, and Nyanga. In ward 38, the NNP received only 40 votes out of a total of 12,378 votes cast, which brought the party to 0.32 percent.

The NNP's massive losses in the 2004 election were in large part due to the party's strategic choices, including its strategy to enter into an alliance with the ANC and appeal to voters on the basis of this cooperative approach. The election results suggest that NNP supporters either misunderstood the strategy of cooperation or rejected it. The NNP lost most of its white and coloured support to the DA's adversarial brand of opposition politics, and failed to win over African voters, which could have compensated for these losses. With its support being decimated the NNP's claim that the party represents minority groups in government becomes almost trivial.

The Aftermath

Did the NNP's substantial loss of support in the 2004 election signal the party's demise? Although NNP leader Van Schalkwyk was awarded by the ANC with a post in the new cabinet, it certainly looks that way. In early August, four months after the election, the NNP announced that it would be taking its cooperation agreement with the ANC a step further. The NNP Federal Council urged all its representatives to become ANC members and to cross the floor to the ANC once the window period for floor crossing reopens in September 2005. The party had decided that it would fight all future elections under the banner of the ANC. Until then, the NNP has to remain in existence so that elected representatives can retain their positions.

The NNP's decision to join the ANC raised criticism from most of the other opposition parties and prompted former president F.W. De Klerk to leave the NNP. And it remains to be seen whether all NNP representatives and, more important, the remaining NNP voters will follow the NNP party leadership in this move. Either way, the NNP seems set to cease its existence in 2005.

But was there a feasible alternative? Could the NNP try to rebuild a shattered support base and prove itself a relevant and effective political force during the second decade of democracy in South Africa? The party would clearly be facing a very difficult future. NNP MPs and local councilors would probably regard their party's electoral performance in the 2004 election as a threat to their livelihoods and be motivated to cross the floor to the ANC or other parties. NNP supporters would probably also defect to other parties in great numbers.

However, the relatively low turnout in the 2004 election did signal an opportunity for the NNP to win back support through skilled campaigning. The 2004 election results also showed that the DA's style of campaigning did not invite overwhelming success in coloured communities, although the DA's aim was to consolidate support in this constituency. In addition, the new ID constitutes an unknown entity and may, in time, present a challenge to the DA, which could be beneficial to the NNP.

The NNP's longer-term prospects would probably have depended to a large extent on how the party would tackle the first challenge of the local government election in 2005. Had the NNP not decided to disband and join the ANC, it would have had to reestablish a niche on the electoral market for itself while working toward genuinely broadening its support base. Building popular support would have depended on the party's ability to define a cohesive agenda that reflects the needs and concerns of its target audiences. In the short term, the NNP's survival would have been dependent on maintaining the ANC-led coalition, yet the long-term problems of this relationship were abundantly clear. Influencing policy while retaining an independent identity that attracts voters would probably be extremely challenging, given the parties' ideological differences and the ANC's ability to dictate the terms of their cooperation.

But the biggest challenge would have been to convince voters that there is a place for consensual opposition in the new South Africa, especially since this message would have come from the former apartheid party. The failure of the GNU and the growing support for robust opposition suggest that such a message of inclusion and cooperation is increasingly unpopular. The NNP has chosen not to face this challenge and to dissolve instead. Thus, the 2004 election marks the end of the road for the former party of apartheid.

Notes

1. The decision to disband was taken by the party leadership at its Federal Council meeting during August 2004.
2. The 1980 elections in Zimbabwe saw Ian Smith's Rhodesian Front (which changed its name to the Republican Front in 1981), campaign on a platform of protecting white economic and cultural interests in a postindependence Zimbabwe. Although it won all twenty seats reserved for whites in the first democratic election it ceased to exist ten years later. See Andrew Reynolds, *Electoral Systems and Democratization in Southern Africa* (New York: Oxford University Press, 1999), 173.
3. For more on the formation of the coalition government, see Lia Nijzink and Sean Jacobs, "Provincial Elections and Government Formation in the Western Cape: The Politics of Polarisation," *Politikon* 27, no. 1 (2000): 37–49, 47.
4. The South African Constitution was amended to remove the anti-defection clause that prohibited MPs from changing parties. A set of legislations was passed that amended the constitution to allow for an individual or group of parliamentarians who constitute 10 % of a particular party to either defect to another party, form a new party, or merge with another party. Floor crossing can only take place during two "window periods" of fifteen days each that occur between elections. Floor crossing is permitted at all three spheres of government, namely national, provincial, and local. For more on floor crossing see Nijzink and Piombo, "Parliament and the Electoral System," this volume.

5. Roger Southall, ed., *Opposition and Democracy in South Africa* (London: Frank Cass, 2001), 3.

6. Tom Lodge, *Bus Stop for Everyone: Politics in South Africa* (Cape Town: David Phillip, 2002), 158.

7. Ibid., 158.

8. Ibid., 64.

9. Ibid., 158.

10. Joint Statement of the ANC and NNP, issued on October 26, 2003 and author's interview with Carol Johnson, Media Director of the New National Party, April 29, 2004.

11. Southall, *Opposition and Democracy*, 2.

12. Excerpt from a speech by Mr. Daryl Swanepoel, NNP secretary general, at a symposium organized by the ANC Youth League at the University of the Western Cape on April 19, 2003.

13. Markdata Opinion Survey, "An Estimate of the Election Outcome: Results of the Latest Markdata Pre-Election Opinion Poll," (Cape Town: April 2004).

14. For a more detailed discussion of this process, see Nijzink and Piombo, "Parliament and the Electoral System," this volume.

15. Lodge, *Bus Stop for Everyone*, 159.

16. Electoral Institute of Southern Africa, "Results at the Close of the Period for Municipal Floor Crossing," (Johannesburg: Electoral Institute of Southern Africa, 2002).

17. Cherrel Africa, Robert Mattes, and Collette Herzenberg, "Political Party Support in South Africa: Trends Since 1994," Afrobarometer Briefing Paper, no. 6 (July 2003).

18. SABC/Markinor Opinion Survey, "Political Party Support And Possible Voter Turnout" (March 18, 2004). Fieldwork for this latest poll in the SABC/Markinor Opinion 2004 series was undertaken from January 29 to February 20, 2004.

19. Ibid.

20. Africa, Mattes, and Herzenberg, "Political Party Support."

21. Ibid.

22. Ibid.

23. Ibid., 10.

24. Markinor Opinion Survey, "Are you an ANC supporter?" (April 12, 2004). The survey results were collected in February 2004, released in April.

25. Hennie Kotzé, "A Consummation Devoutly to be Wished? The Democratic Alliance and Its Potential Constituencies," in *Opposition and Democracy in South Africa*, ed. Roger Southall (London: Frank Cass, 2001),120.

26. Ibid., 132.

27. Willie Breytenbach, "The New National Party," in *Election '99 South Africa: From Mandela to Mbeki*, ed. Andrew Reynolds (Cape Town and New York: David Philip and St Martin's Press, 1999), 120.

28. Markinor Opinion Survey, "Opposition and Leadership" (April 12, 2004). These figures are based on the universe of eligible voters, 18 years and older, who are registered to vote in the election on April 14, 2004.

29. Johnson interview.

30. "Election to Decide if SA Becomes Second Zim," *The Independent Online*, January 26, 2004; accessed at www.iol.co.za.

31. SABC/Markinor, "Government Performance: Expectations and Perceptions" (January 2004).

32. Views of supporters of the ANC, DA, IFP, and NNP (Pretoria and Cape Town: Markinor 2003).

33. Johnson interview.

34. Jessica Piombo, "The New National Party: Sunset for the Architect of Apartheid?" in "Constructing Dominance: Institutions, Cleavages and Parties in Post-Apartheid South Africa, 1994–1999" (Ph.D. dissertation, Department of Political Science, Massachusetts Institute of Technology, 2002).

35. Andrew Reynolds, ed., *Election '94 South Africa: The Campaigns, Results and Future Prospects* (Cape Town: David Phillip, 1994), 56.

36. Tom Lodge, *Consolidating Democracy: South Africa's Second Popular Election* (Johannesburg: Witwatersrand University Press, 2001), 131.

37. Joint Statement of the ANC and NNP issued on October 26, 2003.

38. SABC/Markinor Opinion Survey, "Political Party Support."

39. Drew Forrest, "We are Not the Power-Mongers," *Mail & Guardian*, April 8, 2004, p. 4.

40. Douglas Carew and Willem Steenkamp, "Kortbroek to Get the Boot," *Sunday Argus*, April 11, 2004, p. 1.

41. Johnson interview.

42. Gavin Davis, "Bridges and Bonds: List PR and Campaigning in South Africa," CSSR Working Paper No. 50 (Cape Town: University of Cape Town, October 2003), 97.

43. Johnson interview.

44. "HSRC Survey—NNP Grows/Performs Well," NNP Document: Key Facts No.19, 2003, www.nnp.org.za. The NNP maintain that they have now firmly established themselves as a truly rainbow party and use this report as evidence.

45. Hermann Giliomee, "The National Party's Campaign for a Liberation Election," in *Election '94 South Africa: The Campaigns, Results and Future Prospects*, ed. Andrew Reynolds (London, Cape Town, and New York: James Currey, David Philip, and St. Martin's Press, 1994), 66.

46. Johnson interview.

47. Ibid.

48. Jeremy Michaels, "De Klerk Has High Praise for NNP/ANC Link," *The Star*, February 3, 2004.

49. Source from televised speeches by Marthinus van Schalkwyk on April 15 and 16, 2004.

50. In April 2004 newspaper articles reported that the NNP's account with ABSA Bank was R6-million overdrawn. The bank was reportedly using donations to the party to decrease the overdraft.

51. All election results in this chapter are from the Independent Electoral Commission, http://www.elections.org.za.

52. Willie Breytenbach, "The New National Party," in *Election '99 South Africa: From Mandela to Mbeki*, ed. Andrew Reynolds (Cape Town and New York: David Philip and St. Martin's Press, 1999), 117.

53. Christelle Terreblanche, "Voter Numbers Down as Alienation Takes Hold," *The Sunday Independent*, April 18, 2004, 3.

54. Kotze, "A Consummation," 128.

55. Author's interview with Garth Stracham, African National Congress, MPL Western Cape, April 28, 2004.

56. For an overview of the style of ANC's 1999 election campaign in the Western Cape see Tom Lodge, "The African National Congress," in *Election '99 South Africa: From Mandela to Mbeki*, ed. Andrew Reynolds (Cape Town and New York: David Philip and St. Martin's Press, 1999), 76. Rassool is from the Western Cape and Muslim, so he appeals to a variety of constituencies in the Western Cape.

57. Stracham interview.

58. Ibid.

59. Johnson interview.

60. Markinor Opinion Survey, "Uncertain Voters" (April 12, 2004).

61. Marianne Merton, "ANC Romps Home but Now the Hard Bargaining Begins," *Mail & Guardian*, April 16, 2004, p. 4.

CHAPTER TEN

Struggling to Represent the Left: The Pan Africanist Congress, the Azanian People's Organization, and the Independent Democrats

THABISI HOEANE

South African politics has a rich tradition of leftist political movements. During the struggle against apartheid, the African National Congress (ANC) was the foremost of these movements, though the less prominent Pan Africanist Congress (PAC) was, ideologically speaking, more radical than the ANC. Since 1994, most political parties in South Africa have moved to the center of the political spectrum, leaving the ideological Left wide open. Aside from the South African Communist Party (SACP), which is represented in government due to its alliance with the ANC, the parties that occupy this space barely receive any electoral support. In fact, were it not for the proportional representation system, most of the parties of the Left would not be represented in the National Assembly (NA) at all.

In a political context where large portions of the South African public desire radical change, where socialism appeals to many and a strong communist party exists, why are the leftist parties performing so poorly? The PAC and the Azanian People's Organization (Azapo) were important players in the fight against apartheid, yet they have consistently fared poorly in postapartheid electoral contests. The one new contender on the Left, the Independent Democrats (ID, formed in 2003 by former PAC leader Patricia de Lille), did reasonably well in the 2004 election but has not lived up to preelection predictions that it would emerge as a viable and strong party in South African opposition politics. This chapter is structured around a number of themes and within these discusses the parties in turn, starting with the PAC, followed by Azapo, and then the ID.

This chapter describes how the three parties fared in the 2004 electoral process by analyzing their election campaigns and the election results. The chapter also provides an assessment of the parties' performance. It aims to contribute to a broader understanding of the role and position of black and Left parties in South African electoral politics.

The Campaigns

These parties, the PAC, Azapo, and ID, are parties bound together by their common roots in radical, leftist, and black politics. This section discusses the main features of the parties' election campaigns, specifically addressing their backgrounds, the content of their manifestoes, the voter groups they targeted, the strategies adopted to attract these groups, and the nature of their candidate lists. It also includes a discussion of the parties' prospects through an interpretation of preelection public opinion surveys.[1]

The PAC

The PAC was formed in 1959 after a group of ANC members broke away from the ANC when it adopted the Freedom Charter, accusing the ANC of betraying the African struggle by following a nonracial path. The PAC's most significant contribution to resistance politics of that era were the anti-pass campaigns of the late 1950s that led to the Sharpeville shooting of March 1960, resulting in the banning of the party and ANC. The two organizations were subsequently forced into exile where they embarked on armed struggle.

Through the exile years the PAC was considered one of the major players in the liberation movement, but it was always more disorganized and received less international attention than the ANC. Operating from bases in Zimbabwe, the PAC did not receive the degree of foreign assistance and backing as did the ANC, and as a result was not able to launch covert operations within South Africa in the manner as had the ANC. Thus at the moment of liberation in 1994, the PAC started off with far fewer advantages than the ANC and the Inkatha Freedom Party (IFP).

In the post-1994 era, the small support that the party had been able to mobilize within the country has been further eroded by the PAC's consistently poor (and declining) electoral performance. The PAC's electoral performance has been unimpressive given its liberation credentials, coming in at number six out of the seven opposition parties that came to be represented in the National Assembly (NA). Its poor showing continued in the 1999 elections when it lost over 40 percent of its 1994 support.

The PAC registered to contest the 2004 elections both nationally and in all nine provinces, just as it had done in the 1994 and 1999 elections. In 2004, the PAC was one of ten parties in this category. The PAC launched its election manifesto in Tembisa, a black township on the East Rand, in the province of Gauteng.

The manifesto emphasized how the socioeconomic condition of the black majority had not improved appreciably since 1994 and offered solutions to this problem.[2] It detailed the perceived failures of ANC government policies to address the legacy of apartheid. In a rally to commemorate the PAC's forty-fifth anniversary in Soweto, party President Dr. Motsoko Pheko declared, "Our people are still without the wealth and land they fought for. . . . these people are being told today by the African National Congress government to celebrate ten years of democracy, but there is nothing to commemorate."[3]

The PAC manifesto identified a number of major points around which the party planned to contest the election. In line with its campaign messages in 1994 and 1999, the PAC prioritized land distribution to the black majority in order to achieve redistribution of wealth. In an interview with the *City Press* newspaper, PAC Deputy President Themba Godi asserted that ". . . redistribution of land and wealth continue to remain the party's permanent issues of contention."[4] The PAC also argued that the clause in the constitution, which recognizes the right to private property, must be scrapped because it legitimized racial economic inequality and was the main obstacle to land reform.[5]

The second priority listed by the party was the provision of free education from primary school to the tertiary level. The party regarded unemployment as another main concern and called for the establishment of an unemployment fund to disburse R500 per month to every unemployed South African. In addition, the PAC called for the increase of the old-age pension grant from R600 to R1,000 per month, and said that this grant should be extended to the disabled.

On health issues, the PAC focused specifically on HIV/AIDS, calling for free treatment and provision of drugs to HIV-positive pregnant women, to reduce the chances of infecting their offspring, as well as to other South Africans living with the condition.

On the economic front, the PAC called for support to emerging black businesspeople and farmers in the form of state subsidies. The party also mentioned corruption as one of the most serious problems facing the country that had to be dealt with decisively. In addition, the PAC came out against the privatization of state assets especially in sectors that are responsible for the provision of basic services such as water and electricity.

The manifesto called for scrapping the country's apartheid debt and increasing the compensation for all victims of apartheid abuses. It argued that the R30,000 compensation for victims identified by the Truth and Reconciliation Commission (TRC) was inadequate, adding that the number of apartheid victims was more than the 22,000 named in the final TRC report.[6]

In terms of target groups, the manifesto specifically mentioned policies with regard to women, workers, the youth, rural communities, pensioners, and the disabled. To reach these groups, the PAC campaigned in black residential areas such as townships and squatter camps in urban areas.

The PAC's election campaign was mostly focused in the northern and central provinces of the country: Gauteng, Limpopo (formerly the Northern Province), Mpumalanga, North West, and the Free State. It did not have a particularly strong focus on the southern and eastern provinces of KwaZulu-Natal (KZN), Eastern Cape, Northern Cape and Western Cape. The campaign was especially notable for its relative neglect of the Eastern Cape considering that the party's origins lie in this province and it won representation in the provincial legislature in 1994 and 1999. PAC President Dr. Pheko did not make a single visit to the province during the election campaign.

The party utilized conventional methods of campaigning including posters and political rallies by its prominent leaders, as well as advertisements on radio and in newspapers, but the latter were almost negligible. The party did not make much use of new means of technology in spreading its campaign message. Its Web site was poorly managed, containing outdated information, and was only revamped in the run-up to the election. Even then, it did not contain much information on the election. Although the site had a 2004 election page, the only information available was the election manifesto.

One notable feature of the 2004 electoral campaign was the fact that several political parties forged alliances and the PAC was no exception. It formed pacts with two former Bantustan political parties, the Dikwankwetla Party of South Africa (DPSA), that had ruled the former Qwaqwa, and the Sindawonde Progressive Party (SPP) that was active in the former KwaNdebele.[7] The basis of these agreements was that, as these parties were not contesting the election nationally, their supporters would give the PAC their vote on the national ballot.[8]

The PAC's candidate list was dominated by black candidates. This was not surprising given the party's Africanist views. The list included a few coloured and Indian candidates and no white candidates. The only white candidate of the party, Costa Gazi, was removed from the party list, after it was discovered that he was also on the list of the Socialist Party of Azania (SOPA).[9] The dominance of black candidates is incongruous with the PAC's view that it has impeccable nonracial credentials, a fact asserted by party President Dr. Pheko, who stated in a newspaper interview, "we have been nonracial from day one."[10]

With regard to gender representation, the PAC was doing well compared to other political parties. With 33 percent of its candidates being women, the party found itself in fourth position, after the SOPA (39 percent), the United Christian Democratic Party (UCDP) (38 percent) and the ANC (35 percent).[11]

Electoral forecasts consistently indicated that the PAC was not going to do well in the 2004 election. An omnibus survey, carried out by the South African Broadcasting Corporation (SABC) and Markinor, tracing the likely support of each party in November 2002, April/May 2003 and October/November 2003, had the PAC at 1 percent support during all these phases.[12] The South African Social Attitudes Survey (Sasas) of the Human Sciences Research Council (HSRC), released in November 2003, indicated that the party would win 0.51 percent of the vote.[13]

Measuring the level of trust in party leaders, the PAC President Dr. Pheko was rated last in a Markinor survey released in April 2004, two days before the elections. On a scale from 0 to 10 South Africans gave him an average score of 1.90. Notably, PAC supporters trusted the leader of the ANC, Thabo Mbeki, more than their own president. Among PAC supporters, Mbeki scored an average of 6.72, while Pheko's average was 6.29.[14] The PAC was very skeptical of such findings, arguing that surveys were biased in favor of the ANC and that the PAC was going strong, estimating its support between 12 and 20 percent.[15]

Azapo

Azapo was formed in 1977 after the banning of major black consciousness (BC) organizations. Azapo sought to continue to uphold the BC ideology, which was dominant in internal opposition politics to apartheid in the late 1970s. It asserted the centrality of black

South Africans in the struggle against apartheid. Thus, Azapo's political orientation largely echoed that of the PAC but was fundamentally different in that it defined black people without reference to colour but mainly in political terms (i.e., meaning all oppressed peoples in South Africa), therefore, including coloureds and Indians in this definition. Azapo differed from earlier BC organizations as it explicitly embraced radical Left ideas, arguing for a socialist South Africa. Unlike its predecessors such as the South African Students' Organisation (SASO), it identified the black working class as the most potent force to provide a viable and qualitative alternative to apartheid.

It is not possible to put the party's 2004 election campaign into a ten-year perspective, because Azapo had boycotted the 1994 elections. At the time, the party argued that the political settlement that resulted in the formation of the Government of National Unity (GNU) was flawed due to its power sharing nature. The party joined the electoral process in 1999, but only managed to win one seat in the NA, indicating its weakness as an effective opposition party in the new dispensation.

Azapo's campaign message in 2004 was crafted on the premise that ten years into South Africa's democracy most citizens had yet to enjoy the economic benefits that were brought about by political freedom. In its preface to the election manifesto, Azapo President Mosibudi Mangena cited the inequitable racial distribution of wealth as the main problem facing South Africa since 1994. The party specifically identified the black majority as suffering the brunt of the inequality and argued that only with changed economic conditions of this community could South Africa truly be regarded as a democracy.

Azapo's manifesto summarized the party's demands by listing policy areas that needed critical solutions such as education, health, employment, housing, crime, social security, infrastructure, rural development, land distribution, and corruption. Azapo cited the reorganization of the state machinery in order to deliver more resources to the black majority as its first priority. The most significant way in which the party planned to do this was through the abolishment of provincial governments that, according to Azapo, were a burden on national resources.

Azapo's second priority was education. The party demanded free and compulsory education, called for education to be open to all South Africans and emphasized the centrality of government in this area. Another demand listed in the election manifesto was the creation of an efficient health system. The party specifically emphasized the problems of HIV/AIDS and called for special grants to be paid to people living with the condition, especially women.

With regard to economic policy, the party stressed the centrality of government in controlling the economy, adding that privatization of state enterprises should be scrapped. Azapo specifically called for the boosting of small and medium enterprises through the creation of a ministry of small businesses in order to assist black businesspeople. In a newspaper interview, Mangena said this was imperative as black businesses like spaza shops and hawkers generated about R32 billion per year.[16] In keeping with its roots in the Black Consciousness Movement, Azapo urged black communities to patronize black businesses as opposed to white-owned concerns.[17]

The party also called for "meaningful black economic control and affirmative action" a clear critique of ANC policies, which, according to Azapo, favored a small black elite at the expense of the poor. In addition, the manifesto called for land redistribution to the black majority and emphasized the need for an independent labor movement, a criticism aimed at the Congress of South African Trade Unions (Cosatu), the country's main labor federation that is allied with the ANC.

On the cultural front, Azapo encouraged the promotion of African values, specifically proposing that the government recognize black traditional leaders.

In line with its overall focus on the black majority, Azapo's electoral campaign specifically targeted the sections in this group the party identified as being most vulnerable: women, the youth, and the disabled.

Azapo's election campaign was mainly focused in the northern provinces of Limpopo, Gauteng, North West, and Mpumalanga. This was significantly indicated by the fact that the party held its manifesto launch in Mankweng, a black township near the city of Polokwane in the Limpopo province. Azapo focused scant attention on the other provinces, especially the seriously contested KZN and Western Cape. In line with the specific policies it advocated in its election manifesto, the campaign targeted mainly black residential areas.

Azapo utilized the usual campaign methods of rallies, posters, and door-to-door campaigning, relying especially on its senior leadership in the campaign. The party made very few visible media efforts in terms of advertisements on the radio and in the print media, possibly due to its limited election budget.[18]

Azapo did not make use of modern technology like cell phones and the Internet in its campaign. The party's website was poorly maintained and seldom updated. It was revamped in the run up to the election, but did not contain much information on Azapo's electoral activities. Under the link "Election Information," there were only two available pages, including an abridged version of the party's manifesto. The site also had a link called "Vote Online" but when this was accessed, it contained a message noting "Check Back in Future for Azapo Polls."

Azapo's national and provincial party lists were dominated by black candidates. The lists included a few coloured and Indian but no white candidates, despite the party's policy decision in 2002 to open membership to whites.[19] Azapo had 22 percent women candidates and thus a lower gender representation than the PAC.

Azapo did not follow the trend of forming alliances with other political parties. The party did not enter into any alliances to contest the 2004 election. The reason could have been that past efforts by black parties such as Azapo, Sopa, and the PAC to form an electoral alliance did not work.

Looking at the party's electoral prospects, the SABC/Markinor preelection survey found Azapo in the group of parties with less than 1 percent support among the electorate. The HSRC/Sasas survey indicated 0.49 percent of support for the party in November 2003. In terms of trust in party leadership, the Azapo President Mosibudi Mangena, did not even feature on Markinor's list of trusted leaders.

The ID

The ID—the first party to be led by a woman in South Africa—was formed by former PAC member, Patricia de Lille. Regarded as the most vocal and visible of the three PAC Members of Parliament, she defected from the party in March 2003, during the first window period for floor crossing. Rather than defecting to an existing political party, she broke with the current alignment of party politics and created a new organization, dedicated to represent workers, leftists, and those unhappy with the current selection of political organizations.

The main message contained in the ID's election manifesto was that the party wanted to provide an alternative to both the ANC government and the existing opposition. The ID promised to address the policy issues on which it thought the ANC had failed. Its manifesto specifically focused on HIV/AIDS, corruption, accountability in government, and the protection of vulnerable groups in society such as women and children. The document also detailed a number of "divides" that the party identified as obstacles for the creation of a democratic and united society: the cultural, rural/urban, economic, inequality, human security, HIV/AIDS, educational, and global divides.

The ID's election manifesto was further divided into a number of sections that elaborated the party's guiding principles. The first two sections covered the party's vision, which can be summarized as offering a viable alternative to the policies of the ruling ANC by being a strong and principled opposition. The other sections addressed topics such as the economy, job creation, and poverty eradication, HIV/AIDS, crime, corruption, arts and culture, environmental policy, and social development.

The IDs campaign largely targeted the most vulnerable groups in society: women, children, and the youth. The party promised tough action against physical and emotional abuse of women and children, coupled with effective legal measures. With regard to the youth, the ID emphasized the need to deal with problems they face in the modern world such as unemployment, crime, and HIV/AIDS. The party showed its commitment to confront the HIV/AIDS pandemic when its national leadership led by de Lille took a public HIV test at Baragwanath Hospital in Soweto and challenged other political leaders to do the same.[20] In an effort to destigmatize the condition, the ID also revealed that it had six active members that were HIV-positive and that one of these was in the top ten of its national list.[21]

The ID ran one of the most sophisticated and technologically advanced election campaigns of 2004. In addition to the traditional methods of campaign rallies and media advertisements (both radio and print), the ID concentrated on novel technological methods such as connecting potential voters to the party through sending of SMS messages and placing advertisements in classified sections of newspapers.

The ID website was one of the most impressive party sites, with colorful graphics, an array of links to information on the elections, and a prominently displayed party leader de Lille. The website included a digital democracy forum with a (working) link to e-mail de Lille. The link to the party's election manifesto was prominently displayed on the front page, with brief information indicating what each part of the manifesto dealt with. There was also a link to an Election 2004 page, and the Young Independent Democrats page. The Young ID page was dominated by graphics of de Lille and various ways to contact her, including SMS and e-mail. The Election 2004 page contained links to the national and provincial lists and information on why it was important to vote and how to vote, which was clearly targeted at young, first-time voters.

The ID campaigned in all nine provinces of the country, although much of its campaign was concentrated in Gauteng, the Western Cape, and Northern Cape. The party launched its manifesto in Newtown, a newly revamped part of downtown Johannesburg that is popular with the youth for its shopping malls and cultural facilities. The ID campaign message was largely carried by de Lille, who visited a cross section of residential areas of all racial groups, but mainly concentrated on the working class and poor coloured communities of the Western Cape and Northern Cape. Like Azapo, the ID did not enter into alliances with any party and in fact heavily criticized alliance politics, which it interpreted as not working for the country.[22]

In terms of gender representation, the ID did reasonably well with 30 percent female candidates on its party lists. This is perhaps lower than expected, considering the party's female founder and leader and the fact that the election manifesto strongly stressed the need to address women's issues. However, the ID *is* the first party led by a woman to be represented in the NA.

The ID projected itself as a party with the most impeccable nonracial credentials and indeed had a racial mix of coloured, Indian, white, and black candidates on its lists. Number six on the national list was, a South African of Chinese origin, Yi-Zhu Wang, who made history by being the first person from this community to become a Member of Parliament (MP).

Because the ID was formed in March 2003, the SABC/Markinor partnership did not include the party in its surveys conducted in November 2002 and April/May 2003. The October/November 2003 survey indicated 1 percent support for the ID, while the HSRC/Sasas survey reported that the ID would win 0.44 percent of the national vote. These preelection forecasts seem to have been slightly off the mark as the ID managed to get 1.73 percent of the national poll. This result was, however, far below the 10 percent that the ID had forecast for itself.[23]

In terms of popularity and trust, ID leader de Lille scored high in the Markinor survey, released on April 12, 2004, just two days before the election. The survey indicated that de Lille was the most popular opposition leader. The ID leader was also number four on the list of political leaders most trusted by the electorate.

The Results

This section outlines the national and provincial performance of each party in the 2004 election and provides the basis for an assessment of their overall performance in the following section. Unless otherwise noted, all election results presented here were obtained from the Independent Electoral Commission (IEC) of South Africa.

The PAC

The PAC's performance in 2004 indicated a general trait that has defined the party's performance in all postapartheid electoral contests—the weakness of the PAC despite its stature as a major liberation movement. In 1994, the PAC managed to win only 1.25 percent of the national vote, becoming the fifth largest opposition party, with five members in the NA. Provincially, it won representation in only three legislatures: the Eastern Cape, the Pretoria, Witwatersrand, Vaal area (now Gauteng) and KZN. In each of these provincial legislatures, the PAC had one representative.

In the 1999 election, the PAC's weak national standing declined further when it lost 43 percent of its national support, registering 0.71 percent of the national vote. As a result, the party's parliamentary representation declined from five to three MPs. Its provincial support was also reduced to representation in only two provinces, the Eastern Cape and Limpopo. Again in each provincial legislature the PAC had one representative. Significantly, the party lost more than half its support in the Eastern Cape.

In the 2004 election, the party won 0.73 percent of the national vote, maintaining its three members in the NA. Thus, the party showed some recovery after its representation had been reduced to two members by the defection of Patricia de Lille when she formed the ID in March 2003. What is interesting about the PACs national support in the last two elections, is that the party had almost exactly the same number of votes: 113,125 votes in 1999 and 113,512 in 2004. The party is now represented in two provincial legislatures, Gauteng and the Eastern Cape, with one representative in each.

Azapo

Azapo boycotted the 1994 election on the basis that the negotiated settlement that called for a GNU was unfair to the black majority. The party did not want to participate in a government that might include parties associated with the apartheid system such as the NP.[24]

Azapo changed its mind in the run up to the 1999 election, as the GNU would cease to exist after the election. The party won 0.17 percent of the vote and one seat in the NA, but failed to win representation in any of the nine provincial legislatures. In 2004, Azapo increased its support, registering 0.27 percent of the national vote. This seemed to give the party two members in the NA. However, the electoral court, in a case brought by the African Christian Democratic Party (ACDP), ruled that there had been a counting error and 2,666 votes had been incorrectly allocated to Azapo. As a result, the party was awarded one seat in the NA instead of two. The ACDP gained the contested seat and ended up with seven NA members. Again, Azapo failed to win any representation in the provincial legislatures.

The ID

The ID performed well given that the party was only one year old at the time of the 2004 election. The party polled 1.73 percent of the national vote and earned seven members in the NA. At the provincial level, the ID is represented in three provincial legislatures: Western Cape (three members), Northern Cape (two members), and Gauteng (one member). The party's support is heavily concentrated in the Western Cape province, from where its draws 47 percent of its national support.

The national significance of the ID's performance is that it managed to do better than more established parties, such as the New National Party (NNP), the Freedom Front+ (FF+), the UCDP and De Lille's own former party, the PAC. Quite significantly, the ID polled more than twice the support of the PAC.

An Assessment

This last section of the chapter focuses on an assessment of the parties' performances, drawing out the main factors that accounted for how they fared in the 2004 election. It discusses three broad themes: party leadership and unity, campaign strategies, and the quality of campaign messages in relation to the groups each party targeted.

Leadership and Ideology

A factor that is useful in assessing a party's performance is leadership strength or lack thereof. This is linked to party unity or disunity. The impact of a party in terms of electoral outcomes partly depends on the caliber and quality of its leadership and the degree of unity within its structures. Thus, a political party that has weak leadership and lacks coherency is likely not to perform well as this reflects poorly on its image and undermines its effectiveness to attract potential voters.

The PAC's weak electoral performance since 1994 can be attributed to weak leadership, which has been a perennial problem within the organization since the 1960s when it was forced into exile.[25] Leadership problems have continued to beset the PAC in postapartheid South Africa. They occurred during the run-up to the 1994 election under the leadership of Clarence Makwetu and in the period before the 1999 election under the leadership of Reverend Stanley Mogoba.

> Summarizing these problems, a veteran leader of the PAC, Phillip Kgosana stated: The PAC was not ready in 1994. In fact, it was a divided party. Between 1994 and 1999, the PAC was facing a rather bumpy ground, especially on the leadership side. Makwetu on that side and Mogoba on this side and key factors like internal discipline, everybody saying whatever they liked in the press, personal attacks and so on—the internal cohesion was just not there.[26]

The PAC was once again embroiled in leadership battles in the run-up to the 2004 election, which probably had a negative effect on its ability to raise its electoral profile. Patricia de Lille's defection from the party to form the ID in 2003 is exemplary of the extent of these leadership problems and not only led to the PAC losing one of its three seats in Parliament, but also to the departure of its most notable MP. De Lille alluded to the leadership problems shortly before she left the party in a critical newspaper article in which she admitted that the PAC's incessant leadership squabbles were the main problem confronting the party.[27] To give just a few examples: in April 2003, the party dissolved its provincial branch in Limpopo and expelled the leader Maxwell Madzivhanani for indiscipline. In October of the same year, the PAC's own Secretary General, Wonder Masombuka, was expelled after being found guilty on charges of corruption and fraud.[28]

The problems within the PAC were compounded by the annulment of the results of the party's national congress elections held in Umtata in 2002, following a flawed and corrupt process. The most damning accusation was leveled at then deputy president Motsoko Pheko. He was accused of bringing nonparty members to the congress, some of whom were even too young to vote.[29] The congress was rescheduled for Johannesburg six months later, in mid-2003, but once again ended in disarray after a walkout by a section of the leadership led by Thami Ka Plaatjie, the secretary general, who complained of corruption and flawed voting procedures. The congress elected Deputy President Pheko as president, and the party later expelled Ka Plaatie and his group.

The most serious admission of these problems by the PAC leadership was when in the period leading up to the 2002 Congress, Mogoba conceded that "[t]he PAC has been greatly divided on issues of leadership." Mogoba significantly added that in addition to power struggles he had tried to deal with "ethnic and tribal issues within the party."[30]

These leadership battles and confusion most likely discouraged the target voters of the PAC, black South Africans, from voting for the party. Yet leadership squabbles are not restricted to the PAC. They also occur in other political parties, so why does leadership stand out as one of the primary factors preventing the PAC from becoming a stronger political organization?

The answer is that the PAC's leadership problems occur at such a high level that they disrupt party processes, such as the party's ability to organize local branches and to conduct its national congress. The party is consistently consumed with resolving internal politics, and has little energy left to spend on attracting new voters. Not only does this pose problems for the party as an organization, it also creates a public relations problem, as most of these issues are public knowledge. Therefore, infighting among leaders and factionalism within the party become a liability to their credibility as well as to the party organization.

Compounding the leadership difficulties, the PAC's ideology has failed to evolve with changing conditions in postapartheid South Africa. Ideologically, the PAC has remained mired in its apartheid-era mindset. In the post-1994 era, the PAC has fundamentally questioned the new dispensation by refusing to fully embrace the tangible changes that have occurred in dismantling apartheid. It has stuck to a pre-1994 mould of analyzing South African politics. The PAC's hostility toward the consensus politics that have been a significant feature of this era largely contradicts the feelings of the majority of its target constituency—black voters—who have endorsed the new dispensation. Thus, instead of addressing the real needs of black voters in advancing policies to effectively dismantle apartheid, the PAC is still overly arguing as if nothing has changed—thus pitting it against the wishes of its potential supporters.

Azapo had its own problems, as is apparent from the two major splits the party has experienced since 1994. The first was the breakaway in 1997 by Lybon Mbasa to form the SOPA. The most current was the breakaway in 2002 by a faction that formed the Black Consciousness Forum (BCF). The founders of the BCF accused the leadership of Azapo of being blind to the ANC strategy to undercut the black consciousness movement by co-opting its senior leadership in government positions, as exemplified by the appointment of Azapo president Mosibudi Mangena as the deputy minister of education after the 1999 elections.[31] However, if indeed Azapo has not improved its popular support because of the ANC "poaching" its leadership, then the party has a serious dearth of leadership to begin with, as there was only one Azapo member in a senior position in the ANC government.

The BCF accusation does raise the more general question of how black parties to the left of the ANC *should* position themselves in relation to the ruling party. The PAC has steadfastly refused to be involved in any ANC government, while Azapo has been receptive to work with the ANC. The PAC claims that such cooperation would dilute its message, as voters would fail to see any difference between the two parties. However, in opposition to the ANC government the party has not been able to improve its popular support.

Whereas the PAC has chosen to remain outside government, Azapo, has chosen to remain separate from the ANC, but to work with the government to pursue its agenda. Thus, Azapo is represented in the cabinet and theoretically has a degree of input and influence that the PAC does not. Azapo, however, has not been able to gain any more influence and support at the voter level than has the PAC, despite this strategic positioning. In this respect, whereas Azapo, unlike the PAC, has adapted its tactics and strategy in the postapartheid context, it has also failed to develop its ideological position, same as the PAC. The party consistently articulates radical and leftist positions, while the country is liberalizing economically and faces the pressures of a globalized market economy, which makes the party's programs seem out of date. Azapo has failed to convince the black electorate that its programs will be workable. Its insistence on calling for socialism based on the black working class seriously hampers its prospects as it is not altogether clear how the party will be able to successfully implement this program in this postcommunist world.

Thus both the PAC and Azapo are limited in their appeal by their rigid ideological positions that do not articulate with the outlook of their target constituencies. Rather than adopting socialist programs that are in touch with current realities, the parties espouse a brand of socialism that seems dated and stuck in the mindset of the 1970s. As the ANC, the premier "socialist" organization, has moved to the right, the political left has been vacated, yet neither of these two organizations have filled the gap with credible and convincing political platforms, capable of winning over significant electoral support. The ideological rigidity of these parties has negative consequences as it leads to acute internal contestation over the direction of the parties, which in extreme cases results in leaders being expelled form the parties and breakaways, an image that does not inspire confidence in the electorate.

In direct contrast to the PAC and Azapo, the leadership of the new ID seemed strong. It was one of the factors that accounted for the party's good showing in the 2004 election. This is supported by preelection surveys and media reports. The Markinor survey released in April, just two days before the elections, indicated that de Lille was the second most popular party leader after President Thabo Mbeki.

De Lille had carved a position for herself on the South African political landscape as a politician with strong convictions. When she was a PAC member, she often differed from the party line on controversial issues like Zimbabwe. De Lille's image as a strong leader and a potent threat to other parties was buttressed when the Democratic Alliance (DA) launched a bitter attack on her during the election campaign. The DA saw her as a critical threat to its opposition credentials and later admitted that it had tried to attract her to join its ranks.[32]

Thus, the success of the ID can to a large extent be attributed to its image of a party with strong leadership. Evidence in the Markinor survey suggests that de Lille's popularity correlated with her party's performance, whereas the consistent unpopularity of PAC and Azapo leaders reflected the relatively poor showing of these parties at the polls.

The Quality of the Campaigns

The PAC and Azapo ran relatively weak campaigns. In contrast, the ID had a strong and attractive campaign strategy. This was recorded in the Markinor survey "Opinion 2004," which indicated that people thought the PAC was declining in strength and the ID was ascending the political ladder. Significantly, Azapo did not even feature in the results.[33]

The use by the ID of new technological methods such as cell phones, e-mail, and the internet was also instrumental in distinguishing the party's election campaign from the campaigns of the PAC and Azapo, which continued to rely heavily on old methods and strategies. The main strength of the ID campaign was that it was specific and appropriately targeted at the youth, a sector of the population that does not necessarily identify with any of the old parties and is receptive to the usage of modern technology.

The ID also effectively presented itself as having no baggage of the past. It successfully portrayed itself as a new party that was prepared to take on the ANC, engaging in constructive rather than destructive opposition. This position was described by de Lille herself as based not on "ideology but constitutionalism."[34]

Thus, the ID campaign was two pronged—to challenge the ANC while at the same time projecting itself as different from existing opposition parties. This strategy was vital to the ID's success. The ANC's main criticism against opposition parties was that they were preoccupied with bringing down the ruling party, rather than serving the interests of the country. The ID was effective in exploiting the notion of being a "patriotic opposition."

Target Groups and Campaign Issues

The competition between parties over a given constituency is another factor that determines how well a party is able to perform in elections. The performance of the PAC and Azapo can be understood cogently through the prism of their target constituency, the black vote. This constituency was also targeted by the powerful ANC and was thus highly contested. Furthermore, the ANC was contesting this constituency on more or less the same basis as the PAC and Azapo, using such issues as land redistribution and the reversal of the legacy of apartheid. Thus, the PAC and Azapo had serious competition from the ANC in the 2004 election.

The PAC's main election platform, its position on the land question slightly differed from that of the ruling ANC. The PAC called for a more radical redistribution of land, whereas the ANC government advocated a more cautious approach. This seems to have been a dividing line between the parties in terms of drawing popular support. It might have been a critical factor in the 2004 election, because the PAC had exhibited a rather unpopular position with regard to the land question in 2002, when the party supported land invasions in Gauteng, which were widely condemned around the country.

Azapo's campaign message, based on black people's aspirations, showed little difference to that of the ANC. This was exemplified by Azapo's participation in government. Through its position as governing partner Azapo presented itself as sharing the ruling party's objectives. As noted earlier, Azapo has not been able to significantly improve its popular support based on this message.

Another drawback of the PAC and Azapo campaigns was that they were isolated from organized labor, which is a critical electoral force in South Africa. This was especially problematic because both parties were on the left of the political spectrum and would therefore be expected to maintain close ties with this constituency.

The PAC exacerbated the isolation by attacking the main trade union federation. The party accused Cosatu of misleading the workers by being in an alliance with the ANC and acting as a privileged trade union that did not take the interests of the unemployed into account. Azapo implicitly criticized Cosatu's alliance with the ANC by calling for an independent labor movement in its manifesto. This kind of policy was unlikely to entice black workers to support the PAC or Azapo. Instead it contributed to existing weaknesses because it further distanced the parties from worker's organizations.

In terms of target groups, the ID's success in the 2004 election can in large part be attributed to the party successfully carving a niche of support for itself by way of the issues it addressed. The ID had a very clear and effective message that matched the policies espoused by party leader de Lille. In this regard, the ID had the advantage of not competing for the traditional constituency of the ANC, the black majority. In fact, it was a conscious strategic move by the ID to distance itself from a black perspective of politics and project itself as a truly nonracial party.[35]

The ID's strength was that it ran a targeted campaign that singled out specific issues—HIV/AIDS, corruption, child and women abuse—that were not the main priorities of the ANC. The ID campaign was not primarily based on the issues on which the PAC and Azapo were challenging the ANC. Thus, the ID managed to avoid direct competition with the ANC.

Conclusion

The parties that are considered be to the left of the ANC and have their roots in Africanism and Black Consciousness had mixed fortunes in the 2004 elections. The PAC and Azapo managed to retain their representation in Parliament with low levels of support. Their weakness can be traced to internal problems, the nature of their campaign strategies and messages and the competition they faced from the ANC in terms of aiming for the same constituency of black voters. The ID, on the other hand, has performed reasonably well in terms of South African electoral standards. As a new party it managed to gain representation in the NA and three provinces and stay ahead of many more established parties, such as the NNP. The success of the ID can be largely ascribed to its strong leadership, its targeted campaign, and its focus on niche issues that did not pit it directly against the ANC.

Notes

1. The survey data used in this chapter includes a study carried out by the Human Sciences Research Council (HSRC), a research body that is partly funded by the government. The HSRC survey is titled "South African Social Attitudes Survey" (Sasas), and reports on the opinion of

South Africans of voting age with regard to economic, social, and political issues. It used a random sample of 7,501 South Africans and was conducted in 1,000 census areas around the country between August and October 2003. The other surveys used are conducted by the South African Broadcasting Corporation (SABC) in conjunction with the private marketing company Markinor. These surveys traced the political attitudes of South African voters leading up to the 2004 election.

2. It is important to note that the PAC uses the terms "black" and "African" interchangeably, despite the party's assertion that it regards those who identify themselves with the African continent as Africana regardless of their racial background.

3. SAPA, "PAC: Black Living Conditions Not Improved," April 10, 2004.

4. Jimmy Seepe, "PAC Manifesto Focuses on Land and Wealth," *City Press*, February 8, 2004, p. 4.

5. This point was asserted by Dr. Pheko in an interview with Chris Barron of the *Sunday Times*, January 18, 2004, p. 19.

6. Ibid.

7. See Khangele Makhado, "PAC Woos Free State," *Sowetan*, January 28, 2004, p. 4; and Caiphus Kgosana, "PAC Stakes Poll Hope on Civic Structures," *The Star*, March 19, 2004, p. 5.

8. The DPSA contested the provincial election in the Free State; the SPP in Mpumalanga. They did not win any seats in the provincial legislatures.

9. Eric Naki, "PAC Expels Gazi for Having Name on Another Party's List," *The Herald*, April 7, 2004, p. 1.

10. Ibid.; see also Pheko Interview with Barron.

11. Nazma Dreyer, "Record Number of Women Candidates for the Polls," *The Cape Times*, April 6, 2004, p. 6.

12. SABC/Markinor Opinion 2004, "If There Were An Election Tomorrow," Press release (Cape Town and Pretoria: Markinor, January 15, 2004).

13. HSRC, "South African Social Attitudes Survey," November 2003.

14. SABC/Markinor Opinion 2004, "Opposition and Leadership," Press release (Cape Town and Pretoria: Markinor, April 12, 2004).

15. Mzwandile Hlangani, "PAC Scoffs at Survey Findings," *The Star*, March 19, 2004, p. 5; and Khangele Makhado, "PAC Woos Free State," *Sowetan*, January 28, 2004, p. 4.

16. Selby Makgotho, "AZAPO Launches Election Manifesto," *Sowetan*, February 16, 2004, p. 4.

17. Kingdom Mabuza, "Rotate the Rand-AZAPO," *Citizen*, February 23, 2004, p. 4.

18. Dan Habedi, "Democracy that Benefits the Rich," *The Star*, January 15, 2004, p. 8.

19. Khathu Mamaila, "Whites can now Join AZAPO," *The Star*, June 18, 2002, p. 5.

20. "De Lille to Set Example," *The Star*, April 5, 2004, p. 1.

21. Moipone Malefane, "SA Needs Role-Models for AIDS Battle—De Lille," *The Star*, April 6, 2004, p. 6.

22. Sam Mkokeli, "Current Opposition Ineffective," *The Herald*, January 9, 2004, p. 2.

23. Caiphus Kgosana, "ID Could Get 10% of the Vote-Poll," *Cape Times*, April 8, 2004, p. 6.

24. Author's interview with Pandelani Nefolovhodwe, Deputy President of Azapo, Johannesburg, May 2000.

25. Tom Lodge, "The Pan Africanist Congress 1959–1990," in *The Long March: The Story of the Struggle for Liberation in South Africa*, ed. Ian Liebenberg, Fiona Lortan, Bobby Nel, and Gert van Westhuizen (Pretoria: Haum, 1994), 186.

26. Author's interview with Philip Kgosana, PAC National Organizer, Pretoria, May 2000.

27. Rapule Tabane, "Suzman versus De Lille," *Mail & Guardian*, March 26–April 1, 2004, p. 4.

28. See Jimmy Seepe, "PAC Splits Over Expelled Official," *City Press*, October 20, 2002, p. 2; and Selby Makgotho, "Dark Cloud Over PAC Leader," *Sowetan*, April 25, 2003, p. 10.

29. Kingdom Mabuza, "PAC Pheko Camp Refuses to Accept Other Leaders," *Citizen*, December 23, 2002, p. 7.

30. Mpumelelo Mkhabela and Jimmy Seepe, "Mogoba Set To Relinquish the PAC Presidency," *City Press*, June 8, 2003, p. 2.

31. Siza Ngqebo, "Leader of the Pack," *Sowetan Sunday World*, August 18, 2002, p. 15.

32. Rapule Tabane, "Suzman Versus De Lille," *Mail & Guardian*, March 26–April 1, 2004, p. 4.

33. "Ideology is Dead, Long Live ID-OLOGY," *Mail & Guardian*, April 27, 2004.

34. Ibid.

35. Janet Cherry, "Elections 2004: The Party Lists and Issues of Identity," in *Election Synopsis* 1, no. 3, 2004, ed. Maxine Reitzes and Roger Southall (Pretoria: HSRC), 6–9, 6.

CHAPTER ELEVEN

The Smallest Parties: The ACDP, UCDP, FF+, MF, and UDM

SANUSHA NAIDU AND MBOGENI MANQELE

In the course of South Africa's first decade of democracy, the role of small political parties has become the subject of much speculation. The smallest parties on the South African political landscape seem trapped in what has become a fish bowl of opposition politics. Questions have emerged around their relevance and future prospects. What do these parties stand for and to which part of the electorate do they appeal?

The performance of small parties in the 2004 national election was mixed. Some parties retained or increased their presence in the National Assembly: the ACDP, FF+, UCDP, and MF. Others, like the Nasionale Aksie and Peace and Justice Congress (PJC), were not able to obtain a single seat, pointing to their relative obscurity on the national political scene, or saw their presence in Parliament decrease, like the UDM, which lost five of its fourteen seats. Some small parties, including the ACDP, MF, and UDM, performed better in provincial ballots, thus continuing a trend established in the 1999 election.

This chapter reviews five small parties, each of which won representation in the National Assembly in the 2004 elections: the African Christian Democratic Party (ACDP), Freedom Front Plus (FF+), Minority Front (MF), the United Christian Democratic Party (UCDP), and the United Democratic Movement (UDM). These parties have diverse ideological orientations, but all tend to have regional bases and tend to lie on the political right of the ideological spectrum. Additionally, several have their roots in the apartheid era. They represent either a re-creation of apartheid-era parties (the UCDP, created by former Bophuthatswana homeland leader Lucius Mangope) or were created through a merger of apartheid-era political organizations (the FF+, pieced together from a variety of small Afrikaner parties). Only one of these parties was created in the first democratic decade: the UDM, founded in 1997 when former members of the ANC (Bantu Holomisa) and the NNP (Roelf Meyer) collaborated to create a new political organization. The ACDP was created just prior to the 1994 elections, and since its inception has been strongest in the Western Cape. The MF had existed as a regional political organization in KwaZulu-Natal (KZN) throughout the decades of National Party (NP) rule and its leader had held office in apartheid-era governments.

Given these commonalities and differences, what were the salient features of the election campaigns and strategies of these small parties? What does the future hold for these parties as part of South Africa's opposition? One hallmark of the South African political system is that most of the smallest parties simply would not exist if the country were to use an electoral system based on plurality instead of proportional representation. Given that the continued inclusion of the smallest parties in the National Assembly could be considered an artifact of a permissive electoral system, this chapter concludes by asking: is there space for their continued existence in South African politics?

Party Campaigns and Strategies

Rebuilding South Africa's Morality: The African Christian Democratic Party

Founded by Reverend Kenneth Meshoe in 1993, the ACDP sees itself as representing "Bible Believing Christians" and "those who have a high regard for moral values." In response to the secular nature of the democratic South African state, the aim of the ACDP is to infuse Christian principles and values into the decision-making process. As the party sees it, the implosion of HIV/AIDS, legalization of abortion, free distribution of condoms, and television and radio campaigns encouraging safe sex, have all contributed to an erosion of family values and the demise of a moral code of conduct. The ACDP's message of defending and upholding Christian values is therefore aimed at voters who want to preserve morality and protect the integrity of the family structure. According to ACDP Member of Parliament (MP) Might Madasa, "many Christians are turning to the ACDP as the only moral custodian of their values in the face of rapid moral degeneration."[1]

The ACDP's appeal appears to be dovetailing with a rise of religion as a primary source of social identity.[2] Since 1994, evangelical Christian institutions have grown and captured the imagination of their audiences by speaking to the issues of morality and family values. Contrasting with the ruling party's relatively liberal stance on social issues (pro-abortion, anti-death penalty, support for family planning, and safe-sex education), the social conservatism of these religious platforms seems to resonate with many South Africans. Furthermore, many Christians see high crime rates and social problems related to unemployment as signs that the social fabric of society is disintegrating. Such sentiments seem to cut across racial divisions and appear to be fertile ground for the ACDP's message of moral regeneration. The ACDP thus appears to be enjoying "cross-racial support from members of new fundamentalist churches that have mushroomed across the country."[3]

The ACDP campaign for the 2004 election did not depart much from the party's campaigns in 1994 and 1999.[4] The ACDP kept its electoral strategy close to its founding manifesto by reiterating its commitment to Christian principles, freedom of religion, a free market economy, family values, and the protection of family and individual rights. In its 2004 campaign the party identified five critical issues: crime, affirmative action, poverty and unemployment, HIV/AIDS, and education, all under the slogan "Its About Real Hope."

Campaigning along these lines displayed a political agenda that was conservative and at times contradictory in nature. Its "zero tolerance on crime" policy saw the ACDP advocate a repeal of the parole system, no bail for crimes like robbery and vehicle hijacking and the reintroduction of capital punishment for offences like murder and rape. At the same time, the party argued against abortion, euthanasia, and homosexuality as part of its message of moral regeneration. This not only effectively negated the ACDP's claims of upholding individual rights, it placed the party in a position of opposing constitutionally protected rights.

Central to the ACDP's position on economic policy, was the party's belief that foreign direct investment (FDI) and economic growth would create opportunities for employment and poverty alleviation. The ACDP saw crime and corruption as deterrents to FDI and, by extension, to economic growth. The party was critical of Black Economic Empowerment (BEE) and felt that the net of BEE needed to be expanded and not confined to a few black elites.

On the issue of affirmative action, the ACDP argued that the policy as currently applied was racist in its foundation. The party advocated that the focus of the policy should change from "previously" disadvantaged[5] to disadvantaged individuals. The ACDP did concede that this would be a symbolic rather than a substantial change. Given the racial and socioeconomic nature of poverty in the country, the results of the proposed policy would not differ dramatically from the results of a race-based policy.[6] However, according to the ACDP, the change of focus would make the policy a matter of social welfare, while the proposed creation of a separate Apartheid Restitution Fund would focus on the redressal of the wrongs of apartheid.

Defectors from other parties fared well on the ACDP candidate lists. The floor-crossing legislation had enabled the ACDP to increase its six seats in the National Assembly to seven through the defection of NNP MP Adriaan Blaas. Another defector, Graham McIntosh, who left the Democratic Alliance (DA) in February 2004 to join the ACDP, was elevated to a relatively high place on the ACDP list. In the Western Cape, Pauline Cupido, who also crossed over from the DA, was the ACDP's premier candidate. In KwaZulu-Natal, the party presented former SABC CEO Reverend Aash "Hawu" Mbatha as the ACDP candidate for the premiership. Mbatha's candidacy was a strategic move by the ACDP to capitalize on the popularity of the reverend and make inroads into the black section of the electorate in the province.[7]

A Shrinking Legacy: The United Christian Democratic Party

Like the ACDP, the UCDP is a quasi-religious party with a strong regional base. Whereas the ACDP is primarily based in the Western Cape, the UCDP's regional focus is the North West province, the location of the former Bophuthatswana homeland that gave birth to the party. Unlike the ACDP, the UCDP is one of the parties that were "recycled" from the apartheid era. The UCDP was formed after the 1994 election by former Bophuthatswana leader Lucas Mangope, when he revived an organization that had existed in the Bophuthatswana homeland in the 1980s.[8]

Despite its historical background and the political baggage of its leader, the UCDP was able to become the official opposition in North West. In the 1999 election, support for the ANC was 4 percent lower on the provincial than the national ballot, which indicated that the UCDP was able to steal away some of the ANC's support in the province. The UCDP's popularity among the Twsana-speaking electorate clearly represented a challenge to the ruling party. The UCDP's share of the national vote in 1999 was relatively small, but large enough to secure three seats in the National Assembly.

The appeal of the UCDP was similar to that of the UDM. Both parties did well in provinces with large former homeland areas and both parties seemed to appeal to sections of the electorate that might have "had it better" under apartheid, due to their relatively privileged positions in the apartheid-homeland administrations. The core of the UCDP's support base stemmed from disgruntled civil servants in the urban centers of North West and tribal chiefs and headmen from the rural areas in the province. The latter may have harbored residual loyalty to Chief Mangope or become incensed by the reversal of their fortunes under the ANC government. The UCDP also benefited from a perception that the ANC had failed to keep its promises of service delivery in the province. Many voters chose the ANC on the national ballot, but when it came to the provincial ballot, they gave their vote to the UCDP.[9] In the Eastern Cape, the UDM benefited from a similar dynamic in 1999.

Similar to its strategy in 1999, the UCDP's electoral strategy in 2004 was designed to expose the failures of the ANC. At the launch of the UCDP election campaign in Mmabatho, Mangope criticized the ANC's failure to deliver, which he saw as an indictment of the government's responsibility and a betrayal of the trust and support of those who voted for it.[10] Mangope claimed that this betrayal would lead people to seek alternative leadership, which he believed the UCDP provided. Unlike the ACDP, the UCDP campaign did not rely primarily on a religious angle. It focused instead on the credentials of the UCDP leadership and on promises of delivery and improved standards of living in North West. The party hoped to attract voters with the slogan: "Ready to deliver where others have failed."

The core issues of the UCDP campaign were HIV/AIDS, poverty and unemployment, crime, education, health care, nepotism and corruption, infrastructure, and the situation in Zimbabwe. The party used rallies and house meetings in an attempt to capitalize on the perceived failures of the ANC in these areas. While the house meetings gave party officials the opportunity to develop a rapport with the electorate and the space to try and win them over to vote for the UCDP, the impact of the rallies was harder to gauge. Similar to the other small parties, the UCDP campaign was constrained by a lack of resources, which, according to party officials, precluded the UCDP from achieving more.

The Last Bastion of Afrikanerdom: The Freedom Front Plus

The FF+ contested the 1994 and 1999 elections under the banner of the Freedom Front (FF). Founded in the early 1990s by General Constand Viljoen, Chief of the South African Defence Force under apartheid, the party aims to protect and advance the interests of the Afrikaner population. In the 1994 election, the FF managed to secure nine seats in the National Assembly, capitalizing on uncertainty among minority voters about their existence under a black government. Afrikaner voters clearly saw the FF as a party willing to fight for their rights in a nonracial, multiparty, democratic South Africa. But the appeal of the FF extended beyond the protection of Afrikaner political and cultural rights. What attracted part of the Afrikaner electorate to the FF was the party's promise to fight for an Afrikaner homeland and self-determination,[11] thus entrenching group identity in the face of majority rule. In contrast, the NP's negotiations with the ANC were seen as a collusion with the former enemy that would not produce any tangible benefits for the Afrikaner.

The conservative platform of the FF continued in the 1999 elections but the party could not sustain its 1994 performance and lost six of its nine seats in the National Assembly. Commentators attributed the decline in support to a rejection of General Viljoen's "constructive engagement" with the ruling party to protect and advance Afrikaner identity. Some analysts believed that FF supporters had become exhausted waiting for their "Volkstaat," which, in the face of continued opposition from the ANC, seemed nothing more than a pipe dream.[12]

Following the FF's poor showing in 1999, General Viljoen retired, paving the way for the party to reorganize itself behind a new leader: Dr. Pieter Mulder. During the window period for floor crossing in March–April 2003, the FF joined forces with the Conservative Party and the Afrikaner Eenheids Beweging (AEB) in order to contest the third democratic election as a new entity, the Freedom Front Plus. Instead of fighting for an Afrikaner homeland, the FF+ focused on advancing the cultural rights of Afrikaners.

The FF+ campaign in the 2004 election can be characterized as taking the offensive. The party attempted to reestablish its connection with Afrikaner voters by "calling on government to stop subjecting white matriculants to affirmative action when they applied for their first jobs."[13] The FF+ also spoke out against attacks on farmers and urged voters to

say NO to the ANC's centralization of political power and its marginalisation of Afrikaners and other minority communities, unfair affirmative action and discrimination, crime, immorality and corruption; the deprivation of property rights and the nationalization of assets and resources; and freedom without justice in this country.[14]

The party clearly hoped to attract undecided Afrikaner voters by playing on their fears of exclusion and marginalization. The FF+ campaign tried to tackle the ANC on its mistakes and missed opportunities. It challenged the ruling party on the issues of poverty and unemployment, the brain drain and its "quiet diplomacy" approach to the political and economic crisis in Zimbabwe.

In the Western Cape, the FF+ formed a cooperation pact with the Cape People's Congress (CPC) in order to keep the ANC-NNP alliance from gaining control of the province and prevent the ANC from gaining a two-thirds majority in the national parliament.[15] The pact with the CPC was a strategic move by the FF+ to appeal to the coloured section of the electorate. In a similar move the FF+ pursued a preelection agreement with the Inkatha Freedom Party (IFP) in KZN. Given the fact that the parties in question continued to contest the election independently, these alliances seemed to primarily serve the function of promoting minority group rights and interest representation of specific communities in the context of majority rule.

Keeping Alive the Indian Vote: The Minority Front

Of all the small parties contesting the 2004 elections, the Minority Front (MF) has by far the most flamboyant leader, Amichand Rajbansi. Mixing metaphors with colloquial Indian speech, Rajbansi has had an illustrious political career. In the 1980s, Rajbansi, known as "The Raj" and "the Bengal Tiger," served in the tri-cameral parliament as a member of the House of Delegates. He was forced to resign after the James Commission investigating fraud, corruption and other irregularities deemed him "unfit for public office."

In 1994, Rajbansi returned to politics as the head of a new party, the MF. The party's identity seems to be intrinsically linked to its leader, and there is every indication that without Rajbansi the MF has little organizational cohesion. The departure of Visvin Reddy, a rising star in the MF, just before the 2004 election, was a clear sign that the party had become Rajbansi's personal vehicle. There was simply not enough room in the party for more than one charismatic personality. In this respect, the MF resembles the UCDP rather than the ACDP and the FF+, which do not rely so heavily on the personal charisma of their founding leaders.

The MF solely concentrates on the Indian vote and is thus an ethnically based party. Most of its support is found in KZN, which has the largest Indian population in the country. Stemming from Rajbansi's experience in the House of Delegates in the 1980s, the strategy of the MF is to work for change from within the system. Whether one regards this as collaboration or mere pragmatism, the MF has become a crucial player in coalition politics. The party's ability to command the support of a large portion of the KZN electorate puts the MF in the position of king maker in the province at times when support for the ANC and IFP is evenly balanced. Following the 2000 local elections, the MF threw its weight behind the ANC and enabled the party to gain control over the Durban city council. Similarly, after the 1999 elections, the MF agreed to use its one seat in the National Assembly to help the ANC control 267, or two-thirds, of the NA votes.

The core of the MF strategy is to safeguard Indian interests under an African-led government. The party aims not to create tensions between Indian and African sections of the electorate and promises to make a deal with the African majority so as to ensure that Indians get their share of government services and other benefits.[16] In the 1994 and 1999 elections, the MF campaigned on the platform that it would work with whatever party won a majority of the votes in KZN and at the national level. Rajbansi believed that the MF "should stand in 'co-operative co-existence' with ruling parties," and asserted that opposition politics that criticized the government merely for the sake of opposition did not "contribute to the reconstruction and development of South Africa."[17] In 2004, the MF conducted its campaign along the same lines of constructive engagement.

Unlike the campaigns of the other parties discussed in this chapter, the MF campaign steered clear of attacks on the ANC about missed opportunities and service delivery failures. Like most parties, the MF campaigned around the issues of poverty and unemployment, crime, affirmative action, education, HIV/AIDS, and social grants. However, unlike the parties that criticized the ANC's policies in these areas, the MF supported the ANC's approach but argued that Indians needed to be included in the government's efforts.

A core element of the MF campaign was to remind its supporters and the Indian community in general that the party had advanced Indian economic and social interests through quiet diplomacy. In a newspaper article published ten days before the election, Rajbansi outlined that the MF had intervened on numerous occasions to ensure that Indians were given "their place in the sun." He noted that this was only possible because of the MF's policy of good relations with the majority, which enabled the party to gain a sympathetic ear from the government.[18] In the same article, Rajbansi cautioned Indian people not to fall prey to charismatic politicians or parties who only come courting for their votes once every five years. Such appeals tied in with the MF's overall strategy of uniting the Indian vote under its auspices, which would enable it to engage with the ruling party and to hold sway especially in KZN where the electoral race is close.

In contrast to the MF's message of including Indians in ANC policies and programs, the DA campaign emphasized that the ANC government excluded minority voters and their interests. In other words, the DA played the racial and ethnic card in the hope of scaring Indian voters into supporting the party. Thus, the DA presented itself as the party that would defend Indian interests against African ones. The MF saw the DA campaign as divisive and criticized the DA's strategy of presenting Indians and Africans as being at odds. According to the MF, such an approach would marginalize and isolate the Indian community from mainstream politics. The MF urged that Indian voters be cautious voting for parties that would only pay attention to them during election time and thereafter ignore their interests.

As in previous election campaigns, the MF staged a number of glamorous rallies that dazzled the audience. At a cost of R1.5 million, the party mainly campaigned in the traditionally Indian suburbs of Phoenix and Chatsworth. Both of these suburbs are working-class areas, which reflects the fact that the party enjoys more popularity among the working- and lower-class segments than among the middle- and upper-class segments of the Indian community. Where middle-class Indians see Rajbansi as a caricature of that which is Indian, for the working-class Indian in Chatsworth and Phoenix he is a Robin Hood of sorts. Members from these communities assert that the MF leader is easily accessible and is a part of the community he represents; that he listens to their grievances and takes up their cause. Rajbansi's high profile at social, business, and religious functions further entrenches his popularity at the grassroots level.

A Flash in the Pan? The United Democratic Movement

In the 1999 election the UDM had burst on the scene as a contender for power in the Eastern Cape. The surprise performance of the UDM in the Eastern Cape provincial poll had given rise to speculation about the party's potential of becoming a serious opponent to the ANC.

Christened as the "new kid on the block," the UDM won fourteen seats in the National Assembly and managed to become the official opposition in the Eastern Cape, winning nine of the sixty-three seats in the provincial legislature. At the time, the party's success was deemed all the more important because it took place in a province that traditionally had been the backbone of the ANC's support base. It was significant that the UDM could make inroads in the area that many ANC leaders "including Nelson Mandela, Govan and Thabo Mbeki, Chris Hani and Walter Sisulu have viewed as their ancestral home."[19]

The UDM had been established in September 1997 through a merger of Roelf Meyer's New Movement Process (NMP) and Bantu Holomisa's National Consultative Forum (NCF). Both Meyer and Holomisa had positions of power under the apartheid government, and both had fallen out of favor with their respective parties in the postapartheid era. Both resigned from their parties after conflicts with party leadership, and both subsequently formed alternative political organizations. Meyer had belonged to the NP and had been the chief role player in the NP's negotiations with the ANC. Holomisa had been the military leader of Transkei in 1987 and later gained favor with the ANC by granting the movement and its military wing Umkhonto we Sizwe the space to operate from the homeland.

Following its creation, the UDM attracted disaffected voters from a variety of political backgrounds. Nationally, the dual leadership of Meyer and Holomisa enabled the party to project a multiracial image, and Meyer's presence brought experienced former NP party organizers into the party. In the Eastern Cape, Holomisa's appeal helped the UDM to capitalize on widespread poverty and unemployment among the electorate. With promises of a return to capable leadership, the UDM was also able to win support among former elites, chiefs, and dissatisfied civil servants in the Eastern Cape.[20] As a result, the new kid on the block was seen as a serious opponent to the ANC provincially as well as nationally.

Shortly after the 1999 election, Meyer left the UDM to work with the Rhema church, leaving Holomisa as the party leader. While Meyer did not fault the party for his leaving (instead he claimed it was simply time to get out of politics), the timing of his departure was suspicious. His departure deprived the UDM of much of its nonracial appeal and caused internal problems.[21] It seemed to signal the beginning of a declining trend for the UDM. Thereafter, opinion polls consistently reported the party's support to be in the single digits, and in the March–April 2003 window period for floor crossing the UDM lost ten of its fourteen MPs to the ANC. The UDM appeared to have become an ethnically based party with appeal only in the Eastern Cape.

As the 2004 election approached, the UDM faced a challenge. The party had to prove that it was more than just a regional force, which meant mounting a nationally visible campaign, while its efforts in the Eastern Cape had to entrench the loyalty of its core support base. With only limited funds, the UDM concentrated its campaign efforts in the Eastern Cape. The party invested most of its resources in adorning the walls and lampposts of the province with its election posters. Nationally, the UDM chose to campaign along the lines of poverty and unemployment, with billboards noting that South Africa had experienced ten years of joblessness.

The UDM hoped that it would continue to attract the disaffected voter. The focus of the UDM campaign was to attack the ANC's electoral strategy of a people's contract and to convince voters that the ANC had abandoned them through neoliberal policies that tended to exacerbate poverty and unemployment. The party also sought to discredit the ANC's call for volunteerism by asserting that it was the responsibility of the government to provide jobs and economic security.

The UDM broadly addressed the same issues as the other parties reviewed in this chapter. First, the party promised to set up a sustainable development program to create jobs and a productive and safe environment for the electorate. Second, it argued for a domestic-led growth strategy through small business development. Third, the party pledged to devote 1 percent of income tax to fund a properly paid, trained, and resourced police force and a skills development program to train people to find work. The UDM also promised to increase public expenditure for education and health care, and reduce the budget for defense. In addition, the party proposed a basic service subsidy for the poor. Finally, the UDM said it would develop a national consensus plan of action around HIV/AIDS.

In spite of the fact that the UDM was contesting the 2004 election more to maintain than increase its support, the party leadership was optimistic about the election. In a Sunday newspaper, Holomisa cautioned against writing off the UDM and insisted that the party was growing despite what opinion polls were predicting.[22] Such confidence meant that the UDM felt its electoral strategy of attacking the ANC was going to find appeal among the economically marginalized.

Election Results

At the start of the 2004 election, each of the five parties reviewed in this chapter had a regionally concentrated support base: the ACDP in the

Western Cape, the UDCP in the North West, the MF in KZN, the FF+ in the Transvaal, and the UDM in the Eastern Cape. The five parties could be regarded as both economically and socially conservative, with only slight variations in their policy positions. Most attacked the ANC's record on crime, unemployment, management of the economy, and the HIV/AIDS crisis. The MF stressed opposition through cooperation, while the others emphasized that it was necessary to challenge the ANC on its mistakes and failures.

The five parties differed more with regard to the constituencies to which they appealed. The ACDP attempted to attract a Christian support base, the FF+ tried to develop a cadre of Afrikaner supporters, the MF appealed directly to Indians, while the UCDP and the UDM primarily ran regionally based campaigns, focusing on former homeland areas. Given these differences and similarities, how did these five parties fare in the 2004 election?[23]

They failed to make major inroads into the national electorate, although the ACDP, FF+, and MF slightly improved their results from 1999. They held onto their regional bases, but in the case of the MF, the UCDP, and the UDM with less support than in 1999. Although not winning a large number of seats, some parties managed to become critically important to the balance of power in provincial politics, specifically in KZN. They became "kingmakers" in the formation of a provincial government, providing crucial support to the ANC that had not managed to win a majority. In the past, the MF played this role in KZN (and nationally), but after the 2004 election, the ACDP and the UDM also took on this role.

The African Christian Democratic Party

Following its success in the 1999 elections, the ACDP slightly increased its showing in 2004. The party received 1.6 percent of the national vote, compared to 1.4 percent in 1999 (see table 11.1), and ended up with seven seats in the NA.[24] The ACDP also did well at the provincial level, increasing its total number of provincial seats from four to eight. Both in the Western Cape and KZN, the party managed to double its seats in the provincial legislature. The ACDP also captured one seat each in the Free State and the Northern Cape legislatures. Undoubtedly, the decline of the NNP contributed to the ACDP's success in the Western and Northern Cape, whereas using a popular religious leader (Rev. Mbatha) to head the campaign in KZN helped to retain the party's support there.

The most notable election outcome for the ACDP occurred in KZN. With neither the ANC nor IFP having won an outright majority, the

Table 11.1 Election results at national level

Party	Vote share (%)			Seats		
	1994	1999	2004	1994	1999	2004
ACDP	0.45	1.43	1.6	2	6	7
FF+	2.17	0.80	0.89	9	3	4
MF	0.07	0.30	0.35	—	1	2
UDM	n.a.	3.42	2.28	n.a.	14	9
UCDP	n.a.	0.78	0.75	n.a.	3	3

Source: Independent Electoral Commission of South Africa.

Table 11.2 ACDP provincial results

	Vote share (%)			Seats		
	1994	1999	2004	1994	1999	2004
Eastern Cape	0.51	0.96	0.78	—	—	—
Free State	0.45	0.9	1.32	—	—	1
Gauteng	0.61	1.16	1.64	1	1	1
KwaZulu-Natal	0.67	1.81	1.78	1	1	2
Limpopo[a]	0.38	1.1	1.26	—	1	1
Mpumulanga	0.48	1.12	1.09	—	—	—
Northern Cape	0.40	1.53	1.85	—	—	1
North West	0.35	0.94	1.1	—	—	—
Western Cape	1.20	2.79	3.44	1	1	2

[a] Formerly Northern Province.

Source: Independent Electoral Commission of South Africa.

ACDP became critical to the bargaining that subsequently took place. The two seats that the ACDP acquired enabled the party to become one of three kingmakers in the province. Even though the ANC won thirty-eight seats in the provincial legislature, it was short of three seats to establish a ruling majority, while the IFP had to bargain with the smaller parties if it was to retain control of the province. In other words, the support of the ACDP was indispensable for the formation of a provincial government.

The fragile political situation in the province placed the ACDP in a position to play the role of peacemaker. The party argued that if peace and stability were to be maintained the ANC and IFP had to seek ways of working together. Thus, the ACDP declared its support for the ANC on the basis that the party had won the plurality of votes in the province and asserted that the ANC should use its control over the provincial government as an opportunity to establish enduringly peaceful relations with the IFP. The ACDP's diplomatic brokering was further entrenched when the party declared that it would decline a portfolio in the provincial government in return for supporting the ANC. According to the ACDP leadership, this strategic choice was motivated by a need for transparency and accountability. If the ACDP were to enter into government, it would be less able to hold the ruling party accountable.

The United Christian Democratic Party

The UCDP contested the 2004 election at the national level and in all nine provinces, which reflected a change in strategy. In 1999, the UCDP had participated in only four provincial ballots, in Mpumulanga, North West, Free State, and Gauteng. Comparing the 1999 and 2004 results in these four provinces shows little change in the UCDP's performance: the party very slightly increased its showing in Gauteng and slightly decreased in Mpumalanga and the Free State (see table 11.3). In its stronghold of North West, the UCDP remained the official opposition and retained its three seats in the provincial legislature despite a 0.63 percent drop in support. The party did not manage to win seats in any of the provinces in which it contested for the first time. At the national level the UCDP's support remained more or less constant at 0.75 percent of the vote, compared to 0.78 percent in 1999. Thus, the party maintained its three seats in the NA.

Table 11.3   UCDP provincial results

	Vote share (%)		Seats	
	1999	2004	1999	2004
Eastern Cape	n.a.[a]	0.12	n.a.	—
Free State	0.78	0.77	—	—
Gauteng	0.23	0.26	—	—
KwaZulu-Natal	n.a.	0.14	n.a.	—
Limpopo[b]	n.a.	0.22	n.a.	—
Mpumulanga	0.23	0.17	—	—
Northern Cape	n.a.	0.33	n.a.	—
North West	9.57	8.94	3	3
Western Cape	n.a.	0.23	n.a.	—

[a] n.a. indicates that the party did not contest the election in that province.
[b] Formerly Northern Province.

Source: Independent Electoral Commission of South Africa.

These results paint a picture of stability: the UCDP has neither raised its profile enough to attract new supporters nor lost a significant degree of its support between 1999 and 2004. The ANC won the North West provincial ballot with a sizable majority and, unlike the ACDP, the UCDP did not acquire any seats in KZN. Therefore, while the ACDP could leverage its small number of seats for influence in the formation of a provincial government, the UCDP did not have this option. Another difference between the UCDP and the ACDP was that the latter explicitly presented itself as a Christian party and decided to campaign on a religious platform, while the UCDP based its campaign on the personal appeal and former stature of party leader Mangope. This gave the UCDP little credence in provinces other than the North West. The "Christian" aspect of the UCDP seemed to many South Africans to be a convenient ploy to help the party position itself in the postapartheid landscape. As a result, the party was not able to match the performance of the ACDP, which attracted small pools of voters throughout the country.

With the UCDP's performance being more or less the same than in 1999 the prospects of the party making serious inroads into the ANC support base seem rather bleak. However, for the first time since the UCDP became the official opposition in the North West, the party has been given the chairmanship of the Standing Committee on Public Accounts (Scopa). This is seen in UCDP circles as a positive sign for future cooperation with the ANC. Thus, while the UCDP campaigned with a strong anti-ANC message (similar to the message of the UDM), in the postelection political landscape the party switched to a more collaborative relation with the ANC. This may seem as expediency on the side of the UCDP, it certainly indicates that the future of the party may well depend on how its relationship with the ANC in the North West is nurtured and sustained.

The Freedom Front Plus

The 2004 election results revealed a stable level of support for the FF+. Overall, the party neither advanced nor declined compared to its performance in 1999. Despite the fact that the FF+ only slightly increased its national support from 0.80 percent in 1999 to 0.89 percent in 2004, the party's representation in the NA increased from three to four seats. At the provincial level, the results also indicated that the FF+ was neither increasing nor losing support. With a few smaller gains and losses balancing each other out, the party retained its single seats in five of the provincial legislatures and Gauteng remained the party's main support base.

Table 11.4 FF+ provincial results

	Vote share (%)			Seats		
	1994	**1999**	**2004**	**1994**	**1999**	**2004**
Eastern Cape	0.80	0.33	0.26	—	—	—
Free State	6.03	2.11	2.47	2	1	1
Gauteng	6.17	1.25	1.34	5	1	1
KwaZulu-Natal	0.51	0.23	0.28	—	—	—
Limpopo[a]	2.15	0.65	0.6	1	—	—
Mpumulanga	5.66	1.70	1.24	2	1	1
Northern Cape	5.97	1.66	1.55	2	1	1
North West	4.63	1.38	1.32	1	1	1
Western Cape	2.06	0.40	0.62	1	—	—

[a] Formerly Northern Province.

Source: Independent Electoral Commission of South Africa.

Almost one-third or 42,000 of the 139,465 votes the FF+ received nationally came from the Gauteng province.

The stable level of support for the FF+ can best be interpreted against the background of three developments. First, the FF+ of the 2004 election was actually an umbrella organization, containing within it three different Afrikaner parties. That this joining of forces did not yield better results signals that the appeal of Afrikanerdom could only just sustain but not extend the existing FF support base. Similarly, the alliances of the FF+ with other parties did not yield any electoral payoffs: the CPC could not frighten the coloured voter with its "swart gevaar" tactics, and the IFP was facing a losing battle in KZN. Finally, one would have expected the FF+ to benefit from the massive decline of the NNP. However, the evidence suggests that the FF+ was not able to scoop up conservative voters fleeing the NNP, who seemed instead to have moved to the ACDP and the DA.

Yet, the FF+'s evaluation of the election results was not negative. The party saw its stability in the face of the NNP's decline as a positive sign. In a media statement issued just after the election, the FF+ expressed satisfaction at its performance. The statement pointed out that the FF+ had successfully recovered from a disappointing performance in 1999, while the NNP had disintegrated, and that this was the benchmark against which to measure success.[25] However, the fact that the NNP's decline did not result in at least some new supporters for the FF+ suggests that the party lacks appeal among Afrikaners and raises questions about Afrikaner nationalism and the FF+'s future as an ethnically based party.

The Minority Front

The MF contested the 2004 election both nationally and in KZN. After a successful campaign, the MF emerged with gains at both levels. The party managed to slightly increase its share of the national vote from 0.30 percent in 1999 to 0.35 percent in 2004 and also saw its presence in the NA increase from one to two seats. Unsurprisingly, most of the party's national votes came from KZN.[26] In the province, the MF received 2.61 percent of the votes. This was less than the 2.93 percent the party got in 1999 but it nevertheless made a virtual clean sweep of the two working-class Indian areas. It won pluralities in twenty-four out of thirty-one voting districts in Phoenix and thirty-one out of the thirty-six districts in Chatsworth.[27] This meant that the MF gained the largest share of the vote here, eclipsing the DA, which in 1999 had won a plurality of votes in these areas. When interviewed about the MF victory in Phoenix and Chatsworth, Rajbansi stated that the DA's campaign against the MF had actually worked in favor of the party "and for that I must thank them."[28]

The MF's performance in the provincial poll saw the party retain its two seats in the KZN legislature. Like the ACDP, this placed the MF in the role of kingmaker when the ANC and IFP sought support in order to establish a majority and form a provincial government. In the past, the MF had supported the ANC both in KZN and in the National Assembly. This time, the MF had made a campaign pledge that it would work with the party that won the plurality of votes in the province, which constrained the postelection maneuverability of the MF. Bound by its campaign promise and in line with its cooperative strategy toward the ANC, the MF helped the ANC form the KZN provincial government. Its cooperative strategy paid off when following the inauguration of ANC provincial leader Sbu Ndebele as KZN premier, Rajbansi was given the MEC portfolio for sport and recreation. This could have been the reason why the MF party leader chose to stay in provincial politics and not take up one of the party's two seats in the National Assembly. On the other hand, Rajbansi's choice was probably part of a long-term strategy to remain close to his electorate, continue to consolidate his image as the people's politician, and build on the party's success in Phoenix and Chatsworth.

Rajbansi's position and leadership are important factors in the future prospects of the MF. Currently, the MF is to a large extent Rajbansi's party. Especially after Visvin Reddy's defection to the DA (and subsequently the ANC), there is no tier of MF leadership to take over the reins in the future. It remains to be seen whether the MF can retain and consolidate its success without The Raj. Given the fact that its support base is, by choice, limited to the Indian community, primarily within KZN, the party will have to continue to use its kingmaker role to gain influence. But, as the peace process in KZN progresses, and if the ANC continues to consolidate its hold on the electorate, the MF may find its pivotal position undermined.

The United Democratic Movement

The UDM's performance at the national and provincial level revealed a shrinking support base. In the national poll, the party's vote share decreased from 3.42 percent in 1999 to 2.28 percent in 2004, which gave the UDM nine seats in the NA. At the provincial level, the party lost support in every province and received less than 10 percent of the vote in its stronghold, the Eastern Cape. As a result, the UDM lost three of its nine seats in the provincial legislature but retained its status as the official opposition in the province. In Mpumulanga, the UDM failed to hold on to the one seat it won in 1999. The party retained the single seats it held in four other provinces: KZN, Limpopo, Gauteng, and the Western Cape (table 11.5). Thus, the UDM was able to hang onto some semblance of national appeal, but was unable to break out of its regional concentration in the Eastern Cape.

The decline of the UDM demonstrated the limitations of the party's appeal both nationally and in the Eastern Cape. In 1999, the party had offered something new to the Eastern Cape electorate: the prospect of a

Table 11.5   UDM provincial results

	Vote share (%)		Seats	
	1999	2004	1999	2004
Eastern Cape	13.6	9.23	9	6
Free State	1.67	0.88	—	—
Gauteng	1.95	0.99	1	1
KwaZulu-Natal	1.17	0.75	1	1
Limpopo[a]	2.51	1.72	1	1
Mpumulanga	1.42	1	1	—
Northern Cape	0.9	0.45	—	—
North West	1.29	0.96	—	—
Western Cape	2.4	1.75	1	1

[a] Formerly Northern Province.

Source: Independent Electoral Commission of South Africa.

serious opponent to the ANC and a change in the socioeconomic conditions in the province. Yet, the UDM failed to live up to its promises. While the party undoubtedly gained a great deal of media attention from the court case it lodged against the floor-crossing legislation and from its support for the investigation into the arms deal, there was little evidence of party activities related to the concerns of poor, unemployed people in the Eastern Cape and elsewhere. Therefore, the UDM's claim that it stood for the interests of the poor and disenfranchised did not have the same appeal this time around.

The most notable outcome of the 2004 election for the UDM was its position in KZN. Like the ACDP and the MF, the party's one seat in the provincial legislature enabled it to attract the attention of the ANC in its quest for a majority. Like the other two kingmakers, the UDM declared its support for the ANC and encouraged the party to repair its relationship with the IFP for the sake of peace in the province. Given the UDM's clear anti-ANC message during the election campaign, its alignment with the ANC may have seemed somewhat surprising especially when the party subsequently accepted the ANC's offer of a deputy minister post in the national government. However, the fact that the UDM was not able to develop the national support it needed to become a serious opponent of the ANC combined with the specific outcome of the 2004 election in KZN made a shift in its strategic relationship with the ruling party opportune and is perhaps even crucial to the party's future.

Conclusion

At first glance, there seems to be little that ties the five parties reviewed in this chapter together. Yet deeper inspection reveals that there are common trends. Each of these smaller parties appealed to a particular constituency, that is, Christians, Afrikaners, Indians in KZN, and former homeland residents in the Eastern Cape and North West. Some of these constituencies have the potential to deliver sizable electoral payoffs, but none actually delivered large shares of the vote in the 2004 election. All five parties tried to attract voters through a mix of socially and economically conservative programs and positions. Among the two "Christian" parties, the one that actually campaigned on a religious platform performed better than the other. The religious appeal seems to have some pull among the electorate. At the same time, despite higher levels of religious identification among South Africans, neither of the two religious parties succeeded in building a more than small political presence nationally or provincially.

The way the smaller parties gained influence was by taking on the role of kingmakers and coalition partners. The parties with a presence in KZN (the ACDP, MF, and UDM) had an advantage over their counterparts, which received their main support in less fiercely contested provinces. Among the kingmakers in KZN, there were differences in strategy toward the ANC, ranging from cooperation in government to offering support while retaining the independence to criticize the ruling party. The role of small parties in opposition politics therefore seems to resist settling into a particular mould, but overall it looks as though the smallest parties are becoming increasingly regionalized. What this means for the future is still unclear.

Each of the five parties seems to have developed a strategy of seeking power by representing a minority or regional interest. The electoral payoffs of such a strategy are uncertain. In the 2004 election, it worked for the ACDP and the MF, but was less successful for the FF+, the UDM, and the UCDP. This raises the question whether the representation of certain interests is as valid a goal for opposition parties as is challenging the ANC for power. After all, allowing for the political representation of smaller identity groups was an important motivation for the adoption of a system of proportional representation in South Africa.

In this context, the apparently shrinking overall space for opposition parties becomes even more interesting. Do various minority voters feel they no longer need to be represented by their "own" parties? If not, do they vote for the bigger parties instead or not vote at all? The fact is that none of the parties reviewed in this chapter significantly increased its support levels, even though the NNP lost over three-quarters of its 1999 support. Combined with the decline in turnout, this seems to indicate a turn toward non-voting rather than vote switching. What this means for the future of opposition politics is still unclear, but the evidence does not seem to indicate an impending realignment in South African party politics just yet.

Notes

1. *Business Day*, March 19, 2004, p. 4.
2. Institute for Democracy in South Africa (Idasa) opinion poll data indicate a growing level of religious identification. From 1994 to 2004, there has been an increase in people who respond that they are religious and identify themselves with their religions as a primary source of social identity.
3. *This Day*, February 24, 2004, p. 5.
4. For an overview of the party's performance in the 1994 and 1999 elections see Jessica Piombo, "The Smallest Parties: The UCDP, Minority Front, ACDP and Federal Alliance," in *Election '99 South Africa: From Mandela to Mbeki*, ed. Andrew Reynolds (Cape Town, London, and New York: David Phillip, James Currey, and St. Martin's Press, 1999), 133–146.

5. The South African colloquial term used to refer to those discriminated against by apartheid without using racial labels.
6. See http://:www.acdp.org.za/policies/trade.asp.
7. *The Mercury*, February 23, 2004, p. 2.
8. See Piombo, "The Smallest Parties," 134–136, for an overview of the party.
9. Ibid., 136.
10. "UCDP Kicks off Election Drive," press release accessed at http://www.ucdp.org.za/news/manifesto_launch.htm.
11. The party had signed an accord with the ANC seeking Afrikaner self-determination through a Volkstaat. See http://www.vryheidsfront.co.za/english/history_accord.asp for more details of the accord.
12. Patrick Cull, "Moment of Truth for Squabbling Parties," *The Herald,* April 12, 2004, accessed at http://www.theherald.co.za/colarc/cull/cu120404.htm.
13. "The Freedom Front Plus for a Volkstaat," January 29, 2004, accessed at http://iafrica.com/news/saelectionfocus/parties/299136.htm.
14. See the Freedom Front Plus 2004 Election Manifesto.
15. The CPC had formed during the window period for floor crossing in March 2003, to represent coloured people in the Western Cape. Both the FF+ and CPC saw their common ground of promoting Christian values, protecting and promoting Afrikaans as an indigenous language, reintroducing the death penalty for certain crimes, empowering their respective communities, zero tolerance on crime and ending affirmative action that had negatively impacted on their constituencies as the basis for cooperation. *This Day*, February 25, 2004, p. 5.
16. Adam Habib and Sanusha Naidu, "Transcending Race in the Fight for the 'Indian Vote,' " in *The Mercury*, April 2004, accessible online at http://www.sabcnews.com/features/elections_2004/ issues/isindian.html.
17. Piombo, "The Smallest Parties," 137.
18. *The Herald*, April 4, 2004.
19. Roger Southall, "The Struggle for a Place Called Home: The ANC Versus the UDM in the Eastern Cape," *Politikon* 26, no. 1 (1999): 155–166.
20. Since the Eastern Cape contains within it elements of two separate former Bantustans (Ciskei and Transkei) there were many civil servants who had been excessed since 1994. Additionally, the province's capital had been moved from Umtata to Bisho, which created another group of disaffected civil servants. Many of these people initially flocked to the UDM when it was created.
21. Following Meyer's departure, the UDM lost capable party organizers, many of whom left to join the new Democratic Alliance. In addition, the UDM has experienced difficulties in the middle tier of leadership, which have hampered its ability to operate as a coherent organization.
22. *The Sunday Times*, February 1, 2004, accessed at http://www.sundaytimes.co.za/2004/02/01/ politics/politics02.asp.
23. Unless otherwise noted, all election results in this chapter were obtained from the Web site of the Independent Electoral Commission, www.elections.org.za.
24. Initially, the ACDP was awarded six seats in the National Assembly. A few weeks after the election, however, it was discovered that a number of ACDP votes had been incorrectly awarded to Azapo. The ACDP brought the matter before the Electoral Court and as a result a seat that was initially awarded to Azapo was given to the ACDP, bringing its number of seats in the NA to seven.
25. Source: http://www.vryheidsfront.co.za/english/media.asp?language=e&id=429.
26. At the national level, the MF polled 55,267 votes, 51,339 of which came from KZN.
27. *Sunday Times Extra*, April 18, 2004, p. 1.
28. Ibid.

PART 3

Results and Assessment

CHAPTER TWELVE

Media Coverage in Election 2004: Were Some Parties More Equal Than Others?

Gavin Davis

Citizens in democracies the world over increasingly rely on the media and less on family, community, and other intermediary organizations for political information.[1] The growing importance of the media can also be observed in South African politics. This is why the main political parties employ media strategists and allocate a great deal of money to obtain prominent news coverage. It is also why the South African media remain a site of struggle, particularly during election campaigns.

The first part of this chapter considers how the mass media covered the 2004 election. Historical divisions in the media still influenced which parties were covered in which media. At the same time, increasing diversity has led to less partisan media. Parties got media coverage because of their ability to generate "news" and not because sections of the media were bent on promoting a specific party. The second part of this chapter discusses how the parties themselves used the media to get their message across to voters. The evidence suggests that the well-resourced parties increased their dominance of media coverage through their ability to advertise extensively in print, radio, and the outdoor media.

How the Media Covered the 2004 Election

Questions of media ownership and the demographic profile of newsrooms are raised regularly by those who feel that media transformation is too slow. Some analysts and politicians argue that the South African media (particularly the print media) are inherently elitist and therefore, by their very nature, will serve reactionary interests.[2] In 1999, an African National Congress (ANC) Member of Parliament (MP) told the National Assembly that the "liberal media" (i.e., the English language press) were "racist and unpatriotic" and that they "suppressed and distorted the truth, encouraging a negative mood in the country."[3] In 2001, the ANC noted a tendency for the media to "oppose the government at every turn," because newsrooms did not reflect a diversity of perspectives and experiences among journalists, editors, subeditors, managers, and photographers.[4]

ANC criticism of the independent press has led to concerns among the opposition that the ruling party will begin to use the state-owned South African Broadcasting Corporation (SABC) as an ANC mouthpiece. An Inkatha Freedom Party (IFP) representative recalled remarks allegedly made by an SABC spokesperson on radio that the SABC had to "compensate" for the "Mbeki-bashing" characteristic of other sections of the media.[5]

How the media relate to the ruling party and the opposition is particularly important in the course of an election campaign. This chapter attempts to ascertain whether the broadcast and print media exhibited any bias in their coverage of the 2004 election campaign.

Broadcast Media

The broadcast media are the main source of political information for most South Africans. Their reach into South African society has expanded significantly since 1994. A 1997 research report found that 52 percent of South Africans listened to the radio on a daily basis, 44 percent watched television, whereas only 16 percent read newspapers.[6] In 2004, over 23 million South Africans watched television at least once a week and over 27 million listened to the radio. The number of television sets in South African homes has grown from 5.9 million in 1994 to 8.2 million in 2004, while radio sets have tripled from 10.4 million to 33.7 million.[7] Given these trends, the impact of the broadcast media on the electorate should not be underestimated, and questions of ownership, diversity, and bias become increasingly important.

The radio sector has diversified markedly since 1994 when radio broadcasting was the sole preserve of the SABC and the former Bantustan-based broadcasters.[8] New and independent voices have emerged through the sale of six SABC stations to private shareholders in 1996, the rapid growth of community radio stations, and the arrival of E-TV, an independent television channel with its own news service, in 1998. However, the SABC still dominates broadcasting. Of radio listeners, 77 percent tune in to SABC stations, and 65 percent of radio listenership is accounted for by the SABC's African language services.[9] With regard to television, the SABC is responsible for most free-to-air television programs through its three channels: SABC 1, 2, and 3.

During apartheid, the SABC had served to advance apartheid propaganda. Questions of control, racial composition, news content, language policy, and ideology thus became paramount in the run-up to the first democratic election in 1994.[10] In their assessment of the SABC's role in that election, Silke and Schrire found that radio and television had been "able to steer a reasonably impartial ship," and that "the SABC had shed its shackles of overt or covert government control and was ready to enter into a new era of impartiality even if it was just for the duration of the election."[11]

However, since 1994, the SABC has come under considerable fire for perceived bias toward the ANC government. The appointment of known ANC loyalists to the SABC board fueled perceptions that transformation simply meant the replacement of one set of political masters by another.[12] In 2003, critics alleged that the ANC had attempted to sway the Communications Portfolio Committee in its nominations for the SABC board.[13] SABC board member Thami Mazwai stated that the SABC could not afford to be "driven by old clichés, such as objectivity or the right of the editor." Opposition parties interpreted these statements as evidence that Mazwai was linking SABC news to the ANC government's objectives.[14]

The SABC's role in the 2004 election was controversial. In January, the SABC aired live coverage of the ANC's election manifesto launch in Pietermaritzburg, a privilege not granted to any of the other parties. The meeting, which ANC president Thabo Mbeki began with a cry of "Viva, ANC, Viva," was undeniably a party rally, and the SABC coverage predictably raised outcries from the opposition. The Democratic Alliance (DA) complained that the SABC was acting as a public platform for the ANC government, while United Democratic Movement (UDM) leader Bantu Holmisa used the event to accuse the SABC of consistently favoring the ANC. The IFP claimed that the SABC decided to cover the ANC manifesto launch because the new SABC board chairperson, Eddie Funde, had been in charge of the ANC's party list selection process.[15] Media analysts Mandla Seloane and Simon Ndungu agreed that the SABC had given "undue advantage" to the ruling party.[16]

SABC spokesperson Paul Setsetse responded that the SABC was not favoring the ANC but recording the "first important presidential speech of the year."[17] The matter was taken to the Independent Communications Authority of South Africa (Icasa), which ruled in favor of the SABC on the grounds that the election period had not yet commenced. Since the election date had not yet been set by the president, this was not an unfair coverage of an election campaign event. The UDM reacted by calling Icasa's independence into question, while the DA's Dene Smuts stated: "The SABC seems to be settling into the role of state broadcaster, perpetuating ANC rule instead of serving democracy."[18]

Meanwhile, it emerged that Diane Kohler-Barnard, a well-known talk show presenter on the SABC radio station Safm, was a candidate on the DA party list for a seat in the National Assembly. The ANC stridently condemned the DA for "infiltrating" the SABC.[19] The SABC swiftly relieved Kohler-Barnard of her duties at the station, justifying the action on the grounds that "we must be seen to be objective and impartial and not be motivated by party political things in what we do."[20] For analyst Guy Berger, the dropping of Kohler-Barnard and the decision to broadcast an ANC election event smacked of double standards on the part of the public broadcaster.[21]

Party Coverage on Television

Despite accusations of SABC bias, analysis of television news coverage showed that the public broadcaster did not give undue coverage to the ANC or any other party. Data released by the Media Monitoring Project (MMP) indicated that the ANC did get the lion's share of the television news coverage. However, comparing the government-owned and independent television stations, the ANC actually received more coverage on the independent channel E-TV than on the SABC (see table 12.1). The DA and the IFP received a good proportion of coverage on television. The IFP received more coverage on E-TV than on SABC, while the DA got a higher proportion of coverage on SABC. Notably, the New

Table 12.1   Television news coverage of parties (% of total airtime devoted to parties)

	ACDP	ANC	DA	FF+	ID	IFP	NNP	UDM	Others
SABC	3.3	31.7	16.3	3	6.7	10.3	8.7	2.7	17.7
E-TV	4	47	14	4	4	16	0	0	12

Source: Media Monitoring Project.[22]

Table 12.2   Television news coverage of parties (% of total airtime devoted to parties)

	ACDP	ANC	DA	FF+	ID	IFP	NNP	UDM	PAC	Others
SABC (Afrikaans)	4.5	26.1	14.4	6.7	4.6	10.7	10.1	5.1	5.5	12.3
SABC (English)	5.6	22.8	14.1	3.8	4.9	14.1	9.6	6.3	6.7	12.1
SABC (Nguni)	3.4	29.3	14.0	3.7	3.0	15.1	9.2	6.0	5.9	10.4
E-TV	3.8	28.9	8.7	6.1	4.4	11.2	4.9	5.2	5.5	21.3

Source: Media Tenor.[23]

National Party (NNP) and UDM did not feature at all on E-TV during the period covered by the MMP.

A monitoring project by Media Tenor (see table 12.2) found that the ANC enjoyed slightly more coverage on the SABC Nguni news than on the Afrikaans and English news of the public broadcaster. The proportion of coverage for the ANC on the SABC Nguni news and on E-TV was almost the same. Again, the DA received a higher proportion of coverage on the SABC than on E-TV.

Media Tenor also measured how favorable television news coverage was to each party. They found that television coverage of all parties was mainly neutral, if not slightly positive. The study also showed that coverage of the ANC on SABC was less sympathetic than ANC coverage on E-TV, and that reports about the ANC were less positive on the Nguni news than on the English and Afrikaans news. Coverage of the DA tended to be negative on SABC news, but positive on E-TV.

Party Coverage on Radio

Analysis of radio news showed a similar picture with the ANC receiving most of the coverage across all radio stations (see table 12.3). The radio stations included in the monitoring project were a cross section of South African radio stations. Umhlobo Wenene (isiXhosa), Ukhozi (isiZulu), and Motsweding (seTswana) are SABC African language stations. SAFM is broadcast in English by the SABC and has a diverse listenership. YFM is an independent station that targets young, urban black people, while Algoa, OFM, and Radio Sonder Grense (RSG) are all commercial stations with a predominantly white listenership.

On all stations the ANC received the most coverage, with the proportion of ANC coverage being the highest on Ukhozi, Motsweding,

Table 12.3   Radio news coverage of parties (% of total airtime devoted to parties)

	ACDP	ANC	DA	FF+	ID	IFP	NNP	UDM	Others
U. Wenene	0	40	23	0	3	10	10	3	13
Ukhozi	1	45	10	1	2	24	5	5	7
Motsweding	4	45	12	3	3	7	4	4	17
YFM	2	32	24	2	9	17	8	4	13
SAFM	1	39	16	3	4	15	9	3	10
Algoa	7	43	21	0	5	2	7	14	0
OFM	9	33	24	4	4	9	11	4	2
RSG	1	35	21	4	8	14	11	4	2

Source: Media Tenor.

and Algoa, and the lowest on RSG, OFM, and YFM. The DA got the second highest proportion of airtime on all stations, except Ukhozi, which gave more coverage to the IFP, no doubt because this station uses isiZulu and broadcasts mainly in KwaZulu-Natal (KZN). The Independent Democrats (ID) made a relatively strong showing on radio news, especially on the stations RSG and YFM.

Parties got covered on the radio not only in the news but also through radio talk shows and radio advertising. There has been no systematic study of radio talk shows but data for advertising showed that the ANC and the DA got by far the most exposure through radio advertising, both in terms of paid adverts and Public Election Broadcasts (PEBs).

A PEB is a free two-minute advertising slot for political parties partic-ipating in the national ballot during prime listening time on all national radio stations. PEB slots were allocated to parties based on the number of seats held in the national and provincial legislatures and the number of candidates put forward in the 2004 election. Obviously, this formula was to the advantage of bigger parties, specifically the ANC with its large share of parliamentary seats. Icasa defended the policy by referring to the "international convention" that "the public is entitled to hear more from and about political parties more likely to influence policy decisions affecting the electorate, nationally and provincially."[24] In any event, the formula meant that the ANC received most of the PEBs.

Overall, the ANC received the most coverage on both radio and television, probably because, being the largest party, it generated the most news. As the ruling party, the ANC also received substantial media coverage through being mentioned by other parties and journalists. Media Tenor found that only 23 percent of the ANC's coverage (across all media) could be considered "own voice" coverage, with the party being the source of the statement. In contrast, the percentages of "own voice" coverage for the DA, IFP, and NNP were 42 percent, 32 percent and 39 percent respectively.[25]

Print Media

Newspapers may not have the reach of the broadcast media, but they are important for at least three reasons. First, newspapers are likely to be the media of choice among opinion makers who influence others in their communities. Second, newspapers provide a deeper analysis than radio and television, which increasingly report just sound bites. Third, the press has an investigative capacity unrivaled by the broadcast media. Major stories often break in the press and are then taken up by radio and television journalists.

In 1994, the newspaper industry was dominated by the pro-apartheid Nasionale Pers and the Anglo-American Corporation (AAC), which supported the parliamentary opposition. Nasionale Pers owned the Afrikaans press and the AAC controlled the English "liberal" press through the Argus Group and Times Media Limited. The print media was viewed by the ANC government as reflecting "the perspective and interests of a small group of South Africans" and being "almost totally exclusive of the experiences of black South Africans."[26] This perception was compounded by the fact that most of the English language press endorsed the DP in the 1994 election.[27]

Since 1994, print media ownership has diversified (see table 12.4). In 1996, the black empowerment group, the National Empowerment Consortium (NEC), acquired a controlling stake in Anglo-American's Johnnic, owners of Times Media Limited. Johnnic subsequently acquired the black empowerment company, New Africa Publications, with its popular titles, the *Sowetan* and *Sowetan Sunday World*. In 2004, Johnnic owned these two publications plus the *Business Day, The Herald, Daily Dispatch, East Cape Weekend Post*, and the *Sunday Times*. The Nasionale Pers (renamed Media 24) owned all four Afrikaans medium newspapers, *Die Burger, Die Volksblad, Rapport and Beeld*, plus the *Daily Sun*, the *Sunday Sun*, and the *City Press*, all with a predominantly black readership. In short, the duopoly of the Independent News Group and Media 24 has effectively been broken by Johnnic and the profile of print media ownership has changed. In 2004, approximately one-third of South Africans who read newspapers read black-owned publications.

In his assessment of the role of the media in the 1999 election, Jacobs argued that the print media had little influence on voter preferences because whites made up the bulk of the readers of mainstream newspapers and most

Table 12.4 Ownership and readership of mainstream newspapers

Title	Ownership	Readership	% White	% Black	% Coloured	% Indian
Beeld	Media 24	319,000	91	8	0.6	0.3
Volksblad	Media 24	118,000	86	7	7	0
Rapport★	Media 24	1,652,000	64	5	30	0.2
East Cape Weekend Post★	Johnnic	163,000	56	23	21	0
Mercury	Independent	189,000	47	21	3	30
Cape Times	Independent	270,000	44	13	41	3
Business Day	Johnnic	117,000	46	40	9	6
Witness	NWP	159,000	42	31	0	27
Isolezwe	Independent	339,000	0.3	99	0.3	0
Sowetan	Johnnic	1,853,000	0.3	98	1	0.4
City Press★	Media 24	2,211,000	1	98	1	0.3
Daily Sun	Media 24	1,755,000	0.7	96	3	0.6
Daily Dispatch	Johnnic	230,000	23	73	5	0
Pretoria News	Independent	97,000	31	64	1	4
Mail & Guardian★	M&G	237,000	30	61	8	2
Sunday Times★	Johnnic	3,440,000	24	58	9	9
The Citizen	Caxton	493,000	34	55	6	5
The Star	Independent	618,000	37	53	5	5
Sun. Independent★	Independent	230,000	29	48	11	13
Cape Argus	Independent	390,000	33	11	53	4
D. F. Advertiser	Independent	50,000	26	34	40	0
Die Burger	Media 24	577,000	44	1	55	0.2
The Post (Fri)★	Independent	1,440,000	3	3	0	94
Daily News	Independent	291,000	25	23	6	46
Sunday Tribune★	Independent	693,000	29	27	4	40
Independent on Sat.★	Independent	308,000	31	25	5	39

★ weekly newspapers.

Source: Ownership figures provided by Print Media South Africa; readership figures by South African Advertising Research Foundation.

journalists and editors were white.[28] In 2004, this situation has changed. Out of the 8 million newspapers read daily in South Africa, over 5 million are read by black South Africans. Whites account for 1.7 million, coloureds 879,000, and Indians 339,000.[29] As table 12.4 shows, the only newspapers that have a near exclusively white readership are the Afrikaans-medium newspapers, *Beeld* and *Volksblad*. *Isolezwe, Sowetan, City Press*, and the *Daily Sun* all have an almost totally black readership and *The Post* is read mainly by Indians. The other newspapers all have very diverse readerships. Similarly, the demographic profile of editors has changed substantially since 1994 when editors were almost without exception white males. By June 2000, twelve out of thirty editors of the country's main daily and weekly newspapers were black.[30] Therefore, Jacobs's arguments no longer apply. In 2004, the print media reached voters in both black and white communities.

Editorial Endorsements

Did the print media exhibit any bias in their coverage of the 2004 election campaign? Editorial endorsements provide some indication of the preferences of newspapers. A survey of a number of the main newspapers' editorials showed that most newspapers were less willing to endorse a particular party in 2004 than in previous elections. Only the *Sowetan, Sunday Times,* and *Mail & Guardian*—all newspapers with a relatively high proportion of black readers—endorsed the ANC. Both the *Sowetan* and the *Sunday Times* bemoaned the state of opposition in South Africa and endorsed the ANC as the only party capable of leading the nation forward. The *Mail & Guardian* noted several problems with the ruling party, but nevertheless endorsed the ANC because it was "still closest to the newspaper's core values."[31]

Almost all newspapers owned by the Independent group chose not to endorse a party in the 2004 election. The *Sunday Independent* ran an editorial calling for America to withdraw its troops from Iraq.[32] The *Cape Argus, The Star, Cape Times, Weekend Post,* and the *Sunday Tribune* urged readers to not shirk their civic duty and vote for the party of their choice.[33] Only the *Pretoria News* appeared willing to indicate its preference and tried to convince readers to go to the polls and vote against the ANC: "Every non-vote is in effect a vote for the ruling party—and that's not good for democracy."[34] Similarly, most Afrikaans and English language newspapers owned by Media 24 abstained from endorsements.

The fact that most of the "liberal" and Afrikaans newspapers chose not to endorse any party was a sign that the print media was less partisan than sometimes suggested. The cautious endorsement of the ANC by some publications with a predominantly black readership indicated that, if anything, it was the ANC that enjoyed support in the press.

Party Coverage in the Press

In terms of influence on the electorate, editorial endorsements are probably less critical than news articles about political parties. Therefore, it is important to ascertain whether there was any bias in the amount of coverage parties received in the print media. Tables 12.5 and 12.6 show how much coverage each party received in the press as measured by the Media Monitoring Project (MMP) and Media Tenor (MT).

Table 12.5 Newspaper coverage of parties (% of total space in main news sections)

	ACDP	ANC	DA	FF+	ID	IFP	NNP	UDM	Others
Star	1	36	22	3	14	9	6	3	6
Citizen	1	40	22	1	8	10	8	5	5
Bus. Day	2	45	17	0	12	10	8	1	3
Cape Times	3	40	19	2	9	6	10	2	8
EP Herald	1	47	23	3	5	7	5	3	6
Mail & Guardian	6	28	13	4	7	11	7	5	19
Sunday Times	2	57	15	2	7	13	4	0	0
Sowetan	2	42	18	1	13	10	4	3	7
Daily Sun	10	40	10	0	0	20	10	10	0
Ilanga	2	35	5	2	0	51	0	2	4
Isolezwe	1	49	6	0	0	33	0	6	4
City Press	3	43	14	3	3	19	7	4	5
Beeld	4	31	17	6	9	13	10	4	9
Die Burger	3	34	18	5	8	7	14	3	8
All	2.9	40.5	15.6	2.3	6.8	15.6	6.6	3.6	6

Source: Media Monitoring Project.

Table 12.6 Newspaper coverage of parties (% of total space in main news sections)

	ACDP	ANC	DA	FF+	ID	IFP	NNP	UDM	PAC	Others
Star	3.8	36.5	21.2	1.8	3.9	9.6	8.2	3.5	4.6	6.9
Citizen	2.2	36.0	30.0	2.2	2.3	7.4	11.6	2.1	1.8	4.4
Business Day	1.7	42.9	24.0	1.0	4.5	10.0	7.8	2.6	1.9	3.6
Pretoria News	4.2	36.2	21.4	4.1	4.1	11.8	9.9	2.3	2.7	3.3
Sunday Ind.	1.9	52.0	20.5	0.6	1.5	6.1	5.0	2.1	8.5	1.8
Sowetan	1.1	46.7	22.1	1.0	2.9	10.9	5.4	2.5	3.9	3.5
City Press	2.8	39.4	15.2	0.6	1.8	17.4	2.9	3.8	10.3	5.8
Sunday Sun	3.8	40.0	8.8	1.7	7.1	9.2	7.1	10.9	4.2	7.2
Mail & Guardian	2.4	52.4	18.0	1.4	1.8	9.7	7.4	1.6	3.6	1.7
Sunday Times	1.6	55.6	15.4	0.5	1.0	11.1	7.0	2.1	2.5	3.2
Beeld	2.5	36.7	21.5	4.5	3.0	13.3	10.0	2.5	2.5	3.5
Rapport	4.0	28.8	23.6	6.9	3.0	6.8	17.6	2.0	0.9	6.4
All	2.7	41.9	20.1	2.4	3.1	10.3	8.3	3.2	4.0	4.3

Source: Media Tenor.

According to MMP, the ANC received most of the coverage in all newspapers except the Zulu-medium *Ilanga*, which devoted more space to the IFP. The proportion of ANC coverage was highest in the *Sunday Times* and *Isolezwe*, both publications with a large black readership. It was lowest in the *Mail & Guardian, Beeld,* and *Die Burger.* In the *Mail & Guardian* the proportion of space devoted to the ANC (and other main parties) was lower because the very small parties received more coverage. The Freedom Front Plus (FF+) and the NNP received a higher share of coverage in the Afrikaans dailies. The DA received a good deal of coverage in all newspapers, with the exception of *Ilanga* and *Isolezwe.* The IFP's extensive coverage in these two newspapers meant that the party averaged the same proportion of coverage as the DA overall, though less evenly spread.

According to Media Tenor, the ANC enjoyed the highest proportion of coverage in all newspapers. ANC coverage was highest in the *Sowetan, Sunday Times, Sunday Independent,* and the *Mail & Guardian*, which have a significantly high black readership. The proportion of ANC coverage was lowest in *Rapport*, one of the two Afrikaans newspapers included in the study. The DA enjoyed a good deal of coverage in all papers except the *Sunday Sun*, which devoted relatively more space to the UDM. Again the FF+ and the NNP were covered more prominently in the Afrikaans press than elsewhere.

Newspaper coverage was generally neutral, but, unlike on television, parties received more negative than positive coverage in newspapers. One exception was the NNP, which enjoyed favorable coverage in most titles monitored by Media Tenor. The *Sowetan* was the only publication that gave the ANC a good deal more positive than negative coverage and only the *Sunday Independent* was positive about the DA, indicating that the two main parties were critically reviewed in the press. The IFP received negative coverage in most of the black and "liberal" press and were covered positively only in *Rapport*. The FF+ struggled to get good publicity, although the party seemed to be most favorably covered in the *City Press* and *Beeld*. Coverage of the PAC was favorable only in the *Mail & Guardian* and *City Press*.

It is clear from these data that the ANC and the DA received the lion's share of print media coverage. The fact that the DA got more coverage than other opposition parties and the ANC's dominance of coverage across all media, are less an indication of media bias than a sign that these two parties probably generated the most news. The ANC and the DA were most active between elections as well as on the campaign trail. The high profile leaders of both parties attracted the media to cover their election campaign events. Media Tenor found that out of all politicians, Tony Leon received the most media coverage, 30 percent, followed by Thabo Mbeki with 26 percent.

The advantage of high profile leadership is encapsulated in a remark made by UDM spokesperson Siviwe Nzwelini: "We would organize a rally and then the ANC would organize a rally nearby with a high profile speaker. The media would then be more concerned in covering the ANC than the UDM."[35] The ID's Media Officer Marlon Kruger believed that the ANC and the DA got a lot of coverage because Thabo Mbeki was the president and the DA was effective in getting publicity.[36] As the next section shows, the ANC and the DA were able to boost their media profile further through paid advertising.

How the Parties Used the Media

The main parties all have media strategists and departments that aim to get the party covered in the media by writing press releases and alerting the media to the movements of the party leaders on the campaign trail. In addition, parties can be assured of a good deal of media exposure through paid advertisements, whether on posters, billboards, or through newspaper and radio adverts. The remainder of this chapter provides an overview of the advertising strategies of the major parties. The ANC and the DA had unrivaled access to resources through public and private funding. This meant that they enjoyed a great deal more coverage than other parties through paid advertising.

Posters and Other Outdoor Media

Most parties waged a national poster campaign with little variation from province to province in terms of content. The ANC posters called on voters to support the ANC in order to help the ruling party create work and fight poverty. A large number of ANC posters contained no programmatic messages, simply reading: "Vote ANC 14 April." Many ANC posters featured a smiling and benevolent looking Thabo Mbeki, accompanied by the election slogan: "Vote ANC: A better life for all."

The DA posters were more issue based, promising to put 150,000 cops on the street, to convict corrupt politicians, to provide free AIDS drugs and the creation of "1 million *real* jobs." Many DA posters featured a picture of a smiling Tony Leon with the slogan: "South Africa Deserves Better."

This was a significant departure from the main DP poster in the 1999 election, which had depicted a grim-faced Tony Leon, with his arms folded, urging South Africans to "Fight Back." Another prominent DA poster in 2004 urged voters to "Vote DA for Real Change." A number of DA posters, prominent in the Western Cape, simply read: "The NNP and ANC are the same—Vote DA." The black and red colors of this particular poster were not consistent with the DA's usual yellow and blue election material, possibly indicating that the DA was not entirely comfortable associating itself with the negative undertones of the poster.

The NNP responded to the DA's red and black posters with its own posters in black. One variation read: "Stop DA race politics," and another: "The DP + right-wing = DA." Both were aimed at black and coloured voters and attempted to portray the DA as the party of white privilege. The NNP projected itself as a Cape-based party, through posters declaring: "Keep the Cape NNP" and "Marthinus for Premier." The NNP's strategy of minority protection through cooperative government was apparent in posters that read: "You deserve a fair share," "It's your country too," and "The NNP—Your key to government."

The FF+ pleaded with voters to "Se Nee vir die ANC" ("Say no to the ANC") and told disaffected minorities that "Daar is weer hoop" ("There is hope again"). The UDM called for the "arrest of arms-deal crooks" and declared that "ten years of unemployment undermine the people's freedom." The ID posters sought to bank on the popularity of their leader by featuring a large picture of Patricia de Lille giving the thumbs-up sign and telling prospective ID voters that they would get more voice for their vote. The IFP urged people to come together and vote for the IFP, featuring Mangosuthu Buthelezi surrounded by female IFP members of all races. PAC posters consisted of a picture of party leader Motsoko Pheko with the rather cumbersome caption: "Together restoring the dignity of the African people through an equitable distribution of wealth."

Placement of Posters

Aside from content, the placement of posters gives an indication of the groups that parties targeted in their campaigns. Research conducted during April 2004 in the Western Cape, Gauteng, and KZN showed that the ANC and DA produced by far the most posters and that poster placement tended to correlate with the strategic imperatives of parties.[37] The ANC dominated African townships, but the DA also placed posters in these areas of "uncharted territory" for the party. The DA, NNP, and FF+ dominated the white suburbs, whereas coloured and Indian areas were targeted by a broad range of parties that probably viewed these voters as "swing voters."

In the white middle-class suburb of Edgemead in the Western Cape, the FF+, the NNP, and the DA were the most prominent and there were very few ANC posters. Lampposts in the white upper-middle-class area of Houghton and the Afrikaans-speaking suburb of Florida, both in Gauteng, were dominated by the DA. The DA was again the most prominent party in the white working-class area of Oribi village in KZN, but researchers reported a dearth of DA posters in the white middle-class suburb of Berea where the ANC and the NNP dominated.

The ANC saturated the African townships of the Western Cape with posters, billboards, and painted murals of Thabo Mbeki. UDM posters were few and far between, while PAC posters showed up only occasionally. On the major thoroughfare between Guguletu and Nyanga, there was approximately one DA poster for every three ANC posters. A large number of these DA posters were in Xhosa. One read: "Umzantsi Afrika Ufanelwe Zizonte Ezingcono" ("South Africa deserves better"), while another stated: "Isigidi semisebenzi eyiyo" ("One million *real* jobs"). Along Masithandane Street in Kayamandi township near Stellenbosch, just over 55 percent of the posters were ANC, including two large ANC billboards. The UDM also had a fairly strong presence in this township, accounting for roughly one-third of the posters. Imbali, a black working-class township outside of Pietermaritzburg in KZN was dominated by ANC billboards and posters. Of all the posters counted 63 percent were ANC, while the DA accounted for about 30 percent. Only ANC posters could be seen in the black rural area of Willowfontein, although there were a few DA posters at the intersection leading into the area. In Richmond, roughly 60 percent of the posters were ANC and only 4 percent were IFP. ANC posters also dominated in Alexandra township in Gauteng. Along Roosevelt road, there were forty ANC posters to the DA's twenty-two and the PAC's eighteen. Three African Christian Democratic (ACDP) posters were seen and six IFP posters. Along Lombardy street in Richmond, our researcher counted twenty-two posters each for the ANC and the DA, but none for any other party.

In the predominantly coloured area of Athlone in the Western Cape, the ANC, the NNP, and the DA had a fairly equal amount of posters. Along Klipfontein road, approximately 36 percent of the posters were ANC, 28 percent NNP, and 32 percent DA. The Peace and Development Party, the African Muslim Party, the Moderate Independent Party and the African Christian Democratic Party all placed some posters here. Peter Marais's New Labour Party posters attempted to woo the "coloured vote," with a smiling Marais urging these voters to "Come Home." Posters were also diverse in the coloured working-class suburbs of Newlands, Montclare, and Westbury in Gauteng with the ANC, DA, and NNP featuring most prominently.

Reflecting the spirited competition for the "Indian vote," various parties put up posters in the Indian working-class area of Chatsworth in KZN. Here the Minority Front was the most prominent, with thirty-six out of eighty-three posters along the Higgenson Highway. The DA accounted for roughly a quarter of the posters, and their red and black "NNP and ANC are the same" posters featured strongly. The placement of the poster here and not in other parts of the province indicated that the DA's strategy in the Indian areas of KZN was similar to its strategy in the coloured areas of the Western Cape. The ACDP, ANC, and IFP had twelve, nine, and five posters respectively, while the NNP had no posters in Chatsworth. In the predominantly middle-class Indian area of Westville North, ANC and DA posters were the most prominent with both parties having placed about 35 percent of the posters along Dawncliffe Road. The MF followed with 25 percent of the posters and the ACDP with 4 percent. As in the Indian areas of KZN, Lenasia in Gauteng featured a good variety of posters. Here ANC and DA posters dominated, although Azapo and the NNP were well represented.

One should be cautious in generalizing from these data, but poster placement appears to be a good indicator of party strategy on the ground. The ANC had an unrivaled dominance in the black townships, although the DA did place part of its poster campaign there. For all its bluster as a nonracial, catchall party, the NNP did not target black areas. All three parties featured prominently in coloured and Indian areas, indicating that these residents were regarded as relatively uncommitted voters that could be won over. Posters of the IFP, UDM, PAC, ID, and others were far less prominent in all areas, which was probably due to their limited campaign resources.

Financial resources played an important role in the use of other outdoor media. The ANC made the most extensive use of outdoor media other than posters, spending R12 million on billboards, murals, and moving media (such as adverts on taxis, buses, and trucks). The UDM spent R1.4 million on other outdoor media, while the DA spent R200,000, the IFP R15,000, and the UCDP R11,990.[38] Many other parties, like the NNP, did not use billboards, probably because of their cost.[39]

Radio Advertising

In addition to the Public Election Broadcasts (PEB) discussed earlier in this chapter, parties were allowed to place paid advertisements on the radio but not on television. Nielsen Media Research calculated how much parties spent to purchase airtime. These so-called Adspend data revealed that in the period from January to the end of March 2004, political parties collectively spent over R12 million on radio advertisements.[40] In the use of radio for their election campaign, the DA and the ANC were far ahead of the competition. Both parties spent more on radio advertising and used radio advertisements to reach a much broader audience than their competitors.

The DA spent R5.9 million on radio advertisements, outspending the ANC by some R1.1 million. According to DA Director of Communications, Nick-Clelland Stokes, "The DA wants to get every South African. We focus on radio because it is the most effective way of targeting people."[41] The DA spent over R2 million advertising on stations with a predominantly black listenership, spending R775,000 on the isiZulu-medium station Ukhozi alone. The DA spent R1.3 million advertising on stations with a white listenership such as 5FM, Cape Talk, Highveld, OFM, and Radio Sonder Grense. The party allocated the remainder to stations with a more diverse listenership such as East Coast Radio, Jacaranda, Radio 702, and SAFM. Common themes on DA radio adverts were assertions that the DA, with its partners, would win 30 percent of the vote; that Thabo Mbeki's biggest ally was Robert Mugabe; that the NNP and MF had betrayed their supporters by joining forces with the ANC, and that a vote for the ID was a wasted vote.

The ANC spent R4.75 million on radio advertising. Like the DA, the ANC advertised on a wide range of stations, although it spent over 80 percent of its radio-advertising budget on stations with a predominantly black listenership. The ANC produced eight types of adverts around the following themes of job creation, fighting poverty, fighting crime, fighting corruption, improving service delivery, and building a united nation.

Other parties spent far less than the DA and ANC on radio advertising and tended to target niche markets. The NNP spent R1.1 million and only advertised on radio stations with a predominantly white, coloured, and Indian listenership. The FF+ spent just under R450,000 advertising on KFM, Jakaranda, OFM, and Radio Sonder Grense, all Afrikaans stations with a mainly white listenership, as well as on Afrikaans-medium university campus radio stations: Matie FM (Stellenbosch), Radio Tuks

(Pretoria University), and Radio RAU (Rand Afrikaans University). The UDM and the IFP spent R300,000 and R490,000 respectively, both choosing to advertise mainly on the African language stations. The ID and ACDP spent a meager R70,000 and R23,000 respectively.

Newspaper Advertising

Parties devoted the smallest portion of their advertising budgets on the print media. The ANC dominated the market, spending R3.8 million on advertisements in newspapers, far more than any other party. The ANC advertised in nearly every title, spending over R700,000 on advertising in *Beeld*, *Die Burger*, and *Rapport*, and R550,000 on advertisements in the "black" newspapers *City Press*, *Sowetan*, and the *Daily Sun*. The DA allocated only R790,000 to newspaper advertisements. This was five times less than the ANC and R110,000 less than the UDM's budget for newspaper adverts of over R900,000. Unlike the DA's "catch-all" advertising on radio, the party targeted newspapers with minority readerships such as *Beeld*, *Die Burger*, *Cape Argus*, *Daily News*, and *Rapport* and did not advertise in *City Press, the Daily Sun*, or *Sowetan*. The NNP and FF+ spent R550,000 and R115,000 respectively, both advertising mainly in the Afrikaans press. The IFP and the ACDP only advertised in community newspapers. The ACDP, IFP, and ID all cited a lack of funds for not advertising extensively in the print media.[42]

Conclusion

This analysis points to the increasing media dominance of the ANC as the ruling party and the DA as the voice of opposition. Disparities in public and private funding gave the ANC and the DA an unrivaled ability to ensure a strong media presence in the run-up to the election. Both parties could afford to run extensive and sustained advertising campaigns in the press, on the airwaves, and on posters and other outdoor media.

The extensive coverage given to the ANC and the DA was not the result of media bias. Both parties enjoyed coverage across *all* media: in the "liberal," "Afrikaans," and "black" presses, as well as on an assortment of television and radio stations. However, coverage of the ANC was comparatively higher in the black press. The liberal press tended to cover the DA slightly more than other parties, while the FF+ and the NNP enjoyed comparatively more exposure in the Afrikaans media and the IFP in the isiZulu media.

In general, the South African media were less partisan than they have been. There seemed to be a sufficient plurality of media voices to act as a counterweight against the possible development of an uncritical or biased media. This is not to say that debates about the role of the media will not or should not continue. While the media was far more diverse in 2004 than 1994 in terms of ownership, personnel, and audience, there is still some way to go before media transformation can be considered complete. The SABC's broadcasting of an ANC rally in the run-up to the 2004 election, coupled with the postelection appointment of ANC loyalist Snuki Zikalala to a senior position at the SABC gives cause for concern. Time will tell whether the DA's prophecy that "the SABC is set to become Mbeki's broadcaster outright" will prove correct.[43]

Notes

1. Anthony Mughan and Richard Gunther, "The Media and Nondemocratic Regimes: A Multilevel Perspective," in *Democracy and the Media—A Comparative Perspective*, ed. Richard Gunther and Anthony Mughan (New York: Cambridge University Press, 2000), 3.

2. See e.g., Sean Jacobs, "The Media and the Elections," in *Election '99 South Africa: From Mandela to Mbeki*, ed. Andrew Reynolds (Cape Town, London, and New York: David Philip, James Currey, and St. Martin's Press, 1999), 147–158.

3. Cecil Valentine-Burgess, "South Africa," in *So This is Democracy? Report on the State of the Media in Southern Africa 1999*, ed. Rashied Galant (Windhoek: Media Institute of South Africa, 2000), 121.

4. ANC Press Statement, "What South Africa Needs is a Truly Critical Media," May 7, 2001, accessed at www.anc.org.za/ancdocs/pr/2001/pr0507.html.

5. "Mbeki's Radio Slot Raises Political Eyebrows," *Independent Online*, January 22, 2004, accessed at www.iol.co.za.

6. Soraya Kola and David Everatt, "Analysing Radio Listenership Patterns" (Johannesburg: Community Agency for Social Enquiry, 1997), 2.

7. Luise Allerman, "What a Difference a Decade Makes," *Marketing Mix* 22, no. 3 (April 2004): 28.

8. Michael Marcowitz, "Regulation Ten Years On," *Marketing Mix* 22, no. 3 (April 2004): 37.

9. Sarah Crowe, "Local Media Freedom is Not Set in Stone," *Focus* 31 (September 2003), accessed at http://www.hsf.org.za/focus31/focus31crowe.html; Africa All Media and Products Survey (AMPS) conducted by the South African Advertising Research Foundation (SAARF), accessed at http://www.saarf.co.za.

10. Ruth Teer-Tomaselli and Keyan G. Tomaselli, "Reconstituting Public Service Broadcasting: Media and Democracy During Transition in South Africa," in *Media and Democracy*, ed. Michael Bruun Andersen (Oslo: University of Oslo Press, 1994), 217.

11. Daniel Silke and Rober Schrire, "The Mass Media and the South African Election," in *Election '94 South Africa: The Campaigns, Results, and Future Prospects*, ed. Andrew Reynolds (Cape Town, London, and New York: David Philip, James Currey, and St. Martin's Press, 1994), 128 and 142.

12. Teer-Tomaselli and Tomaselli, "Reconstituting Public Service Broadcasting," 98.

13. S'Thembiso Msomi, "ANC 'Selects' SABC Board Members," *Sunday Times*, October 5, 2003.

14. Gordon Bell, "News Objectivity Just a 'Delusion,' " *The Herald Online*, June 4, 2003, accessed at http://www.epherald.co.za/herald/2003/06/04/news/n21_04062003.htm.

15. Charles Phahlane and Bheko Madlala, "ANC Using SABC in Massive Push for KZN," *The Independent on Saturday*, January 9, 2004.

16. Ndivhuwo Khangale, "SABC Must Cover Other Parties Too," *The Star,* January 12, 2004.

17. Raymond Louw, "SABC Breaks the Rules and ICASA Turns a Blind Eye," *Election Update South Africa 2004,* no. 1 (Auckland Park: EISA), 10.

18. "Opposition Parties Condemn Icasa's Decision," *Independent Online,* January 20, 2004, accessed at www.iol.co.za.

19. ANC Press Statement, "ANC Calls for Firing of Diane Kohler-Barnard," February 9, 2004, accessed at www.anc.org.za.

20. Sam Sole, "SABC's Double Standards," *Mail & Guardian,* February 13–19, 2004.

21. Guy Berger, "Practise What You Preach," *Mail & Guardian,* February 13–19, 2004.

22. The Media Monitoring Project (MMP) counted the number of times a party was mentioned on the news. The data do not give any indication as to whether statements were by the party itself or by a third party. MMP monitored election coverage from March 22 until April 16.

23. Data provided by Media Tenor (MT). MT measured coverage in terms of whether a party was the source of a statement. MT monitored the media from January 1 until April 14.

24. Icasa, "Regulations relating to party election broadcasts, political advertisements, the equitable treatment of political parties by broadcasting licensees and related matters in respect of the 2004 general elections," Report available at www.icasa.org.za, 18.

25. See www.media-tenor.co.za/index1.html.

26. ANC Press Statement, "Debate on Media Control," December 1, 1995, accessed at www.anc.org.za/ancdocs/pr/1995/pr120a.html.

27. ilke and Schrire, "The Mass Media," 122.

28. Jacobs, "The Media," 148.

29. Figures provided by the South African Advertising Research Foundation (SAARF).

30. Media Development and Diversity (MDDA) "Draft Position Paper," 20 (2000), available at http://www.gov.za/documents/2000/mdda/mdda2.pdf.

31. *Sunday Times,* April 11, 2004; *Sowetan,* April 13, 2004; *Mail & Guardian,* April 8–15, 2004.

32. *Sunday Independent,* April 11, 2004.

33. *Cape Argus, Cape Times,* and *The Star,* April 13, 2004; *Sunday Tribune,* April 11, 2004; and *Weekend Post,* April 10, 2004.

34. *Pretoria News,* April 13, 2004.

35. Interview with Nzwelini conducted by the author in Cape Town, May 6, 2004.

36. Interview with Kruger conducted by the author in Cape Town, May 6, 2004.

37. Alexandra Paddock, Sarah Meny-Gibert, and Gavin Davis carried out the poster research in KZN, Gauteng, and the Western Cape respectively. Researchers counted the number of posters for each party along a one-kilometer stretch of a major artery in representative areas of each city.

38. Data provided by AC Nielsen.

39. Author's interview with Carol Johnson, NNP Media Director, in Cape Town, May 7, 2004.

40. AC Nielsen measured adspend for forty-three commercial and seventy community radio stations.

41. Moshoeshoe Monare, "No Transparency Over Election Budgets," *The Sunday Independent,* March 14, 2004.

42. Interview with Selby Khumalo, National Media Director of the ACDP, Marlon Kruger, Media Officer of the ID, and Musa Zondi, IFP Director of Communications, May 6, 2004.

43. "Zikalala's Appointment No Accident: DA," SABC News, April 22, 2004, accessed at http://www.sabcnews.com/politics/elections/0,2172,78121,00.html.

CHAPTER THIRTEEN

The Results of Election 2004: Looking Back, Stepping Forward

JESSICA PIOMBO

On April 14, 2004, South Africans voted for the third time in democratic national and provincial elections. This third test of majority rule demonstrated that the institutionalization of democracy in South Africa is well under way and that politics are normalizing to an extent that can be observed in many established democracies around the world. Now that the 2004 election has come and gone, we can begin to evaluate what the results mean for the state of democracy and party politics, and the future of a democratic South Africa.

In contrast to the politically tense situation that surrounded the 1994 election, in 2004 the electoral process was calm. There were very few incidents of politically motivated violence and the remaining issues revolved around the more technical aspects of electoral administration. To many South Africans, for whom the memories of the heady days in 1994 are still fresh, electoral politics in 2004 may even have seemed dull. One of the factors contributing to this seemingly unexciting electoral process was the fact that the results were known well before the first ballot had been cast. There was no doubt that the ruling African National Congress (ANC) would retain its position and remain in government. The main questions were: how large would be the ANC's margin of victory, and would there be a further fragmentation of the opposition? By the evening of April 15, the answer to these questions became apparent: the ANC was heading toward winning a two-thirds majority, while the opposition remained as fragmented as it had become after the 1999 election.

In the end, the ANC won 279 out of the 400 seats in the National Assembly (NA), and the power to form the government in all nine provinces. Thus, the ruling party increased its dominant position in South African politics. On the other side of the benches, the opposition failed to band together behind a few larger parties, and returned to parliament with thirteen parties sharing 121 seats. The Democratic Alliance (DA) performed well and increased its support above the levels that the DP reached in 1999, yet failed to reach the 30 percent threshold that it had projected it would win along with its alliance partners. The DA was the only opposition party that increased its representation in the NA by more than one seat. The New National Party (NNP) experienced a devastating defeat as it saw its national support decline to less than 2 percent. As the results came in on election night, many pronounced the NNP dead. By August 2004, they were proven right, when NNP leader Marthinus van Schalkwyk announced that the party would disband in the next year. Ten years after the advent of democracy in South Africa, the architect of apartheid decided to close up shop.

In order to assess what the election results mean for the future of South Africa, this chapter aims to discuss various aspects of the 2004 election. It aims to draw out electoral trends during the past decade of majority rule. In these pages, I revisit one of the questions raised in the beginning of the volume: how should we interpret the increasingly dominant position of the ANC, and offer a slightly different interpretation from the normal pessimism. I also investigate the increasing fragmentation of the opposition. Finally, I turn to an examination of the new parliament and cabinet, and pose the question, "What comes next?"

Trends in Political Violence and Turnout

The 1994 election exhibited a duality common to political transitions: the period was filled with the spirit of hope and renewal, but within a climate of insecurity and political intimidation. Politically related violence spiked the year before the election with a large number of political assassinations, violence between supporters of rival political parties, and fears that the White Right or Inkatha would destabilize the electoral process. Violence monitors estimated that before the April polls, hundreds of people died each month in politically related violence, with the highest number of incidents occurring in KwaZulu and Natal between members of the ANC and the Inkatha Freedom Party (IFP). Monitors were also worried that members of the White Right would stage a violent incident capable of derailing the electoral process. In the end, the election took place without major incidents, but the process was on a knife's edge.

In 1999, there were still incidents of violence and intimidation, but on a much smaller scale. KwaZulu-Natal (KZN) remained a hotspot, but whereas in the six months preceding the 1994 poll, over 300 people died each month, in the entire five months before the 1999 election, fewer than 300 people were killed in the province.[1] Other hotspots included areas where the United Democratic Movement (UDM) was growing and posed a challenge to the ANC, such as in the Cape Flats, Richmond in KZN, and several townships outside of Johannesburg. The White Right, which had threatened to derail the election in 1994, remained passive. The relative calm of the 1999 election was a sign that politics were beginning to normalize.

The decrease in political violence can be traced against not only a growing acceptance of electoral means to resolve political conflict, but also the increasing dominance of the ruling party at national and provincial levels. In the opening chapter of this volume, Friedman argued that in a country dominated by identity politics, the ANC is secure in its position, and therefore does not need to intimidate opposition parties or voters. I would like to suggest that the ANC's dominance in itself contributed to the peacefulness of the 2004 election, regardless of whether or not this dominant position is due to identity politics. In a context where there is no doubt that the ruling party will win an overwhelming majority, there is little reason for political tension to rise to violent levels. The only problem remaining could be when despondent opposition supporters resort to intimidation and violence to prevent the ruling party from winning. This did not happen in 1994, 1999, or 2004.

In fact, remaining incidents of electoral violence and intimidation occurred with highest frequency in the provinces in which the ANC did not already hold a majority—the Western Cape and KZN. In 1999, in addition to these two areas, electoral violence had spiked in the Greenfields area of Johannesburg and in the Eastern Cape, where the UDM mounted what seemed to be a serious challenge to the ANC's position (though in hindsight, the extent of this challenge may have been miscalculated). Consistently across all three elections, in the regions and areas where the outcome was uncertain, violence and intimidation arose. In the areas where there was little question that the ANC would win, electoral violence was much diminished. Thus, the ANC's security in its dominant position can be interpreted as one of the factors underlying the increasing peacefulness of the electoral process.[2]

By April 2004, the electoral process had become so routine that many described the campaign and voting day as boring and reporters searching for controversial stories had little to cover. There was no large-scale political intimidation, the number of politically related deaths was minimal, and there were very few "hotspots" of conflict between rival parties. The list of potential trouble areas identified by the Independent Electoral Committee (IEC) included mostly informal settlements where fires had destroyed people's identity documents, preventing them from voting.[3] The IEC worried that these people would try to vote anyway, and could get violent when denied.[4] There were reports of intimidation in KZN and a few other areas, but overall the campaigns and voting day were overwhelmingly peaceful. The electoral process was perceived to be on track to such an extent that the European Union, United Nations, Commonwealth, and Carter Center all declined to send delegations to monitor and observe the 2004 election.

In 2004, not voter *intimidation* but voter *apathy* was a major concern among political leaders and analysts. As in 1999, people had to be registered on the voters' roll in order to cast their ballots on election day. The responsibility to register lays with the individual South African, who must be in possession of a specific form of identification, a bar-coded identity document, and apply to be included on the voters' roll by registering at a local office of the Department of Home Affairs. While people could register at any Home Affairs office at any time up until the election date was announced by the president, most people either did not know about or were unable to take advantage of this opportunity. Therefore, as it had done in 1999, the IEC held special "registration weekends," during which local voting stations opened for the purpose of registering eligible voters and allowing those already registered to check the voters' roll to make sure that they were listed. Originally, the IEC planned to hold only one registration weekend for the 2004 election, but during the initial weekend in September 2003, so few potential voters registered that the IEC resorted to holding another weekend in November.[5] In the end, 75.4 percent of eligible voters (i.e., those over the age of 18) registered to vote, a decline of 5 percent compared to the registration figures of 1999 (see table 13.1).

South Africa has witnessed a steady decline not only in voter registration, but also in turnout on voting day. Participation in the national election, calculated as a percentage of the voting age population, decreased by almost 30 percent between 1994 and 2004, reaching a low of just under 58 percent in 2004. However, due to doubts about the accuracy of the census data on which the voting age population figures are based, this is

Table 13.1 Registration and turnout 1994–2004, national ballot

	Voting age population (VAP)	Registered voters	VAP-registered (%)	Turnout-registered (%)	Turnout-VAP (%)
1994	22,709,152	na	na	na	86.0
1999	22,589,369	18,172,751	80.4	89.3	71.8
2004	27,436,819	20,674,926	75.4	76.7	57.8

Source: The 2004 VAP is based on the 2001 census figures (of people who are 18 years or older) obtained at http://www.statssa.gov.za/SpecialProjects/Census2001/Census/Database/Censuspercent202001/Censuspercent20 2001.asp. The 1999 and 1994 VAP figures are from Andrew Reynolds (1994:187; 1999:178). The registration figures are from the IEC at http://www.elections.org.za. In 1994, there was no voters' roll.

not the turnout figure that is commonly cited. The IEC and the ANC government prefer to use turnout rates calculated as a percentage of all citizens registered to vote, rather than a percentage of all citizens over 18, thus presenting a different picture. Based on the number of registered voters, the decline in national turnout looks less dramatic: 12.6 percent between 1999 and 2004. An impressive 89.3 percent of registered citizens turned out to cast their ballots in 1999, while a still rather high 76.7 percent of registered voters turned out in 2004. However, using the number of registered voters as the basis for turnout calculations, one needs to take into account that the population has steadily grown since 1994. Even if one maintains that the official demographic statistics of the census cannot be trusted, it raises the question whether all new potential voters have indeed been included on the voters' roll.

The turnout picture does not change substantially at the provincial level (see tables 13.2 and 13.3). The 2004 turnout for the national ballot does vary across provinces, with KZN registering the lowest turnout on the national ballot (51.4 percent) and the highest turnout (64.9 percent) occurring in the Eastern Cape. Nevertheless, all provinces fall within 13 percentage points of one another. Using voting age population as a basis for calculation, on both the provincial and national ballots, not a single province witnessed a 2004 turnout above 65 percent, and half of the provinces showed a turnout in the 50s. This stands in marked contrast to 1994, when some provinces saw turnout rates of more than 90 percent, and the lowest turnout was 81 percent (in KZN, which was probably due to the tense political climate in the area prior to the election). Even in the ANC's stronghold provinces, turnout has shown a relatively sharp decline across the three democratic elections. Around the world, "second elections" tend to demonstrate lower levels of turnout than founding

Table 13.2   Turnout 1994–2004, national ballot by province

	2004 Voting age population (VAP)	2004 Registered voters	2004 VAP-registered (%)	2004 Votes[a]	2004 Turnout-registered (%)	1994 Turnout-VAP (%)	1999 Turnout-VAP (%)	2004 Turnout-VAP (%)
National	27,436,819	20,674,926	75.4	15,863,554	76.7	86.0	71.8	57.8
EC	3,559,309	2,849,486	80.1	2,310,226	81.1	91.6	68.7	64.9
FS	1,692,978	1,321,195	78.0	1,042,120	78.9	82.7	73.5	61.6
GP	6,325,393	4,650,594	73.5	3,553,098	76.4	86.3	80.0	56.2
KZN	5,467,448	3,819,864	69.9	2,807,885	73.5	79.9	64.3	51.4
LP	2,756,231	2,187,912	79.4	1,686,757	77.1	84.0	70.1	61.2
MP	1,805,135	1,442,472	79.9	1,157,963	80.3	85.4	74.7	64.1
NC	519,481	433,591	83.5	329,707	76.0	91.9	69.8	63.5
NW	2,286,637	1,749,529	76.5	1,353,963	77.4	89.2	70.4	59.2
WC	3,024,207	2,220,283	73.4	1,621,835	73.1	88.9	69.7	53.6

[a] Including spoiled ballots.

Source: The 2004 VAP is based on the 2001 census figures (of people who are eighteen years or older) obtained at http://www.statssa.gov.za/SpecialProjects/Census2001/Census/Database/Census percent202001/Censuspercent 202001.asp. The 1999 and 1994 VAP figures are from Andrew Reynolds (1994:187; 1999:178). The registration figures are from the IEC at http://www.elections.org.za.

Table 13.3   Turnout 2004, provincial ballot by province

	Votes[a]	Turnout-registered (%)	Turnout-VAP (%)
National	15,516,324	75.0	56.6
EC	2,259,903	79.3	63.5
FS	1,027,401	77.8	60.7
GP	3,452,225	74.2	54.6
KZN	2,782,565	72.8	50.9
LP	1,636,461	74.5	59.4
MP	1,129,585	78.3	62.6
NC	323,894	74.7	62.3
NW	1,321,787	75.6	57.8
WC	1,582,503	71.3	52.3

[a] Including spoiled ballots.

Source: The 2004 VAP is based on the 2001 census figures (of people who are eighteen years or older) obtained at http://www.statssa.gov.za/SpecialProjects/Census2001/Census/Database/Censuspercent202001/Censuspercent202001.asp. The registration figures are from the IEC at http://www.elections.org.za.

elections,[6] so it is not surprising that turnout rates declined between 1994 and 1999. But the fact that turnout continued to decline with the 2004 election has given rise to speculations about a slow descent of South African democracy. Yet, the 2004 turnout rates are not so low as to jeopardize the quality of democracy. In fact, South African participation rates are beginning to approximate those in other countries at similar levels of economic development and with similar dominant party systems. Pippa Norris, in her work *Democratic Phoenix: Reinventing Political Activism*, has found that most countries at South Africa's level of economic development and length of democratic rule tend to demonstrate turnout rates averaging around 70 percent of the voting age population, whereas dominant party democracies record average turnout rates of 57 percent.[7] Given the position of the ANC, South Africa seems to fit into the dominant party category and indeed witnessed a turnout of 57.8 percent in the 2004 national election.

Interpreting the decline in turnout has become a heated debate among political analysts. On the one hand, supporters of the ANC claim that "apathy" is not a problem and the decline represents the normalization of the democratic process. On the other hand, critics of the ANC's predominant position argue that the decline in turnout is a symptom of a declining democracy in which people do not think that their vote will make a difference, and are, thus, less inclined to register and vote. Regardless of the position one takes in this debate, there are a number of factors underlying the lower level of registration for the 2004 election (75.4 percent of the voting age population compared to 80.4 percent in 1999, see table 13.1). These include inability to get to a registration point, lack of the proper identity document, confusion about the registration process, and probably disinterest.[8] The decline in turnout could reflect similar problems. In addition to these underlying factors, there is the issue of the timing of the 2004 election. It was held on the tail end of the Easter holiday, a four-day weekend during which many people travel. Those who were traveling may have voted less than those who did not because many registered voters did not know that they were not restricted to the voting district where they registered but could cast their ballots anywhere in the country.[9] This lack of knowledge is partly attributable to the IEC, because some provincial electoral officers (PEOs) intentionally did not publicize the information.[10] In combination with the extent of traveling during the Easter weekend, it may partially explain why KZN, Gauteng (GP), and the Western Cape exhibited the lowest turnout rates in the country.

On the positive side, one cannot argue that the relatively low turnout in 2004 was due to political intimidation or a poorly organized electoral event. On the morning of April 14, most voting stations opened on time, and most also closed on schedule. Stations at which there were still queues at closing time allowed all people in the queue to vote. The presiding officer at each polling station could decide to extend voting hours until midnight, instead of closing at the official time of 9 PM. Voting proceeded smoothly, with few of the impediments that had been experienced in the previous elections, such as a lack of ballot papers, inadequately trained staff, and wrong sections of the voters' roll.[11] Unlike 1994 and 1999, there were relatively few incidents of overcrowded polling stations at which people had to wait the entire day to vote. Overall, the process was judged free and fair, with only a few complaints about irregularities and intimidation lodged with the IEC.

The biggest problem encountered on election day pertained to the fact that the IEC had difficulty projecting how many voters were likely to turn up at each station. The new provision enabling voters to cast ballots anywhere in the country created an organizational problem: without knowing how many people would take advantage of this option of the so-called 'Section 24a' vote, planning for bottlenecks was difficult.[12] On election day, reports came in that election officials were at times unclear on how to process voters who were trying to cast ballots outside the districts where they were registered, and occasionally turned people away. This administrative difficulty was, however, the only major obstacle on voting day.

As Kabemba argued in his chapter on the electoral administration, this represents a remarkable achievement ten years into a democratic South Africa. Similarly, the fact that political leaders and analysts worried about voter apathy, rather than electoral violence, signifies that politics have become increasingly routine. Certainly, this is a sign of the institutionalization of democracy in South Africa. Whether or not the decline in participation holds negative implications for the quality of democracy in South Africa, is a topic that will be discussed at the end of this chapter. Here, it is important to note that, given the high levels of electoral fraud and voter intimidation elsewhere in Africa, and South Africa's own history of political violence as well as the often tense situation surrounding elections, it is significant and positive that we can discuss the electoral process in terms of "normal" politics.

Electoral Outcomes 1994–2004

It is undeniable that the electoral dominance of the ANC has been steadily increasing since 1994 at both national and provincial levels (see tables 13.4 to 13.14). The 2004 election will probably be remembered particularly for the fact that the ANC secured its "Parliament of Hope," winning over two-thirds of the seats in the National Assembly and the power to form the government in all nine provinces.[13] The ANC increased its share of

Table 13.4 National election results, 1994–2004

	Votes			% of Votes			Seats		
	1994	1999	2004	1994	1999	2004	1994	1999	2004
ACDP	88,104	228,975	250,272	0.45	1.43	1.60	2	6	7
AEB	—	46,292	—	—	0.29	—	—	1	—
ANC	12,237,655	10,601,330	10,880,915	63.12	66.35	69.69	252	266	279
AZAPO	—	27,257	39,116	—	0.17	0.27	—	1	1
DA[a]	338,426	1,527,337	1,931,201	1.75	9.56	12.37	7	38	50
FA	—	86,704	—	—	0.54	—	—	2	—
FF+	424,555	127,217	139,465	2.19	0.80	0.89	9	3	4
ID	—	—	269,765	—	—	1.73	—	—	7
IFP	2,058,294	1,371,477	1,088,664	10.62	8.58	6.97	43	34	28
MF	13,433	48,277	55,267	0.07	0.30	0.35	—	1	2
NNP	3,983,690	1,098,215	257,824	20.55	6.87	1.65	82	28	7
PAC	243,478	113,125	113,512	1.26	0.71	0.73	5	3	3
UCDP	—	125,280	117,792	—	0.78	0.76	0	3	3
UDM	—	546,790	355,717	—	3.42	2.28	—	14	9
Other	145,683	28,866	113,161	—	0.20	0.75	—	—	—
Valid Votes	19,533,498	15,977,142	15,612,671	100	100	100	400	400	400

[a] DA results reported for 1994 and 1999 are results of the DA's predecessor, the Democratic Party (DP).
Source: The results were obtained from the Independent Electoral Commission (IEC) at www.elections.org.za, and Andrew Reynolds, *Election '94 South Africa: The Campaigns, Results and Future Prospects* (Cape Town and New York: David Philip and St. Martin's Press, 1994) and *Election '99 South Africa: From Mandela to Mbeki* (Cape Town and New York: David Philip and St. Martin's Press, 1999).

the national vote to almost 70 percent. The party won a plurality of votes in all nine provinces, and a majority in seven, with the Western Cape and KZN being the exceptions. The ANC became a party in government in all the provinces, and announced the premiers within a week of the election.

In contrast to the ANC's consolidating hold on the electorate, the opposition's share of the vote has steadily declined and fragmented since 1994. Within this broad trend, there is a difference between the periods 1994–1999 and 1999–2004. The largest increase in the number of opposition parties represented in the National Assembly occurred between 1994 and 1999. Between 1999 and 2004, there has been a slight concentration of the opposition vote behind the largest opposition party, though as a bloc, the opposition saw its share of the vote decrease. The largest opposition party in Parliament in 2004 (the DA, with fifty seats) has over one-third fewer seats than the largest opposition party in 1994 (the NP, which had held eighty-two seats). The share of the vote held by opposition parties in 2004, just over 30 percent, was contested among twenty different parties, thirteen of which gained entrance into Parliament. In 1994, just six opposition parties got into the National Assembly, while in 1999 this doubled to twelve. At the same time, however, the largest opposition party in Parliament has gotten larger, in terms of absolute number of votes, share of the vote, and parliamentary seats. After the 2004 election, the DA holds just over 12 percent of the national vote and fifty NA seats, while in 1999 the largest opposition party (the Democratic Party, the predecessor of the DA), held less than 10 percent of the vote, and thirty-eight seats.

The DA, as the largest opposition party, promised that in 2004 it would make inroads into the black vote but the party seems to have won the support of only a tiny percentage of this population group. Although the DA became the "official opposition" in six provinces, it has not earned this position by cultivating a broad support base that reflects the diversity of South African society. The party's support remains over-whelmingly urban and is confined primarily to minority-group voters. The DA lost a great deal of the Indian vote it had earned in 1999, but picked up a fair amount of coloured voters who jumped ship from the sinking NNP. The DA seems to have won virtually all the moderate white-Afrikans and liberal-English votes. So, despite proclamations of becoming an alternative to the ANC, the DA remains a minority, con-servative, urban-based opposition party. Whether this will prove a base from which to broaden out remains as doubtful after 2004 as it was before the election.

Other trends among the opposition saw the NNP decimated: its share of the national poll reduced to just 1.7 percent, down from 6.9 percent in 1999 and 20.6 percent in 1994. The party that dominated South African politics for fifty years is now represented in only two provincial legislatures, and will cease to exist after September 2005.[14] A number of small parties managed to hold on to or slightly increase their repre-sentation in the NA: the PAC, Azapo, ACDP, MF, UCDP, and FF+. There seems to still be room for small parties in South African politics, though whether this is an artifact of the electoral system remains an open question.

The UDM increased its position to fourth in the NA, despite losing more than half of its MPs during the floor-crossing period in late 2003, which weakened the party's ability to wage an effective election campaign. The UDM lost support, compared to its 1999 performance, and shows every indication that its role in the future will be limited to that of a regional political force, centered in the Eastern Cape. Interestingly, the newcomer in the 2004 election, the Independent Democrats (ID), in existence for less than a year, broke into the national political arena with a larger vote share than the NNP but smaller than the UDM. Analyses in the wake of the election, however, lauded the ID for its impressive showing, whereas five years earlier, the UDM had been castigated for winning a comparable percentage of the national vote. The different reactions were probably caused by different expectations. Before the 1999 election, many had anticipated that the UDM, given the leadership profile of its founders, Roelf Meyer and Bantu Holomisa, would enter the national political arena as a significant contender, while in 2004 expectations for de Lille's ID were clearly less ambitious and proved more realistic.

Provincial Results

In addition to its national success, the ANC also consolidated its dominance in the provincial electoral contests, for the first time forming the government in all nine provinces. The party has yet to secure a majority in KZN and the Western Cape, but it won a plurality of the vote in the KZN provincial election, another first for the ANC.

The ANC took the initiative to nominate premiers for all nine provinces, and eight of these were new to the position. As Lodge noted in his chapter in this volume, the ANC declined to announce its premier candidates before the election, arguing that this way all party members would work harder for the election campaign. Unofficially, the move was meant to curb factional infighting in a number of provinces. When the list of nominees finally became known, there were more than a few surprises. Only one of the premiers serving before the election, Sam

Table 13.5 Seat allocation in provincial legislatures, 2004

	Eastern Cape 63 seats	Free State 30 seats	Gauteng 73 seats	KwaZulu-Natal 80 seats	Limpopo 49 seats	Mpumalanga 30 seats	Northern Cape 30 seats	North West 33 seats	Western Cape 42 seats
ACDP	—	1	1	2	1	—	1	—	2
ANC	51	25	51	38	45	27	21	27	19
DA	5	3	15	7	2	2	3	2	12
FF+	—	1	1	—	—	1	1	1	—
ID	—	—	1	—	—	—	2	—	3
IFP	—	—	2	30	—	—	—	—	—
MF	—	—	—	2	—	—	—	—	—
NNP	—	—	—	—	—	—	2	—	5
PAC	1	—	1	—	—	—	—	—	—
UCDP	—	—	—	—	—	—	—	3	—
UDM	6	—	1	1	1	—	—	—	1

Source: IEC website, http://www.elections.org.za/library1.asp?KSId=19&iKid=3.

Shilowa of Gauteng, was renominated. This does not mean that the new premiers came to office without any government experience: all the new premiers had been Members of the Executive Council (MECs) in their respective provinces, showing that the ANC is consistently developing its leadership capacity. The ANC selected four women to be premiers, an increase over the single female premier (Winkie Direko) serving before the 2004 election. When the ANC released its premier nominations, the party stated that the candidates were all relatively young, and would have the energy and motivation to "pull the provinces into shape" and increase service delivery across the country.[15]

Eastern Cape

In 1999, the big story in the Eastern Cape involved the performance of the UDM, as it broke onto the political scene, secured the second highest number of votes in the province and became the Eastern Cape's official opposition. While the UDM managed to hold onto this position in 2004, its support declined, with the party winning only six seats in the EC provincial legislature, compared to the nine it had earned in 1999. Furthermore, the UDM held on to its position by just a single seat. The decline in support for the UDM is tied to the party's poor performance running the Umtata municipality since 2000, and that the ANC has increasingly won over the chiefs in the province. The DA increased its representation in the EC from four to five seats, thus retaining its position as the third largest party in the province, but this time much closer on the heels of the UDM than in 1999. The PAC held on to its single seat in the Eastern Cape legislature, while the NNP lost all its representatives in the province. The ANC increased its hold on the EC electorate and made most of its gains at the expense of the UDM. The latter party was clearly not able to hold on to many of the supporters it had wooed away from the ANC in 1999. The ANC's support came from all areas of the province, while the UDM supporters were concentrated in rural areas, mostly in the former Transkei. The DA's supporters were primarily located in the urban areas of the Eastern Cape.

After the election, the ANC replaced Eastern Cape Premier Makhenkesi Stofile with the former arts, sports, and culture MEC, Zisiwe Beauty (Nosimo) Balindlela. Stofile's administration had been marked by poor service delivery, especially in the rural areas of the province, and infighting within the provincial ANC. Stofile had been elected in 1999, and therefore could have served a second term, so his replacement demonstrated that the ANC was committed to "redeploying" premiers who had not performed well or who had not been able to control factional fighting within their provincial party organizations. Incidentally, Stofile got a position in the new national cabinet as minister of sport and recreation.

Balindlela's appointment came as a surprise in the Eastern Cape, as in 1998 she had been fired from her position as Education MEC by Stofile after she failed to improve matric results and demonstrated poor financial management of her department. Soon after she took office as the new Eastern Cape premier, she alienated the provincial party structures by nominating a provincial cabinet (executive council) without consulting them. When the provincial party leaders complained to ANC Secretary General Kgalema Motlanthe, they were told that appointing the MECs was Balindlela's prerogative, and that the national leadership would not interfere.[16] This exchange provides an example of the national organization's policy of supporting its chosen provincial leaders even in the face of resistance from provincial party structures, pointing to the national leadership's continuing efforts to control the party organization from the top down.

Table 13.6 Eastern Cape provincial election results

Party	Votes 2004	% of votes 2004	Seats 2004 (63)
ANC	1,768,987	79.3	51
DA	163,785	7.3	5
PAC	22,324	1.0	1
UDM	205,993	9.2	6
Others	70,454	3.2	0

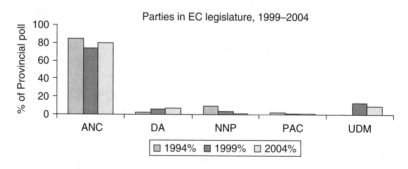

Source: IEC website, www.elections.org.za, the bar graph presents the percentage of the provincial vote for each party represented in the legislature between 1994 and 2004.

Free State

Election results in the Free State saw the ANC retain the twenty-five seats it had won in 1999. Change only occurred within the ranks of the opposition. The DA increased its representation from two to three seats and the ACDP won its first seat in the Free State legislature. The NNP lost its representatives in the Free State, while the FF+ retained its single seat. In 1999, the official opposition in the Free State had been the DA, and in 2004 the party retained that position, though with the ANC's lead so overwhelming, the position becomes almost symbolic.

Following the election, the choice of premier in the Free State reflected the dissatisfaction of the ANC's national leadership with factional infighting in the province. Provincial party leader Ace Magashule, who had repeatedly stirred up conflict in the provincial ANC structures, did not get nominated for the premiership. Instead, the party put forth Beatrice Marshoff, former social development and welfare MEC. Marshoff was not a prominent figure in Free State politics prior to her nomination, nor was she considered popular in the provincial party organization. Marshoff had only been included in the provincial cabinet in 2001, when then Premier Isabella (Winkie) Direko reshuffled the executive council in the wake of provincial infighting. And, Marshoff was not included in

Table 13.7   Free State provincial election results

Party	Votes 2004	% of votes 2004	Seats 2004 (30)
ACDP	13,119	1.3	1
ANC	827,338	81.8	25
DA	85,714	8.5	3
FF+	24,946	2.5	1
Others	60,489	5.9	0

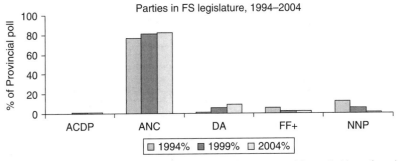

Source: IEC website, www.elections.org.za, the bar graph presents the percentage of the provincial vote for each party represented in the legislature between 1994 and 2004.

the top thirty of the candidate list that the Free State party branches had sent to the national ANC office. Supporters of Magashule, upset that he had been passed over, argued that Marshoff would further widen the gap between the national ANC organization and the Free State party structures.[17] In fact, some branches went so far as to threaten that they would boycott the local election in 2005, in protest over Magashule's demotion. Magashule himself publicly accepted the appointment of Marshoff, and rejected claims that he had been snubbed by the National Working Committee of the ANC.[18]

Gauteng

In 2004, Gauteng, where the NNP used to be relatively strong, turned its back completely on the former ruling party and denied the NNP even a single seat in the provincial legislature. The DA picked up most of the fallout from the NNP and increased its seats in the Gauteng legislature

Table 13.8   Gauteng provincial election results

Party	Votes 2004	% of votes 2004	Seats 2004 (73)
ACDP	55,991	1.6	1
ANC	2,331,121	68.4	51
DA	708,081	20.8	15
FF+	45,648	1.3	1
ID	51,921	1.5	1
IFP	85,500	2.5	2
PAC	29,076	0.9	1
UDM	33,644	1.0	1
Others	67,326	2.0	0

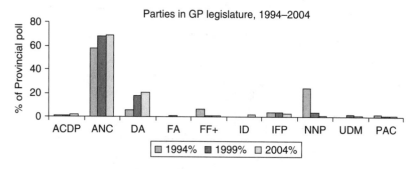

Source: IEC website, www.elections.org.za, the bar graph presents the percentage of the provincial vote for each party represented in the legislature between 1994 and 2004.

from thirteen to fifteen. In 1999, the DP wooed many of the moderate Afrikaners who in the past had supported the NP, and in 2004 the DA continued to build on this support. Testament to this trend, the DA won wards in Centurion and the East Rand, former NNP support bases, while retaining its hold over Houghton and other more traditionally liberal suburbs. The ACDP, FF+ and the UDM retained their single seats in the Gauteng legislature, while the PAC and the new ID also won one representative each in the province. The IFP lost one of its three representatives in Gauteng.

Among all the provinces, Gauteng is the only one that did not see a change in premiership after the 2004 election. Between 1994 and 1999, Gauteng had been beset by factional disputes within the provincial ANC structures, leading to the mid-term removal of Premier Mathole Motshekga. After the 1999 election, the party nominated Sam Shilowa for the top position in the province, in the hope that he would be able to bring some stability to provincial politics. The fact that the ANC retained him in this position is a signal that he successfully improved party relations in the province. Shilowa's continued position as premier also attests to the way the ANC manages its continuing alliance with Cosatu and the SACP. High-ranking officials of the two organizations are incorporated into the ranks of government, in an attempt to keep Cosatu and the SACP, which have a tendency to criticize the government's right-leaning economic policies, in line.

KwaZulu-Natal

The 2004 election saw ground breaking results for the ANC in KZN. For the first time, the ANC won a plurality of the vote and soundly beat the IFP on its home ground. Not only in Durban, which the ANC has held since the local election in 1996, but in many of the rural areas as well, the ANC polled enough votes to become the largest party in the province. The ANC also won back many of the Indian voters who had flocked to the DP in 1999, thus making significant inroads in Indian voting areas.[19] Whereas the ANC increased its representation in the KZN legislature from thirty-two to thirty-eight seats, the IFP lost four of its thirty-four seats and ended up with thirty representatives. The DA held onto the seven seats it had won in 1999, while the ACDP and the MF both got two seats in the KZN legislature. The UDM managed to hold on to its single seat, while the NNP lost its representation in the province.

The IFP found the election results difficult to swallow, and immediately launched a court case to protest the certification of the provincial result. The party claimed that it had lodged complaints with the IEC about the conduct of the poll in forty-seven voting districts, but that the IEC had certified the provincial result without hearing the IFP's case. The party argued that approximately 367,000 votes in KZN had been tampered with, enough to overturn the ANC's plurality in the provincial poll. A week later, the IFP dropped the court case, in the "interests of national unity," on the same day as IFP spokesperson Reverend Musa Zondi was nominated to serve in the new national cabinet as a deputy minister. In the end, the IFP did not become part of the national government. Thus, the IFP emerged from the 2004 election as a much reduced political force, with a tenuous position in its traditional stronghold, and needing to resort to tantrum tactics to retain influence on the national scene.

The ANC included members of the IFP and the MF in the new KZN provincial government, thus extending an olive branch to the IFP in pursuit of provincial stability. The ANC refused, however, to let the IFP nominate the premier, and instead put forth their own provincial chair, Sibusiso (S'bu) Ndebele. Before the election, rumors had circulated that Deputy President Jacob Zuma might be deployed to the province as the

Table 13.9   KwaZulu-Natal provincial election results

Party	Votes 2004	% of votes 2004	Seats 2004 (80)
ACDP	48,892	1.8	2
ANC	1,287,823	47.0	38
DA	228,857	8.3	7
IFP	1,009,267	36.8	30
MF	71,540	2.6	2
UDM	20,546	0.8	1
Others	74,340	2.7	0

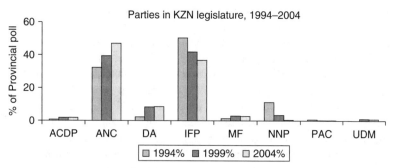

Source: IEC website, www.elections.org.za, the bar graph presents the percentage of the provincial vote for each party represented in the legislature between 1994 and 2004.

premier, in response to allegations of impropriety in the arms deal scandal,[20] but the ANC, true to its policy of supporting beleaguered members until proven guilty, retained Zuma as the deputy president in the national cabinet.

Ndebele was a somewhat controversial candidate for the premiership, as he has been involved in hostilities between the IFP and ANC in the province, and therefore may not be the most suitable candidate to repair relations between the two parties. Yet, as the leader of the provincial ANC, it would have been insulting to the KZN party organization to nominate anyone else for the top post in the province.

As an initial assertion of its newfound power in KZN, the ANC announced that the provincial legislature would sit once again solely in Pietermaritzburg, finally putting an end to the IFP's attempt to relocate the provincial government to Ulundi, the former capital of KwaZulu. The issue of the location of the provincial capital, whether in the apartheid-era Pietermaritzburg or the former homeland capital of Ulundi, had for the past decade divided parties and people in the province. Interestingly, the DA's support of the IFP position on the issue seems to have cost the DA 50,000 votes in Pietermaritzburg.[21]

Limpopo (Formerly Northern Province)

The ANC increased its overwhelming share of the seats in the Limpopo legislature, from forty-four to forty-five, whereas the official opposition, the DA, increased its representation from a single to two seats. The ACDP and the UDM both retained their single seats, but the NNP and the PAC lost their representatives in Limpopo.

The new Limpopo Premier Sello Moloto (former health MEC), is considered by many to be a rising star within the ANC, and the most effective MEC in the province.[23] Moloto's appointment is significant not only because it is an example of a promotion of a well-functioning party member, but also because Moloto is a member of the SACP. The nomination of an SACP member for the position of premier can be seen as an attempt by the ANC to shore up its relationship with the SACP, just as it had done with the nomination of Cosatu leader Sam Shilowa as premier of Gauteng.

Moloto will have to remain vigilant about preventing provincial party politics from degenerating into the factional infighting that in 2001 had caused the ANC to disband its provincial structures. Since then, Premier Ngoako Ramathlodi had been able to control the problem, and had reportedly rebuilt a solid party organization. Nevertheless, the new premier needs to avoid the tensions that led to the 2001 dissolution, while he is facing an urgent need to improve service delivery in the context of widespread unemployment in the province.

Table 13.10 Limpopo provincial election results

Party	Votes 2004	% of votes 2004	Seats 2004 (49)
ACDP	20,418	1.3	1
ANC	1,439,853	89.2	45
DA	57,930	3.6	2
UDM	27,780	1.7	1
Others	68,533	4.2	0

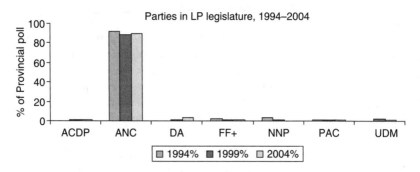

Source: IEC website, www.elections.org.za, the bar graph presents the percentage of the provincial vote for each party represented in the legislature between 1994 and 2004.

Mpumalanga

Party politics in Mpumalanga are ANC politics, as the opposition has never been able to gain much of a foothold in the province. In 2004, the opposition parties performed even worse than they had in 1994 and 1999, with the DA being the only exception. The DA managed to increase its representation in the Mpumalanga legislature from one to two seats. The NNP and the UDM had both earned seats in 1999, but lost these in 2004. The FF+ managed to hold on to one representative in the province.

When forming the provincial government, the ANC decided not to retain controversial Ndaweni Mahlangu as premier. In 1999, when one of his subordinates was found to have made fraudulent claims about licencing in national parks, Mahlangu had stated that it was "okay" for politicians to lie under certain circumstances. This caused much uproar. Yet, the party backed up its premier at the time, and insisted that despite his statement he was a competent public official. However, following the

Table 13.11 Mpumalanga provincial election results

Party	Votes 2004	% of votes 2004	Seats 2004 (30)
ANC	959,436	86.3	27
DA	77,119	6.9	2
FF+	13,732	1.2	1
Others	61,405	5.6	0

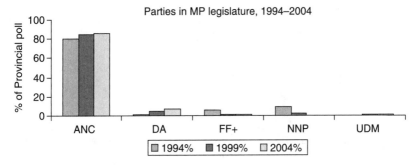

Parties in MP legislature, 1994–2004

□ 1994%   ■ 1999%   □ 2004%

Source: IEC website, www.elections.org.za, the bar graph presents the percentage of the provincial vote for each party represented in the legislature between 1994 and 2004.

2004 election, the ANC replaced Mahlangu, although he could have served another term. Former safety and liaison MEC Sampson Phathakge (Thabang) Makwetla, a member of the ANC's National Executive Committee, became the new Mpumalanga premier.

Makwetla is thought to represent the ANC's attempt to select premiers who embody youth and dynamism. In 2002, he was deployed from his position as an ANC whip in the national parliament to Mpumalanga in order to stabilize politics in the province, which at the time was being torn apart by corruption scandals and infighting.[22] Before the 2004 election, despite evidence of corruption and incompetence, Mpumalanga MECs had been retained in office. Thus, Makwetla is facing a serious challenge in addressing the problems that have characterized Mpumalanga politics over the past few years.

Northern Cape

The most remarkable electoral trend in the Northern Cape has been the performance of the NNP. In the 1999 election, the NNP had retained some of its strength in the Northern Cape, primarily among rural, coloured residents. After the 2004 election, the NNP's position was markedly

Table 13.12   Northern Cape provincial election results

Party	Votes 2004	% of votes 2004	Seats 2004 (30)
ACDP	5,995	1.9	1
ANC	219,365	68.8	21
DA	35,297	11.1	3
FF+	4,948	1.5	1
ID	22,485	7.1	2
NNP	23,970	7.5	2
Others	6,642	2.1	0

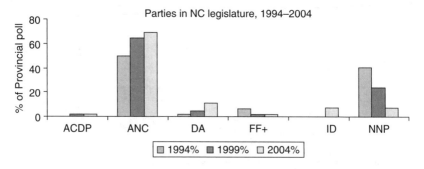

Source: IEC website, www.elections.org.za, the bar graph presents the percentage of the provincial vote for each party represented in the legislature between 1994 and 2004.

diminished. The party saw its support in the province decline by more than 50,000 votes, compared to 1999, and retained only two of the eight seats it had earned in the 1999 election. The DA benefited from the NNP's decline and increased its representation in the Northern Cape legislature from one to three seats. The new ID won two seats in the Northern Cape legislature, while the ACDP won its first seat in the province. The FF+ retained its single seat.

Regarding the formation of the Northern Cape provincial government after the 2004 election, Premier Mannie Dipico, having served two terms, had to be replaced and found his way into the NA. In his place, the ANC nominated former health MEC Dipuo Peters. Peters is one of the four new female premiers.

North West

In 1999, the UCDP entered the electoral contest in North West for the first time, and managed to become the second largest party in the province. Based primarily in the former Bophuthatswana homeland area, the UCDP

Table 13.13   North West provincial election results

Party	Votes 2004	% of votes 2004	Seats 2004 (33)
ANC	1,048,089	80.7	27
DA	64,925	5.0	2
FF+	17,123	1.3	1
UCDP	110,233	8.5	3
Others	58,193	4.5	0

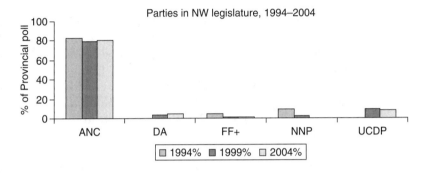

Source: IEC website, www.elections.org.za, the bar graph presents the percentage of the provincial vote for each party represented in the legislature between 1994 and 2004.

managed to secure a traditional, rural support base, comprising mainly people loyal to Lucius Mangope, the former homeland leader. In 2004, the party retained its three seats in the North West legislature as well as its status as official opposition in North West, but with a diminished share of the vote. Many of the party's supporters from 1999 returned to the ANC in 2004. North West is one of the three provinces in which the DA was not able to become the official opposition, though with two representatives it became the third largest party in the province. The NNP lost its seat in the North West legislature, whereas the FF+ managed to hold on to its single representative in the province.

After the 2004 election, North West Premier Popo Molefe, who had served two terms, was redeployed to a seat in the national parliament and replaced by former economic affairs MEC Edna Molewa. Molewa had been popular in the provincial ANC structures, and was considered a front-runner in the competition for the premier nomination before the 2004 election. She is a former MEC, former MP, and ANC Women's League provincial chair. Molewa's appointment was hailed as an attempt to forge unity among the various ANC factions in North West, which had supported different candidates for the premiership in advance of the election.[24]

Western Cape

In the Western Cape, the most notable result of the 2004 election was the decimation of the NNP, which lost twelve of its seventeen seats in the provincial legislature and witnessed an all-time low of less than 11 percent of the vote in its last remaining provincial stronghold. In 1994, the NNP had won 53 percent of the vote in the Western Cape and seats in all nine provincial legislatures. Ten years later, the Western and Northern Cape were the only provinces in which the party won any representation. The 2004 result for the NNP in the Western Cape was one of the many signs that the once powerful party was near ruin. All of the NNP's remaining representatives in the NA came from its Western Cape list, another sign that the party was reduced to, at most, playing the role of a small regionally based party. In contrast to the NNP's decline, the DA and the ACDP demonstrated that their support in the Western Cape was rising. Both parties increased their vote share and their number of seats in the provincial legislature, the DA from five to twelve and the ACDP from a single to two. The UDM managed to hold onto its single seat, while the new ID entered the Western Cape legislature with three representatives.

The ID, DA, and the ANC were the principal beneficiaries of the collapse of the NNP in the province. The ANC succeeded in making inroads into different communities, including the working-class coloured townships around Cape Town, which were traditionally NNP strongholds. Despite the problems that had plagued the provincial ANC before the election, the party waged a successful campaign and emerged as the party with the plurality of votes in the Western Cape. In 1999, the ANC had also been the largest party in the province, but the NNP and the DP had been able to come together and, with a majority between them, had formed a coalition government. In 2004, the situation was different, as the ANC and NNP had brokered an agreement before the election that they would form a coalition to govern the Western Cape.

Thus, once the election results were announced, the ANC formed the provincial government together with the NNP, and elected ANC provincial leader Ebrahim Rasool as Western Cape premier. Rasool's appointment put to rest any speculation about whether the ANC would uphold its preelection pact with the NNP, in which the party had supposedly promised multiple cabinet positions, including the premiership, to the NNP. Prior to the election when opinion polls started to show just

Table 13.14   Western Cape provincial election results

Party	Votes 2004	% of votes 2004	Seats 2004 (42)
ACDP	53,934	3.4	2
ANC	709,052	45.3	19
DA	424,832	27.1	12
ID	122,867	7.8	3
NNP	170,469	10.9	5
UDM	27,489	1.8	1
Others	58,306	3.7	0

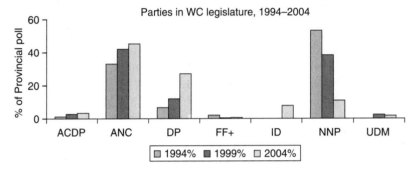

Source: IEC website, www.elections.org.za, the bar graph presents the percentage of the provincial vote for each party represented in the legislature between 1994 and 2004.

how low the NNP's support had shrunk, the ANC had begun to float rumors that the NNP would not be given the premiership, and only a small number of cabinet positions. Both parties denied the rumors at the time. Yet, the ANC also claimed that it had not committed itself to any specific number of positions for the NNP, and that it would accord its coalition partner representation in the provincial cabinet commensurate with the NNP's level of support in the province. The NNP subsequently received two provincial cabinet posts.

Given the Western Cape election result, Rasool's nomination as premier came as no surprise. It also showed that the ANC's national leadership had decided not to impose an outsider on the province, as it had previously done with other provinces that demonstrated tensions within the provincial party organizations. By late 2003, the ANC in the Western Cape had begun to show cracks that revolved around financial difficulties and internal tensions that split the party into "Africanist" and "Charterist" camps.

These tensions had led to rumors that senior ANC leaders wanted to appoint a premier from outside the province, in an attempt to avoid favoring one faction over the other. Another supposed motivation behind the wish to nominate an outsider was the fact that Rasool had at times been accused of questioning national leadership's directives.[25]

Interpreting Electoral Trends

The ANC

There are many ways to interpret the electoral trends described earlier. First, the ANC's increased share of the vote must be considered against a decline in the levels of registration and turnout. The decline has occurred in the context of a growing population, in other words an increase in the number of citizens eligible to vote.[26] As noted by both Mattes and Seeking in their chapters in this volume, the South African electorate has changed in the past ten years. There were 5 million more people in the Voting Age Population (new potential voters) in 2004 than in 1999. Over 2 million more people registered to vote in 2004. Yet, the ANC only increased its absolute number of votes by 279,585. What this means is that the party won a larger share of the poll, but the result could also be interpreted as a decrease in "real" terms. If turnout had increased in proportion with the increase in population, the overall number of ballots cast would have been much larger. Therefore, the ANC's result of near 70 percent could well be an artifact of the decline in turnout.

Second, interpreting the election results raises the question of how one should understand the electoral dominance and centralization of power within the ANC. The debate on the ANC as a dominant party tends to overlook one important aspect of the phenomenon: becoming a dominant party was not an automatic process, and retaining that position has required effort. The ANC has worked hard to prevent the organization from following in the footsteps of liberation movements throughout Africa that fractured soon after independence in the 1960s and 1970s. The mid-1990s were an arduous time for the ANC as the organization refashioned itself from a liberation movement into a governing party and began the transformation of South African government and society. The past ten years have truly been a test of majority rule, as the ANC has faced a myriad of challenges, stemming from both within and outside the party.

Internally, the ANC faced a number of demands. First of all, it had to reconcile divergent organizational cultures. In exile, the organization had been forced to function in a top-down, hierarchical manner, enforcing strict party discipline. Within South Africa, the United Democratic Front (UDF) fought the struggle against apartheid as an umbrella body of grassroots organizations that were loosely aligned with the ANC. The UDF, in contrast to the ANC in exile, governed itself through a system of consultation and discussion, as the numerous subunits retained their autonomy. After the National Party unbanned the ANC in 1990, the two organizations began to merge, a process of integration that has created many challenges. The tension between "internals" and "exiles" still underlies power rivalries that exist within the ranks of the ruling party. In addition, once the ANC had won seats in national and provincial governments, it had to fill the positions from within its ranks. This left the party apparatus without many of its most talented individuals, as they moved into government positions. Therefore, the ANC not only had to reconcile the different UDF and exile communities, it also had to virtually rebuild its organizational structures when active members from the branches were deployed in government positions.

While facing these internal challenges, the ANC had to take over a government that had been designed to oppress the majority, and turn it into an organization capable of empowerment and upliftment. The liberation-movement-turned-governing-party had to transform the apartheid bureaucracy into a civil service that would transform and uplift, manage the demands of a modern, industrial economy as well as the needs of traditional, small-scale farmers, and confront the problems of endemic poverty, unemployment, underdevelopment, and poor education. In other words, the demands were many and the party faced them with varying success.

Throughout the first decade of majority rule, the ANC never took its position as a "dominant party" for granted. Instead, the ANC strategically used its position to influence the creation of political institutions that provided the party with mechanisms with which it could insulate itself from centripetal pressures, such as an electoral system of proportional representation with closed party lists and a centralized federal system, which focuses lines of power and accountability upward to the national leadership. The fact that the ANC refused to nominate premier candidates prior to the 2004 election, and instead nominated people to be "deployed" as premiers three days after the polls is the latest example of such centralizing tactics. It defused factionalization within the provinces, while reinforcing the party's control.

The ANC has also pursued less formal mechanisms to preserve its status, such as maintaining the strategic alliance with the South African

Communist Party (SACP) and the Congress of South African Trade Unions (Cosatu). This alliance enables the ruling party to internalize and co-opt criticism from the left and provides it with the ideological flexibility to curtail the organizational ground for opposition parties. In addition, the ANC has frequently contributed to a political discourse that demonizes the opposition as racist and reinforces the social cleavage between blacks and whites. The resulting image of black government versus white opposition has prevented the successful politicization of competing lines of division, whether based on interest groups, ethnic identities, or class. On top of all these long-term strategies, the party runs a formidable election machine that brings disaffected supporters back to the party at election time.[27]

The electoral performance of the ANC and its dominant position must be interpreted against all these factors. The tendency to centralize power in the presidency, to strictly enforce party discipline, and to crack down on public dissent outside of party structures are all defensive mechanisms to strengthen party unity. The ANC has apparently felt that this was necessary to begin and manage the transformation of South African society. Similarly, the ANC seems to view its dominant position as enabling continued transformation without derailment. Yet, the party's tendencies toward intolerance of public criticism and centralization of power are worrisome from the perspective of democratic accountability, responsiveness, and transparency. Where one party controls so many seats in Parliament, the most important debates take place within the party caucus. If the party then exhibits signs of intolerance of dissent and centralization of power, it hinders vibrant public debate and raises concern about the continued democratic development of South Africa.

The Opposition

To date, the opposition has barely presented itself as a viable alternative to the ANC. It remains a group of parties with leadership and policy platforms that fail to attract a wide range of South African voters. Several trends among opposition parties are worth noting here. First of these is the decline of the NNP, which seems to be an almost inevitable conclusion for the party that created the apartheid system. In 1994, the NP still emerged from the election as the second largest party in Parliament, with representation in all nine provincial legislatures. In 1999, the "New" NP was reduced to third position, with its remaining support concentrated primarily in the Western and Northern Cape. Although, the party retained members in all nine provincial legislatures, in seven of these its representation was down to three seats or less. In 2004, the NNP's performance was disastrous. The party won seats in just two provincial legislatures (in the Western and Northern Cape), and had to share the ranking of the fifth largest party in the NA with the African Christian Democratic Party (ACDP) and the new ID.

The NNP's poor performance can be attributed to many factors, but chief among them is the fact that since 1994 the party has frequently changed its opposition tactics. The NNP's involvement in a number of coalitions and alliances has confused its image among voters. The last straw seems to have been the coalition agreement the NNP worked out with the ANC in 2001, which gave the ANC government power in the Western Cape. This deal put the NNP back into a close relationship with the ruling party, which made it difficult for the NNP to present itself as a genuine opposition party. In 1996, the NP had withdrawn from the Government of National Unity precisely because of this problem, so it should have been no surprise that it resurfaced in the 2004 campaign.

When the 2004 election results began to filter into the IEC on the evening of April 14, the rumors began that the NNP was considering disbanding.[28] The party denied these claims, and continued to present itself as a coherent organization. Yet, in July 2004, three and a half months after the election, the party announced that it would disband during the next defection window in September 2005. Party leader van Schalkwyk announced his intention to join the ANC and urged other NNP members to follow his lead. The NNP had been unable to carve out a role for itself in the new South Africa, and the party's attempts to reinvent itself drove even its core supporters away. Alliances with and then withdrawals from the DP and ANC contributed to the image of a party that is lost, unsure of which way to turn, and without any core principles to guide it in the postapartheid period. Ultimately, the party was forced to concede that its experiment in creating a moderate, Christian-Democratic party, capable of attracting credible leaders and transforming into a nonracial organization, had failed.

Together with the decline of the NP/NNP, the rise of the DP/DA represents an important realignment in South African party politics during the past decade. The transformation of the Democratic Party (DP) from a liberal, English-dominated voice for freedom into its current conservative form took more analysts by surprise than did the decline of the NNP. After the 1994 election, the DP had seven representatives in the NA, and decided that it would operate as a moderating voice and attempt to persuade the larger parties to adopt DP policy perspectives. The DP tactics changed by 1998, as the party began to position itself for the 1999 election. The DP shifted to a more aggressive stance, becoming a very vocal opposition party, which earned party leader Tony Leon the moniker, "the Chihuahua."

In its bid to become the largest opposition party in 1999, the DP pursued the NNP's Afrikaner support base, and subsequently created an alliance (the Democratic Alliance) with the NNP in June 2000.[29] Following the withdrawal of the NNP from the new party in 2001, the DP decided to maintain the new creation and officially became the DA in April 2003.[30] In its current form, the DA's strategy of "aggressive opposition" seems to alienate many South Africans. Regardless of DA claims that it represents the interests of all South Africans, the party is widely perceived as a conservative protector of minority interests opposing all ANC propositions on principle.[31] Therefore, the DA's potential to develop into a party capable of mounting a genuine electoral challenge to the ANC will remain limited, unless the party radically changes tack and recruits a large cohort of black supporters. The DA made small inroads into the black electorate in the 2004 election, but has yet to break through to significant support levels among this group. Similarly, the DA has yet to genuinely transform its leadership to include black, coloured and Indian leaders. At present, most of its leaders are white, and those who are not have histories from the struggle era that render them suspect to many South Africans.

The IFP emerged from the 2004 election as the third largest party in the NA, the same ranking as in 1994 and 1999. The IFP's bid to increase its performance outside KZN had failed in 1999, and after the 2004 election its presence in other provinces declined even further. But the most negative outcome of the 2004 election for the IFP was that the party lost its position as the largest party in KZN, and failed to secure a ministerial position in the new national cabinet. Analysts had speculated that the ANC would want to retain Buthelezi in his cabinet position, in order to prevent him from returning to an exclusive focus on KZN politics,[32] but the ANC leadership evidently did not consider this a serious enough threat to retain Buthelezi at the national level. The ANC gave the portfolio of home affairs, which Buthelezi had held since 1994, to his former deputy minister.[33] Initially, two IFP members were selected to serve in the national cabinet as deputy ministers, but shortly before the swearing-in ceremony the appointees sent a letter to President Mbeki, explaining that they could not take up their seats until the issues around the formation of a provincial government in KZN had been resolved. Mbeki retaliated by withdrawing the nominations, saying that he would only appoint ministers who were willing to work, which left the IFP without representation in the national cabinet. Both the IFP's defeat in KZN and the exclusion from the national cabinet are highly significant, as KZN is the IFP's stronghold and the party previously retained national relevance by serving in cabinet.

The UDM, which entered the national political scene in 1999, had briefly raised hopes that a nonracial or multiracial opposition party had arrived. Yet, in 2004, the UDM did not perform well, and seems to have been reduced to a primarily black, Eastern Cape based, regional force. In the 2004 election, another newcomer represented a sign of hope for multiracial opposition. The ID, formed just one year before the election, performed reasonably well, securing seven seats in the National Assembly. Led by fiery politician and ex-Pan Africanist Congress member Patricia de Lille, the new party seems to have the potential to become a multiracial voice for the poor, if it can build a party organization that does not sustain itself solely through the charisma of its leader, de Lille. Finally, among the smaller opposition parties in Parliament, the African Christian Democratic Party (ACDP), though representing a small percentage of the overall vote, continues to perform relatively well. The ACDP has consistently increased its vote share since 1994.

Underlying these trends is the decline in voter turnout. At this point, one can only speculate as to which categories of eligible voters declined to exercise their right. The decreased share of the vote earned by the opposition as a whole would suggest that it is mainly opposition voters who stayed at home. However, the fact that the ANC's absolute number of votes increased by only 279,585 indicates that, while ANC supporters did not shift their votes to the opposition, the ruling party failed to motivate a large number of its potential supporters to make the trip to the polling station.

Alternative Electoral Systems

What would the election results look like under alternative electoral formulas? Would there be more fluidity in the South African political landscape? Would smaller parties band together? Would the ANC's position be as secure? These questions are central to the ongoing debate about electoral reform (discussed by Nijzink and Piombo in this volume) but not easy to answer. It is difficult to meaningfully map the 2004 election results onto a simulated constituency system. Leaving aside the thorny issues of constituency boundaries and the most appropriate number of constituencies, parties and voters would have behaved differently under a first-past-the-post constituency system, which makes it almost impossible to accurately predict electoral outcomes under such an alternative system. If the 2004 election results would in fact have been tabulated on the basis of plurality in a number of geographical units both parties and voters would have chosen campaign strategies and made voting choices appropriate in the context of these new electoral rules.[34] The same is true if a certain threshold would have been introduced. Parties would probably change their strategies to best suit the new electoral rules. However, it is fairly easy to assess how many of the parties that gained entrance into the National Assembly in 2004 would have won representation under different electoral thresholds, while retaining the system of proportional representation with closed party lists.

Based on the 2004 election results, imposing even a 1 percent threshold would reduce the number of parties represented in the National Assembly from twelve to seven. Furthermore, the three largest parties in Parliament would increase their share of seats, while the remaining four smaller parties would not have benefited. Imposing a 5 percent cutoff would increase the ANC's share of the 400 NA seats to well over 300 and reduce the number of parties in Parliament to just three. Clearly, the current system in which the number of votes necessary to win a single seat is determined by the total number of votes cast in the election, works to the advantage of smaller parties. It enables a variety of parties to be represented in Parliament. Yet, there is a trade-off to the fact that small parties are able to gain entrance into the NA. With only one or two MPs, it is difficult to cover all portfolio committees and have an impact on public policy making.

Table 13.15   Electoral results under different thresholds[35]

	No threshold		One percent		Five percent	
	Seats	**% vote**	**Seats**	**% vote**	**Seats**	**% vote**
ANC	279	69.7	290	72.4	313	78.3
DA	50	12.4	51	12.9	56	13.9
IFP	28	7.0	29	7.2	31	7.8
UDM	9	2.3	9	2.4	—	—
ID	7	1.7	7	1.8	—	—
NNP	7	1.7	7	1.7	—	—
ACDP	7	1.6	7	1.7	—	—
FF+	4	0.9	—	—	—	—
UCDP	3	0.8	—	—	—	—
PAC	3	0.7	—	—	—	—
MF	2	0.4	—	—	—	—
AZAPO	1	0.3	—	—	—	—
Total	400	100	400	100	400	100

There is no doubt that imposing different thresholds would limit representation. Imposing a 1 percent threshold would eliminate small parties with a regionally concentrated support base, such as the UCDP and MF, while a 5 percent threshold would eliminate most opposition parties. In other words, based on the 2004 results, such thresholds would simply benefit the ANC. However, if parties knew beforehand that they would have to get a certain number of votes in order to pass the threshold, they might alter their campaign strategies and group together before the election, in order to increase their vote share. Even with a 1 percent threshold in place, the logic of party campaigning and alliance building would probably change significantly, which could alter the party political landscape and electoral outcomes. In this way, imposing a threshold could eventually even lead to the emergence of a credible alternative to the ANC, to replace the current opposition of a fairly large number of parties with different ideological and policy platforms that rarely work together to present a coherent alternative to the ANC's policy proposals.

The Representation of Women

How do women fare in South African politics? Many argue that whatever the disadvantages of the current electoral system, one of the benefits has been that it promotes the representation of women and other minority groups. This is because in the current system of proportional representation with closed party lists, party leaders can place women in "electable" positions on candidate lists, thus ensuring that they will be represented in Parliament and the provincial legislatures. In a candidate-centered constituency system, women may not achieve the same level of representation. Particularly in the context of a traditionally patriarchal society in which women are often not represented in formal power structures, the closed list variant of proportional representation is useful to ensure that women make it into Parliament.

So how do women fare in South African politics? There are no legal requirements for women (or other minorities) to be included in the parties' candidate lists. Measures to increase the political participation of women are within the discretion of the individual political parties. They must decide to give priority to the representation of women when generating their candidate lists. In fact, parties employ different procedures to compile their lists, and also follow different criteria for including women and other minorities. The ANC has a formal requirement that at least 30 percent of its candidates must be women. No other political party sets

Table 13.16   Women in Parliament, 2004

	Women in both Houses of Parliament		Women in NA		Women in NCOP	
	No.	**%**	**No.**	**%**	**No.**	**%**
Total	150	33	131	33	19	35
ANC	118	38	106	38	12	34
DA	15	25	10	20	5	50
IFP	8	26	7	25	1	33
UDM	4	40	3	33	1	100
ID	2	25	2	29	0	0
MF	1	50	1	50	na	na
ACDP	1	14	1	14	na	na
NNP	1	11	1	14	0	0
FF+	0	0	0	0	0	0
PAC	0	0	0	0	na	na
UCDP	0	0	0	0	0	0
Azapo	0	0	0	0	na	na

Source: The list of members posted on www.parliament.gov.za and a list of members of the NA and NCOP provided by parliament's public information office. The NCOP section of the table refers only to the fifty-four permanent delegates and excludes the thirty-six special delegates who are rotating according to the topic under discussion. In the table, "na" indicates that the party in question does not have any permanent delegates in the NCOP.

a similar earmark, but all claim to promote the advancement of women in their processes of candidate selection. Yet, not all achieve comparable results, as table 13.16 shows.

Setting a target for the representation of women, like the ANC has done, seems to work. The ANC has produced most women MPs, both in terms of absolute numbers (not surprising given the fact that the ANC is by far the largest party) and as a percentage of the party's representatives. More than one-third of the ANC's parliamentarians in both houses are female (38 percent). Only the UDM and the MF perform better than the ANC. One of the MF's two NA members is a woman, while one-third of the UDM's representatives in the NA are women, as is the UDM's sole permanent delegate to the NCOP. Other parties perform dismally when it comes to representing women: the FF+, PAC, UCDP, and Azapo have no women representatives, whereas only 14 percent of the ACDP and NNP representatives in the NA are women.

Clearly, whether or not women are adequately represented in Parliament is not just a function of the type of electoral system, but also, and perhaps more important, a result of the policies of the individual political parties.

Therefore, whether or not women would do as well in a constituency system remains an open question. Parties could make a similar effort to select female candidates in such a system, which could mean that the closed-list variant of proportional representation is not necessary to ensure adequate representation of women in Parliament. The debate on electoral reform prior to the 2004 election did not touch on the representation of women, instead it focused on the effects of the electoral system on political party representation. However, the effect of the different types of electoral systems on the representation of women remains an issue worth considering, especially in light of the fact that the debate over whether or not South Africa should alter its electoral system will be reopened in advance of the 2009 national and provincial elections.

The New Parliament

What do the 2004 election results mean for the composition of the National Assembly, not only in terms of political party representation but also with regard to the mix of new and experienced members? How many elected representatives are new to parliamentary politics? What is the level of experience that is retained? Comparing the 1999 and 2004 results, turnover in the National Assembly has increased, while at the same time a fair amount of experience has been retained in the form of MPs who have served in Parliament since 1994.

In 1999, 40 percent of the politicians who won a seat in the National Assembly were new MPs (159 out of 400). One-third of ANC MPs had not served in the first parliament, while 87 percent of the DP contingent was in Parliament for the first time. The IFP and NNP returned the most experienced group to the NA in 1999: only 15 percent of IFP MPs and 29 percent of NNP MPs were first-time MPs. Thus, in 1999, the NA saw a large number of fresh faces, with 60 percent of its members having served in the first parliament.

In 2004, turnover in the National Assembly was even higher than in 1999. The third parliament saw 198 new members take up their seats (almost 50 percent), while just under one-third of its members have ten years of experience, that is, have been in Parliament since 1994 (30 percent). Among the various parties, the largest number of new members can be found in the ranks of the ANC: 124 new MPs are ANC members. This means that 44 percent of the ANC caucus consists of new MPs. The DA, with 60 percent, has a higher rate of new MPs, which is not surprising since the party has shown significant growth since 1999.

Table 13.17   Retention and turnover, National Assembly

Party	Total MPs 1999	New MPs 1999	% New MPs 1999	Total MPs 2004	New MPs 2004	% New MPs 2004	MPs serving 10 yrs	% MPs serving 10 yrs
ACDP	6	4	67	7	2	29	2	29
AEB	1	1	100	—	—	—	—	—
ANC	266	86	32	279	124	44	100	36
AZAPO	1	1	100	1	1	100	0	0
DP/DA	38	33	87	50	30	60	6	12
FA	2	2	100	—	—	—	—	—
FF	3	0	0	4	2	50	2	50
ID	—	—	—	7	6	86	1	14
IFP	34	5	15	28	15	54	5	18
MF	1	1	100	2	2	100	0	0
NNP	28	8	29	7	3	43	3	43
PAC	3	1	33	3	3	100	0	0
UDM	14	14	100	9	8	89	0	0
UCDP	3	3	100	3	2	67	0	0
Total	400	159	40	400	198	50	119	30

Source: The 1999 data was obtained from the IEC and Parliament. The 2004 data was provided by parliament's public information office, but their list of MPs for 2004 included only 393 of the 400 NA members. The members missing from the list were all ANC members. The figures of MPs who served in all three parliaments from 1994 to 2004 include members who switched parties during this time.

Some of the "new" faces in the National Assembly in 2004 are actually members who served in the first parliament but not the second: fourteen of the ANC's new MPs and three of the IFP's new representatives fall into this category. The UDM's contingent is composed almost entirely of new entrants into Parliament. The only UDM MP who has served in Parliament before is party leader Bantu Holomisa. Some of the UDM's MPs from 1999 left the party during the March 2003 defection window and are now serving in the third parliament as members of other parties, such as Annelize van Wyck and Gerard Koornhof, both of whom are currently ANC parliamentarians. Only 12 percent of DA MPs have been in Parliament since 1994 (this figure includes DA MPs who previously served in other parties in Parliament).

The Cabinet

The cabinet selected after the 2004 elections demonstrated the ANC's commitment to cultivate leadership and expertise and promote loyal party members. The ruling party has also paid careful attention to its many constituencies, balancing the tensions between those who were in exile and those who stayed in the country during the apartheid era and rewarding its partners in the Tripartite Alliance by granting top positions to Cosatu and SACP members. The ANC ensured that at least 30 percent of the positions went to women and that minorities were represented, though the latter were incorporated more on the deputy rather than the ministerial level. Notably, the number of African ministers has increased since 1994. There are now six minority ministers in the cabinet; 79 percent of ministers are black/African, up from 52 percent in 1994.[36]

Like the new National Assembly, the new cabinet demonstrates a mix of experience and new recruits. Thirteen of the twenty-eight ministers retained their positions, and most of the new ministers have either served as deputy ministers or in Parliament before assuming their new positions. Four ministers moved from one portfolio to another, two deputy ministers became ministers; two of the new ministers came from the National Assembly, and three from service in other areas of government. The cabinet also includes members of two other parties: Marthinus van Schalkwyk from the NNP (though in 2005 he will become an ANC member), and Mosibudi Mangena from Azapo. IFP leader Buthelezi lost his portfolio and an ANC member took his place. Sixteen of the ministers come from the ranks of the ANC in exile, five from the United Democratic Front (UDF), one is the former minister of the Transkei homeland, and two each are Cosatu and SACP members.

In contrast to the relative stability at the ministerial level, there was a great deal of turnover among the deputy ministers. Almost half of the new deputies are women (ten out of twenty-one), and many started their political careers in the UDF. There are more "internals" than "exiles" (sixteen versus two) among deputy ministers and a relatively high percentage are from minority communities (52 percent compared to 21 percent of ministers). Seven deputies are white, one is coloured, and three are Indian.

In 1994, the ANC had balanced NP with ANC ministers and deputy ministers. In 2004, the party retained some ministers who had not performed well, and balanced them with deputies whom the party thought would ensure that the department would run smoothly. For example, the party retained Manto Tshabalala-Msimang in the health portfolio, despite criticism of her handling of the HIV/AIDS crisis, and brought in a deputy minister, Noziziwe Madlala-Routledge, to whom the party planned to quietly transfer responsibility for HIV/AIDS programs. Reportedly, the decision to retain Msimang was based on the ANC leadership's irritation at the condemnation of the government's position on HIV/AIDS by the press and the international community.[37] Similarly, Ngonde Balfour was moved from sports and recreation to correctional services, where Cheryl Gillwald, formerly the deputy minister of justice, became his deputy minister. Balfour's tenure in the sports and recreation portfolio had not been noted for its success, while Gillwald's reputation as a hard-working, competent deputy minister earned her the position as deputy in Balfour's new portfolio.[38]

Overall, the new cabinet represents a mix of old and new. The trend toward increasing the proportion of African ministers at the expense of minority cabinet members points to the ANC's increasing confidence in its position, and marks the fact that the party has moved away from the power sharing arrangements of the 1994 interim constitution. This trend could also mean that the ANC feels it no longer needs to attend to the fears of minority groups by overrepresenting them in cabinet positions, which could be interpreted as a sign of the maturation of South Africa's democracy. The ruling party seems committed to balancing abilities and incorporating minority members at the deputy level, but in the more visible, ministerial positions, is beginning to bring appointments in line with the demographics of the country.

Conclusion

In the final analysis, democracy is taking firm root in South Africa. There are definite signs of increasing party dominance, which could be creating voter apathy, but the country's levels of voter participation are not unusually low when compared with other countries in similar situations. The increasing dominance and centralization of the ANC are reasons for concern from the point of view of democratic accountability and transparency, but at the same time the ANC's dominance has increased political stability in postapartheid South Africa.

The continuing "irrelevance" of the opposition may become a threat to democratic stability. If voters de-aligning from the ANC do not find an alternative political home through which to express their political aspirations, the party system could become divorced from the realities of political life. In a system with proportional representation based on closed party lists, this disconnect could ultimately prove destabilizing.

But such pessimism is not yet warranted. The 2004 election pointed to areas that need to be monitored but mainly demonstrated that politics are normalizing in South Africa. Democracy is stable and performing well. If South Africa can avoid the pitfalls of permanent party dominance and a slow erosion of the democratic freedom it has enjoyed during the past decade, the second ten years of democracy will be worth celebrating.

Appendix: The Cabinet as Appointed after the 2004 Election

President: Thabo Mbeki
Deputy President: Jacob Zuma[a]

Portfolio	Minister	Deputy Minister
Agriculture and Land Affairs	Didiza, Thokozile	Du Toit, Dirk Cornelis (NNP) Botha, Ntombazana Gertrude
Arts and Culture*	Jordan, Pallo	Winifred Padayachie, Radhakrishna "Roy"
Communications	Matsepe-Casaburri, Ivy	Lutchmana
Correctional Services	Balfour, Ngconde	Gillwald, Cheryl Ellen
Defence	Lekota, Mosiuoa k	George, Mluleki Editor
Education	Pandor, Grace Naledi	Surty, Mohamed Enver
Environmental Affairs and Tourism	Van Schalkwyk, Marthinus (NNP)	Mabudafhasi, Thizwilondi Rejoyce
Finance	Manuel, Trevor	Moleketi, Philip Jabu
Foreign Affairs*	Dlamini-Zuma, Nkosazana	Pahad, Aziz Goolam Hoosein Van der Merwe, Susan Comber Madlala-Routledge, Nozizwe
Health	Tshabalala-Msimang, Mantombazana	Charlotte
Home Affairs	Mapisa-Nqakula, Nosiviwe	Gigaba, Knowledge Malusi Nkanyezi
Housing	Sisulu, Lindiwe	—
Intelligence	Kasrils, Ronald	—
Justice and Constitutional Development	Mabandla, Brigitte	De Lange, Johannes Hendrik
Labour	Mdladlana, Membathisi	—
Minerals and Energy	Mlambo-Ngcuka, Phumzile	Xingwana, Lulama Mary Theresa
Minister in the Presidency	Pahad, Essop	—
Provincial and Local Government	Mufamadi, Sydney	Hangana, Nomatyala Elizabeth
Public Enterprises	Erwin, Alexander	—
Public Service and Administration	Fraser-Moleketi, Geraldine	—
Public Works	Sigcau, Stella	Kganyago, Ntopile Marcel (UDM)
Safety and Security	Nqakula, Charles	Shabangu, Susan
Science and Technology*	Mangena, Mosibudi (Azapo)	Hanekom, Derek André
Social Development*	Skweyiya, Zola Sidney Themba	Benjamin, Jean
Sport and Recreation	Stofile, Makhenkesi	Oosthuizen, Gerhardus Cornelius
Trade and Industry	Mpahlwa, Mandisi Bongani	Hendricks, Lindiwe Benedicta
Transport	Radebe, Jeffrey Thamsanqa	—
Water Affairs and Forestry	Sonjica, Buyelwa Patience	—

NB: unless otherwise noted, all ministers and deputy ministers are ANC members.
* Three new departments were created in 2004. The former ministry of Arts, Culture, Science and Technology was split into a Department of Arts and Culture and a separate Department of Science and Technology. A new Department of Social Development was created. An additional deputy minister was allocated to the Department of Foreign Affairs.
[a] Replaced by Phumzile Mlambo-Ngcuka in July 2004. President Mbeki relieved Zuma of his cabinet position after charges of corruption were brought against him.

Notes

The author would like to thank the Centre for Social Science Research at the University of Cape Town for supporting her research on the 2004 election. All opinions expressed in this chapter are those of the author and do not reflect the official position or view of the government of the United States.

1. Author's interview with Fran Fearnley, head of the Electoral Code of Conduct Observer Coalition in Berea, KZN, April 1999.

2. The reasons for the ANC's dominant position are many and varied, and the central debate revolves around whether or not racial politics underpins the ANC's dominant position. R.W. Johnson and Laurence Schlemmer (*Launching Democracy in South Africa: The First Open Election April 1994*, New Haven: Yale University Press, 1996) and Hermann Giliomee and Charles Simkins (*The Awkward Embrace: One Party-Domination and Democracy*, Cape Town: Tafelberg, 1999) provide the now classic formulations of the "racial census" argument for the ANC's dominance, while Friedman's contribution to this volume could be read as a nuanced version of the argument. Jessica Piombo ("Political Institutions, Social Demographics and the Decline of Ethnic Mobilisation in South Africa, 1994–1999," CSSR Working Paper No. 63, Cape Town: CSSR, November 2004) argues that, instead, a combination of institutional and social factors account for the ANC's dominant position.

3. The informal settlements in Hout Bay and Khayelitsha, which had experienced devastating fires ahead of the election, are examples of areas on which the IEC kept close watch for possible violence from those disfranchised when their identity documents were destroyed.

4. Author's interview with Courtney Sampson, Provincial Electoral Officer of the Western Cape, Cape Town, April 8, 2004.

5. See Patrick Hlala, "IEC Wants Another 9 Million Voters," *Pretoria News*, October 9, 2003.

6. Michael Bratton, "Second Elections in Africa," *Journal of Democracy* 9, no. 3 (1998), 51–66.

7. Pippa Norris, *Democratic Phoenix: Reinventing Political Activism* (New York: Cambridge University Press, 2002).

8. See, e.g., Christelle Terreblanche, "South Africa's 10 Million Missing Voters," *The Sunday Independent*, July 13, 2003, and Donwald Pressly, "South Africa's Youth Spurn the Electoral Process," *Mail & Guardian Online*, November 5, 2003, http://www.mg.co.za/Content/l3.asp?ao=23105. On another note, the decrease in registered voters also points to the fact that while creating a voters' roll helps to guard against electoral manipulation, it can also present as a barrier to the full participation of all eligible voters.

9. In 1994, South African voters had not been required to register, so the IEC had to base its projections of voter turnout on population figures. Since the census tends to undercount the population in informal settlements, the IEC was less prepared for the volume of traffic through the voting stations in those areas. Therefore, these voting stations were characterized by lines that took hours, if not all day, to get through. However, voters could cast their ballots at any station in the country. Thus, in some areas parties transported voters from crowded stations in the townships to empty stations in city centers. In 1999, the IEC could use the voter's roll to estimate potential turnout, because South Africans were required to register in specific voting districts and to cast their ballots in those districts on election day. In theory, this made it relatively easy for the IEC to anticipate how many people would come to specific voting station, even though in practice they still underestimated the number of people who showed up in townships, especially in informal settlements, throughout the country.

10. Philani Makhanya and Sipho Khumalo, "IEC Official Tells of Voting Nightmare," *The Mercury*, April 24, 2004. "Section 24a" refers to the amendment to the Electoral Law that enables people to cast their ballots outside of the voting district where they are registered; the PEO of KZN admitted that he had intentionally not publicized the enactment of Section 24(a) because of the administrative difficulties it would create.

11. Many of these problems were observed by Piombo while she was an election monitor in the Western Cape during elections in 1999 and 2000.

12. Sampson interview; see also Philani Makhanya and Sipho Khumalo, "IEC Official Tells of Voting Nightmare."

13. This is significant because a two-thirds majority enables the ANC to unilaterally change the Constitution.

14. In August 2004, party leader Marthinus van Schalkwyk announced that the NNP would disband at the next national and provincial floor crossing window.

15. Rapule Tabane, Vicki Robinson, Marianne Merten, and Yolandi Groenwald, "All the Provinces' Women and Men," *Mail & Guardian*, April 22, 2004, accessed at www.mg.co.za/Content/ 13.asp?o=65880.

16. "E Cape Premier Alienates Provincial Leadership," *Daily Dispatch*, April 30, 2004.

17. Tabane et al., "All the Provinces' Women and Men."

18. Sable Ndlangisa, Xolisa Vapi, S'Thembiso Msomi, and Wally Mbhele, "Agony and Ecstasy," *Sunday Times*, April 25, 2004.

19. For a detailed analysis, see Buddy Naidu, "Why Indians Ditched the DA," *Sunday Times*, April 18, 2004; accessed at www.sundaytimes.co.za/2004/04/18/news/durban/ndbn01.asp.

20. uddy Naidu, "Speculation About a Zuma Premiership Rife," *Sunday Times*, April 18, 2004, and "Eight New Faces Among Provincial Premiers," *The Star*, April 22, 2004.

21. See Xolisa Vapi, "Ulundi Issue Cost IFP Dearly," *Sunday Times*, April 18, 2004. The DA earned 47,573 lesser votes on the provincial than the national ballot in Pietermaritzburg's voting districts.

22. Thabang et al., "All the Provinces' Women and Men." See also Ndlangisa et al., "Agony and Ecstasy."

23. Naidu, "Eight New Faces."

24. Ndlangisa et al., "Agony and Ecstasy."

25. See "Pandor Tipped for Premier," *News 24*, April 16, 2004, accessed at http://www.news24.com/News24/South_Africa/News/0,,2-7-1442_1513632,00.html.

26. The increase in citizens eligible to vote is especially important as we calculated the 2004 registration and turnout figures on the basis of the 2001 census, which more accurately captured African township dwellers than the 1996 census, on which the 1999 registration figures were based. Given that the data we used were three years old, and had some problems, it's likely that we still undercounted the South African population. The impact of HIV/AIDS, however, may have altered the population figures somewhat in a way not yet captured by the census.

27. For an extended analysis of these dynamics, see Jessica Piombo, "Political Institutions and the Decline of Ethnic Politics in South Africa, 1994–1999," *Party Politics* 11, no. 3 (May 2005), and Jessica Piombo, "Constructing Dominance: Institutions, Cleavages and Parties in Post-Apartheid South Africa, 1994–1999" (Ph.D. dissertation, Department of Political Science, Massachusetts Institute of Technology, 2002).

28. Jeremy Michaels, "We Will Not Be Disbanding—NNP," *Cape Times*, April 26, 2004.

29. This party existed only at the local level, as the parties were prevented from merging at the national and provincial levels by constitutional provisions that then existed against floor crossing in the national and provincial legislatures.

30. In March April 2003 the defection window enabled DP (and NNP) representatives at national and provincial levels to cross the floor to the DA, thus ending the existence of the DP.

31. The series of opinion polls released by the Institute for Democracy in South Africa, the South African Broadcasting Corporation and Markinor in 1999, called "Opinion '99" revealed that most South Africans did not perceive the DP as inclusive, and little evidence since has disconfirmed this trend.

32. Makhudu Sefara and Eleanor Momberg, "It's Deal Time for Choosing SA's Premiers," *The Star*, April 19, 2004.

33. The ANC was forced to include an IFP representative in the cabinet in 1994, due to power sharing provisions in the interim constitution. After 1999, the ANC retained party leader

Mangosuthu Buthelezi as minister of home affairs, as part of a deal that the ANC made with the IFP in KZN.

34. See Piombo, "Constructing Dominance."

35. Results were tabulated by imposing a cutoff of 1 and 5%, respectively, and then distributing the seats among the parties above the threshold. To do this, I employed the following procedure. Once the parties below the threshold were eliminated, percentages for each party were recalculated based on the aggregate number of votes earned by the remaining parties. These percentages were then translated into seats via the largest remainder method: a quota of votes per seat was calculated by dividing the remaining number of votes by the number of seats. The quota is called the Droop quota, where the number of votes cast in the election is divided by the number of seats to be filled, plus one. If the number of seats based on the whole vote shares is not 400, then additional seats are added to the parties whose remainders (the decimal portion of their quota) are the highest, until all seats are allocated.

36. 1994 figure from Andrew Reynolds, "The Results," in *Election '94 South Africa: The Campaigns, Results and Future Prospects*, ed. Andrew Reynolds (Cape Town, London, and New York: David Philip, James Currey, and St. Martin's Press, 1994), 214.

37. Author's anonymous interview with ANC speechwriter, Cape Town, May 5, 2004.

38. Ibid.

CONTRIBUTORS

Susan Booysen is a Professor in the Graduate School of Public and Development Management at the University of Witwatersrand and a Johannesburg-based research consultant. Prof. Booysen is President of the South African Political Studies Association. A South and Southern African politics specialist, she has a particular focus on government, party political trends, and opposition politics. She has published widely on democracy, transitional politics, elections, and citizen attitudes. Her most recent research and publications concern the liberation movement governments of Southern Africa. She regularly acts as media commentator and analyst. She is a former research fellow in Southern African Research Program (SARP) at Yale University (United States of America). Her Ph. D. is from RAU, Johannesburg. Until mid-2005, she was with the Nelson Mandela Metropolitan University (NMMU), where she was Professor of Political Studies and leader of the Master's Programme in South African Politics and Political Economy.

Gavin Davis is a researcher in the South African Parliament. He holds a BA (Hons) in politics from Rhodes University and an MA in democratic governance from the University of Cape Town. He is the author of "Proportional Representation and Racial Campaigning in South Africa" (*Nationalism and Ethnic Politics* 10, no. 2, 2004, 297–324), and "The Electoral Temptation of Race: Implications for the 2004 Election" (*Transformation* no. 53, 2004, 4–28). He has worked as a researcher for the Centre for Development and Enterprise in Johannesburg and the Democracy in Africa Research Unit at the University of Cape Town.

Steven Friedman is a senior research fellow and former director of the Centre for Policy Studies, Johannesburg. He is a social theorist with a particular interest in democratization, grassroots social, political, and economic dynamics, and development policy. Friedman writes regularly for leading newspapers, and is frequently interviewed on radio and television. He often delivers papers at international conferences, and is consulted by donor agencies, local and international NGOs, businesses, international journalists, and other analysts.

Collette Schulz-Herzenberg is a doctoral candidate in the Political Studies Department of the University of Cape Town. Prior to this, she was a Senior Researcher with the Political Information and Monitoring Service (PIMS) of the Institute for Democracy South Africa (Idasa). She has also worked as the Parliamentary Portfolio Committee for Justice and Constitutional Development Secretary and was a parliamentary journalist and presenter for DSTV. She also trains on how to advocate and lobby in government institutions and has completed research projects for various NGOs and the European Union. She holds a BA Honours in the Politics of Africa and Asia (SOAS, University of London) and an M.Sc. in Democratic Governance from the University of Cape Town, South Africa.

Thabisi Hoeane is a lecturer in the Department of Political and International Studies at Rhodes University, Grahamstown. He holds a BA degree in Political Science and Public Administration from the National University of Lesotho, MA and Ph.D. degrees in Political Studies from the University of the Witwatersrand. His current research interests include South African Political Parties, Race and Ethnicity in Electoral Studies, and South African Social Movements.

Claude Kabemba is a senior researcher specializing in Sub-Saharan Africa's political economy at the Electoral Institute of Southern Africa. He holds a BA in International Relations from the University of Lubumbashi, a BA (Hons) and MA in International Relations from the University of the Witwatersrand. His research interests include conflict management, good governance, regional integration, and democracy in sub-Saharan Africa. He coedited the book *Whither Regional Peace and Security? The Democratic Republic of Congo after the War.* Kabemba contributes to conferences and seminars and writes regularly for local and international newspapers and magazines.

Tom Lodge is a professor of Politics at the University of Limerick in Ireland. Prior to this appointment, he was a professor of Political Studies at the University of the Witswatersrand and research director at the Electoral Institute of Southern Africa. His research interests include nationalist movements, African politics, and political biography. He is the author of *Black Politics in South Africa since 1945* (1991), *Consolidating Democracy in South Africa: The Second Open Election* (1999), and *South African Politics Since 1994* (1999). Born in the UK, he was educated in Nigeria, Malaysia, and Britain, receiving a D.Phil. from the University of York.

Robert Mattes is Associate Professor of Political Studies and Director of the Democracy in Africa Research Unit in the Centre for Social Science Research at the University of Cape Town. He is also an associate with the Institute for Democracy in South Africa (Idasa). He is a cofounder and codirector of the Afrobarometer, a regular survey of Africans' attitudes toward democracy, markets, and civil society. With Michael Bratton and E. Gyimah-Boadi, he is coauthor of *Public Opinion, Democracy and Market Reform in Africa* (Cambridge University Press, 2004) and author of *The Election Book: Judgement and Choice in the 1994 South African Election* (Cape Town: Idasa, 1996). He has authored or coauthored articles in leading journals such as the *British Journal of Political Science, World Development, Journal of Democracy, Democratization,* and *Party Politics.*

Mbogeni Manqele is a research intern with the Democracy and Governance at the Human Sciences Research Council based in Durban. He is also the Woodrow Wilson Fellow of the Social and Public Policy Program at the University of KwaZulu-Natal, Pietermaritzburg Campus.

Sanusha Naidu is a research specialist in the Integrated Rural and Regional Development research programme of the Human Sciences Research Council, Durban. After completing a BA Law degree and an honors degree in Political Science at the University of Durban-Westville, she obtained an MA in International Relations from Staffordshire University, England. Her areas of interest include the impact of free trade arrangements on poverty-reduction strategies, the implications of SA's multilateral approach to international relations and democratic change and consolidation in Africa. Prior to joining the HSRC, Naidu was Senior Africa Researcher at the South African Institute of International Affairs. She has also lectured in the Department of Political Science of the University of Durban-Westville. Naidu has authored and coauthored a number of articles in accredited journals.

Lia Nijzink is the Project Manager of the African Legislatures Project, a comparative research project on the role of African legislatures in democratic governance, based at the Centre for Social Science Research of the University of Cape Town. Her research interests concern the comparative study of representative political institutions, democratic transition and consolidation, and parliamentary politics and practices in Africa. Having received an MA in Political Science from the University of Amsterdam and an LLM from the University of Maastricht (the Netherlands), she is completing her doctorate degree in the Political Science Department at the University of Stellenbosch (South Africa). Nijzink has recently lectured in the Department of Political Studies at the University of Cape Town; has conducted training sessions for the National Assembly of South Africa; has consulted with the Gauteng provincial legislature to codify their procedures; and is the coauthor of *Building Representative Democracy* (with Christina Murray and published in 2002 by the European

Union Parliamentary Support Program), which is a review of the functioning of South African legislatures during the first decade of democratic governance.

Jessica Piombo is an assistant professor in the Department of National Security Affairs at the Naval Postgraduate School (NPS), USA, specializing in Comparative and African politics. She joined NPS in 2003 after completing her Ph.D. at the Department of Political Science of Massachusetts Institute of Technology in 2002. Piombo is the author of, among others, "Political Institutions, Social Demographics and the Decline of Ethnic Mobilization in South Africa, 1994–1999," *Party Politics* (May 2005), "Opposition Parties and the Voters In South Africa's 1999 Election," (with Robert Mattes, *Democratization*, Autumn 2001), and "The Smaller Parties," (in *Election '99: From Mandela to Mbeki*, St. Martins Press, 1999). Piombo has worked with the Institute for Democracy in South Africa, the University of Durban-Westville, and as an election monitor and member of the Steering Committee of the Peace Monitoring Forum of the Western Cape. Piombo is a research associate of the Center for African Studies of the University of California at Berkeley and the Centre for Social Science Research of the University of Cape Town.

Laurence Piper is a senior lecturer in the School of Politics at the University of KwaZulu-Natal, Pietermaritzburg. He received his BA (Hons) from the University of Natal, and his M.Phil. and Ph.D. from Cambridge. His Ph.D. was on the rise and fall of Zulu nationalism in South Africa's transition to democracy, and he has published extensively on this subject, the IFP, and KwaZulu-Natal politics. More recent research interests include democracy and racial desegregation in South Africa.

Jeremy Seekings is Professor of Political Studies and Sociology at the University of Cape Town. Seekings has a D.Phil. from Oxford University. His research interests cover Political Sociology, Comparative Politics, Public Policy and the Sociology of Law. His books include *The UDF: A History of the United Democratic Front in South Africa, 1983–1992* (2000) and *Class, Race and Inequality in South Africa* (2005, with Nicoli Nattrass).

INDEX

Note: Page numbers in italics indicate tables.